.500

POLITICS AND SOCIETY IN DE GAULLE'S REPUBLIC

POLITICS AND SOCIETY IN DE GAULLE'S REPUBLIC

PHILIP M. WILLIAMS
and
MARTIN HARRISON

LONGMAN

LONGMAN GROUP LIMITED
LONDON

Associated companies, branches and
representatives throughout the world

First published 1971

ISBN 0 582 12785 8

Printed in Great Britain by
Ebenezer Baylis and Son Limited
The Trinity Press, Worcester, and London

CONTENTS

PART V REPUBLICAN MONARCHY— AND BEYOND

ACKNOWLEDGEMENTS

This volume is a successor to *De Gaulle's Republic* which we published in 1960, very early in the life of the new regime. At that point we naturally concentrated our attention on the crisis which had destroyed the Fourth Republic and on the new constitutional arrangements, though we tried to use the limited material then available to assess the likely evolution of the new system. With the exceptional conditions of the Algerian War now only an evil memory, a full decade of the Fifth Republic has transformed both the balance of the subject and our perspectives on it. We have therefore made no attempt to bring the old text up to date, but instead have written, without reference to it, an entirely new work. Much of this was in draft before the General's departure, but major developments up to that date are included in the relevant chapters and the narrative is completed in chapter 15. As the title suggests, however, we have not attempted to deal with events in the new reign. Most of chapters 1, 9, and 12–16 were drafted by MH and chapters 2–8, 10 and 11 by PMW; but each of us has helped to revise and redraft parts of the other's text.

We greatly appreciate the help of our academic colleagues and political and other friends in France, without whom this book could never have been written. We are very grateful to our patient secretaries, Miss J. Brotherhood and Miss M. Young and to David Steel, who read the proofs. We are also obliged to Malcolm Anderson, Vernon Bogdanor, Claude Brosse, Serge Hurtig, Joël Le Theule, Graham Thomas and Frank Wright for helpful comments on parts of the manuscript; and especially to David Goldey who read and criticized it all. They corrected and clarified many of our errors and obscurities; for those that remain we are jointly responsible.

ABBREVIATIONS

APEL	Association des Parents d'Elèves de l'Enseignement Libre
CAPEB	Confédération de l'Artisanat et des Petites Entreprises du Bâtiment
CD	Centre Démocrate
CFDT	Confédération Française Démocratique du Travail
CFTC	Confédération Française des Travailleurs Chrétiens
CGAF	Confédération Générale de l'Artisanat Français
CGC	Confédération Générale des Cadres
CGPME	Confédération Générale des Petites et Moyennes Entreprises
CGT	Confédération Générale du Travail
CNCM	Comité National des Classes Moyennes
CNEJ	Centre National d'Etudes Judiciaires
CNI(P)	Centre National des Indépendants (-Paysans)
CNJA	Centre National des Jeunes Agriculteurs
CNMCCA	Confédération Nationale de la Mutualité du Crédit et de la Coopération agricole
CNPF	Conseil National du Patronat Français
CODER	Commission de Développement Economique Régional

COPA	Comité des Organisations Professionnelles Agricoles
DC	Democratic Centre (Centre démocrate)
EDC	European Defence Community
EEC	European Economic Community
ENA	Ecole Nationale d'Administration
ESC	Economic and Social Council
FEN	Fédération de l'Education Nationale
FGDS	Fédération de la Gauche Démocrate et Socialiste
FLN	Front de Libération Nationale
FNEF	Fédération Nationale des Etudiants de France
FNPL	Fédération Nationale des Producteurs du Lait
FNSEA	Fédération Nationale des Syndicats d'Exploitants Agricoles
FO	Force Ouvrière
GNP	Gross National Product
GPRA	Gouvernement Provisoire de la République Algérienne
JO	*Journal Officiel*
MODEF	Mouvement de Défense de l'Exploitation Familiale
MRP	Mouvement Républicain Populaire
NATO	North Atlantic Treaty Organization
OAS	Organisation Armée Secrète
ORTF	Office de Radiodiffusion-Télévision Française
PCF	Parti Communiste Français
PDM	Progrès et Démocratie Moderne
PME	*See* CGPME
PR	Proportional representation

PSA	Parti Socialiste Autonome
PSU	Parti Socialiste Unifié
RFSP	Revue Française de Science Politique
RI	Républicains Indépendants
RPF	Rassemblement du Peuple Français
SAFER	Sociétés d'Aménagement Foncier et d'Etablissement Rural
SFIO	Section Française de l'Internationale Socialiste
SICA	Sociétés d'Intérêts Collectifs Agricoles
SNESup	Syndicat National de l'Enseignement Supérieur
SOFRES	Société Française d'Enquêtes par Sondages
TVA	Taxe sur la Valeur Ajoutée
UDR	Union des Démocrates pour la République
UDT	Union Démocratique du Travail
UFD	Union des Forces Démocratiques
UFM	Union Fédérale des Magistrats
UGS	Union de la Gauche Socialiste
UNAF	Union Nationale des Associations Familiales
UNEF	Union Nationale des Etudiants de France
UNR	Union pour la Nouvelle République

I

CHANGING FRANCE

FRANCE MARRIES HER CENTURY

The stalemate society

'Throughout her existence France has traversed periods when the course of events obliged her to renew herself on pain of decline or death. . . . This is certainly the case today, because the age in which we find ourselves, which is notable for the acceleration of scientific and technical progress, the need for greater opportunity for all, the advent of a swarm of new states, the ideological rivalry of empires, impose on us at home and in our relations with others an immense renovation. The problem is to carry this through without France ceasing to be France.'[1]

The difficulty of wedding change to tradition which so preoccupied General de Gaulle has been common to every established nation in western Europe in recent years. But none has experienced it more swiftly and sharply than France since 1945, and few reveal the tensions and contrasts between old and new more starkly. For during the postwar years she has not only acquired the familiar attributes of the contemporary mass economy, but after so long being retarded by structures and attitudes rooted in the nineteenth and even the eighteenth century, she is at last leaping forward economically and socially to 'marry her century'—to employ the term (and ambition) formulated by de Gaulle himself.

Prewar France had languished in economic backwardness, social stalemate and political instability, her creative vitality drained by historical cleavages, acute inflation and the appalling physical and psychic toll of the 1914–18 war. The prevailing attitudes of the twenties and thirties were the caution, pessimism, defeatism and hostility of groups to whom

---

[1] General de Gaulle, 2 Feb. 1962.

change was perceived primarily as a threat—the self-sufficient peasant, the independent craftsman, the provincial and even the Parisian bourgeoisie and the local notables, the traditional elites of a still largely pre-industrial society whose political influence remained immense. For them the prime hope of security seemed to lie in immobility. Diplomatically this brought appeasement, militarily the Maginot Line. Economically it meant a relatively self-contained economy sheltering behind high tariff barriers, and composed overwhelmingly of family firms, subsistence farms and an overcrowded tertiary sector, with its vast army of shopkeepers and intermediaries predisposed towards high profits and low turnovers. Family companies valued security, stability and autocratic independence above the risks involved in expanding on borrowed money and possibly losing control to outsiders. Right up to 1939 this prevailing economic malthusianism discouraged expansion and competition; French industrial development remained localized, incomplete and stunted. The same underlying attitudes moulded a legal framework which—in matters like land-ownership, inheritance, marriage law and company legislation—enshrouded existing rights and privileges in a protective cocoon which actively inhibited change and efficiency. These were the years of the cult of 'the little man', zealously courted by the politicians and philosophically justified by the fashionable theories of Alain. Those who had their *situation acquise* enshrined by law and custom thought more of clinging to it than improving it.

Yet as long as economic stagnation continued society had little in reserve to satisfy the aspirations of the small but increasingly impatient industrial working classes. Consequently their demands were not simply a threat to the pockets of the 'haves', but seemed to jeopardise the entire precarious, jealously guarded equilibrium on which this static society survived. Between the wars France experienced the class struggle and ideological conflicts of more advanced societies without in fact achieving the benefits of widespread industrialization. This was only one of the ways in which economic immobility hardened and engrained social tensions where expansion would have provided greater scope for either attenuating or dissolving them.

These were not the only conflicts within a fragmented and defensively-minded society. Frenchmen were divided rather

4

than drawn together by their historical memories, by such symbols as Marianne (the Republic), the Cross and the Tricolour. Well into the Third Republic there were still groups working to undo the French Revolution, while the long and bitter war between Church and State, priest and schoolteacher, raged on with the educational system as its special Flanders. There were also tensions between employers and workers, peasants and townsmen, soldiers and civilians, intellectuals and bourgeois, as well as the regional and local rivalries which proliferated in the absence of a system of strong national pressure groups—itself a consequence of the failure to develop a national market. The dominant social units remained the family and the State: the State remote and centralized in Paris, arbitrary and suspect, yet seen as the prime source of social initiative and constantly appealed to as a crutch against change or encroachment by a rival interest; the family, closely knit and dominated by its elders, trusting to its own resources in a hostile world. There was little in between. For to the Republican heirs of Rousseau, defending a centralized system against the constant threat of centrifugal or anarchic tendencies, and to many orthodox Catholic social thinkers before the thirties, there was no respectable place within the one and indivisible Republic for intermediary social forces. What groups there were tended to be preoccupied with defending vested interests, and reinforced social cleavages by the way they organized sporting, recreational or cultural activities. Individualism and mutual suspicion rarely allowed voluntary associations and cooperative civic action to take root on any significant scale.

This splintered individualistic society attempted to stabilize and contain its potentially disintegrative tensions by an authority structure characterized by remoteness, impersonality and hierarchy, both in the State administration and, wherever the scale was large enough, in industry and commerce. Authority, it was felt, could be maintained only by keeping one's distance—an expression of what Michel Crozier has called the characteristic French horror of face-to-face confrontation. The *fonctionnaire's* limited sphere was minutely spelled out to avoid jurisdictional disputes (thereby creating inflexible patterns of established rights and relationships which themselves inhibited change), but within it, if he knew his rights and responsibilities, he had considerable freedom—

which he often exercised autocratically. This helped to intensify the ordinary man's suspicion of the remote and authoritarian arbiter—Paris, the State, *Them*. There was a yawning gap between the politico-administrative system and the 'real' country. Alone against powers he neither knew, trusted nor controlled, the Frenchman was confirmed in the tradition of suspicion and civic indiscipline which had its origins in the *ancien régime*. Though hostile to the State he was also unusually dependent on it, since the *étatiste* tradition (which also antedated the Revolution) meant that he was accustomed to social and economic initiatives coming from the government in Paris. Within a system which at national level gave him little feeling of effective participation, the citizen reacted by behaving like an angry subject.

The unwillingness to accept government was matched by a lack of the will to govern. Political parties ceased to try to win power but limited their ambition to sharing the places in a coalition cabinet. Electorally, though there were emergent national parties on the Left, parties either competed for the favours of restricted clienteles or existed on paper only, as mere syndicates of provincial notables. Yet the failings of the politicians were more the symptoms than the true causes of the deepening inability of the political system to solve the problems of the interwar years. Effective democratic government had little hope of evolving from a society where individualism, localism and ideological animosity had so long been bred by social and economic fragmentation and preserved by industrial stagnation; where a sense of community or adequate consensus over essentials was therefore lacking; and where the political system was called on to perform tasks exceeding its capacities. The Third Republic survived as the form of government which divided France the least, its cabinets reshuffling frequently, its policies changing little. But while static equilibrium was tenable during the years of peace and limited government before 1914, it could not cope with the economic and international problems of the thirties. The system reeled impotently from crisis to crisis until the final defeat of 1940 ended its agony.

In many ways defeat and occupation irretrievably shattered the old stalemate society. But if the old order could never be recreated, in the four years between defeat and Liberation no adequate social and economic basis for a reformed political

6

order could develop. Once the brief surge of national unity at
the Liberation had evaporated it was clear that despite the
new constitution governments were not strong and stable
enough to deal effectively with the strains of decolonization
and to fight the Cold War both abroad and at home. The worm
was in the fruit right from the adoption of the Fourth Republic's constitution in 1946, by only 9 million to 8 million, with
8½ million people not troubling to vote at all. Less than twelve
years later the revolt of the colonels in Algiers drew attention
to the fact the Fourth Republic was dead in turn, ending its
days as ignominiously as its predecessor. The politicians were
rightly condemned for their failures of courage, imagination
and leadership. But, as before, the parliamentary paralysis
only reflected a political incoherence rooted in the history
and social structure of the country.

Problems of affluence

Yet behind the unwept, unsung Fourth Republic's political
instability, economic and social change were at long last under
way. France was to emerge from relative poverty among her
European neighbours in the thirties to overtake or rival even
her wealthy neighbours.[1] While the deeper origins of the
process remain elusive, the war seems to have been the
turning point. As elsewhere in continental Europe the shocks
of war, defeat and occupation threw accepted structures and
attitudes into the melting pot. For differing reasons and in
differing ways both Vichy and the Resistance in effect if not
always in intent found themselves challenging the past.
Clandestinity, inadequate communications and the division
of the country into occupied and unoccupied zones breached
the tradition of centralization from Paris and threw the
provinces back on their own resources. Vichy's flirtation with
corporatism, though rooted in nostalgia, encouraged the
participation of intermediary groups in the consultative process. Fleeting though the ideal of Resistance unity proved to
be, the common fight against the invader brought together
across the traditional political and social fissures men of very

---

[1] GNP per head at market prices, 1967: France $2,210; West
Germany, $2,030; Belgium $2,050; Holland, $1,810; Switzerland,
$2,620; United Kingdom, $1,980; USA, $4,040.

different backgrounds and beliefs—*ceux qui croyaient au ciel, et ceux qui n'y croyaient pas*, in Aragon's famous line. The economic and political fiascos of the thirties and wartime collaboration discredited the conventional wisdom and customary elites of the Third Republic, leaving minds more receptive to the social critics of the prewar years and to new ideas which matured during the enforced inactivity of the occupation years. The defection of their elders also gave a younger and more progressive generation their chance to step from their leading roles in the Resistance to wield power during their twenties and thirties to an extent unparalleled since Napoleon's day. This new blood rejuvenated both industry and the higher administration—though initially not politics—intellectually as well as physically.

One of the best indications that attitudes were changing fundamentally was the birth rate. Demographic stagnation had been a constant element in French society since at least the eighteenth century; without the family limitation of the nineteenth century the population would today be closer to ninety million than its present fifty. Between 1911 and 1945 there was not a single year when the net reproduction rate exceeded 100.[1] Then from 1946, due to some extent to a policy of high family allowances, the rate shot up brusquely to over 130. Though it flagged in the fifties it moved back into the 130s during the sixties. From 40·5 million in 1946 the population rose to exceed 50 million in 1968, and by about 1985 it should reach 60 million. De Gaulle and some French demographers have even looked forward to one hundred million Frenchmen some time in the next century. Although critics brand this expansive population policy as 'national rabbitism', with a population density only 40 per cent of the United Kingdom's, France can still be considered lightly populated in relation to resources by West European standards. However, fertility tends to respond to deeper attitudes than the requirements of national grandeur. Whatever the innermost significance of this major shift in public taste, *le baby boom* has

---

[1] 100 means that the population is reproducing itself. Thus the 1935 figure of 87 indicated a 13 per cent decrease in the population if the rate continued, while the peak of 137·3 for 1964 corresponds to a projected 37·3 per cent increase from one generation to the next. The low birth rate between the wars was a consequence of the 'lost generation' as well as attitudes to family size.

produced an exceptionally young population and focused attention as never before on *la jeunesse*.[1] It has also altered attitudes towards geographical, social and job mobility, weakened the hold of the tightly closed authoritarian family, and led to a continuing preoccupation with provision of housing, schools, social services and industrial training facilities.

This gently inflating population has been one of many nails in the coffin of the old static economic thinking. But neither the demand induced by population growth nor the contribution of the postwar generation to the labour force is sufficient to explain the sustained vigour of economic expansion. Growth has continued beyond the immediate reconstruction stage to reach 5·5 per cent in 1954, and to average over 5 per cent ever since, double the British rate and comparable to West Germany's. The origin of this sustained expansion lies less in considerations of inherent demand, technology or economic structure—though these had their part—than in the restaffing of the economy with new men holding new ideas.[2] The new generation in charge of nationalized and private industry (where the traditional owner of the family firm was increasingly giving way to the professional manager) took change rather than stability as their watchword; they were set on expansion, innovation and efficiency and prepared to compete, even in foreign markets. The effects of this change, as yet incomplete, began to show in the early fifties. Although the steel industry remained a bastion of the old autarchic defensive thinking right up to the last-ditch fight against the European Coal and Steel Community in 1950–51, only five later the *patronat*'s cautious acceptance of the European Economic Community showed the shift to a more competitive outlook.

The alteration of managerial attitudes owes something to the missionary activities of the Commissariat-Général au Plan, which under Jean Monnet and a band of devoted technocrats has preached expansion, smoothed the way for

---

[1] The proportion of the population under twenty reached a peak of 34 per cent in 1966; it will decline slightly to 32 per cent in 1980–5. The over-sixty-fives were 11·8 per cent of the population and will rise to about 14 per cent in 1980–5. The effects of two world wars are still noticeable on the age pyramid, and have meant that a small working population has had to support the burden of both old and young.
[2] Cf. Charles Kindelberger in S. Hoffmann, ed., *France — Change and Tradition* (London, 1963), pp. 156–7.

orderly growth, and in the old *étatiste* tradition helped the process on its way with a combination of threats, blandishments and incentives aided by the government's control of subsidies and access to capital. But it also needed wider and subtler alterations in social attitudes for the expansionism of the technocrats and managers to meet the positive responses from workers and consumers without which sustained growth would have been impossible. One factor has been the diminished ferocity of the class war as professional managers, and large groups of technicians and executives have emerged as buffers between the manual workers and the bosses. The industrial worker, moving away from the poverty line, has become less revolutionary and more practical and 'reformist' in his demands. Change which was once seen primarily in terms of threats to vested interests is more likely now to offer hope—if not for oneself, then for one's children.

In the defensively-minded atmosphere of the thirties saving was both a cardinal virtue and essential to dynastic hopes of either moving into the bourgeoisie, marrying one's daughter well, or extending the family holding. But affluence, optimism and the demise of the arranged marriage (with its crushing burden of saving for the dowry) have all contributed to the emergence of the more consumption-oriented mood and the readier resort to credit which were essential to swelling sales of consumer durables. This has also been helped by the decline in the aristocratic and individualistic preference for elegant hand-produced goods, which had previously hampered the development of large-scale production. Today, factory-standardized products are accepted to the point of penetrating even that last bastion of extravagantly labour-intensive production—the kitchen.

The structure of industry has also changed. When Herbert Lüthy surveyed France in the early fifties he described the new large-scale industry, then largely limited to the state sector, as an isolated enclave of modernism within old France. But since then dynamic industries like chemicals, electronics, petroleum, building and car production have come to the fore to constitute a far larger share of the economy than the dwindling and defensively-minded industries like paper and textiles. Greatly aided by the transfer of workers from the inefficient agricultural sector to industry, productivity has surged forward to overtake Germany and, of course,

Britain. Although there are still some great family firms like Michelin and Peugeot, during the fifties and sixties a spate of mergers (450 in 1957, 1,500 in 1965) produced many public companies capable of holding their own within EEC—in domestic appliances alone, from forty companies a few years ago, three today share over 90 per cent of French production. Yet there is still far too large a non-competitive sector of small firms, one-man shops and independent craftsmen. Two-thirds of employed Frenchmen work for firms with under two hundred employees. Of some 18,000 furniture firms, 17,000 employ fewer than ten workers. For all the impressive record of mergers, in 1964 not one French firm was among *Fortune*'s sixty-four 'world-class' companies with an annual turnover exceeding one billion dollars. France still suffers from an inadequate capital market which reflects the Gaullist neglect of the financial aspects of economic growth, from low outlays on advertising, and from a reluctance to adopt fully modern management methods which stems back to the tradition of individualism and hierarchy as against teamwork. Industrialization and rationalization still have much further to go, but France can at last boast a sizeable advanced industrial sector capable of holding its own at home, and of achieving significant exports despite the disappearance of the captive colonial market.

The benefits of this modernization have not been equally shared. Economic inequalities have steadily widened during the Fifth Republic, largely because the remains of the old economic structure hold back many peasants and independent craftsmen, while unions are weak and divided, but also because taxation changes have favoured those deriving income from dividends and profits, while social benefits have lagged behind inflation. The chief beneficiaries have been the growing army of managers and executives, followed by the technicians and foremen, who have left the less skilled workers far behind.[1]

---

[1] Between 1956 and 1966 pre-tax real income of executives and managers rose 48·7 per cent, while the increase for manual workers as a whole was 31·6 per cent — but it was only 6 per cent for workers on the official minimum wage. A survey of 1967 earnings of male workers in industry and commerce showed 29·8 per cent with under £15 per week (pre-tax but also pre-family allowances), while 11·1 per cent had over £36 per week. This does much to explain the events of May 1968. (Conversion rate £1 = 13·3 francs = $2·40; 1 franc = approx 7·5 N.P. = 18c.)

These have been hard years for those on fixed incomes, and particularly pensioners.

Not surprisingly, this has been resented by many of those who have been hurt by economic progress or benefited little. Poujadism,[1] which flared briefly but dangerously in the fifties, was launched by a small-town stationer from an impoverished rural department and supported most actively by shopkeepers and independent craftsmen threatened by modernization. Although it snowballed into an expression of much wider national frustrations, at bottom it was the rebellion of static France against change and the economic ascendancy of more advanced regions. The attitudes from which Poujadism had been born persisted after its founder's eclipse, though their expression, if at times as virulent, was normally more limited. A classic instance of the blind defence of *droits acquis* and the rejection of change was the Decazeville strike of Christmas 1961. When the State decided to close their mine, which was played out and hopelessly uneconomic, eight hundred miners stayed down at the pit bottom. They refused jobs in other coalfields because they were unwilling to move; instead they insisted not just that the pit should remain open until new industry had been brought to their isolated and dying town in the south-west, but also that on transferring to this new industry all miners, regardless of age, should retain their existing right to retire ten years earlier than other workers, and all the social and medical benefits of being a state employee while working for private industry. For a few weeks Decazeville was a national *cause célèbre*, rallying an emotional upsurge of support, much of it from others who were threatened by change, before it eventually collapsed—as it had to if economic progress were not to be paralysed. Generally, however, workers have struck to demand work rather than against change as such.

Change in the factory has been more than matched in the countryside. Today the French peasant is better equipped, better informed and more efficient than ever before. Since the early sixties an increasing proportion of his national leaders

---

[1] A small shopkeepers' pressure group which became a short-lived political party, winning 2,600,000 votes and 52 seats in the election of January 1956. Its leader opposed de Gaulle in 1958, but was supporting him by 1967.

have been able, modern-minded men with a grasp of the industry's problems. The prewar farm was typically a tiny holding rooted in the pre-machine age; the two million farms of 1938 had only 30,000 tractors. Change came rapidly after 1945. There were 120,000 tractors by 1950 and 960,000 by 1964. Nevertheless the few new large and semi-industrial farms remained very much the exception. With the reform of landholding lagging seriously, half the new tractors were on farms too small ever to earn an economic return on them.

In the 1967 census 1,108,500 farms (out of 1,689,000) were under 50 acres, and only 24,000 over 250 acres. Only about half the 700,000 wheat farmers send more than a single truck load of wheat to market in a year. Though productivity has risen steadily, this has brought with it surpluses which contributed to the fall in real terms of 16 per cent in farm prices between 1959 and 1969. The average income of peasants is about 30 per cent below the average for industrial workers. Consequently, despite an increase in state expenditure on agriculture from £254 million in 1958 to £1,480 million in 1969 (11·5 per cent of the national budget),[1] the drift from the land continues. The proportion of the working population engaged in agriculture fell slowly from 44 per cent in 1906 to 36 per cent in 1936, more rapidly to 27 per cent in 1954, then even faster to 16 per cent in 1961. By the close of the seventies under 10 per cent of workers will be in agriculture.

It is scarcely surprising that despite the signs of progress the countryside has been potentially explosive ever since the wartime sellers' market ended in 1950. The farmers were encouraged to put high hopes in a succession of changes like mechanization, cooperative marketing or the EEC agricultural policy. But though the large, efficient operators have prospered, the small family farmer has seen every hope crumble in turn. Ultimately the great majority of the small men are doomed. By the end of the seventies nearly half the existing farms are expected to have either merged or gone out of

---

[1] That is, the Treasury subsidizes each farmer an average of £870 per year. In 1969 the cost of storing, destroying or dumping surpluses at cut prices was equal to about a quarter of the gross income from farm products.

cultivation.[1] As few as one farm in twenty is thought to be fully viable. Sometimes governments have sought to stem the tide or provide temporary respite, at others they have tried simply to ease the long and painful contraction. But sporadically the peasants' frustration and despair has flared up; scarcely a year has passed since 1954 without more or less serious outbreaks of direct action. It will be at least a generation before the transformation of agriculture is complete. These will inevitably be years of even greater social and political tensions, fraught with the danger of political upheavals.

All told, well over three million people have left the land since the war. More and more hamlets are deserted or have lost their ablest children to the towns—a pattern familiar in Britain and the United States in earlier decades, now belatedly but rapidly repeated in France. Mechanization and improved communications have not only killed the old rural crafts, but have also put an end to the village as a self-contained economic and social unit. Today its inhabitants seek their purchases, their pleasures and often their work further afield. Television and improved roads have narrowed the physical and mental gap between the peasant and the townsman—though often this means that the countryman acquires the material wants of his urban cousin with much less hope of satisfying them. While the spread of school bus routes has given country children a better chance of a decent education, even today only one in a thousand children of farm workers reaches university, compared with 55 per cent of those whose fathers are in the liberal professions. Rural society has traditionally been dominated by its elders, who have monopolized the leadership of the farmers' organizations and seats on local councils. In 1963 50 per cent of farm holders were over fifty-five; many were holding back sons whose technical knowledge and understanding of the industry's problems were greater than their own. However, during the fifties and sixties, first in the Catholic rural youth movement, later in the Centre National des Jeunes Agriculteurs, and then in the national farmers' organizations, the younger generation has

---

[1] A small number of efficient farms will produce far more than today's 1,650,000 holdings. An official committee suggested in 1969 that it would be necessary to take one-third of existing farmland out of production by 1985 to keep production down to levels approximating to demand.

been making itself felt, and has at times influenced policy more than its elders. There are more young councillors and mayors in the countryside today than would have been conceivable a generation ago. Even in the remotest areas the old patriarchal family is disappearing, and deference to the rural 'squirearchy' has almost vanished. Socially the countryside is changing more and faster than at any time in its history.

The modernization of distribution is little nearer completion than the 'silent revolution' in the countryside. Even now 60 per cent of the country's 370,000 food shops are strictly family affairs with no employees, many of them scraping a bare living despite high markups. France has one food shop for 175 inhabitants, compared with 1 : 239 in Germany, and 1 : 306 in the United States. While the number of middlemen in the grocery trade has fallen dramatically since the war, distribution of fruit and vegetables remains expensively inefficient even after the long overdue transfer of the congested and anarchic Paris central market to the suburbs in 1968. Even the Fifth Republic has so far failed to break down the byzantine and corrupt meat marketing arrangements which can still turn a fall in farm gate prices into rises in the shops. Although France introduced the department store to the world it was left to others to exploit the potentialities. The old restrictive mentality, the readiness of manufacturers to back price-fixing by cutting off supplies to the discounters, and the conservatism of the consumer long shielded shopkeepers from competition. The first signs of change go back to 1949, when Edouard Leclerc opened his first cut-price store near Brest and fought off all the attempts of his competitors and suppliers to sink him by fair means or foul. The first true supermarket did not open until 1958; by 1968 there were 800, with about 3 per cent of retail food turnover, and in 1970, 1,600 with over 14 per cent of food sales—compared with 72 per cent in the United States. Nevertheless, though restrictionism remains embedded in every level of the distributive system, the retailing revolution is gathering pace.

Socially as well as economically attitudes and structures have been shifting, though it is harder to isolate the significant elements from the more trivial. With industrialization and the rural exodus the French are for the first time predominantly an urban nation. The proportion living in communes with over 10,000 inhabitants rose from 39 per cent in 1946 to

exceed 50 per cent in 1968. Despite official policies of decentralization, the population of greater Paris has swelled to
more than eight million. Paris still remains the goal of the
ambitious, though its central area is dirty and noisy, more a
victim of the car than even Los Angeles, with the heaviest
housing costs in Europe and population densities higher than
inner London or Manhattan. Yet despite the capital's unchallenged ascendancy in politics and administration, the
arts, industry and commerce, there has been a gradual
renaissance of the provinces. Cities like Rennes and Grenoble
which were quiet backwaters only a decade or so ago now
have new life and energy, and are attracting able men who in
earlier days would have headed for Paris. While North
America and most other countries in Europe are grappling
with urban renewal, France is setting about providing herself
with a sizeable number of large provincial cities for the first
time. Eventually it is intended to end the era of 'Paris and the
French desert' by creating eight *metropoles d'équilibre* with
populations between 500,000 and a million. Though there are
still only five conurbations outside Paris with populations
exceeding 400,000, there are now almost a hundred with over
50,000 (compared with sixty-three in 1954) and more than
forty over 100,000. Increasingly the French are discovering
such novelties as new towns, dormitory areas, suburbs and
commuting. As just one consequence, lengthening journey
times may now make the traditional leisurely midday meal at
home impossible, promoting a trend to shorter lunch breaks
and longer evenings at home.

France today shows most of the characteristic superficial
traits of modernism and affluence: computers, pop, super-
markets, Wimpy bars, convenience foods, soaring ownership
of washing machines and cars and (to a lesser extent) the cult
of youth. Consumption habits are moving closer to the British
and American pattern in such ways as the rapidly rising
share of expenditure on leisure in family budgets, with the
growing popularity of holidays in the country or abroad—a
novelty in a nation which has traditionally combined a land-
locked geography with insular attitudes.[1] Possibly one reason
for the popularity of *le weekend* in the country and holidays

---

[1] A legal entitlement to two weeks holiday with pay was established
in 1936, three weeks in 1956 and four weeks in 1969.

from home is the desire to escape from cities deficient in green spaces and adequate housing. As a result of the straitjacket of rent controls originating in the first world war, the low priority assigned to public housing, bureaucratic delays and uncontrolled land speculation, France has a large stock of overcrowded and substandard housing and a sluggish building programme. Although the French are spending a higher proportion of their incomes on shelter than ever before (but still less than their neighbours), the situation remains a major social blackspot.[1] Here, as in the inadequate system of *autoroutes,* the lack of public lending libraries, and a telephone system described by President Pompidou himself as a 'disaster', France is suffering from the familiar ailment of public indigence amid private affluence.

'Depoliticization'?

Whether in industry, agriculture, trade or the professions, structural and psychological change are far from complete, but the achievements of the quarter century following the Liberation were impressive. Though not yet dead, the cult of the 'little man' has lost much of its potency during the last fifteen years. The French as a nation seem to have rediscovered an economic optimism and a hope of progress they had lost since the time of Saint-Simon. A superficial yet revealing sign of the new confidence has been the flood of articles, conferences and exhibitions on the theme of 'France of the Future' or 'Paris 2000'. Gaston Defferre's 1965 campaign theme of 'Horizon 80' would have been unthinkable less than a generation earlier. More striking still for the milieu was Laurence Wylie's observation of change in the village of Roussillon. In 1950 he found the peasants reluctant to replant

---

[1] In the 1962 census 61·7 per cent of houses were built before 1914 and 32·2 per cent before 1870; 22·6 per cent lacked running water, 50 per cent had no inside toilet and 28 per cent no bath or shower. The average size of a Paris flat was 2·2 rooms compared with 3·1 in London and 3·3 in New York. It was reported in 1966 that 20 per cent of new housing units had no bath or shower. In 1969 fifteen million people were estimated to live in overcrowded conditions, including 38 per cent of those in the Paris conurbation, and five million were suffering extreme overcrowding. There is as yet no sign of measures to overcome this situation.

orchards which they feared were destined to be the battle-grounds of World War III. In 1960 he found them ready to go into debt to lay down olive trees which would take twenty years to bring to maturity.

Thus, while many have been left behind by progress (and forcefully signalled their resentment in 1968 and 1969), the 'average' Frenchman has 'never had it so good'. The occasional ostentatious vulgarity accompanying the new prosperity has its detractors, who speak with the assured austerity of the comfortably endowed. More serious social commentators wonder whether France will emerge from the onslaught of Anglo-American influences—most irritatingly evident in the spread of that barbarous hybrid 'language', *franglais*—and establish a civilization which is both modern and distinctively French. While the external signs of change are obvious to the most casual eye, it is naturally harder to discern deeper and subtler shifts in social attitudes or to surmise how these may affect the political system. However, it is plain that the relatively superficial changes mentioned, together with the advent of television, are gradually diminishing the difference in attitudes and life styles of Parisian and provincial, towns-man and countryman, worker and clerk, although even now great regional and social differences remain. It is still a fairly non-egalitarian society in which class divisions are more rigid (though more taken for granted) than in Britain and social mobility is fairly limited.

While even today French society is associationally under-developed (apart from the many groups devoted to the defence of particular economic interests), there is now a far wider range of social, cultural, sporting or professional organizations cutting across many of the old barriers, and a greater readiness to join in sustained collective action. In some areas, like Brittany, the increased solidarity and discipline of the farmers have allowed the emergence of effective marketing coopera-tives in place of the anarchy which used to leave the individual farmer at the middleman's mercy—though old habits die hard, and the great fruit glut of 1968 became so severe because the growers of the south-west had failed to reach the modest 20 per cent membership required for the marketing organizations to receive official backing. *Etatisme* also dies hard. One still finds an arch-apostle like Debré proclaiming that 'it is the business of the State to choose, to command, to impose. . . . [The State] is the expression of the general interest, the rights of the nation and the needs of freedom. This lofty responsibility is matched by a power of decision and intervention which certainly have limits, but the principle of which cannot be challenged in any domain.'[1] Yet in the field of social welfare, where the French have traditionally wanted the initiative to come from the State, the success of the Mouvement Français pour le Planning Familial suggests that even here there may be a new readiness for joint civic action. Steadily France is becoming more cohesive, developing a greater feeling for community cooperation and private initiative.

Among the most important changes are those within the family—whether it be the steadily improving status of women, the disappearance of the dynastic marriage, the loosening of family ties, greater leisure easier divorce and birth control, or the cautious emergence of a teenage subculture. Perhaps the most noteworthy development is the tendency for relations between parents and children to be less formal and autocratic, with all this implies for the child's early experience of authority relationships.[2] The other major formative influence is the school (for to date the new rival, television, has been less influential in France than elsewhere). The educational effort of recent years has been impressive. By 1970 the national education budget was at almost six times the 1958 level in money terms, and had doubled its share of GNP. About 30 per cent of French children now receive full-time schooling up to eighteen—three times the British figure (though a worker's child has less hope of graduating from university in France than in Britain). Education has been in the throes of structural change ever since the fifties. The *baccalauréat* examination designed for an elite of 20,000 is now struggling to cope with 200,000, and has been 'reformed' so often that the ministry admitted in 1969 that 'it is time to put an end to the disquiet, confusion and damage that the multiple reforms it has undergone have entailed for teachers, parents

[1] *Le Monde*, 11 Jan. 1966.

[2] But old attitudes die hard. In March 1968 a national poll asked for views on the Minister of Education's decision that, with their parents' permission, adult women students might visit the rooms of adult male students in university residences: 57 per cent disapproved.

and pupils'. But so far the enormous expansion in numbers[1] has largely met political timidity and academic conservatism in tackling the reform of outdated structures, methods and attitudes. The secondary system has remained a bastion of the older bourgeois values, with its emphasis on examinations, encyclopaedic syllabuses and abstract exposition, and with its impersonality, its neglect of discussion and out-of-school activities, and its lack of interest in fostering responsibility among its pupils. More even than the family, the schools and universities have clung (with noteworthy but infrequent exceptions) to the older formal, remote and non-participatory authority structure. The educational system remains a resilient and potent (if slowly weakening) barrier to greater equality and social mobility. It was scarcely surprising that the great explosion of 1968 began in the universities and spread rapidly to many *lycées*.

The society which is emerging from this pattern of rapid if incomplete social and economic change is more prosperous, confident and self-aware, and less divided by history than at any time since 1789.[2] Even the old division over *laïcité* in education has lost much of its intensity. Although as late as 1960 the cause roused millions to sign petitions and tens of thousands to flock to meetings throughout the country protesting at the extension of the subsidies to church schools, since then feeling has subsided. The split between Resisters and Vichyites means less to the older generation now, and nothing whatever to the young. Algeria, which threatened at one time to inflict fresh scars, has sunk into collective amnesia, though the refugee organizations remain active and sporadically influential. Since the end of the Algerian war the extreme Right has almost disappeared as a distinct intellectual or political force. Even the Communist Party has lost much of its revolutionary and ideological zeal and, despite Czechoslovakia, it is no longer wholly frozen out of the political

[1] There were 122,000 registered university students in 1939, 156,000 in 1955, 349,000 in 1965 and 643,000 in 1969–70. The University of Paris had 154,000 students in 1968 compared with 65,000 in 1955.

[2] However, John Ardagh, in *The New French Revolution* (London, 1968), comments on the dangers of the *civilization des gadgets* for the sense of community, and notes the preoccupation of much modern French literature, the cinema and even pop music with alienation and the solitude of modern life.

community. Apart from a small and vocal element on the revolutionary Left, the breadth and intensity of ideological divisions have declined. Old slogans and symbols have been devalued; more potent ones have not as yet been found. Today perhaps a third of Frenchmen are almost innocent of ideological baggage, while most of the rest are better described as belonging to one of several broad political 'families' or temperaments than to precisely identifiable ideological sects.[1] Since the fifties France has been experiencing all the influences which were once diagnosed as leading to the 'end of ideology'—with the difference that for more than a decade the void was apparently filled by the unique personality of de Gaulle, proclaiming his unwavering hostility to party government and his ambition to remove major problems from politics.

Whether or not France has become 'depoliticized' has been argued ever since the advent of the Fifth Republic. The political parties were deeply discredited by the failure of the Fourth Republic, and since 1958 the older parties have been struggling continuously to survive. Under de Gaulle even the Gaullist party had for years only a marginal and episodic role, and public attitudes have naturally reflected awareness of this.[2] As in Britain, membership of parties and participation in their activities is well below the levels of the early postwar years. Yet neither the lessening of the ideological conflict nor the relative disaffection from the parties constitutes depoliticization. Several of the older parties, so repeatedly dismissed as representing nobody but themselves, have survived in one form or other the General's attempt to disrupt them. Despite limited funds and weak organization the opposition has continued collectively to win over 40 per cent of the popular vote. For whatever reason, the parties appear to be more deeply rooted in society than their opponents realized. Turnout for elections and referendums, too, has remained consistently high by modern democratic standards, while the

---

[1] Explored more fully in E. Deutsch, D. Lindon, P. Weill, *Les Familles politiques aujourd'hui en France* (Paris, 1966).

[2] In 1962 a national sample was asked: 'Do you think that the interests of people like yourself are best defended by pressure groups, deputies and senators, or political parties?': 54 per cent said interest groups, 10 per cent deputies and senators, only 8 per cent parties.

presidential campaigns of 1965 and 1969 raised a degree of interest which few other western countries could match. Despite the diminished power and prestige of parliament, competition for seats remains keen, while almost half a million people sit on local councils.[1] Although the number concerned actively with politics is small, levels of interest in France seem in line with those in neighbouring countries.[2]

In fact, political interest seems to have been diverted rather than diminished. Energies and ideas which in earlier days might have found expression through the parties have more often been channelled through political clubs or interest groups (which in consequence have sometimes become more politicized), or else they have erupted right outside the conventional political channels, whether in the giant demonstrations in 1962–63 against the terrorism of the French Algeria diehards, the recurrent resort to direct action by groups like the farmers, shopkeepers and independent craftsmen, or the riots and general strike of 1968. The hopes of the powers-that-be that they could have certain issues treated as purely technical rather than political have been dashed time and again.

Moreover, despite the ebbing of doctrinal and historical feuds the new France is by no means free of divisions and antagonisms. In a 1967 poll, 44 per cent of those questioned said they believed that the class war was a reality; only 14 per cent thought that prosperity was being shared equitably. But resentments are more likely to find expression these days in clashes over specific issues, or to cumulate until there is an explosion (as in 1968), than to be aggregated into a coherent political programme. The disarray of the party system has produced chronic issue fragmentation rather than depoliticization.

---

[1] Turnout at parliamentary elections (first ballots, percentages): 1958 – 73; 1962 – 69; 1967 – 81; 1968 – 80. Referendums: 1958 – 85; 1961 – 76; 1962(1) – 76; 1962(2) – 77; 1969 – 81. Presidential elections: 1965 – 85; 1969 – 78. (These figures would be reduced by about 3 per cent if people eligible to vote but not registered were counted.)

Candidates for 465 Assembly seats: 1958 – 2,809; 1962 – 2,172; 1967 – 2,190; 1968 – 2,267.

[2] In a 1962 cross-national survey, those declaring themselves 'very' or 'moderately' interested in politics were (percentages): Belgium 30; Italy 33; France 43; Germany 47; Britain 52; Holland 54.

And this goes to the heart of France's political ills. Many of the old structures have been swept away or modified. With them have gone something of the old individualism, suspicion and social isolation which prejudiced the development of a stable political order. But the curing of the paralysis which afflicted the Third and Fourth Republics is not solely a matter of destroying the old order. It requires the development of fresh attitudes and structures sustaining an adequate sense of political community and effective democratic authority relationships—including the emergence of a limited number of parties capable, singly or in alliance, of ensuring stable and effective government. Social and economic change cannot be comfortably relied on to produce the emergence of a sounder political order. In fact, to the extent that the upheaval of 1968 arose from the system's failure to cope satisfactorily with the resentments and insecurity arising from change, it clearly showed that the creation of more modern economic and social structures may easily push France further from long-term political equilibrium. It is not within the power of governments to dictate the detailed evolution of either the political culture or its socio-economic underpinning. But ultimately any regime must be assessed not only on its achievements on the international stage or on the increase in the material wellbeing of its citizens, but also on the extent to which it promotes or hinders the emergence of the modern political order which France has lacked for so long.

2

RETREAT FROM EMPIRE
1958–1962

The new regime installed

Today's Fifth Republic was born of its predecessor's inability to maintain just such a viable political order in the face of the cumulative stresses of a protracted war of decolonization in Algeria. Defeat in Indo-China and governmental instability in Paris had sapped the strength of the Fourth Republic, but essentially it was the disintegration of civilian authority in Algiers which precipitated the return of General de Gaulle to power after the long years at Colombey watching and waiting for the demise of the regime. By 1958, after more than three years of cruel fighting, the enthusiasts for the Algerian war had lost their majority in parliament. Pierre Pflimlin, the Christian Democrat nominated for the premiership in May after a particularly long and bitter cabinet crisis, was known to oppose escalation of the war by invasion of Tunisia; he was suspected of favouring an attempt at negotiation with the nationalists. The Algiers settlers promptly rioted, took over Government House with some army connivance, and persuaded General Massu to set up a Committee of Public Safety, hoping to frighten parliament out of nominating Pflimlin. Instead they provoked some deputies into supporting him. Thirty-six hours later the C-in-C in Algeria, the time-serving General Salan, was induced to launch a public appeal to de Gaulle which received an immediate response: on that same afternoon of 15 May de Gaulle announced his readiness to 'take over republican authority'.

The Fourth Republic survived for two more weeks. Parliament was reluctant to capitulate to a show of force from Algiers, but public opinion gave no support to the regime. The ordinary Frenchman did not believe that de Gaulle, who had restored the Republic in 1944, meant to subvert it fourteen years later; to most of his countrymen the General appeared as the miracle-man who could avoid civil war in France, preserve democratic liberties without national humiliation, settle the conflict across the Mediterranean, and keep Algeria French. If these objectives were to prove incompatible, every section of opinion assumed that its own priorities were also the General's. He was at pains to maintain this ambiguity.

On 24 May the government's isolation was demonstrated to the world—and to the ministers—when a handful of parachutists seized Corsica for the Gaullists without resistance from the authorities or the population. Salan told his cheering audience in Algiers 'We shall march down the Champs Elysées and they will cover us with flowers', and after ostentatious preparations for a paratroop descent on Paris, and private negotiations between Pflimlin and de Gaulle, the Premier resigned on 28 May. It took three more days to persuade enough Socialist deputies to accept de Gaulle, but on 1 June he was elected by a majority of a hundred, with the Communists, half the Socialists and a few others (notably Pierre Mendès-France and François Mitterrand) in the minority. He obtained from parliament temporary powers to govern and legislate,[1] and the authority to draft a new constitution which would be submitted to referendum; the members were then promptly sent on a (paid) holiday which for many was the road to political oblivion.

De Gaulle's cabinet was designed to reassure the French, not the Algerian settlers; along with many unknown but respectable civil servants and some faithful Gaullists, it included the most influential leaders of the traditional Right and Left, Antoine Pinay and Guy Mollet, and the man de Gaulle had just overthrown, Pierre Pflimlin—but the Gaullist leader who was regarded as the architect of the Algiers revolt, Jacques Soustelle, was at first given no post.[2] Having produced a safe cabinet to appease anxiety in France, the General on 4 June flew to Algiers and won over the cheering crowd in the Forum with his brilliantly ambiguous first sentence, 'Je vous ai compris'. As the sequel was to show, this was Gaullish for

---

[1] For four months, prolonged for another four by the provisional clauses of the new constitution itself.

[2] He joined in July, just *after* the Socialist party conference had decided to support the new government.

'I have taken your measure', not for 'I have taken your side'. Over the next few months the officers who had been most active in organizing the Algiers insurrection were promoted one by one—to positions of less influence. The government's main public preoccupation during the summer was the drafting of the new constitution. Undertaken by a team of young lawyers under Michel Debré, the old Gaullist who had become Minister of Justice, the draft was submitted to the Fourth Republican leaders in the cabinet and then discussed by a constitutional consultative committee (CCC) chosen as to two-thirds by parliament and as to one-third by the government. While many details were altered the original draft underwent only one major change of principle, and that was the result not of the formal consultations but of de Gaulle's African tour in August: the African colonies, now offered the status of member states of the French Community, could repudiate that status and claim their independence by simply voting No at the constitutional referendum on 28 September. One territory, Guinea, did vote No by a majority as impressively monolithic as that by which twelve others voted Yes;[1] all French assistance to her was severed instantly.

In France itself the new constitution was approved by all major parties except the Communists and a very few opponents on the extreme Right, though there were sizeable minorities among the Radicals and Socialists, some of whom now left their parties. With such widespread support, the ministers were confident of a substantial majority—but taken aback by the magnitude of their victory. In a record poll, 17,700,000 people supported the new constitution against a minority of 4,600,000—which included many non-Communists, but was a million below the Communist vote of 1965. As in 1945–46, the referendum was revealed as a machine for blowing up the political parties.[2]

---

[1] The majority was 64 per cent in Polynesia; over 75 per cent in Madagascar, Niger and French Somaliland; over 90 per cent everywhere else.

[2] Referendum and election results in the Fifth Republic are given more fully in Chapter 4. In October 1945 most Radical voters, in June 1946 some Socialists and in October 1946 most MRP supporters had refused to follow party advice in the three constitutional referendums: see P. M. Williams, *Crisis and Compromise* (3rd edn, London, 1964), pp. 20–3.

In Algeria, the referendum was thoroughly organized by the army, which succeeded in demonstrating its effective control of the territory: 80 per cent went to the polls, of whom 96 per cent voted Yes. Two months later, elections were due: Algiers was instructed that they were to be freely conducted and all points of view allowed to find expression.[1] In wartime this was hardly to be expected, but de Gaulle hoped the war would be over, for he was already secretly negotiating with the FLN. Offers of lavish economic aid were accompanied by proposals for a 'peace of the brave'—but with his inveterate love of ambiguity de Gaulle combined this unprecedented tribute to his adversaries' courage with a reference to 'the white flag of parley' for the benefit of the army and settlers. This destroyed any psychological impact on the FLN, and the olive branch was spurned. But de Gaulle was not unduly discouraged. Though Salan could not now be compelled to conduct free elections, the Elysée rightly remained confident that even Muslim deputies handpicked by the army would soon reflect the changing views of their own people. Salan himself was appointed Inspector-General of the Army amid much flattery in December; three weeks later his new office was abolished and he was made Military Governor of Paris (an honorific post in which his chief duty was to lead ceremonial parades down the Champs Elysées).

Both in consolidating and exploiting his position, de Gaulle's technique was already evident. The referendum was a device not only to scatter his domestic opponents but also to impress the country and the world—and, not least, the army—with the extent of his domestic support. Having demonstrated the strength of his position de Gaulle would then offer concessions in the hope of bringing the FLN to a quick settlement on favourable terms, so freeing his hand for the independent foreign policy which was always his main objective. Thus his first attempt to reassert French influence in the world coincided with his first moves to end the Algerian war, and they failed together. Just before the referendum he sent to the United States and Britain a note demanding reorganization of the Atlantic alliance to give France an equal share in a tripartite directorate. No doubt he hoped that a

---

[1] Also that all army officers were to quit the Committees of Public Safety; they did, and the settler leaders did not react.

27

sweeping victory in the referendum and a settlement with the FLN would improve his chances within NATO—perhaps also, and alternatively, that concessions from NATO would strengthen his position towards the FLN. But the FLN refused his offer, and the note about NATO (still unpublished in 1970) was never answered; only the French voters showed overwhelming confidence in him to settle the war on favourable terms.

Time would show, however, that he needed a settlement on any terms, for without it his foreign policy was paralysed. The problem was thus mainly one of convincing his countrymen, and for that he would require the freest possible hand throughout. He wanted no pressure from a parliament dominated by his own most strident supporters, whose leading figures were often intransigently determined to make no political concessions in Algeria. This desire for a free hand explains the President's surprising choice of an electoral system for the new Assembly: a return to the prewar arrangements of single-member constituencies and two ballots, which were expected to prevent a runaway victory by his own partisans and provide a strong balancing force on the Left.[1] Instead the voters used the second ballot to discriminate in favour of the Gaullists and against the Communists and the regular Fourth Republic politicians. With a sixth of the vote on the first ballot, but over a quarter on the second, the UNR won 200 seats. There were 130 Conservatives, reinforced at first by 70 members returned under army auspices in Algeria, but only 140 from all the other Fourth Republic parties combined. Isolated and weakened, the Communists had a remnant of only ten members, despite polling a fifth of the vote. The new house would clearly be dominated by the rivalry between two parties, Gaullists and Conservatives, whose deputies had often campaigned as supporters of both the President and *Algérie française*. When those two causes finally proved irreconcilable, the right-wing opposition thus commanded far greater strength in the house than in the country; it was not surprising that de Gaulle and his loyal followers distrusted that National Assembly, for most of his

---

[1] At the first ballot a clear majority of votes cast was needed, at the second a simple plurality; before the war this system had benefited moderate parties.

democratic critics did so too. But hardly anyone outside the Elysée foresaw that when the break came, almost the whole UNR would follow wherever de Gaulle led. When Raymond Aron warned him that he would be a prisoner of the extremists, he is said to have replied: 'Prisoners escape'.

At the beginning of 1959 the new institutions were installed. A new electoral college for choosing the President of the Republic, composed overwhelmingly of local councillors, functioned for the first and last time in December 1958 and gave 80 per cent of 80,000-odd votes to Charles de Gaulle. As his first Prime Minister the new President chose Michel Debré, a loyal Gaullist who had never taken office in the Fourth Republic, had been a violent defender of French rule in Algeria, and had participated vigorously in the May 1958 conspiracy. Soustelle, who had hoped for the Ministry of the Interior in default of the premiership, was sent to preside over deserts and oceans as Minister for the Sahara and for the Pacific Islands. Defence, Foreign Affairs, Interior (except for four months) and other important posts remained in the hands of civil servants. The one front-rank political leader not a Gaullist was Antoine Pinay, the ideal Minister of Finance to reassure respectable conservative opinion. His severe economic measures—devaluation, deflation and economy— amounted to a classical decision to put a strong currency before domestic expansion or social progress; the Socialists resigned from the government in protest, though promising to continue to support de Gaulle over Algeria. The MRP ministers remained (without Pflimlin). Debré met the Assembly in January and was given a massive vote of confidence by 453 to 56, with 29 abstentions.

For most of 1959 Algerian policy was at a standstill and the political scene was dominated by the routine conflicts of domestic politics. For the municipal elections of March 1959 the Gaullists again chose a majority system (except in the biggest cities) in order to polarize opinion between themselves and the Communists and force their way into power in local government as they had in parliament. But the economic situation was worse, and the electorate thought differently in different kinds of election: the Communists partially recovered and the old politicians regained their hold on their former voters. The election of the new Senate in April (by local councillors as usual) was described as 'the revenge of the

Fourth Republic'; in contrast to the Assembly, most former members were returned and so were several prominent victims of the general election, including François Mitterrand, Gaston Defferre and Edgar Faure. The upper house therefore soon became both the stronghold of the critics, and the centre of lively debate. Its quarrel with the government began very early, for the senators with their traditionalist outlook and opposition allegiance resented even more than the deputies the new political style, and especially the restrictive new standing orders with which the government and the UNR sought to limit parliament's opportunities to harass and vote against the ministry.[1] The government ran into worse trouble with the pro-clerical majority in the Assembly, and particularly the Conservatives, on the perennial problem of the church schools at the end of 1959. Debré had no clerical sympathies and had always regarded this as a bogus conflict, stirred up by the politicians, which could soon be solved by a leader with a little goodwill and courage: but the compromise with which he hoped to settle the problem was quickly distorted by pressure from his majority for drastic amendment, the cabinet was split, the Minister of Education resigned in protest against the concessions made to the Right, and the anti-clericals raised ten million signatures for their petition against the bill. But this was an issue ranging Right against Left, not government against opposition. In the long run there was more political danger in problems on which the traditional politicians of Right and Left could combine: agricultural prices, ex-servicemen's benefits, above all Europe.

That lay ahead. In 1959 the President attempted no major new venture in foreign policy, but he began the policy of pinpricks towards a NATO which showed no sign of granting him the increased influence he demanded: in March he withdrew French ships from NATO command, in June he provoked the withdrawal of American bombers by refusing to store bombs or install launching ramps, in August he criticized proposals for a summit meeting, and in November, in a speech at the Ecole Militaire, he roundly declared that the

---

[1] In June, the two ministers re-elected to the Senate had to choose between their offices and their seats: both preferred parliament — officially, and in part genuinely, for reasons of health.

whole concept of military integration had 'had its day'. When the first French atomic device was exploded in the Sahara in February 1960, he telegraphed 'Hurrah for France'. Meanwhile, in December 1959, de Gaulle had enunciated in Senegal a major change in his colonial policy: henceforth a member state of the Community was to be allowed to become independent while retaining its membership.[1]

The Algerian settlement

Above all, on 16 September de Gaulle announced that Algeria was to be allowed self-determination. As at Dakar three months later, the President of the Republic publicly proclaimed a major new policy and emphasized its source: 'On my responsibility and with a full grasp of the situation I have decided the action we must take in Algeria.'[2] The reaction from the Right came quickly—and prematurely—in an attempt to repeat the May 1958 operation, with riots and military disobedience in Algeria coinciding with a parliamentary crisis in Paris.[3] Nine leading extremists resigned from the UNR in a move to start an anti-Debré bandwagon which might sweep Georges Bidault to the premiership. But the plot fizzled out without disorders, and Debré won another huge vote of confidence on the new policy by 441 to 23, with 88 abstentions. At the end of 1959, therefore, his government

---

[1] This promise was given legal form by a constitutional amendment voted in May 1960, by a procedure which, while doubtless justified politically, clearly violated the constitution itself. By the end of 1960 the Community's member states were all independent. Although several remained formally members of the Community, its institutions ceased to be operative, and early in 1961, again setting convenience over constitutional propriety, de Gaulle simply announced that the Senate of the Community was considered dissolved.

[2] From his message to the army of 28 October 1959.

[3] It was in this tense conspiratorial atmosphere, with one prominent Gaullist warning that 'the killer commandos have crossed the Spanish frontier', that François Mitterrand announced he had narrowly escaped an attempt to assassinate him. He was discredited for some time by the subsequent revelation that he had had prior warning of the attempt. Probably he had tried to outwit the fascists but was himself fooled by them. See P. M. Williams, *Wars, Plots and Scandals in Post-War France* (Cambridge, 1970), ch. 5.

had an overwhelming paper majority but was threatened by growing discontent over policy at home, abroad, and above all in Algeria. The attacks came to a head at the beginning of 1960, the decisive year of the early Fifth Republic. For this was the point at which President de Gaulle, faced with the opposition of the parties and much of the public to his domestic and foreign policies and of the army to his Algerian objectives, decided that he could no longer remain an 'arbiter' above the battle but must descend into the arena and take personal command.

In January 1960 Antoine Pinay was dismissed. The pretext was the friction between the Minister of Finance and several of his colleagues, not least the Premier, over domestic legislation; the more important reason was Pinay's opposition to the President's foreign policies, both European and Atlantic. With his departure only one major Fourth Republican figure remained in a cabinet remarkable for its colourlessness: Jacques Soustelle. It was not for long. On 24 January a group of Algiers fascists fired on the gendarmerie and set up barricades in the centre of Algiers; some sections of the army command then tried to use them, as in May 1958, to deflect the Paris government from its course. But de Gaulle stood firm, and after a week of wobbling the army decided to obey the government; the barricades came down and in mid-February Soustelle and another minister, who had openly shown sympathy for the insurgents, were removed from their posts. For the first time for many years a clash between Paris and Algiers had been decided in favour of the former.

President de Gaulle was now at the peak of his popularity with the public, especially on the Left—confirmed in that quarter by Khrushchev's visit to Paris in March. He suddenly became a hero to a large section of the Muslim population of Algeria—and when parliament was recalled to approve special powers in February, the supposedly integrationist Muslim deputies voted for them by fifty-two to seven, while the European members from Algeria opposed by sixteen to nine. But the army was sullen and resentful; and for nine months de Gaulle chose to disappoint his new supporters in an effort to reassure his old ones. In March he visited officers in Algeria and spoke of a long war which could only be ended after a military victory; in June he accepted the first publicly admitted talks with the FLN, only to frustrate them by a display of total intransigence. At home and abroad, opinion became increasingly exasperated. Within France the atmosphere was poisoned by two spectacular political trials, one of the leaders of the barricades revolt, the other of a group of intellectuals accused of working for the FLN.[1] It was in this mood of passion and indignation that the government forced through parliament its bill to create a nuclear strike force, for which it was unable to command a positive majority in either house.

The political lull over Algeria was ended abruptly before 1960 ran out. Not only was the domestic situation deteriorating, events elsewhere suggested that time was no longer on de Gaulle's side. Collaboration with Germany, launched after Adenauer's visit to Rambouillet in July, was being delayed and impeded by doubts about de Gaulle's strength at home. The Soviet Union received Ferhat Abbas in September, though without formally recognizing the FLN's provisional government of Algeria. On 8 November the United States elected as President John F. Kennedy, the first American leader to express (in 1957) public sympathy for Algerian independence. Four days earlier de Gaulle had announced that a referendum would shortly be held to approve self-determination for Algeria, which would have new institutions set up now and would one day become an independent Republic: he had conceded the FLN's war aim. On 9 December the President visited Algeria, but his tour was arranged to avoid the major cities; the Europeans rioted against him and on the 11th Muslim counter demonstrations, originally in support of de Gaulle, soon proclaimed the FLN sympathies of the townspeople who, for four years, had been passive under the tight control of the French police. It was on 11 December 1960 that the French government and people at last shed their illusions about the extent of Muslim support for French rule in Algeria, and began to accept the inevitability of FLN government in the near future.

In the referendum of 8 January 1961 de Gaulle again demonstrated what a powerful weapon he had forged against his domestic opponents. The right-wing opposition to self-determination was led by his former minister Jacques Soustelle,

---

[1] Cf. below, p. 264.

who carried many Conservatives and a few supporters of
other parties with him; Communists, Left Socialists and
Radicals favoured self-determination but voted No because
they demanded direct negotiation with the FLN. At 15,200,000
the Yes vote was 2½ million below 1958, and 55 per cent
(instead of 66 per cent) of the total electorate. The No vote
was just 5 million and the Left element in it was even weaker
than in 1958. In Algeria most rural Muslims voted Yes and
nearly all Europeans No; the electorate divided into 40 per
cent Yes, 20 per cent No and 40 per cent not voting—
principally the town Muslims, now openly following FLN
instructions. Yet the result of the referendum was bizarre.
The French Left had denounced the proposed provisional
institutions as a sham, diverting attention from the real
issue, which was whether or not to negotiate with the
FLN—who had been refusing any negotiation for six months.
Yet no sooner had de Gaulle won his popular victory than
the FLN called for the talks they had refused, and in reply
the French government promptly shelved the bill to set
up provisional new institutions in Algeria, which it had
asked the voters at the referendum to approve. Ironically,
de Gaulle's final appeal to the electorate to ratify his
proposals had assured them that 'Everything is simple and
clear'.

The President was now anxious to liquidate the Algerian
incubus as soon as possible, and turn his attention to matters
of greater moment. His impatience showed in his press
conference of 11 April, with its cynical and demagogic appeal
to the petty motives he usually fought so vigorously: we must
disengage from Algeria, he told his countrymen, because it
does not pay. Nothing was more certain to exasperate the
soldiers who had been assured for years that they were risking
their own lives—and worse, encouraging pro-French Muslims
to risk theirs—in defence of country and civilization. Eleven
days later the army seized power in Algiers under the leadership of General Challe, a former commander-in-chief whose
high reputation for integrity and moderation brought to the
mutineers most of the limited support they received; he had
consented to participate only after de Gaulle's remarks. On
23 April the President took over full powers of government
under article 16 of the constitution—and retained them until
30 September although the emergency in Algeria lasted for

only four days.[1] Opinion in France was overwhelmingly hostile to the rebels, and a token general strike demonstrated popular support for the government; in Algeria itself the conscripts passively resisted the actively mutinous regular officers, whose colleagues mostly waited cautiously to see which side would win. It quickly became clear that the revolt could not succeed, and Challe, overruling associates like Salan, ensured that it was liquidated without any bloodshed; the civilian extremists of Algiers were never allowed any opportunity to act.

Despite de Gaulle's impatience, little progress was made during the summer and indeed the situation deteriorated. Negotiations with the FLN went on between May and July, but were blocked by the French refusal to discuss the Algerian claim to the Sahara, and poisoned by a violent clash between French and Tunisian forces at Bizerta. In August the Berlin wall provided the President with a new motive for reaching a settlement (and a new pretext for bringing his army home). In the next two weeks there were extensive changes in both the French and the exiled Algerian governments; in Paris the reshuffle strengthened Debré, while the rebels brought to the front men reputedly more intransigent, but perhaps therefore better able to make concessions, than their figure-head predecessors like Ferhat Abbas. On 5 September de Gaulle, having recently allowed the negotiations to fail over the Sahara, decided unilaterally to concede the FLN's claim.[2] Three days later he escaped a clumsy attempt to assassinate him. On 12 September the entire opposition walked out of parliament when the President of the Assembly ruled that a censure motion was out of order, and de Gaulle quickly decided to appease parliamentary frustration by abandoning his emergency powers.

The war now entered its last phase. A settlement was so close that the French administration began what was virtually

---

[1] Article 16 provides that in circumstances (of which the President alone is the sole judge) when the State's continued existence is in danger, the President may assume full executive, legislative, judicial and military authority to deal with the crisis. See below, pp. 189–92.

[2] The act was typical of the Gaullist conception of negotiation by unilateral assertion or concession. The General's chief negotiator, Louis Joxe, learned of it from the press.

a reversal of alliances; its main enemies were now the European extremists and their terrorist Secret Army Organization (OAS), while the French forces and the FLN tried not to provoke one another since each knew they would soon be cooperating. OAS terrorism began in Algiers in September, and soon developed first into indiscriminate attacks on Muslims, then into a spiteful 'scorched earth' policy against plant and buildings, intended to deny to independent Algeria any inheritance at all from the 130 years of French rule. Terrorism quickly spread to Paris, with bomb attacks on the homes and offices of prominent Gaullists or left-wing supporters. The harassed Paris police were slow, like some other sections of the French government machine, to adjust their conduct to the new situation. In October there were demonstrations by Algerians in Paris against the restrictive and exasperating curfew to which they were subjected as a check on FLN terrorism; the police replied with even more than their usual brutality and scores of demonstrators were allegedly thrown into the Seine to drown. Frenchmen demonstrating against OAS terrorism also met such police hostility that many people wondered whether the police were going the way of the army, especially after eight Communist demonstrators were killed by the police on 8 February at the Charonne metro station.[1]

This, however, was the turning-point. The obsequies of the victims, five days later, became the greatest left-wing demonstration in Paris for a generation, with 400,000 to 500,000 people marching—and were treated by the authorities almost as a state procession. On 19 March an agreement with the FLN was finally signed at Evian; parliament was called to hear a government statement, but no censure motion was proposed by the Right and no vote was taken. With the OAS busily reducing Algeria to chaos, the French electorate again went to the polls on 8 April to approve the agreement (and give the President full powers to enforce it) by referendum. There were under two million Noes from the far Right, over a million spoiled or blank ballots, largely from the Left. But

---

[1] Roger Frey, the Minister of the Interior, who had successfully evaded all attempts to inquire into the October repression, blamed the Charonne affair first on the Communists themselves, and later on OAS provocateurs disguised as policemen. See also below, p. 221.

the Communists unhappily voted Yes, so that de Gaulle could claim over 90 per cent of the votes cast and as many supporters as in 1958.[1]

The rout of the parties

Michel Debré, having grudgingly followed the President to the bitter end, now urged him to capitalize on the popularity of the peace by dissolving the Assembly and holding a general election. But de Gaulle refused. All the parties had supported the Evian settlement, and unless he could create a sharp conflict between him and them the return to peace would not bring their voters to desert their old allegiance for the UNR. Debré, therefore, was granted neither the election he sought nor the peacetime premiership in which he hoped to find compensation for his three-year martyrdom; instead he was summarily replaced by Georges Pompidou.[2] As Pompidou had never been elected to parliament (or indeed to anything) he went out of his way to conciliate the members, and tried to broaden the government's political base by bringing in a number of moderate critics. Edgar Faure refused his proposal, but MRP, already represented in the government, agreed to his offer of more posts for more prominent leaders, notably Pflimlin. Within a few weeks, however, the President held a press conference at which he made it clear that he sought MRP's collaboration only on his own terms: sardonically jeering at the enthusiasts for a united Europe, he hinted that they would really like to abandon French and replace it by Volapük.[3] Apparently to his surprise, the MRP ministers—old and new alike—resigned within a month of their appointments.[4] Nor did the government fare much better in its efforts to woo

---

[1] Owing to OAS terrorism, Algeria did not vote in April (which probably made the referendum unconstitutional) but ratified the agreements overwhelmingly in a referendum of its own on 1 July — whereupon the Algerian members were at once removed from parliament by presidential ordinance.

[2] 'If there were Olympic games for ingratitude, de Gaulle would win the gold medal': J. L. Tixier-Vignancour.

[3] An obscure international language, invented in the General's childhood, which has never achieved even the modest fame of Esperanto.

[4] Thus retaining their parliamentary seats: see below, p. 208n.

parliament; on 13 June it held a debate on foreign affairs but
refused to allow a vote, and so provoked a second walk-out
by the opposition—which found 293 deputies, a large majority
of the Assembly, to sign a declaration in favour of a united
Europe. A month later the government had some difficulty
passing through parliament its great agriculture act—in which
it was the minister (Edgard Pisani) who was the reformer and
the members, especially the senators, who were the conservatives, so that the Gaullists earned much goodwill from
the progressive younger generation of peasant leaders.[1]

Ordinary political issues were again coming to the fore, but
the remnants of the Algerian problem remained, and the OAS
terrorists were rounded up only slowly. Under article 16 de
Gaulle had set up a special military court to try those accused
of subversion; on 23 May it found mitigating circumstances
for General Salan—who after the putsch of April 1961 had
become leader of the OAS—and sentenced him only to life
imprisonment, not to death. The court was abolished on the
27th and a new one set up three days later under the special
powers conferred on the President by the Evian referendum
(this new court was to be declared illegal by the Conseil d'Etat
in October because no appeal was allowed from its decisions).[2]
Now, with the end of the emergency, de Gaulle was to find
he could no longer act as he chose with complete political
impunity and the grateful support of public opinion.

The moment seemed to have come for which the old
politicians had waited so long. The great man had fulfilled the
national task for which alone they had called him back to
power. Now, with Algeria safely out of the way (and the
responsibility for its loss firmly attached to the President)
they could soon hope to shunt him aside and return to
'politics as usual'. He had neglected his opportunity to dissolve
in April, and failed to reconcile his most moderate critics in
May; a general election was due within a year and after it the
parties could hope, as in 1946, to force de Gaulle to govern
on their terms or retire into private life. But the General was
as well aware of the situation as his rivals, and infinitely their

[1] See below, pp. 292–3.

[2] See below, pp. 264–6 and 284–5. The Conseil d'Etat is an
independent body which acts (*inter alia*) as legal adviser to the
government.

superior as a strategist. All he needed was an issue on which to draw them into battle on ground of his choice. The pretext was provided by a second OAS assassination attempt, far more dangerous than the first: on 22 August at Petit Clamart he escaped death by two inches. As in the previous years, de Gaulle emerged from his summer retreat to start politics on a fresh course. The danger of assassination, he warned on 4 October, made it urgent to amend the arrangements for electing the President of the Republic: a successor without de Gaulle's personal prestige would need a fuller popular mandate than the present electoral college of local councillors could provide. The risk of public turmoil after a successful assassination attempt was therefore to be overcome by summoning all Frenchmen to the polls to choose their new President.

The argument for urgency was tenuous but the proposal itself was highly popular—and brilliantly calculated to embarrass the politicians. Hardly any of them liked it, for it would reinforce presidential power by giving the new President as good a claim to represent the sovereign people as parliament itself. Yet if they opposed it they would appear as selfish, negative men trying to prevent the ordinary Frenchman deciding who should rule over him: a poor platform for electoral success. If they decided to swallow their objections and prudently vote Yes, they would allow de Gaulle at any time to precipitate a new presidential election by declaring that his mandate from the old electoral college was inadequate, and that he felt a democratic duty to seek a new one from the people.[1] Few of them contemplated this course, for de Gaulle (probably deliberately) made it almost impossible for a self-respecting parliamentarian to follow it. He did this by choosing to introduce his reform by a method that was blatantly unconstitutional, neglecting the procedure for amending the constitution under article 89 (by a bill which must go through parliament before being submitted to referendum) and sending his bill direct to referendum under article 11.[2] The decision left the ordinary voter utterly

---

[1] Nothing would induce de Gaulle to encumber himself with a vice-president.

[2] See below, p. 188. Under the regular procedure the bill would probably have failed in the Senate.

indifferent; but it shocked all jurists and all politicians except the most devoted Gaullists, and even some of them; one minister (Pierre Sudreau) resigned in protest and not only the independent Conseil d'Etat but even the hitherto usually Gaullist Constitutional Council disapproved. On 5 October the National Assembly voted to censure Pompidou's government, which bore technical responsibility for the decision, by 280 votes—39 more than the clear majority required—and was at once dissolved. The battle between de Gaulle and the parties was to be fought out on terrain carefully selected by the General.

The referendum took place on 28 October (in the middle of the Cuban missile crisis, to which the French public showed surprising indifference while the French President gave unwonted support to the United States). De Gaulle warned in advance that he would resign, not merely if he lost but if his majority was *'faible, médiocre ou aléatoire'*. Wisely, he did not define his terms, for by his own past standards the victory was not glorious: the No vote was up to nearly eight million, and the Yeses (under thirteen million) were for the first time less than half the whole electorate. Yet if the result was no triumph for de Gaulle, it was a serious warning to the old parties. Between 1958 and 1962 every one of them, except the Gaullists and the Communists, had switched from support to opposition; together they had only managed to knock 4,300,000 off the Yes vote and add 3,300,000 to the Noes.

After this demonstration of weakness the parties faced a difficult choice at the election: they could offer a viable alternative to the regime only by combining against the Gaullists, as at the referendum—but that would suggest a purely negative consortium to restore the Fourth Republic. Making the worst of a bad situation, they negotiated at national level a coalition which did not work in the constituencies, and so appeared at once conspiratorial and futile. The Socialist leader Guy Mollet saved some seats from the wreck by a last-minute partial pact with the Communists, but the blow which had shattered the Left in 1958 now fell heavily on the Centre and Right. While many voters had defied their parties and backed de Gaulle in the referendum, some would not go all the way to the UNR: in October nearly 13 million had voted Yes, a month later little more than half that number supported Gaullist candidates. But many who did not were still unwilling to repudiate the President by returning to their old allegiance, so the turnout was 2½ million below the referendum figure. The Fourth Republican parties polled between them 5 million fewer votes than in 1958, and won 90 fewer seats; Socialists and Radicals gained seats by their local pacts with the Communists, and Right and Centre losses were in three figures. The Communists also gained seats through the pacts, but without recovering the votes lost in 1958. The UNR and its allies took 6½ million votes, almost twice as many as on the first ballot in 1958, and 250 seats—a gain of 60 and a clear majority. The election had installed them more firmly in power than ever. As one commentator put it: 'We say Yes to de Gaulle and de Gaulle says No to the rest of the universe.'

3

GRANDEUR AND DECAY
1962–1968

Stability at home, activity abroad

The Algerian settlement, Raymond Aron once remarked, was the final proof of de Gaulle's political genius. He had been driven to accept everything France had fought against—total independence, exclusive FLN rule, loss of the Sahara, evacuation of the whole European population—and yet still he won a decisive electoral victory on a record which would have ruined any other leader. The nightmare over, the French set determinedly about burying the painful memory as speedily as possible. Two problems threatened to keep the issue from dying: the trials of the OAS terrorists, and the influx of 800,000 refugees—a group whose frustrations and resentments might well fester dangerously. But government provision for resettlement was imaginative, energetically administered, and generous (though claims for loss of property were not conceded).

Aided by the continuing buoyancy of the economy the refugees were absorbed into normal life in France with astonishingly little friction. The treatment of the conspirators was more controversial. The series of special courts, abolished and replaced when they gave the 'wrong' verdict, had created a thoroughly bad impression which the government tried to efface by introducing a bill establishing a new permanent State Security Court, and by allowing parliament to modify some of the more draconian provisions in its draft. One provision of this new law gave parliamentary sanction to all the ordinances made under the special powers conferred in the post-Evian referendum—thereby restoring to legal life the military court which the Conseil d'Etat had found *ultra vires* in the previous October—and de Gaulle's would-be assassins were tried by this revived military court rather than the new

42

one with its greater legal safeguards.[1] But the execution of their leader in April marked the close of the violent period of the conflict. Only four of the OAS murderers were executed; over the next few years the great majority of prisoners were released individually. Even so, all the major parties except the Gaullists and the Communists soon began vying in advocacy of an amnesty for the remaining hard core. Pious Gaullist horror at this politicking over murderers and enemies of the Republic endured until they themselves stood in need of army and right-wing support during the near-revolution in 1968; then within weeks, just over six years after Evian, the last of the OAS prisoners were freed. Fears that the former OAS men would form a new *Freikorps* threatening the stability of the regime had never materialized. The Fifth Republic was not Weimar. The army and the refugees, like the mass of ordinary Frenchmen, wanted only to forget the past and turn the Algerian page.

His hands now freed by peace in North Africa and electoral victory at home, de Gaulle could strike out at last with a more assertive foreign policy. On 14 January 1963 he unilaterally vetoed British entry into the European Community, then eight days later again sidestepped his other partners in the Six by signing a Treaty of Cooperation with Bonn. A Germany docilely accepting the leadership of Paris would give him a broader base from which to launch an attack on the existing international order, and transform it in French interests. But the Bundestag, noting that in vetoing Britain de Gaulle had flouted the consultation specified in the Treaty even before signing it, diluted Adenauer's enthusiasm by unanimously voting a restrictive preamble. The politicians were only reflecting the views of their constituents who, four months earlier in the wake of de Gaulle's visit, had believed by more than ten to one that his policies were favourable to Germany; after the veto opinions had shifted sharply.[2] Before long it became apparent that the American Trojan Horse in Europe was not Britain but Germany, clearly determined that if forced to a desperately unwanted choice she would look to

---

[1] For fuller discussion see below, pp. 264-6.
[2] Replies were 61 per cent 'favourable' in October, and 28 per cent in Feb.–March; 6 per cent 'unfavourable' in October, and 33 per cent in Feb.–March: cf. A. Grosser, *French Foreign Policy under de Gaulle* (Boston, 1967), p. 72.

Washington rather than Paris. By the summer de Gaulle was already lamenting treaties 'that fade, like roses'.

The 1963 failure marked the turning point in the foreign policy of the Fifth Republic, inasmuch as the idea of an independent Europe with a Franco-German basis formed a clear, immediate objective . . . attempts to find an alternative policy [through] the French influence in Latin America . . . and the recognition of Mao Tse-Tung's China did not bring the anticipated satisfactions. Therefore, there only remained the resort to a rapprochement with the USSR.[1]

Together with disappointment abroad, the spring of 1963 brought de Gaulle a grave domestic failure in the mishandling of the great miners' strike of March and April. When the miners came out against their nationalized employers it was calculated in Paris that rank-and-file militancy was shaky; here then was an opportunity for a convincing assertion of State authority against a troublesome sectional interest. The government decided to break the strike by requisitioning the workers, and to commit de Gaulle's prestige by having him sign the order. But it was ignored. The strike, which was completely orderly, continued amid overwhelming sympathy from the general public—from *Algérie française* sympathizers willing to use any stick to beat the Gaullists to bishops with a social conscience (the Elysée privately sought legal advice in the vain hope of deposing one outspoken prelate). Even *Le Figaro*, that unfailing weathercock of bourgeois opinion, took the strikers' side. The government had to back down and accept a compromise settlement very favourable to the workers. It was the President's worst domestic setback yet, and it brought his popularity down to its lowest point during his first decade in power; in a May 1963 opinion poll only 42 per cent approved of him, while 40 per cent disapproved. (In the mining areas the consequences were lasting; four years later the Left made sweeping gains in the parliamentary elections in a region they had never previously penetrated, while the Gaullists lost ground even to those opposition parties which were falling back elsewhere.) The government scored a minor revenge against the unions in July when a

---

[1] Grosser, *op. cit.*, pp. 163–4.

series of lightning strikes in the capital's transport system caused widespread public exasperation; a bill requiring five days' notice of strikes in the public sector passed through parliament with wide support despite loud protests from the unions.[1] But by September there were more serious economic preoccupations; threatened with inflationary pressure the government decided on a 'stabilization plan' entailing a slow-down in economic expansion and a series of austerity measures which were to threaten its popularity both immediately and superficially, and more profoundly in the long term.

Mistakes and misfortunes such as these were manna to opposition politicians, and criticism of the regime was more general and widespread at the summer and autumn party conferences than at any time during the Algerian war. But capitalizing on them was difficult. The criticism had no immediate focus, for the next election lay well ahead, and no clear direction, for opposition could not be planned until the Socialists had chosen their course. No alternative government was credible without their cooperation, yet any clear align-ment with either the Communists or the Centre carried serious dangers of dividing and weakening them. To their leader, Guy Mollet, escape from this dilemma lay in playing down the importance of the forthcoming presidential election; his rival, Gaston Defferre, sought instead to exploit it to build around the party a new Left movement capable of bargaining from strength with Centre and Communists alike. The politics of the next eighteen months were dominated by Defferre's cam-paign and by the successful efforts of the bosses of all the old parties to smother it—with the connivance of the leaders of the new regime, tireless in proclaiming the need for party renewal, unremitting in discrediting any move to achieve it.

Defferre's candidature won support in his party because, unlike Mollet's resolute ignoring of the presidential contest, it offered some hope of reviving the Socialists' waning for-tunes. When on 2 February 1964 the party endorsed his candidature without imposing restrictive conditions, Defferre

---

[1] See P. M. Williams, *The French Parliament 1958–67* (London, 1968), p. 33; the bill proved harmless but futile. Another bill finally passed (against strong resistance by majority members led by Michel Debré), gave grudging recognition to conscientious objection to military service, over which French traditions had been highly illiberal. See below, pp. 287–91.

promptly made it clear that he regarded the presidency as the chief policy-making institution, and would resign it if his policies failed to command a parliamentary majority—thus repudiating the old regime and committing himself to a democratized Fifth Republic. Already the Communists were determined to defeat him. Although at this stage he had shown them no hostility, he had made it clear he would not negotiate his policy and programme with them; he was trying to strengthen his hand by appealing for support in the Centre; and in foreign policy at least his views were further from their own than were de Gaulle's. This was the period when Maurice Thorez solemnly proclaimed that the Communists had never been a party of all-or-nothing, did not believe in opposition on principle, and welcomed the 'positive aspects' of de Gaulle's foreign policy: his recent recognition of China, his support for the neutralization of Vietnam, and his opposition to American influence in the Middle East and Latin America. This new attitude of cautious sympathy for Gaullist foreign policy was to endure after Thorez's death in July, and to impose a quite uncharacteristic ambivalence on the Party's attitude to the regime.

Meanwhile, in the Gaullist camp, Georges Pompidou was emerging as a possible dauphin. In April 1964 he took up a challenge from Mitterrand to debate the prime minister's role in the system, and by common consent got the better of that formidable opponent—a feat which immensely enhanced his prestige with the Gaullist deputies. During the President's prostate operation in April, and the Latin American tour of September, the Prime Minister performed the presidential functions and in between toured his own native department of Cantal quite in the presidential style. In all this activity he was carrying out de Gaulle's alleged advice with possibly excessive zeal: just before the General's return Pompidou's final cabinet meeting was abruptly cancelled on the instructions of the President, who was supposed to have commented, 'I said "Make yourself known", not "Make yourself noticed" '.

Nevertheless, Pompidou's emergence was one sign that the regime was settling down to the new situation of a France at peace and a loyal majority in the Assembly. Another indication was the smoothness with which the parliamentary machine now functioned. A substantial administrative reform was passed in May, the local government of the Paris region reorganized in June, and a compromise arranged on political control of broadcasting—though the government, apparently on instructions from the Elysée, then intervened to upset the compromise and ensure that the Gaullist monopoly remained intact.[1] In the autumn the government introduced—first on television and only later in parliament—a budget whose statistical presentation allowed it to be hailed as the first balanced budget for thirty years; several Gaullist rapporteurs (notably on education) greeted it very critically. The first censure motion of the parliament, in October, reflected the perennial discontents of the farmers and in particular a recent long and unpopular milk strike;[2] it attracted only 209 votes (32 short of a majority) though these included six Conservatives, nominal supporters of the government. Next month the Fifth National Plan was laid before parliament, the first ever to be debated there before it came into operation. Once again the feature of the debate was the criticism from within the majority's ranks, for the most effective critical speech was not Gaston Defferre's but Michel Debré's. Another sign of successful pressure by the government's own supporters was the introduction in December of an amnesty bill for the minor OAS prisoners, which it had refused to consider in November. But the majority remained solid on essentials, and the bill authorizing the French nuclear strike force passed by a comfortable majority of a hundred.

To de Gaulle stability at home was important primarily as a precondition for successful activity abroad. But he was not a man to despise political by-products, and was well aware that foreign policy can in turn bring domestic benefits. The demonstrative gestures of 1964, which served as substitutes for the stillborn Franco-German treaty, were a notable example, for their only practical consequences were in home politics. Recognition of China in January succeeded in embarrassing simultaneously the Americans, the Russians and, most of all, the French Left. The Latin American tour in September was a triumphant success with the crowd and gratifying proof to voters at home that France was again cutting a figure in the world. Neither initiative had any

---

[1] This was to boomerang against them. See below, p. 50 and Williams, *op. cit.*, p. 93.

[2] See below, p. 296.

discernible effect on the policy of any government. In 1965 the new course in world policy was carried further with large-scale sales of dollars for gold, laying the groundwork for an attack on the international monetary system and particularly the dollar, made possible by France's unprecedentedly healthy reserves. The Soviet Union and her East European neighbours were courted, and there were fresh measures to reinforce French standing among the developing countries—announcements of aid, a petroleum deal favourable to the Algerians, and increasingly vigorous criticism of American policy in Vietnam, Cuba and the Dominican Republic.

Meanwhile de Gaulle pursued his campaigns against American economic, diplomatic and cultural influence within Europe, under the slogan of *l'Europe européenne* he had launched in November 1963. Already—notably over agriculture in that same month—he had more than once pursued a policy of brinkmanship within the Six in defence of French interests, but in July 1965 he precipitated a crisis which brought the Community to the verge of complete disruption. Determined to halt the development of supranational decision-making, he seized the pretext of the EEC Council of Ministers' customary failure to meet its deadline for agreeing on agricultural finance, to launch an all-out attack on the role of the Commission and the erosion of the national veto. For six months the French boycotted Brussels. But for once the Five stood firm, and French voters, concerned that the gains from Europe might be lost, helped swell the opposition score (especially Lecanuet's) at the presidential election. At Luxembourg in January 1966 de Gaulle was forced into a tactical withdrawal, in part to mend his domestic fences, in part to concentrate his fire against NATO.

Until this episode de Gaulle's foreign policy was popular with most sectors of opinion, and his successes over the agricultural Common Market even mollified the discontented farmers for a time. The urban workers, who resented the stabilization plan, were harder to satisfy. Although their grievances carried little immediate political weight since the unions were weak, there were large token strikes in the public sector in December 1964 and the following January. More significant for the long term was the decision in November 1964 by the CFTC—usually somewhat more aggressive than either the Communist CGT or the vaguely Socialist

FO—to abandon its official Catholicism and become the Confédération Française Démocratique du Travail (a Catholic minority splintering off with the old title) in the hope of increasing its influence among the irreligious majority of the workers. This was followed by an agreement for united action between CGT and CFDT, in which the latter often made the running.

In spite of the complaints against the government's economic and social policies, the Gaullist position seemed secure in early 1965. Opinion polls in the spring showed the President's popularity slightly higher than before the miners' strike, with 60 per cent approving and only 27 per cent critical. More unexpectedly, this approval now extended to the government too—though by a far smaller margin—and, more strikingly, to the regime itself. Such indications nourished Gaullist complacency and opposition pessimism about the forthcoming presidential election. But they were misleading. The Gaullists were appreciated less for their policies than for the stability they had brought to France. In other circumstances this asset could turn into a liability, as the municipal elections in March and the presidential contest in December were to show.

Electoral survival

The municipal councils, elected once every six years, have always been the chief arena for parties seeking to sink the local roots which are essential to long-term survival. In 1959 the Gaullists had hoped to triumph by polarizing opinion between themselves and the Left; in 1965 they repeated the mistake. They had again altered the election law to extend the majority system to the largest towns, and generally prevent any change in party lists between the two ballots, thus requiring deals between parties to be made before the first round. But the new rules failed to secure the desired polarization, for most towns were governed by coalitions of the centre (including the Socialists wherever they were strong) under a mayor who was already the recognized leader of the local majority. The very opinion poll which showed the impressive Gaullist strength in national politics had reported that an enormous majority (of 51 against 23 per cent) were intending to re-elect the mayor of their town. When the votes were counted in the 159 largest towns only seventeen outgoing mayors had been ousted, with no gain to the Gaullists. Stability therefore could play against the Gaullists as well as for them.

The presidential election was also a disappointment. At the summer's end polls showed the popularity of de Gaulle and the government to be greater than ever, and the disarray of their opponents more complete. Gaston Defferre had hoped to be the standard-bearer of all the Left and much of the Centre. But first he was bitterly attacked by the Communists, and then he failed to launch the new left-centre opposition party which he had hoped would appear as a credible alternative government.[1] When both Socialist and MRP bosses refused, Defferre withdrew his candidature rather than break with his party. Only three months before polling day the sole opposition leader in the field was the right-wing extremist Tixier-Vignancour. De Gaulle's boycott of the Common Market, with its confident indifference to the risk of incurring the farmers' wrath, spoke eloquently of his complacent assessment of the opposition's disarray.

However the opposition parties belatedly found two unexpectedly strong candidates. François Mitterrand attracted the support of the entire Left, while Jean Lecanuet was endorsed by the Conservatives, some moderate Radicals and many extreme right-wingers, as well as his own party, MRP. Then during the two short weeks of the official campaign, television enabled both men to project themselves effectively to the nation as representatives of a younger generation which was quite capable of managing the succession. This was partly because they (Lecanuet particularly) used the medium skilfully, unlike the older party leaders, but also because the unscrupulous way in which the government had normally monopolized the screen for its own friends ensured the maximum impact for men who were saying what they themselves thought rather than what the authorities wanted them to think. Above all it was because de Gaulle himself mishandled the campaign, treating it as a foregone conclusion, confining himself to the familiar attacks on the parties, and giving no sign whatever of concern over the succession problem, though standing for a term of office which he would begin at 75 and end at 82. Over six weeks of electioneering his opinion poll rating fell catastrophically by over 20 per

---

[1] See below, pp. 121–4.

cent, and in a record turnout on 5 December he had just under 44 per cent of the votes cast in metropolitan France; an impressive performance for any conventional politician, but for de Gaulle a rebuff which subjected him to the unexpected humiliation of a second ballot. Mitterrand won about as many votes as the Left in the 1962 election (though a lower percentage), while Lecanuet had more than the parties supporting him had won then. At the runoff ballot between the two leading candidates, Mitterrand attracted the great bulk of Tixier's million voters (mainly refugees from North Africa) and an unexpectedly large minority of Lecanuet's. De Gaulle's 12,650,000 votes were still slightly below the Yeses of October 1962, while Mitterrand's 10,550,000 were higher than the Noes had been. With 55 per cent of the votes de Gaulle was still a remarkably successful political leader, but he was no longer the incarnation of the unity of Frenchmen.

It was now the opposition's turn to display excessive optimism, and assume that de Gaulle and Gaullism were on the wane. Each of the three chief opposition candidates attempted to build a new party from his presidential following; all found their supporters were only partially and intermittently committed to reform. Nevertheless by the time of the general election of March 1967 there was to be some progress towards a new party structure, with only four main contenders taking the field: Gaullists, Communists, Mitterrand's Federation of the Left and Lecanuet's Democratic Centre (the extreme Right was to disintegrate long before the election). Mitterrand brought about the formation of a Federation 'shadow cabinet' in May 1966, but with its air of simply reshuffling the old pack of political figures and its failure to operate effectively as a parliamentary team it remained more shadow than substance—an ironic echo of the old jibe that under de Gaulle the 'shadow cabinet' is the one which holds office. However, despite its divided counsels, the Federation assented after a long hesitation to a close alliance with the Communists, leaving the Centre isolated and unable to present itself as a serious contender for power or even influence. The real struggle was to lie between the Gaullists and the Left.

In this contest foreign policy was an asset to the government. At the presidential election Lecanuet had profited from apprehensions over the President's brinkmanship in Brussels, but de Gaulle's tactical withdrawal at Luxembourg in January 1966 enabled him to resume negotiations which culminated in May in agricultural agreements along highly satisfactory lines for France. With this success the President had satisfied the 'European' opposition among the electorate, while his decision in March to withdraw from NATO (though not from the Atlantic alliance) simultaneously attracted many voters and divided the oppositions. For the first time the Communists refused to vote for a censure motion presented by the other opposition parties, which received only 137 votes—over a hundred short of a majority. Moreover, this fresh assertion of French independence was so popular in the country that within a few weeks most of the Federation leaders (though not those of the Centre) were avoiding the subject or muting their criticisms. Lecanuet's strong support for the American alliance was hampered by the extreme difficulty of defending the Vietnam war before a French audience;[1] and it helped to make the Centre the prime target for Communist attack. The President set the seal on his rapprochement with the East by his visit to Moscow in June, and on his campaign against the United States by a violent speech on Vietnam at Pnom-Penh on 1 September.[2]

Popular though such gestures were, particularly among many on the Left who had fought the regime from its birth, the ordinary Frenchman was more preoccupied with the everyday impact of social and economic policies, where Gaullism's record remained persistently right-wing. A cabinet reshuffle in January 1966 was intended to regain lost votes. Michel Debré, brought back as Minister of Finance, found himself unable to pursue a much more expansionist policy than his conservative predecessor Valéry Giscard d'Estaing (though the staunchly nationalist Debré did relax the costly hostility of the Atlanticist Giscard to American industrial investment). However, the new Minister of Agriculture, Edgar Faure, transformed the style and modified some of the policies of the dynamic but abrasive Pisani. Wooing the traditional conservative farmers' leaders, and profiting from

---

[1] This was because it was only recently (1954) that France had lost her own war in Indo-China.

[2] On his way there he was met by riots in Djibouti, a last outpost of traditional French colonialism.

the end of the Brussels quarrel, he rapidly recovered many of the peasant votes which had defected to Lecanuet. Moreover, when the election came in March 1967 the electorate seemed mainly concerned with choosing a political force which could provide stable government, and the Gaullists' asset was that their claim to do this was more credible than any rival's. The Centre was far too weak to look like a government, while the Left, though better disciplined than ever before, still presented competing candidates everywhere at the first ballot who allied only for the second. At one point the Gaullists had envisaged similar tactics, and in 1966 different views within their camp were encouraged for a time in the hope of attracting votes from both Left and Right. But when the campaign began, desire for a display of conspicuous unity prevailed: there was a single Gaullist candidate in every seat. The outcome showed the wisdom of this course. Independent and minor parties suffered severely, while the weakest of the big four, the Democratic Centre, did worse even than in the 1962 disaster. On a much increased poll everyone else gained votes while holding a stable percentage share, although a more united opposition on the Left (and a new readiness among Centre voters to support it against the Gaullists) cost the government forty seats, over half of which went to the Communists. The Gaullist majority was slashed to two. For the government to survive and maintain its vote after nine years of Gaullist rule was in fact a notable achievement, but the immediate impression to both opponents and ministers, who had come to think themselves invulnerable as long as the General was there, was that the regime had suffered a moral defeat.

Parliament consequently met in an atmosphere of *après-Gaulliste* anticipation. As a leading contender in the succession stakes Giscard d'Estaing was adopting a distinctive 'Yes, but' attitude, declining to merge his Independent Republicans in a unified governmental group in the Assembly—and so leaving the government nominally beholden to him for survival. Irritated at Giscard's obvious intention to extract every scrap of political advantage from his pivotal position, and uncertain of the solidarity of his own troops under pressure, Pompidou rapidly put both his rival and parliament in their places. Outlining the government's programme to the new Assembly he broke with precedent by refusing to submit himself to a vote. Then he forced through special powers to legislate by ordinance for six months on a wide range of social and economic affairs. Among the resulting measures was a highly unpopular 'reform' of the social security system—which ministers intent on avoiding electoral unpopularity had brought to a financially desperate condition.[1] Once more an election had been followed within weeks by the sudden imposition of unpopular policies which had been studiously ignored during the campaign.

Yet parliament proved quite governable. Its very first vote (re-electing the Gaullist President of the Assembly by a majority of 47) showed that, owing to Centrist help, the cabinet was stronger than the nominal balance of forces suggested. Despite some minor inconveniences its legislation never ran into serious trouble. Its real security was confirmed when the opposition failed by seven votes to censure the government over special powers, despite the affront to both parliament and the electorate these involved (of course Gaullist deputies themselves were grateful to the government for relieving them of the need to vote for unpopular measures). For no hesitant member would take the risk of defeating the government, precipitating a dissolution, and incurring the deadly charge of bringing back the Fourth Republic. Neither the Gaullists nor the Giscardians seriously broke ranks, while Progress and Modern Democracy, the new centre party of convenience, so disliked the companionship of the Communists and the risk of courting a dissolution that its votes were carefully calculated to avoid precipitating a crisis. The Left was still preoccupied with its own unity. After eight months of negotiation the Federation and the Communists succeeded in drawing up a common declaration of policy which contained almost as many agreements to disagree as points of harmony, and their mutual suspicions ensured that coordination of their parliamentary tactics remained erratic.

The unexpected crisis

Meanwhile, the President was as preoccupied as ever with France's position in the world. Withdrawal from NATO was widely accepted, as were the closer relations with Eastern Europe and the quiet but steady rapprochement with the

---

[1] See below, pp. 311–12 (on the farmers' advantages).

Arab world since the Algerian war. But when de Gaulle scathingly branded Israel the aggressor in the Arab–Israeli war, imposed a complete arms embargo on her, and made remarks which were taken to reflect on Jewry as a whole, even many lifelong Gaullists were appalled. (There was comparable dismay among some Communists at the way the party disregarded left-wing unity and unimaginatively toed the Moscow line on the issue.) Weeks later a fresh storm broke over the President's echoing of the separatist slogan 'Long live free Quebec!' during his Canadian visit—this from a man who was so hypersensitive to any hint of foreign incursion into French affairs. But de Gaulle contemptuously dismissed his critics and went on to intensify his attack on the international monetary system, and to veto British membership of EEC for the second time. Though relations with Eastern Europe and the Third World were excellent, if slight, among her western neighbours France was more isolated than ever. The Foreign Minister imperturbably commented that 'one never feels lonely when one knows one is in the right', but many of his countrymen were beginning to wonder uneasily whether they were being led by a self-willed old man in a hurry. Giscard d'Estaing's acid suggestion that 'the solitary exercise of power' was scarcely an appropriate preparation for the succession was deeply resented by Gaullist loyalists, but struck a wider chord of anxiety. Polls showed that only 36 per cent approved the General's position on Israel, while a mere 18 per cent thought him right on Quebec (over which just 30 per cent even of Gaullist voters backed him).

Yet as usual the chief determinants of opinion lay in domestic rather than foreign affairs. Prices of public services had been increased sharply, and the social security ordinances would take a long time to live down. Patches of prolonged unemployment testified to the continuing sluggishness of the economy and to mounting competition from EEC countries. The farmers were realizing increasingly that EEC agricultural policy was not going to bring the benefits which they had been promised for years. The mood of discontent found expression in a rash of small but intractable strikes and incidents at the universities, and also in the success of an increasingly united Left at the expense of the Centre in the autumn local elections. Yet despite a widespread feeling of malaise there was no sign of imminent upheaval. Though the optimism of the President's

New Year address was unusually muted, he saluted 1968 'with serenity'. In the spring *Le Monde* headlined a sober analysis of the political situation 'France is bored'. It was thought that the General might soon be preparing to make way for Pompidou—but although the UNR's November conference had been held in a distinctly *après-Gaulliste* atmosphere, de Gaulle himself had given no clear sign of his intentions. After he went there might be difficulties, but as long as he was at the helm a major explosion seemed unthinkable.

But in May this leisurely speculation about the succession was abruptly suspended, and the regime's ability even to outlive its founder hung in the balance. The relatively trivial spark which touched off the conflagration was harsh police action against a student demonstration (a handful of student revolutionaries had been disciplined; more protested in the courtyard of the Sorbonne; the police were called to expel them; thousands gathered to demonstrate and were brutally handled). Night after night students and riot police exchanged blows and missiles across barricades in the Latin Quarter. Two died, thousands were injured or arrested. Outside Paris almost every institution of higher education was quietly occupied by students demanding greater autonomy for universities from Parisian control, and greater student participation within them. Then the contagion spread to the workers, who were impressed by the students and impatient at delays in meeting their own demands. By the third week in May over half the industrial labour force was on strike, and hundreds of factories were occupied by the workers. Disoriented by the force and speed of the storm ministers alternated between concession and repression, mistiming the moment for each. Only Pompidou seemed to keep some grip on affairs. De Gaulle himself was at a loss to deal with a situation he could neither grasp nor understand.[1] After a long silence waiting for a chink to appear in his opponents' position, his address to the nation on 24 May seemed querulous and uncomprehending even to many Gaullists. He announced a referendum in June on reform of the universities and 'participation' in the economy: one of his favourite but least convincing panaceas, to be achieved by a favourite but now discredited method. Once again there was no mistaking that in his view the real

---

[1] He repeatedly described the situation as *insaisissable*.

issue would not be the vaguely enunciated reforms but the choice between de Gaulle or chaos.

Following the angry reception for the speech the crisis deepened. Another night of rioting in Paris, in which the Stock Exchange was burned, saw opinion swinging away from the students. But now militants in the factories with the bit between their teeth rejected the generous package of concessions produced under Pompidou's urging by the government, the union leaders and the employers. The cry now was for a *gouvernement populaire* and the issue was the regime's very survival. The economy was slowing to a halt. It was increasingly unlikely that the referendum (which was in any case judged unconstitutional by the Conseil d'Etat) could be held amid such incipient anarchy—including a strike of broadcasting staff against governmental interference. Graver still, it was feared that the CGT and the Communist Party leaders, who had taken a reformist and parliamentary line, castigating leftist adventurers in the universities and factories, were wavering under pressure from below. With the government daily seeming more impotent and irrelevant, the Left began discussing a caretaker government under Mendès-France or Mitterrand. The former was courted by Centre opinion but rejected by the Communists; the latter counted all too blatantly and publicly the chickens he hoped to hatch from the imminence of chaos. When news came that de Gaulle had left precipitately for Colombey, ten years almost to the day since he had been summoned to power as the Fourth Republic crumbled, even highly placed Gaullists believed the end had come.

Instead de Gaulle returned from his dramatic symbolic withdrawal in fighting mood, having assured himself of the backing of his military commanders, and probably aware that the Communists had decided against any attempt at revolution that risked civil war. Decisive and confident, as 'holder of national and republican legitimacy' he proclaimed his refusal to resign or dismiss the Prime Minister. Instead he adjourned the referendum and dissolved the Assembly—as Pompidou had been urging for a week. The Assembly had in fact been almost irrelevant and blameless during the crisis; the government had comfortably survived a censure motion with eleven votes in hand (though Gaullist solidarity was breached by Pisani who voted against the government, and Capitant who criticized it bitterly and resigned his seat).[1] De Gaulle was gambling that after almost a month of disruption, with the threat of civil war in the air, his countrymen were ready for a return to normal. He was right. For at least a week opinion had been turning against prolonged disorder and in favour of the authorities. The General's brief withdrawal crystallized the mounting fears that the country was drifting towards anarchy and the unknown. Once he had spoken the Gaullists, who had seemed as extinct as the Hittites, rallied and took heart, drawing a reputed million people to the Champs-Elysées to support de Gaulle. The return to normal began in the factories and universities.

The ensuing nineteen-day campaign was the shortest and one of the crudest ever. Fighting as the Union for the Defence of the Republic, the Gaullists crusaded as the bulwark of democracy against the Red peril, enhancing their appeal to the Right by freeing the remaining OAS prisoners (men convicted precisely for attempts to overthrow the Republic). In fact the Communists, with their hostility to the tiny revolutionary groups, had acted as the firemen of the regime. Nevertheless, once the extreme Left had overreached itself, Pompidou showed a shrewd political instinct in summoning the conservative forces of universal suffrage to redress the balance of the situation. The Gaullists romped home with 358 of the 485 seats. They made gains everywhere, notably in the once impregnable south-west (where the UNR had already begun to penetrate in 1967). All their opponents lost ground; the Left lost over half its seats. Unity of left-wing voting on the second ballot was now far less complete than in 1967, while many of the Centre voters who had voted against the Gaullists in 1967 swung sharply back to the Right. The Federation emerged from the election numerically weakened, split over its handling of the crisis and relations with the Communists, its very existence in question.

Pompidou now looked more than ever the heir apparent. The President had earlier paid deserved tribute to his conduct during the crisis; now he had led the Gaullists to an unprecedented electoral victory. Yet even before the new parliament met he was abruptly banished to the back benches

---

[1] René Capitan, ex-minister and leading Left Gaullist of 1940 vintage.

without explanation, just as Debré had been dumped on the morrow of the 1962 referendum. Perhaps he had been too assertive during the crisis; doubtless he now looked too substantial a potential successor in the eyes of a man whose political technique required the possibility of playing off men or forces against each other.[1] The new Prime Minister, Couve de Murville, who was only now entering the Assembly after a decade as foreign minister, was a self-effacing exponent of presidential policy—as Pompidou had been in 1962. Several Left Gaullists were brought into the cabinet, a technocrat installed at the Ministry of Finance to clear up the economic mess, and Edgar Faure dispatched to employ his emollient skills as Minister of Education. Not without restiveness the President's man was also installed as leader of the Gaullist parliamentary group. Charles de Gaulle was at the helm and determined to stay there, running the system in even more overtly presidential a manner than before.

Superficially the regime appeared to have weathered the storm triumphantly. But behind the victorious façade much of the proudest Gaullist mythology lay in ruins. At the moment of crisis the institutions of the regime had been shown, thanks to the President's plebiscitary rule, to have acquired little vitality of their own. The confident challenge of 'de Gaulle or chaos' had turned for a month into 'de Gaulle and chaos' in a way that the most massive electoral victory could never eradicate. De Gaulle still held the Elysée as imperiously as ever, but the spell was broken, and the hand of political death was upon him.

---

[1] There are some grounds for believing that de Gaulle looked on four to five years as a desirable time for a prime minister and had intended to promote Couve in 1967, but Couve failed to gain election to the Assembly.

II

THE INTERMEDIARIES

4

FRENCHMEN AT THE POLLS

The regime consolidated

In the sweeping changes which transformed French life in the twenty years after 1945, the political sector lagged behind. Though the Resistance generation which came to power in the second world war was bent on a total renovation of the political structure, they found themselves within two or three years driven back into the old situation: a dominant parliament with no majority for action, where every obstructive pressure group wielded disproportionate weight because the defection of a few marginal votes could always bring down a government. For France was still burdened by the legacy of bitterness bequeathed by 150 years of recent history. The Catholic Church had fought the Revolution and the Third Republic, and many Frenchmen still saw in it an enemy of political freedom; the working class had twice been massacred in civil war and, feeling alienated from the nation, voted for an extremist party. Beset by dangerous forces on both Left and Right, the moderate groups had to hold together to provide a government: yet they were divided by political conviction and electoral interest on all the social, economic and external issues over which British parties disagree, and on the clerical problem besides.

During the Fourth Republic's short life its political system came to seem increasingly obsolete. The social foundations of individualism were undermined by the urbanization of the country, the intervention of the State in the economy and the rapid organization of interests—labour and business, peasants and professional groups. With the spread of modern communications and the development of education, the old political potentates—the small-town doctor or lawyer, the village *curé* and schoolteacher, the minor provincial newspaper—lost their traditional influence. An impatient younger generation, swollen by a birth-rate increasing at last, pressed for change and expansion rather than the traditional preservation of existing vested interests. The old defensive mood gave way to a pressure for modernization under the Fourth Republic's economic miracle. Yet material progress did not cure the psychological malaise, partly because the Fourth Republic never gave the impression of dynamic government (except under Mendès-France); and partly because progress at home was accompanied by steady retreat abroad.

A succession of attempts to revitalize the political system foundered one after the other. The unity of the Resistance forces, always precarious, was shattered by the outbreak of the cold war. Many of the dynamic forces in the country were attracted by the Communists and Gaullists, but these combined to paralyse the political system, each hoping to seize power from the ruins of the regime; once they were checked (at the price of deliberately reinforcing the political weight of the backward regions where they were both weak against the modern ones where they were strong), and once their original impetus had slackened, they both became partially the captives of the conservative vested interests they had at first tried to fight. Pierre Mendès-France, in the one serious attempt at radical change within the system, was balked by the resistance of the parties and by opposition to his policies abroad; and the hopes placed in the Left's electoral victory of 1956 were rapidly destroyed by the endless Algerian war. For it was external and not domestic affairs which destroyed the Fourth Republic like the Third, and the division cut right across party lines on all the issues arousing intense passion—the European army, Algeria, and finally the advent of de Gaulle.

In the Fifth Republic the parties which had governed in the old regime were discredited by failure and seemed increasingly irrelevant to a public opinion which wanted its government to 'get France moving again'. They were divided on the real issues, plainly incapable of providing stable government either separately or in combination, and increasingly out of touch with the most active, realistic and civic-minded of the younger generation, who were coming to dominate many of the professional organizations. Such men were mainly progressive Catholics alienated from the traditional parties of Right and Left by the conservatism of the one and the anticlericalism of the other. Yet while the vitality of the Catholic sector of opinion and the stagnation of the old *laïque* groups were among the striking features of the new France, these 'living forces' were only minorities and however influential they might prove in the long run, at the moment they commanded few votes.

Thus the men and the groups who wanted to modernize the existing parties faced formidable obstacles. They rightly maintained that without a radical change the old organizations were doomed to a gradual decline. But in appealing for new parties, strong enough to represent viable alternative governments, the modernizers invited immediate present difficulties for the sake of hypothetical future benefits. They were accepting the institutions and much of the political analysis of the regime their parties officially opposed. They were flouting deeply rooted traditional beliefs, and trying to bridge political differences which were not always concerned with obsolete or trivial issues. They were threatening the careers of men and the power of organizations which flourished in the old order and feared the new. They faced the bitter antagonism of the Communist party, hostile to any opposition movement it could not control, and of the Gaullists who could use the political initiative to strengthen their hold on power. They were trying to breathe new life into organizations which the President of the Republic despised and detested, and he was prepared to use his vast resources of skill and power to thwart them. And while the ordinary voter might favour modernization when he was choosing a government for the nation, his traditional loyalties persisted when he had to elect a local candidate—so that referendums and presidential elections helped to promote a new party system, but local and perhaps parliamentary contests tended to hinder change.

Never before has France voted as frequently as under the Fifth Republic. In the eleven years of de Gaulle's rule the people were called to the polls on national issues no fewer than ten times.[1] In 1958 the General summoned them first to approve his new constitution, then to elect a fresh National Assembly.

---

[1] Or even fifteen—for two ballots were required to elect the four National Assemblies and, in 1965, the President.

In 1961 and again in April 1962 he asked them to ratify his Algerian policy by referendum. Later in 1962 he held a further referendum to authorize popular election of the President by universal suffrage—abolishing the electoral college of local councillors he had himself urged the people to ratify just four years earlier. The hostility of the Assembly to this move produced a dissolution and a general election in November 1962—the third major consultation within the year. The pace then slackened. For the next three years there were only local elections—and steadily intensifying speculation and manoeuvring in preparation for the presidential campaign at the end of 1965. De Gaulle's unexpectedly difficult re-election stirred up fifteen months of almost continuous electioneering in advance of the general election of March 1967. Though that parliament had run its course, its successor had lasted only fifteen months when the President dissolved it to produce a *dénouement* to the crisis of May 1968. Ten months later followed the referendum on the reform of the regions and the Senate which brought defeat and an end to the General's reign. If the frequency of national votes was the touchstone of democracy, the Fifth Republic would rank high.

At the September 1958 referendum 85 per cent of the electorate, the highest proportion in French history, went to the polls to vote on the new constitution. Almost 80 per cent of them voted Yes: 17,700,000 people, two-thirds of the whole electorate. At 4,600,000 the No vote was a million less than the Communist party alone had polled at the previous general election in 1956; yet in campaigning against the constitution the Communists had been joined by a tiny group of the extreme Right (notably Pierre Poujade), by 40 per cent of the Radical party (notably Mendès-France), and by 30 per cent of the Socialists.[1] Plainly many left-wing voters had refused to follow their parties' advice. It was the first sign of de Gaulle's two major strategic successes: his brilliant use of the referendum to detach from his political opponents the voters who normally followed them, and his ability to cut deep into the Communist vote for the first time.

The referendum victory, which surprised everyone by its extent, was followed within two months by a general election,

---

[1] Those Radicals and Socialists who also opposed the war now left their parties, to become the nucleus of the future PSU.

at which the General committed an understandable tactical error in his choice of electoral laws. Everyone knew he intended to abolish proportional representation, which he had introduced in 1945, and which had ever since been the basis of the system and the source of the power of the parties he so mistrusted. But few thought he would deliberately reject the demands of the Gaullists and the Right (for majority voting for party lists, each department forming a constituency) in favour of the prewar system favoured by Mendès-France and Guy Mollet: majority voting in single-member districts, with a second ballot if no candidate polled a clear majority of votes cast.[1] And nobody at all foresaw that this system would help the Gaullists instead of hindering them. Since it had in the past weakened party discipline, aided well-known personalities against newcomers, and strengthened moderates against extremists, in the 1958 context everyone thought that, while damaging the Communists, it would protect the other parties against a Gaullist landslide. It was not the General's fault if the voters' psychology had changed so radically that they used the system to achieve results almost the reverse of those predicted by every practising politician and academic observer. While previously the voter had used the second ballot to help the familiar local figure and eliminate the extremists, now he not only discriminated against the Communists, but also against the most solidly established moderates, and in favour of little-known candidates bearing the Gaullist label.

Thus the new Assembly was dominated by the Right: precisely the result de Gaulle had hoped to avoid. With $3\frac{1}{2}$ million votes on the first ballot and nearly 5 million on the second, the Gaullist Union for the New Republic elected 200 deputies. The old-style Conservatives and their allies had a million more first-ballot votes but did less well at the second round, and emerged with 130 seats; the seventy deputies returned under army pressure in Algeria often followed their lead at first. Though the remaining parties of the Fourth Republic collected between them some 7 million votes, these brought them only 140 seats—MRP doing much better than expected, the Socialists much worse, and the divided Radicals

---

[1] To win he also needed to poll a quarter of the registered electorate. At the second ballot, the man with most votes won.

going down to disaster. With only ten deputies for their 3,800,000 votes, the Communists were the chief victims—but of the voters as well as the electoral system, for nearly a third of their own supporters defected and those of all other parties united against them at the second ballot. A month later, in December, an electoral college of some 80,000 (almost half of them rural mayors) chose Charles de Gaulle President of the Republic by an 80 per cent vote, the rest dividing fairly evenly between a Communist and a follower of Mendès-France.

It soon became clear that the violent swing to the Right and against the old politicians did not necessarily represent the pattern of Fifth Republican politics. Municipal elections, held every six years, were due in March 1959 and the Gaullists, counting on repeating their November triumph, hoped to seize the opportunity to secure themselves a base in local politics. They therefore changed the electoral law, replacing proportional representation in all towns between 9,000 and 120,000 inhabitants by a majority system (of list voting, with two ballots; smaller places already had majority voting, while larger ones kept PR). The results were to disappoint them, for the issues were different from those of November; the economic climate had changed, and the voters' reaction was not the same in local as in national elections. The Fourth Republican parties often formed a coalition instead of fighting independently, and the Communists, exploiting the discontent aroused by the government's deflationary economic policies, recovered about half the votes they had lost four months earlier. Many a former deputy who had lost his seat to a Gaullist in November was comfortably returned to his *mairie* against the same challenger in March. A month later these newly installed municipal councillors provided the bulk of the electoral colleges which chose the entire Senate.[1] Being themselves mostly the same men as before, they picked the same candidates and, of the old senators up for re-election, 84 per cent were returned (only 28 per cent of the deputies standing had held their seats in November) while many (29) of the few newcomers were defeated deputies returning to parliament after a few weeks in the wilderness. With

---

[1] It was normally elected by halves (in the Fourth Republic) or thirds (in the Third and Fifth) every three years; but at the start of a new regime it was wholly renewed.

its few Gaullists and Communists the Senate, whose composition changed little at subsequent elections, was to remain the fortress of the old parties in the new regime. Most of the old parties, though hostile to de Gaulle on other grounds, saw him as the one man who could settle Algeria. So did the ordinary Frenchman. To outmanœuvre those politicians, soldiers and settlers who wanted to tie his hands, the President could therefore rely first on the lesson of events, and secondly on his appeal to public opinion by means of the referendum. Although he promised self-determination in September 1959, he did not hold a referendum on it until 8 January 1961—by which time the electorate was becoming exasperated with the settlers and their military sympathisers, aware of the strength of Algerian nationalism, and thoroughly tired of the war. As usual, only one answer could be given to his double question: do you approve of self-determination *and* the proposed provisional institutions for Algeria? Soustelle and his right-wing followers opposed the first half, the Communists and the PSU (Left Socialist critics of the war) opposed the second; among the Radicals a strange alliance of Right and Left wings committed the party to vote No. At 76 per cent the turnout was lower than in 1958, and the Yes vote was also slightly down: 75 per cent of those voting, and 55·6 per cent of the whole electorate (this was 11 per cent below the previous figure). The Yes vote fell from 17,700,000 to 15,200,000, while the Noes rose only from 4,600,000 to 5,000,000; probably between a fifth and a quarter of the latter were Soustelle's followers, so that the left-wing opposition was smaller than before. Non-voting was higher at 6,400,000 (against 4,000,000 in 1958).

By April 1962, when the next referendum invited approval for the peace settlement making Algeria independent, there was an unprecedented Yes majority of 91 per cent of the votes cast. This was because of the Communist vote. In 1961 the Party had preferred to vote No and risk heavy defections among its troops rather than vote Yes and weaken the morale and combativity of its militants. Now it dared not oppose peace, and therefore decided on an affirmative reply even before it knew what the question was to be. In a slightly smaller turnout than in 1961 (75 per cent), those approving were 17,500,000, almost as many as in 1958 and 65 per cent of the whole electorate. There were now 1,800,000 Noes, all from the far Right (6·6 per cent of votes cast)[1]; and twice the usual number of spoiled or blank ballots, 1,100,000 or 4 per cent, no doubt in response to the PSU's attempt to outflank the Communists on the Left by appealing to its supporters to spoil their papers. By these two Algerian referendums, then, the President had undermined the hold of the left-wing opposition on its supporters, and demonstrated that the right-wing opposition had no significant following in the country.

The Gaullists catch up the General

With both extremes already shaken it was now the turn of the old Fourth Republican parties. Most of their leaders had prudently supported de Gaulle over Algeria, hoping that once he had settled the problem they had found insoluble, he would retire (voluntarily or under pressure) and leave them to return to politics as usual. But with his October 1962 referendum he forced them to fight him on ground of his choosing. If they opposed direct election of the President, they would appear selfish politicians denying the ordinary voter the right to choose his government so that they could go on sharing the spoils behind his back. Perhaps to ensure they would oppose him, the President carried his bill by a plainly illegal procedure, bypassing parliament and going straight to referendum. The Assembly censured the government for this and was promptly dissolved.

For de Gaulle, the referendum was disappointing; though 62 per cent of those going to the polls voted Yes, this was only 46 per cent of the electorate compared with 56 per cent in 1961 and 66 per cent in 1958.

Table I: Three Referendums, 1958–1962

	1958	1961	1962 (Oct.)
Yes vote (millions)	17·1	15·2	12·8
No vote (millions)	4·6	5·0	7·9

[1] The Conservatives were so split that they made no recommendation to their supporters.

But for the Fourth Republican parties these results were catastrophic. Socialists, MRP, Radicals and Conservatives had between them polled nearly twelve million votes in 1958, when they were all supporting the General; now they were all on the other side, yet the Yes vote dropped only four million and the No vote increased even less, by only 3,300,000. In a slightly larger electorate there were three and a half million French people who spoiled their ballots or stayed at home.

For the election, three weeks later, the parties contrived to make the worst of a difficult situation. The Gaullist candidates found themselves to their own surprise benefiting not only from the patronage of the hero who had brought peace in Algeria, but also from their loyal support of a stable (if often unpopular) government. This new appeal would make the opposition parties seem negative, unconstructive and futile if they continued to fight one another in the traditional way. But it would not help much to patch up a momentary and opportunist combination behind one (non-Communist) candidate in each constituency—for that would look uncommonly like a conspiracy to bring back the Fourth Republic, with its loose coalitions and its paralysed governments. Faced with this disagreeable dilemma, the parties unerringly impaled themselves on both its horns, forming a national *Cartel des Non* which brought sworn enemies together for a moment in Paris, but never managed to make itself effective in the constituencies. Indeed, three days before polling day the Socialist leader Guy Mollet reverted to his forgotten left-wing past and urged his followers at the second ballot to keep the UNR out at all costs, if necessary by voting Communist—thus enabling his party in return to benefit from Communist support in some districts and Conservative support in others, and so gain twenty seats despite a drop in its own votes. The Communists themselves held their shrunken vote at the first ballot and increased it at the second; having allies on the Left for the first time for twenty years, they gained thirty seats. Conservatives and MRP now suffered, like the Left in 1958, from the justified popular suspicion that their Gaullism was no more than lip-service; and the extreme Right, so violent for the General in 1958 and against him in 1962, was virtually wiped out. Although only half those who had supported de Gaulle in the referendum now voted for his followers in the election, these were still nearly double the UNR's first-ballot

71

vote of 1958; and among those Yes voters who would not support Gaullist candidates, nearly half seem to have abandoned their old party and stayed at home (the turnout was exceptionally low).[1] The UNR thus emerged with sixty extra seats from a campaign they had expected to lose, and found themselves only eight short of a clear majority of the Assembly; plenty of members, notably the Republican Independents (thirty pro-Gaullist Conservatives who followed Giscard d'Estaing) were delighted to make up the difference. Once again the referendum had proved a formidable weapon for shaking voters loose from their political habits and loyalties.

Table II: Votes and Seats, 1958–1962

| | Votes (millions) | | | Seats | |
	Nov. 1962	Since 1958	Since Oct. 1962	Nov. 1962	Since 1958
Gaullists	$6\frac{1}{2}$	+3	−6	250	+60
Communists	4	same		41	+30
Other parties	$7\frac{1}{2}$	−5	$+3\frac{1}{2}$	175	−90
Non-voters, spoiled ballots	9	$+2\frac{1}{2}$	$+2\frac{1}{2}$		

The defeated parties now had a few years' breathing-space to adapt themselves to the new situation. Plainly Gaullism was more than a passing phenomenon condemned to disappear with the Algerian war which had brought it to power; plainly also small parties acting separately were doomed to slow decline. Yet the Fourth Republic parties could not all come together: differences between Socialists and Conservatives went at least as deep as in Britain and a common belief in parliamentary democracy was not enough to unite them. Any new alignment into two parties would split either the Radicals or MRP (or both), while each new party would include one wing which preferred cooperation with the other centre group

[1] The crude figures suggest that of 6 million Yes voters who would not support Gaullist candidates, $3\frac{1}{2}$ million returned to their own parties and $2\frac{1}{2}$ million did not vote. But the former figure would be higher if many of the new abstainers were people who had voted No; one poll suggests that as many as 600,000 were.

and another which looked instead to its Communist or Gaullist neighbour.

The choice was further complicated because local and national elections pointed in opposite directions. A presidential candidate representing one of the old parties only would certainly attract little support from voters who wanted to choose the leader of a governmental majority. But before December 1965, when the presidential election was due, departmental councils were to be elected in the spring of 1964 and municipal councils a year later. These were areas no practising politician could afford to neglect. For as the prestige of the member of parliament declined, that of the mayor of a big city had grown; local government, always the best field for the rising politician to show his constructive powers, had now become the surest base for a career sheltered from the increasing hazards of national swings. Even a leader who might be willing for political experiment on a nationwide scale would never risk offending the party on whose traditional alliance he relied to hold his local seat. For in contests at the local level the voter was likely to follow traditional loyalties.

By similar reasoning the Gaullists concluded that they were unlikely to do well at the local elections. They therefore changed the municipal election law again, as they had done in 1959. Then they had abolished proportional representation in all but the largest towns; now they did so even there. They also provided that party lists could not be altered between the ballots, so that a majority coalition had to be assembled at the first round, no subsequent deals being allowed. As in 1959, the aim was to polarize opinion and shatter the centre parties; the Socialists would be driven into the Communists' arms and everyone else, for fear of the Communists, would rally to the UNR and bring a comfortable victory to the coalition it dominated. But as in 1959 the Gaullists miscalculated. For whereas the moderate parties were weak, divided and unable to influence policy in the Assembly, they were in power in most provincial cities, under a mayor who was their accepted local leader. Including or led by the Socialists in left-wing areas, without them in right-wing towns, this Centre coalition was usually stronger than either its UNR or its Communist rivals. So the same voters who looked to the Gaullists to provide stable government in Paris found the moderate parties already offering it locally, and the new electoral law benefited them rather than its inventors. But centre politicians made the Gaullists' mistake in reverse by concluding from the municipal elections that a similar coalition of Fourth Republican parties could triumph at a general election.

The expiry of President de Gaulle's term at the end of 1965 offered the French people their first opportunity to elect their President directly since the Second Republic. The first challenger in the field was the Socialist mayor of Marseilles, Gaston Defferre, who attempted to use his candidature as a springboard for the creation of a new left-centre party, but was foiled by the antagonism of all the old machines. Instead two candidates emerged from the Centre and Left (together with the extreme right-winger Tixier-Vignancour and two minor figures), both trying to build new parties around their own campaigns. François Mitterrand brought the Socialists and most Radicals into a new Federation of the Left, and won the support of the Communists and a reluctant PSU. Campaigning personally rather than under the official MRP banner, Jean Lecanuet appealed to his own party, a minority of Radicals, anti-Gaullist conservatives, and extreme rightists who thought Tixier had no chance. Lecanuet's accomplished television performances made him a national figure overnight; Mitterrand played successfully on the traditions of a Left united for the first time in thirty years—while for once the President blundered tactically, underrating his opponents and appearing to treat his overwhelming re-election as a near-formality until the opinion polls (which had seemed to justify his confidence at the beginning of the campaign) showed him losing 20 per cent of the total vote in six weeks, and forced him to reverse his refusal to campaign. Even so it was a shock to almost everyone when de Gaulle was taken to a humiliating second ballot.[1]

The 84 per cent turnout at the first ballot was a record for a French election—though a shade below the 1958 referendum. De Gaulle's vote was 7,000,000 fewer than that cast for his constitution in 1958 and 2,500,000 below the Yes vote in October 1962—though at the second ballot he almost regained the 1962 total. Mitterrand won about as many votes as the parties backing him had attracted (on a far lower turnout) in

---

[1] At which only the top two candidates could stand again (unless one of them withdrew in favour of the third man).

Table III: Presidential Election, 1965 (France only)

	Thousands		% of Vote		% of electorate	
	1st	2nd ballot	1st	2nd ballot	1st	2nd ballot
Registered	28,235	28,240				
Not voting	4,233	4,375			15·0	15·5
Spoiled	244	662			0·9	2·3
Valid	23,758	23,203			84·1	82·2
De Gaulle	10,387	12,645	43·7	54·5	36·8	44·8
Mitterrand	7,659	10,557	32·2	45·5	27·1	37·3
Lecanuet	3,767		15·8		13·3	
Tixier-Vignancour	1,254		5·3		4·4	
Marcilhacy	413		1·7		1·5	
Barbu	278		1·2		1·0	

the 1962 general election; he did well south of the Loire, in the rural strongholds of the traditional Left, but in the northern industrial towns where de Gaulle ran strongly he failed to hold even the hard-core left-wing vote. Similarly in the Catholic and Conservative areas which were most favourable to both de Gaulle and Lecanuet, the former polled relatively more strongly in the industrial north-east.[1] At the second ballot the North African refugees who had voted for Tixier followed their leaders' advice and switched overwhelmingly to Mitterrand out of hatred for de Gaulle. About half Lecanuet's supporters probably voted for the President though he advised them not to; some stayed home or spoiled their papers and a large minority, especially among the most politically-minded ones, turned to Mitterrand and helped to swell his second-ballot figure to one not far short of the total opposition vote at the 1962 election. Optimistic opponents of

[1] However, Lecanuet appealed much more strongly to youth than to the ordinary Conservative candidate.

the General, noting that he had always polled far better than his party, concluded that the UNR had lost ground like the President, and was doomed to disaster in 1967. But the campaign was dominated by the errors of de Gaulle himself— perhaps especially his failure (until the second ballot) to sense the voters' mood and their preoccupation with stability not only in his own time but afterwards. Even among those who supported him, nearly half hoped he would be re-elected only narrowly and thus brought down from his Elysian heights to the earth where ordinary Frenchmen dwell.[1]

Drawing the moral, the Gaullists assiduously set about broadening their appeal. The discontented, notably the farmers, were carefully courted; conservative allies and leftish dissidents were encouraged to express their distinctive views. But as the election approached this 'Hundred Flowers' phase gave way to Pompidou's insistence on a single 'Fifth Republic' candidate in each constituency, enabling the majority to make the most of its chief asset: the claim that Gaullism, unlike any of its competitors, could provide France with stable government. This was a claim the opposition had the greatest difficulty in challenging. The decisive choice rested with Mitterrand and the Federation. A national alliance with the Communists would accord with the tradition of left-wing unity and the electoral interest of many of its members, but others looked to MRP and the Radicals. The Federation's voters were as divided as its candidates, some refusing all truck with the Communists and others with the Catholics. In the past this traditional dilemma had been resolved by the local party branches choosing different allies in different regions, so producing Socialist and Radical parliamentary parties which faced both ways. Such a solution was difficult in 1967. Firstly it was redolent of the political habits of the past, and damaging to a party claiming to offer a strong alternative government; secondly the Communists threatened to oppose the Federation at the second ballot unless it accepted a national pact.

After much hesitation the Federation agreed to joint support at the second ballot, in any seat where there was a hope of

---

[1] An opinion poll just before the first ballot found 38 per cent wanting him to lose, 46 per cent to win — of whom only 26 per cent wanted an easy victory, 10 per cent a narrow one and 10 per cent hoped for a second ballot.

victory, for whichever candidate polled best at the first. Its decision, which made the Left appear a more serious contender for power than it had for years, restricted not only Mitterrand's freedom of manoeuvre but also Lecanuet's. With no hope of support from the Left at the second ballot the Centre leader dared not risk splitting the Catholic vote. Lecanuet therefore became more accommodating towards the Gaullists, thereby offending his more committed supporters while suggesting to the politically indifferent voter that there was little real difference between him and the UNR. This proved a fatal impression in an election dominated by the citizen's desire to choose a party capable of forming a stable government. Small groups, from the PSU to the right-wing extremists, were all regarded as irrelevant and polled badly. Rebels and cast-offs of every hue found the personal support on which they counted had melted away. In the entire Assembly only 21 deputies (17 from overseas) were returned without the endorsement of one of the four major formations. Even among these four the Democratic Centre was badly squeezed for its failure to appear a credible alternative government. It had seemed in 1962 that the Conservatives and MRP had reached rock-bottom; their recovery in the 1965 municipal elections, and Lecanuet's showing in the presidential race had persuaded them that the tide had turned. But now Centre candidates (absent in 100 constituencies) polled a million fewer votes than Lecanuet in a disaster even greater than 1962. In a high turn-out (81 per cent) all the other big parties gained votes—a million for the Communists, half a million net for the Federation, and a million and a half for the Gaullists.

While the striking feature of the election was the preference so many voters showed for choosing a government rather than a local or ideological spokesman, personality still counted significantly, and all the main parties also tried to renew their personnel by promoting the young, energetic, technocratic types who were supposed to appeal to the electorate.[1] Here again though, despite some spectacular successes by Mitterrand's young men, and to a lesser extent the Communists (whose range of candidates was more bourgeois than ever

---

[1] However, sitting members did relatively well. Two-thirds of those who stood again were re-elected, compared with a quarter in 1958 and a half in 1962.

before), it was the Gaullists who made the greatest effort, and were rewarded by some spectacular victories for their *jeunes loups* in the poorer and more mountainous regions, to compensate for their heavy losses in the industrial areas.

For although 38 per cent of the votes cast had given the UNR and its allies a comfortable majority in the old Assembly, the same percentage share very nearly lost them control of the new one. At the second ballot the Left opposition offered a more coherent alternative than the quarrelsome, contradictory combinations of 1962—and one which, as at the presidential election, proved capable of attracting an unexpectedly significant fraction of the right-wing anti-Gaullist vote. Resistance to the UNR proved stronger, and fear of the Communists weaker than in the past. But if these changes of mood cost the Gaullists forty seats and left them a nominal majority of only two, it was a remarkable feat to win a majority at all—especially for the third time running and with a flagging economy.

By contrast with the leisurely and protracted preparations preceding the 1967 campaign, the 1968 election broke without warning out of the May crisis. Sensing the swelling tide of exasperation and alarm at the country's apparent slide towards economic paralysis and political collapse, de Gaulle seized the crucial moment to shift the challenge from the factories and streets to the ballot box through the dissolution of the hapless and largely blameless Assembly—making sure of catching the current of opinion by allowing only twenty-three days between the dissolution and the first ballot. Yet again an election was to serve as both an arbitration by the people and a sledgehammer against the opposition.

It was an oddly anticlimactic campaign after the events of the preceding weeks, an episode in the still unfinished crisis rather than an event in its own right. The Gaullists, so recently demoralized by the seemingly imminent collapse of their world, went into battle scenting victory. Pompidou successfully insisted, as in 1967, on a single Gaullist-endorsed candidate per constituency—though in forty seats there was a contest between a Gaullist and a Giscardian 'ally'. He also set the tone in primitivism. For the Gaullists the issue was simply 'for or against totalitarian communism', or, more pithily still, 'order or anarchy' and the 'sacred duty' to defend the Republic. Combined with the amnesty for the remaining OAS prisoners, the virulent anti-Communism of the Gaullist campaign helped ensure that for the first time they fought virtually without enemies on their Right. But the emphasis on the Red peril and the stark polarization of the electorate for which the Gaullists were aiming was also a major embarrassment to the Centre. Frightened by May, the heterogeneous PDM found that its antagonism to the revolutionaries (extended into suspicion of the entire Left) far outweighed its desire to maintain a distinctive stance apart from the Gaullists. The traditional tactic of arranging local alliances with both Right and Left as opportunity offered proved even more difficult than in 1967. Significantly the number of Centre candidates fell from 385 in 1967 to 272. Many of those who did face the electors were to find that the voters had deserted them for the Gaullist without even waiting for the second ballot.

For the Left, the timing of the election could hardly have been more unfortunate. May caught the Federation in the middle of the transformation towards which it had been so tortuously inching, and left it divided and demoralized. Despite the Communists' caution, all the old fears of the Party's massive potential had been reawakened. On paper relations between the Federation and the Communists remained as in 1967. The Communists rejected Mitterrand's proposal for a united left-wing candidate at the first ballot, preferring 'Republican discipline' on the second as in 1967. But the 'dynamic of unity' was shattered. Before the first ballot every section of the Left campaigned independently, marking its distance from the second ballot allies: the PSU (fielding 321 candidates against 117 in 1967) fought to outflank the Communists on their Left, bitterly assailing the Federation for its timidity; the anti-communism of the Radicals was no longer concealed; the Socialists were plainly more attracted to allies on their Right than to an embrace with the Communists, while the Communists, criticizing their partners in turn, sought like the Gaullists to 'bipolarize' the conflict as one against 'Gaullist dictatorship'. With little hope of winning, the Left fought a lack-lustre campaign with the limited hope of holding its 1967 gains. It was to fail even in that.

Despite the students' cries of 'elections—treason', the first ballot turnout was 80 per cent. The General's calculation had worked. Winning a record 46 per cent of the vote, the Gaullists gained ground in almost every corner of the country. They

79

Table IV: Four Parliamentary Elections (Metropolitan France only)

	Gaull.[1]	Cons.[2] etc.	MRP[2]	Rad.[3][4] etc.	Soc.[4]	Comm.	Non-voters	Total
1 Party votes (millions) at first ballot.								
1958	4·2	4·5	2·4	1·8	3·2	3·9	6·2	27·2
1962	6·6	1·7	1·6	1·8	2·3	4·0	8·6	27·5
1967	8·5	—2·9—		—4·7—		5·0	5·4	28·3
1968	10·2	—2·3—		—4·5—		4·4	5·6	28·2
2 Party votes (millions) at second ballot[5]								
1958	5·2	3·9	1·7	1·1	2·5	3·7	6·1	
1962	6·4	1·2	0·8	1·2	2·3	3·2	6·1	
1967	8·0	—1·3—		—4·7—		4·0	5·0	
1968	6·8	—1·1—		—3·2—		2·9	4·7	
3 Party shares of valid votes (%) on first ballot.								
1958	17½	22	12	8	15½	19		
1962	36	9½	9	7½	13	22		
1967	38	—13—		—19—		22½		
1968	48	—10—		—20—		20		
4 Seats								
1958	206	129	56	40	47	10		
1962	268	—55—		43	65	41		
1967	242	—41—		—121—		73		
1968	346	—26—		—57—		33		

performed noticeably better in the provinces than in Paris, and best of all in the most rural areas, thanks in part perhaps to Edgar Faure's agricultural policies, but mainly to the peasants' reaction to the upheavals of May. While the Gaullists and their allies increased their vote by nearly 1,700,000 all the other contenders suffered. The Communists, with 600,000 fewer votes, lost most of the ground they had painfully recovered since 1962. The Federation dropped almost 600,000, while the

---

[1] Includes RI 1962–8.

[2] Includes PDM 1967–8, Extreme Right (0·5m 1958, 0·2m 1962 and 1967, 0·03 1968) and miscellaneous conservatives (0·8 1967, 0·1 1968).

[3] Includes miscellaneous Left (c. 0·4m 1958 and 1962, 0·3m in 1967, 0·2m in 1968).

[4] Joined in Federation of the Left, 1967–8 (includes PSU 0·5m 1967, 0·9m 1968).

[5] Seats which elect their member at the first ballot (39 in 1958, 96 in 1962, 79 in 1967 and 166 in 1968) not included; thus second ballot votes not comparable with first.

Centre (in part because it had fewer candidates) polled almost 1,200,000 votes less than its already disastrous 1967 level—its worst performance since the war. The intermittently revolutionary PSU professed satisfaction at raising its share of the vote to 4 per cent—but this gain came only from running more candidates and it lost ground where it had already fought in 1967. Of the 154 seats won outright on the first ballot, no fewer than 144 went to the Gaullists.

The qualification for remaining in the race, raised from 5 per cent of the vote to 10 per cent of the electorate, automatically eliminated 668 candidates from the second ballot. The final choice was still further simplified by the 'Republican discipline' of the Left, which produced a single left-wing candidate in every seat without the scattered rebellions of 1967—though the Communists would stand down in only three constituencies (as against fifteen in 1967) for Federation rivals with fewer votes but more chance of winning. The Right and Centre in turn showed greater determination to bar the way to the Left by avoiding competitive candidatures. None of the 316 metropolitan constituencies polling the second time had more than three candidates, and 269 had a straight choice—231 between a Gaullist or their ally and a left-winger. On the second ballot the pendulum swung further still to the government. While in 1967 the tide had flowed from the Centre to the Left between the ballots, now many of the remaining Centre voters supported the Gaullists—as did a fraction of the Left. The decline of left-wing unity also showed in a lower turnout and in the failure of the Communists' three 'gifts' to the Federation. The Gaullists had emphasized their claim to be the biggest party in France. Their massive vote was no longer a personal triumph for the General, but did it represent real support for Gaullism or was it a success for the 'party of funk' as de Gaulle himself described his following? With the aid of the electoral system the Gaullists had emerged from the election with nearly three-quarters of the seats in the new Assembly, based on almost half the popular vote. But though it could be termed the greatest electoral victory in the history of the French Republic, even this did not ensure the regime the air of permanency it needed.

Table V: France at the Polls, 1956–1969
(millions of votes)

	1956	1958(1)	1958	1961	1962(a)	1962(b)
Parliament	1956	1958(1)				
President						
Referendum			1958	1961	1962(a)	1962(b)
Electorate	26½	26½		27		
Not voting & Spoiled	5	4	7	7	8	7
Gaullists	1	4				
de Gaulle, Pompidou OUI			17½	15	17½	13
NON			4½	5	2	8
Communists	5½	*	4	*		*
Other Left	5½		4½			*
Right and Centre	9½		8			*

*Supporting NON.

For fuller details see Tables IV (p. 80), VI (p. 348) and VII (p. 353).

1962(1)	1965(1)	1965(2)	1967(1)	1968(1)	1969	1969(1)	1969(2)
$27\frac{1}{2}$	28		28		$28\frac{1}{2}$	29	
9	$4\frac{1}{2}$	5	6	6	6	$6\frac{1}{2}$	10
$6\frac{1}{2}$			$8\frac{1}{2}$	10			
	$10\frac{1}{2}$	$12\frac{1}{2}$				10	$10\frac{1}{2}$
					$10\frac{1}{2}$		
					12		
4			5	$4\frac{1}{2}$	*	5	
$3\frac{1}{2}$	$7\frac{1}{2}$	$10\frac{1}{2}$	$4\frac{1}{2}$	$4\frac{1}{2}$	*	2	
4	6		3	$2\frac{1}{2}$	*	$5\frac{1}{2}$	8

1 Referendums 28 September 1958 and 27 April 1969

Paris

Seine

Corsica

▨	1 *Oui* over 80% 1958, over 50% 1969
-	2 „ „ „ „ , 45 – 50% „
--	3 „ „ „ „ , under 45% „
+	4 „ under „ „ , over 50% „
▢	5 „ „ „ „ , under „ „

(No department is in group 4)

2 Gaullists 1958 and 1968

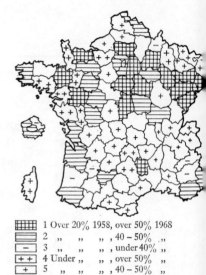

▨	1 Over 20% 1958, over 50% 1968
▤	2 „ „ „ , 40 – 50% „
▢	3 „ „ „ , under 40% „
++	4 Under „ „ , over 50% „
+	5 „ „ „ , 40 – 50% „
▢	6 „ „ „ , under 40% „

(Gaullists 1958 *exclude* those who joined
the party later)

3 De Gaulle for President, 5 and 19 December 1965

▨	1 Over 50% on 5th, over 55% on 19th
▥	2 Under „ „ „ , „ „ „ „
▫•	3 „ „ „ „ , 50 – 55% „ „
▢	4 „ „ „ „ , under 50% „ „
–	5 Over „ „ „ , „ „ 55% „ „

(No department is in group 5)

4 Mitterrand and Lecanuet, 5 December 1965

▨	1 Mitterrand over 50%
▥	2 „ 30 – 50%
××	3 Lecanuet over 20%
▢	4 „ under 20% and Mitterrand under 30%

(Mitterrand over 50% on 19th: see map 3,
group 4)

Percentages of the *vote* on first ballot unless otherwise specified

Federation 1967 and 1968

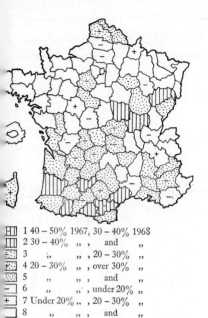

▥	1 40 – 50% 1967, 30 – 40% 1968
▥	2 30 – 40% ,, , and ,,
▦	3 ,, ,, , 20 – 30% ,,
▦	4 20 – 30% ,, , over 30% ,,
▦	5 ,, ,, , and ,,
▭	6 ,, ,, , under 20% ,,
⊞	7 Under 20% ,, , 20 – 30% ,,
▭	8 ,, ,, , and ,,

6 Communists 1967 and 1968

(No department
is in group 7)

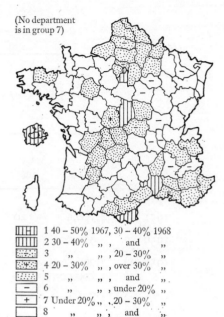

▥	1 40 – 50% 1967, 30 – 40% 1968
▥	2 30 – 40% ,, , and ,,
▦	3 ,, ,, , 20 – 30% ,,
▦	4 20 – 30% ,, , over 30% ,,
▦	5 ,, ,, , and ,,
▭	6 ,, ,, , under 20% ,,
⊞	7 Under 20% ,, , 20 – 30% ,,
▭	8 ,, ,, , and ,,

Catholicism and anticlericalism

▦	1 Most adults attend Mass, *and* over 30% of children in private (Church) primary schools 1959
▨	2 Most adults attend Mass
▭	3 Minority of adults attend Mass
▭	4 Over 70% of voters petition against private schools bill, 1960
▦	5 In both groups 2 and 4

8 Industry, commerce and services 1964

▥	1 Employ over 25% of *total* population
▦	2 ,, 20 – 25% ,, ,, ,,
▭	3 ,, 15 – 20% ,, ,, ,,
▭	4 ,, under 15% ,, ,, ,,

5

THE GAULLISTS

	Votes	Seats	Members
			1947: 1,000,000?
1951	4,100,000	120	
1956	900,000	16	
1958 (1)	3,600,000	187	
(2)	5,200,000		1959: 20,000?
1962 (1)	5,800,000	229	1963: 86,000?
1967 (1)	8,500,000 (all V Rep.)	200 (+32 RI)	
1968 (1)	9,700,000	294	1968: 100,000?

The crisis over Algeria

Of all French parties the Gaullists were the most hetero-geneous. Their nucleus and leadership were provided by the small group of men who had in 1940 defied prudence and sacrificed career and reputation to follow an unknown brigadier-general in revolt against all the leaders and all the respected institutions of the country. These men came from very different backgrounds—a few from the extreme Right and far Left, many from the Socialist and Christian Demo-cratic ranks. In spite of this diversity of origin they shared a common contempt for the safe, comfortable, cautious prudence of the respectable *bon bourgeois*. Yet it was precisely in that bourgeois milieu that Gaullism as a political movement attracted the bulk of its following. When the Rally of the French People was founded in 1947, it drew innumerable adherents from the most opportunistic elements in French public life—Radicals and Conservatives who were aware of their own low political reputation and hoped to borrow that of the General to ride back to power. As their own self-confidence returned these temporary allies quickly abandoned a leader whose objectives, outlook and style were utterly different from their own; the Radicals fell away before the 1951 election, the Conservatives immediately after, when Antoine Pinay tempted them with congenial policies and the prospect of future patronage. In 1953 the General withdrew from the political arena, and his followers were quickly absorbed by the 'System' they had set out to destroy; at the next election, in 1956, three-quarters of their voters deserted them. But as the Algerian problem paralysed governments and broke up majorities the Gaullists began to believe that the catastrophe they had always predicted was indeed imminent. The regime was unable to cope with subversion in Algiers and rebellious discontent in the army; leading Gaullists like Soustelle and Debré worked to precipitate the crisis in which they saw both an opportunity to overturn the regime, and a danger that open fascists would seize the chance if they failed to do so.

In May General de Gaulle was swept back to power by the wrath of rioting settlers and the threats of mutinous soldiers, before which government and parliament capitulated. In November his most vociferous supporters loudly proclaimed their own and their leader's devotion to *Algérie française*. However ambiguous his own acts and statements, it was hardly surprising that so many observers believed the General would be constrained by the pressure of his followers, and that if he wished to pursue a different Algerian policy he would find them deserting him. While commentators of the Right took it for granted (at least in public) that de Gaulle would try to keep Algeria French, those of the Left doubted his ability to take any other course. Their most optimistic assessment was that 80 of the 200 Gaullist deputies might remain loyal to a liberal General—which would leave the *Algérie française* party (Conservatives, Algerian deputies and the rest of the Gaullists) with a comfortable parliamentary majority.

This plausible expectation proved utterly mistaken; barely fifteen members defected from the ranks throughout the course of the war—from self-determination to the division and demoralization of the army, to European terrorism and the final acceptance of an independent Algeria under complete FLN control. For the predictions of 1958 were based on too short a perspective, and on an oversimplified assessment of the men who made up the Gaullist movement. Passionate nationalists, determined to rebuild and reassert French power, the Gaullists had never been unanimously convinced that clinging to every corner of the old empire was the best way to achieve their ends. In the early postwar years they might indeed have seemed intransigent imperialists, and the General himself had gone to astonishing lengths in defending settler interests and prejudices in Algeria in 1947. But the Gaullists were more open-minded and less tied to colonial vested interests than many of the traditional Right, and they came before long to see that colonial wars were sapping the country's strength and reducing its influence. In 1953 when the Sultan of Morocco was deposed and viciously traduced by Conservative journals, the General himself publicly defended the fallen monarch — whose Paris spokesman was a Gaullist deputy. Two years later Edgar Faure chose a group of Gaullist administrators to enforce, against violent obstruction by the local authorities, the reversal of his predecessors' disastrous policy of repression. While a Gaullist high commissioner had borne a heavy share of responsibility for the beginning of the Indo-China war, by the end it was a Gaullist leader who called it 'the Fourth Republic's Mexican expedition'. Gaullists supported Pierre Mendès-France when he came to power in 1954 and made peace in Indo-China, and a Gaullist minister negotiated home rule for Tunisia, even though this was the territory where the settler leaders had been influential supporters of the RPF in Parliament. Subsequently many Gaullists reverted to a more intransigent position, first about Morocco and later over Algeria. But there were always important Gaullist intellectual sympathizers like François Mauriac, and politicians like René Capitant, who protested against torture in Algeria with a courage which many men of the classic Left conspicuously failed to show.

The circumstances of 1958 were bound to minimize the weight of this section of Gaullist opinion. The new party, the UNR, was formed in October to fight the election. Jacques Soustelle was its most dynamic leader, and Léon Delbecque, the architect of the 13 May plot, brought in his own organization, the 'Republican Convention', as a not particularly liberal component of the new party. A few of the most violent ultras from the army, like Colonel Thomazo, or among the civilian extremists, like Maître Biaggi, were returned on the UNR ticket; nearly all the leading left-wing Gaullists stayed outside, and Soustelle made sure none of them was elected. Yet already there were signs that the Right were not in full control. Three other leaders had their names placarded with those of Soustelle and Delbecque on UNR election posters. One, Michel Debré, was a loyal follower of the General first and foremost and an ultra sympathizer only second. Another, Jacques Chaban-Delmas, was a skilful opportunist who was mistrusted by the ultras and had to fight one of their leaders to save his own seat. The third, Edmond Michelet, was a convinced liberal. When Soustelle tried to persuade the party to form an electoral alliance with the Conservatives and other friends of *Algérie française*, the remaining leaders combined to stop him; and on the second ballot the Gaullists infuriated the Right by opposing (and still more by defeating) many of their candidates. Roger Frey, then UNR secretary, announced that it was a party of the centre; and in many constituencies it obtained left-wing votes as a lesser evil than the traditional Right.

These factors alone would not have sufficed to swing the party away from *Algérie française*, and during 1959 the struggle within the UNR continued bitterly. At the beginning of the year it was a UNR member, with the connivance of Chaban-Delmas as President of the Assembly, who succeeded in carrying against the rules of the house a motion in favour of integration. In April over a third of the Gaullist deputies voted for Biaggi as chairman of their group against the 'orthodox' candidate, Louis Terrenoire, who won by only 124 to 72. In June Delbecque announced his candidature for the party secretaryship, presenting himself as a representative of the rank and file, a proletarian by origin and a deputy, against the wealthy unelected new incumbent Albin Chalandon who had loyally described the party's function as that of 'secret agents who owe unconditional obedience to their military chief'.

The decisive moment came in September, when the military chief promised that Algeria would have self-determination to choose between 'secession', 'association', and 'Francization'. Soustelle and Delbecque did not openly attack the decision, but urged the party to campaign for 'the most French solution'; although the executive declined to follow them, a quarter of its members abstained. Two weeks later Algiers seems to have planned a repetition of the 13 May—demonstrations, military pressure on the authorities, and simultaneously a parliamentary revolt against Debré designed to precipitate a split in the UNR and a Bidault government. But the plans were poorly coordinated. The army remained loyal and Algiers stayed quiet. The parliamentary revolt went off at half-cock; only nine members resigned from the UNR and while Biaggi and Thomazo stayed out, Delbecque and three other rebels voted for the government and applied for readmission to the party. On Debré's insistence they were refused. At the UNR's first conference at Bordeaux in November, the integrationist extremists had lost their leadership. They dominated the hall, howling down and intimidating moderates, but the party machinery was safely in the hands of the leaders: somehow an overwhelmingly loyalist executive emerged from the overwhelmingly extremist conference, and though Chalandon gave up the secretaryship his successor was another loyalist. Having seen what their activist rank and file looked like, the party leaders were confirmed in their conviction that they should make no attempt to recruit a following of militants for the UNR.

The integrationists still had sympathizers at the top. The Prime Minister was with them at heart—but put his loyalty to de Gaulle first. Soustelle's priorities were different, and his open support for Pierre Lagaillarde's 'revolt of the barricades' in January 1960 led to his prompt dismissal. The rebels had at least acquired a leader of the front rank, but it was too late, for opinion in France was becoming both alarmed and exasperated at the civilian and military agitators across the Mediterranean. At the self-determination referendum of January 1961, Soustelle (like the Communists) campaigned for No; he could sway little more than a million votes. With the military putsch that April and the OAS terrorism of the autumn and winter, a small difference of priorities between men who had almost agreed became a gulf of hatred and violence; the Gaullists accused the ultras of betraying their leader, and were accused in turn of betraying their cause. The UNR, more even than the anti-war Left, bore the brunt of the OAS murders in Algiers and bomb attacks in Paris; and when the Gaullist authorities imprisoned generals and shot terrorists, the extremists acquired martyrs of their own. With the Evian talks and the peace referendum of April 1962, the wheel had come full circle: Gaullists, many of whom had chosen to champion *Algérie française* at the last election, were vigorously defending a policy of collaboration with the FLN; while ultras, all of whom had proclaimed that only General de Gaulle could save France, were reviling him as the worst betrayer of his country's future. They found under 7 per cent of the electorate to agree with them.

At every turn the extremists had been outmanœuvred. To begin with de Gaulle could count only on the convictions of a handful of liberals and the loyalty of a much larger number of devoted personal followers. But time changed the picture. Some UNR members were gradually educated by events to see that, as in Indo-China, the political price paid for clinging to Algeria was undermining the country's domestic stability and international influence. Some were impressed and influenced by their new Muslim colleagues. For, handpicked though they had been by the army, the Muslim deputies gave steady and growing support to the General's policies; the defection of extremist deputies from the UNR over self-determination was quickly compensated by the adherence of Muslim Algerians, especially after the barricades crisis. Some were appalled as the desperation of the extremists increasingly revealed their fascist character, or ashamed as military disobedience threatened to turn France into a banana republic. Many—notably Debré—had always recognized that a strong government in Paris could afford to make concessions which, extracted from a weak one, would only accelerate the slide downhill to disaster. There were also opportunist reasons for following the General. Politicians who had taken up *Algérie française* in order to win seats in 1958 were likely to abandon it when it endangered their chances of re-election four years later. And the violence of the OAS came at the final point of the struggle to bind all Gaullists together in a common solidarity against the fascist enemy.

By April 1962, therefore, the first phase of the UNR's history was over. Algeria was settled and, to the politicians of the old order, it was time to go back to normal. It was the moment loyal Gaullists had always dreaded, but at least they had expected to be able to capitalize on the return of peace to save their political careers. When the President declined to dissolve the Assembly, and instead replaced Debré by Pompidou, the party was thrown into dismay; they as well as their opponents now took it for granted that they were heading for electoral disaster in the following spring. But they had underestimated their leader's tactical skill.

In challenging the parties on constitutional ground of his own selection, de Gaulle contrived a brilliant manœuvre. His opponents were driven in defence of their traditional conception of parliamentary government to seem to deny the ordinary Frenchman's right to choose his own rulers. The move which disconcerted the opposition also rallied the Gaullists, and the UNR was now reinforced by the adherence of the Left Gaullist UDT, overjoyed that their interpretation of the General's Algerian intentions had come true, and appeased by the sacrifice of their old *bête noire,* Michel Debré. Few though they were in numbers, they included a disproportionate share of potential leaders and several soon acquired positions of influence in parliamentary committees or in the government.

The old lines of division within the UNR were effaced when Algeria ceased to occupy the centre of the stage. Over the constitution, and over the President's foreign policies wherever they seemed to lead, there was little or no criticism within the ranks; but domestic policy provoked sharp divisions not only between Right and Left, but between those who had put loyalty to the government first and those who feared that support for unpopular policies might cost them their seats. These electoral anxieties were at first reinforced by a section of the leadership, including Chalandon himself, who was an ultraloyalist on Algeria but, drawing a sharp distinction between the President and the government, tried hard to give the party an identity and outlook of its own—and lost the secretaryship as a result. The unexpected victory of 1962 weakened these pressures, for the Gaullists' conviction that the country needed stable government was fortified by their renewed gratitude to the General and their new optimism about the electoral appeal of unity, loyalty and discipline.

A party of government

While the 1962 election strengthened the government in

relation to its followers, they became steadily more preoccupied by their political future 'after de Gaulle'. In preparing for the inevitable day they used both traditional and modern methods. They exploited the advantages of official patronage to reward their friends and voters, like all who had controlled the government machine before them, and were able to use the new organization of regional economic development for the same purposes. At the same time the party managers with their modernizing, technocratic outlook and their ample financial resources (which still flowed freely to a government party even when business had become disenchanted) turned the UNR national headquarters into a well-organized, up-to-date, professional political machine with which none of its rivals could begin to compete. With its elaborate offices and files, its receptiveness to new devices such as canvassing by telephone, its sophisticated and systematic use of opinion polls, and its reliance on advertising and public relations techniques to take care of its 'image', the anti-American party pressed forward ruthlessly to Americanize French political life.

Nor did the Gaullists confine their modernization to electioneering. The constitutional reform which endowed France with a strong executive was followed up by a series of major administrative changes. By extensive reforms in other spheres—education, agriculture, industrial equipment, the legal and fiscal systems—they attracted many of the modernizing younger generation. The men who were setting the pace in industry, in the trade unions, in the expanding cities and in the peasant organizations, were mostly progressive Catholics, often on the political Left; while they were disillusioned by the left-wing parties (especially after Defferre's failure) they found comprehension and sometimes active encouragement from the government with which they were in any case obliged in their professional capacities to deal.

Nor was it only a handful of leaders who responded to this Gaullist appeal; as early as December 1962 an opinion poll asking which party was best for economic development found that of 66 per cent who named any party, 29 per cent chose the UNR while none of its rivals was mentioned by more than 9 per cent. But the appeal of modernizing, effective, stable government was much more help to the Gaullists in national contests than in the local battles which were essential to entrenching them in their constituencies, where few had worked assiduously enough to establish a strong local position. Though established and progressive Gaullist mayors often did well, and able young newcomers threatened or even defeated incumbents with poor records, at the 1965 municipal elections the desire for stable and effective government usually worked for the mayor in office and the UNR challenge made little headway. Nor could the Gaullists feel altogether confident that at the parliamentary elections on which their national future depended the voters would continue to put the choice of a government before their preference for a man or a point of view as they had (for the first time) in 1958 and 1962.

Even so, the UNR's impressive electoral strength created a permanent temptation for its strategists. André Malraux had exuberantly announced in the days of the old RPF that there were only two parties left in France—the Gaullists and the Communists. There was always the urge to try to verify Malraux's prediction by arranging the election laws and the Gaullists' appeal and tactical alliances in such a way as to crush the Centre and polarize opinion behind them. (For since most Frenchmen feared to see the Communists in power, if the democratic Left could be forced into their embrace, then the opposing coalition was assured of victory.) Such a strategy presupposed both a concerted effort to destroy the moderate parties and the ultimate development of Gaullism, wholly cut off from the Left, into the nucleus of the modern French Conservative party once advocated by Michel Debré. It also meant that if the country ever became disillusioned with the new rulers the only alternative would be a coalition firmly controlled by the Communists.

Though this strategy offered many attractions to a party seeking electoral success, it never won general approval in the UNR (except in the crisis of 1968). If the Gaullists committed themselves exclusively to conservative slogans, conservative alliances and a search for conservative recruits, they would soon find themselves dominated by the old-fashioned Right who were looking for a new political home.[1] Yet few politicians had more contempt for the cautious, timid, property-minded French Conservatives (who had idolized Pétain) than the men

---

[1] Without a capital letter, 'conservative' refers to social and economic attitudes; with one, it denotes a political party (which is also sympathetic to the claims of the Catholic Church).

who had followed de Gaulle in 1940—not least the adventurer Malraux and the Jacobin Debré. Progressive Catholics like Edmond Michelet and *laïque* ex-Radicals like Jacques Chaban-Delmas always disliked commitment to the conservative Right, and after 1962 they were reinforced intellectually by the entry of the UDT, the small group of left-wing Gaullists who had opposed the Algerian war. And independently of the wishes of the UNR's leadership, three factors worked against the conservative strategy: the President's policies and attitudes, the responses of other politicians, and the reactions of the electorate.

De Gaulle's policies over Algeria after 1959 and foreign affairs after 1962 were detested by most of the Right, who so loathed his tone and style that they were reluctant even to support his conservative domestic policies. But some politicians from all the old Fourth Republican parties became increasingly sympathetic to Gaullism: left-wingers who approved his foreign policy, Conservatives who liked his financial rigour, men of all views who were grateful for stability at home and prestige abroad, or disillusioned with their own parties' failure to adapt, or simply eager for office and a constructive role to play. To attract such men and the voters who might follow them, it was better to appear a flexible centre party rather than an aggressively right-wing one. Other electoral arguments pointed the same way. In 1958 everyone had vied in public devotion to de Gaulle—who prevented any alignment of the UNR with the Right because he wanted a strong democratic Left to give himself room for manœuvre over Algeria. The voters then plainly showed, especially at the second ballot, that they saw the UNR as a centre party, more acceptable to Socialists than the traditional Conservatives and to Conservatives than the old Left; and in the first parliament the Gaullists, lacking a clear majority, could usually rely on the Left and Centre over Algeria and on the Centre and Conservatives on domestic policy. When all their parliamentary opponents combined against them in 1962, the UNR won over from all of them voters who still preferred the Gaullists to their party's traditional opponents.[1]

---

[1] Though an opinion poll in 1963 still showed the UNR seen by 55 per cent as a party of the Right, by 1965 this figure was down to 39 per cent. The proportion seeing it as a Centre party was 22 and 23 per cent respectively. *Sondages*, 1963(2), p. 61; 1966(1), p. 41.

Thus Gaullists who opposed the polarization strategy on grounds of political principle were reinforced by others who thought it would not pay. Jacques Baumel, secretary of the party from 1962 to 1967, prized its tactical flexibility and hoped to turn it into a modern and disciplined version of the old Radical party. The 'Young Turks' newly recruited to Gaullist politics, professional and managerial types too young to have known the Resistance, were usually pragmatic men contemptuous of ideology and eager to 'get things done'—and to advance their own careers in the process. Michel Debré himself had in 1962 wanted to bring Giscard d'Estaing and his Conservative Gaullists within the UNR; but before long he emerged as the leading critic of Giscard (now finance minister), demanded a more expansionist economic policy, and became the hero of his old Left Gaullist enemies. During the 1965 municipal campaign Roger Frey, once secretary of the party and now Minister of the Interior, proposed to merge the UNR into 'a new political formation, larger, broader, open to all who believe in a healthy and rejuvenated democracy . . . the real party of the Centre . . . an organized, structured party such as the Anglo-Saxons understand by the word'.[1]

His proposal offended some of the old loyalists and was not followed up until the presidential election results shocked the Gaullists into action. After the General's humiliation on the first ballot, his followers were strongly tempted to whip up anti-Communist feeling for the second round against Mitterrand. On instructions from above the temptation was resisted; instead the Left Gaullists were given greater prominence than they had ever enjoyed before and Malraux, the star speaker at the main Gaullist rally in Paris, assured his applauding audience of elderly bourgeois that Gaullism was really a movement of the Left.[2] After the second ballot, the preparations for a 'third round' took a new form. The aim now was to widen the party so as to embrace everyone who had supported de Gaulle's re-election, and build a parliamentary majority corresponding to the presidential one. But whereas in 1962 an effort (not wholly successful) was made to bring all Gaullist candidates into a single party, and Frey had proposed in

---

[1] Speech at Asnières on 28 February 1965.

[2] They even cheered his reproach to Mitterrand for not having fought in Spain.

February 1965 to widen that party much further, the new tactic was to stress the diversity of the movement. The reshuffle of January 1966 accentuated the shift to the Centre; Giscard was dropped, a DC minister of state appointed, and two leading ex-Radicals (Edgard Pisani and Edgar Faure), given prominent posts. An attempt was also made to organize the left-wing intellectuals supporting de Gaulle, who were now more numerous than ever before—because of gratitude for his decolonization and foreign aid policies, approval of his opposition to the United States and his rapprochement with the USSR, and disillusionment with the incapacity to adapt of the old parties of the Left.[1]

In the following months the various wings of Gaullism all tried to strengthen their respective positions for the coming election. Giscard d'Estaing, now out of office, exploited his freedom to differentiate his party from the UNR while still proclaiming his loyalty to the President;[2] organizing busily in an attempt to recruit support among provincial Conservatives, he demanded many more seats for his candidates in the new Assembly than the thirty-five they had had in the old. Meanwhile the old Left Gaullists of the UDT also stressed their separate identity by campaigning hard for a profit-sharing scheme (of a kind which had always figured vaguely in the Gaullist programme) and even threatening to vote for a motion of censure on the government if it were not adopted. Pisani publicly condemned his ministerial colleagues for lack of reforming energy, called for a completely new social policy in the new parliament, and set up yet another new Left Gaullist party: while Edgar Faure, abandoning the reforming policies of his predecessors, turned unashamedly for support to the old conservative peasant leaders (and attracted to his banner a forgotten Conservative leader, Roger Duchet, anxious by his new enthusiasm for uniting the Right behind de Gaulle to offset the memory of his former sympathy for the men who had conspired to overthrow or assassinate his new

---

[1] Prominent among these new Left Gaullists were Emmanuel d'Astier de la Vigérie, former editor of the fellow-travelling daily *Libération*, Pierre Le Brun who had led the non-Communist minority in the CGT, and André Philip, an old opponent of Mollet in the Socialist party who had later joined and then left the PSU.

[2] One of his leading supporters described their relation to the UNR as resembling that of France to her Atlantic allies.

hero).[1] The UNR looked sourly on all such last-minute recruits and insisted that there could be only one approved Gaullist candidate in each constituency at the coming election.[2] These candidates would have to follow a common line only on three essential points: maintenance of the institutions of the Fifth Republic, support for a foreign policy of national independence, defence of the stability of the currency. On other matters Gaullists were free to advocate any policy they chose, and among them there were all shades of opinion: Gaullist Conservatives, Christian Democrats, Radicals of Left and Right, moderate Socialists and even a sort of Gaullist PSU.

The stern discipline which their narrow majority imposed on the Gaullists fed the tensions inherent in such heterogeneity. Giscard d'Estaing, who now seemed to hold the government's life in his hands, refused to merge with the main UNR parliamentary group, and was plainly set on extracting the maximum advantage both in concessions and in the succession stakes. 'We are thinking in terms of demanding rather than of asking or begging', commented one of his followers. But Giscard's fatal weakness was that if he moved from mere sniping to decisive action he risked political suicide; many of his nominal supporters—particularly the Giscardian ministers—were clearly unprepared for such a gamble. The decision to seek special powers[3] was motivated at least partly by a determination to dish Giscard, whose impotence Pompidou mercilessly exposed by publicly refusing him even token concessions. The would-be king-maker (or king) was consigned to the ultimate Gaullist gehenna as a 'man of the Fourth Republic'.

But, as Pompidou admitted, there was a general malaise among the majority. Pisani resigned over the special powers issue and began criticizing from the back benches. The loyalty of even Gaullists of the first hour was shaken by the General's repudiation of Israel in the Six Days War. The Left Gaullists unsuccessfully pressed to be allowed to set up a separate parliamentary group to 'balance' the Giscardians. Though most of them agreed to a merger with the enlarged movement

---

[1] On Duchet, see below, pp. 105, 106.

[2] A committee on candidatures represented all the different factions: UNR, Giscard, Left Gaullists, etc., with Pompidou in the chair.

[3] See above, pp. 52–3.

—embracing men like Edgar Faure and Maurice Schumann and rechristened Union Démocratique pour la Cinquième République—their personal hostility to Pompidou intensified. Capitant called for his removal. Others complained that Pompidou was trying to impose a reactionary social policy on the party. Several leading Left Gaullists even refused to attend its first conference for four years at Lille—and the Elysée made no attempt to discourage their offensive. A running debate on party organization, lasting for months, had involved the replacement of Baumel, who was disliked by many of the parliamentarians, by a collective national secretariat which was allegedly under remote control from Pompidou and Frey. The Lille Conference insisted on a single secretary-general, and clearly indicated that the rank and file expected to be consulted more frequently than every four years. The new secretary-general, Robert Poujade (no relative of Pierre Poujade, the Fourth Republic demagogue who had recently become one of the strangest of the regime's strange bedfellows), was widely looked on as a Pompidou man— but acceptable to the Gaullist Left.

Before the 1968 crisis Pompidou had consolidated his control of the government and his influence in the party. During it he alone in the Gaullist leadership succeeded in enhancing his reputation. But then, within days of the electoral triumph of which he was the chief architect, de Gaulle had banished him to 'the reserve of the Republic'. Though bitter at the dismissal, and at a sordid Parisian scandal which party opponents tried to use against him in 1969, Pompidou was not slow to grasp the advantages of his exile. Free of compromising responsibilities in a difficult economic and political situation, something of a martyr figure, he held the gratitude of many of the parliamentarians and the rank and file. What better position from which, while maintaining complete loyalty, to prepare for the post-Gaullist leadership? His chief danger was of falling out of the public eye: by announcing early in 1969 that he was a candidate for the Presidency when it fell vacant, he guaranteed that he would not lapse into oblivion, staked his claim as the leading Gaullist contender—and provided all who felt that the time had come for the General to go with the reassurance that the choice would not lie between de Gaulle and the void.

Pompidou's brusque dismissal was only one cause of the

curious unhappiness which the Gaullists (soon rebaptized twice, ending as Union des Démocrates pour la République) felt with their huge majority.[1] Electoral victory did not dispel their uneasy fears about the fragility of the regime, while the chilly leadership of Couve de Murville was borne rather than accepted. One small satisfaction was to punish Giscard d'Estaing for his 'disloyalty' by evicting him from the chairmanship of the Finance Committee and strictly curbing his TV appearances now that the Gaullists could survive without his support. But though the chairman of the UDR group discreetly echoed the general expectation of having greater influence, ministers were no more disposed to bow to backbenchers' wishes than in the past. The aftermath of the crisis involved swallowing some bitter medicine. Elected to maintain law and order, deputies found themselves voting reforms to placate striking workers and riotous students. A modest extension of union rights on the shop floor, promised in May, was seriously opposed only by Gaullists and Giscardians, to whom it was an 'industrial Munich'—and who listened aghast as a colleague on UDR's furthest Left reported de Gaulle as declaring that 'the capitalist system must be condemned outright'. This was nothing to their fury and frustration over Edgar Faure's university reform. Faure was already suspect of being a 'ghost' from the Fourth Republic scheming to rob the Gaullists of their inheritance after the General's passing. Now he introduced a sweeping reform which was in itself unacceptable to the party's conservatives, won de Gaulle's approval for it, and made no bones about publicly recognizing that his chief enemies lay among the government's own supporters. Armed with de Gaulle's benediction he fought the bill through with few concessions. Although it was carried without a dissenting vote, on a free vote the Gaullists would probably have rejected it.[2] Once the bill was passed, sniping over its implementation continued both on the Gaullist benches and from local Committees for the Defence of the Republic— groups of hard-line Gaullists which were organized in June with the President's encouragement and were acting as

---

[1] 'The party has changed names as often as a pursued criminal.' J. S. Ambler on the UDR in *Rice University Studies*, 54·3 (Summer 1968), p. 39n.

[2] See below, pp. 326–31.

political vigilantes for the party's repressive wing. Spanning the political spectrum more fully than ever, from the bully-boys of the far Right to the occasional sympathizer with student protest on the Left, the Gaullists found that the strains of policy debate within their own ranks were more acute than ever during the closing months of de Gaulle's rule.

The divisions over policy were exacerbated by differences of temperament.[1] There were older leaders like Malraux and Michelet, and others among the rank and file, for whom Gaullism was a quasi-religious faith, and who were likely to withdraw from politics once the General was no longer there (as Malraux did). Then there were the doctrinaires, eager to impose their divergent views on the movement: the former Christian Democrats, the Left Gaullists, Debré with his passion for service to the dominant State. Always present, but now increasingly numerous, were the 'empiricists' (or for Jacques Soustelle the careerists) who had joined Gaullism because it seemed a more promising means than the old parties of forwarding their ideas or ambitions. All these diverse groups were held together by the personality and inspiration of their leader. Many observers were convinced that they would soon fly apart once he was gone.

That was not certain. Ever since the end of the Algerian war and the institution of direct election for the presidency de Gaulle had moved steadily away from his 'above-party' status, and had more readily (but never completely) identified himself with his party supporters. At the same time these followers themselves were more and more concerned with politics 'after de Gaulle', and with developing their own appeal instead of relying on his. From one election to another the change was striking. In 1958 Gaullists depended on their presumed fidelity to the national hero who could avert civil war and settle the Algerian imbroglio. In 1962 this loyalty was still an asset but it was supplemented by the fresh claim to offer France a new and more effective form of government. In 1965 the President's apparent unconcern with his own succession did him great harm; and sixteen months later it was the Prime Minister who played the most active part in the 1967 campaign while Gaullist candidates championed the Fifth Republic rather than the man who had created it. During

---

[1] Defined by J. Charlot, *L'UNR* (Paris, 1967), Ch. 11.

the 1968 crisis the Gaullists were well aware that Pompidou had shown clearer vision than the President, and until the very last moment had provided the only leadership. They also knew that increasingly the electorate wanted to choose a government, and that they were the party with the most credible claim to provide one—if only they could preserve their discipline and unity. The centrifugal forces, from Giscard's ambitions to the Left Gaullists' consciences, would be counteracted not only by habit and sentiment, but also by the unremitting pressures of self-interest.[1]

---

[1] The last paragraph was written before de Gaulle's departure — which had as its immediate political consequence not a defection from Gaullism but the rallying to it of yet another group of centrists —Pleven from UDSR, Fontanet from MRP, Duhamel from the Radicals —who formed another allied group, Centre Démocratie et Progrès, alongside Giscard's Independent Republicans.

6

THE 'PARTIES OF
YESTERDAY'

The common problem

The 'parties of yesterday', as Gaullists complacently or contemptuously called them, were the political groups which had
almost monopolized politics before the second world war and
government after it. From the royalist and revolutionary
enemies of the bourgeois Third Republic there descended
Conservatives and Socialists who by 1914 had come to accept the regime. The ruling Radicals manœuvred between
these rivals, usually relying on Socialist support at elections
against the clerical threat from the Right, and on Conservative
backing for the budget against the menace to property from
the Left. Conservatives were often in office between the wars,
Socialists not until 1936, Radicals throughout. In the Resistance a new party was born, the Christian Democratic MRP,
and these four provided between them all but one of the
premiers and almost all the ministers who served between the
two reigns of de Gaulle. After the first few postwar years
the Radicals were always in office, and Conservatives and MRP
almost always; the Socialists were in every cabinet (except
from 1951 to 1955) between the Liberation and de Gaulle's
election to the Presidency.

The four parties held together because they had to: against
the aggressive challenges of the Gaullists of 1951, the Poujadists of 1956 and the Communists throughout, no government
could long survive without the support of three at least and
usually all four. But, while they believed French democracy
could be saved only by their cooperation, they differed on
the whole spectrum of political issues which divided parties
in Britain; if they made concessions to their governmental
partners at the expense of their own supporters in the country,
there were always active and demagogic rivals on Right and

Left to seize the opportunity to undermine their support, and the coalition with it. Despite these difficulties, the 'parties of yesterday' laid the foundations for French prosperity and modernization. But they failed to meet the challenge of colonial nationalism; and by 1958 their endless deals and quarrels over patronage or policy, their cabinets which fell every six or nine months without ever seeming to change, had discredited their regime with the ordinary voter. Once offered the novel spectacle of a government that was stable at home and respected abroad, he would not go back to the confusion and instability of the past. The future was therefore bleak for small parties. Only the Gaullists could claim to provide a government on their own. An opposition which excluded the Communist party provided no credible alternative; an opposition dominated by the Communists had little hope of winning over the electorate. But if the moderate parties refused both the Gaullist and the Communist embrace, their common belief in parliamentary democracy could not easily withstand the differences on every policy problem which threatened to paralyse or split them—and in either case to discredit them, as in the past. Some MRP and Radical politicians preferred to work with Conservatives, some with Socialists, while the two latter parties could never cooperate for long.[1] After twelve years of the Fifth Republic the 'parties of yesterday', bewildered and divided, had still not adapted to the new world.

[1] In Paris; they could in local government.

The Conservatives (*Centre National des Indépendants-Paysans*, CNIP); and the extreme Right

Year	Votes	Seats	Members
1946	3,100,000	71	
1951	2,300,000	98	A party of notables
1956	3,200,000	97	with no mass
1958	4,500,000	129 (146)	membership
1962	1,700,000	29	
1967	in Democratic Centre		
1968	in Progress & Modern Democracy		

Before the second world war the Conservatives had never belonged to one political party, however loose, but were scattered among several groups which imposed no discipline on their members of parliament and had no organized base in the country. But in the Fourth Republic, enjoying the services of a superb party manager, Roger Duchet, and a popular leader, Antoine Pinay, they built up for the first time an effective party machine. At the 1958 election they proclaimed their allegiance both to de Gaulle and to French rule in Algeria; but while the slogans were the same as those of the Gaullists, the purpose was to capitalize on the supposed mood of the country and contest with the UNR for the leadership of the Fifth Republic. Though disappointed at emerging as only the second strongest party, the Conservatives were the sole challengers for power in the first parliament, and they could hope for some sympathy among the other Fourth Republican parties against the UNR.

They suffered, however, from internal strains far graver than those of their rivals. Whereas the new men of the UNR displayed surprising cohesion and loyalty, the individualism characteristic of the traditional Right was to prove their undoing. There were few divisions of view among them on foreign policy, where they all accepted the European and

Atlantic alignment of Fourth Republican governments, or on the constitution, where they all preferred parliamentary to presidential rule. They differed somewhat on domestic, social and economic issues, since their members ranged from violent reactionaries to moderate sympathizers with Mendès-France; but these conflicts could usually be compromised. The fatal dispute was on Algeria. When the twin allegiances of 1958 proved to be incompatible, nine-tenths of the Gaullists followed the sinuous course of their leader, but many of the Conservatives, frustrated of the power they had expected to wield in the new regime, attempted to use against de Gaulle the emotions and the slogans which had helped to sweep him to power. In January 1960 Pinay's dismissal (mainly over foreign policy) weakened the loyalty felt by Conservatives to a government they had never regarded as theirs; although most of their members of parliament continued to support de Gaulle over Algeria, Duchet controlled the machine and managed in November 1960 to win a three-to-one majority at a party conference for *Algérie française*. At the referendum two months later the party was too divided to advise its followers which way to vote. In April 1961 Duchet went too far in showing his support for the generals' putsch in Algiers, and lost his secretaryship. But the Conservatives' support for de Gaulle over Algeria overlaid only temporarily their hostility to him on other grounds, and with the end of the war they, like the other Fourth Republican parties, felt themselves free to express their criticisms. Paul Reynaud, the leader of those who had steadfastly defended the General over Algeria, attacked his European policy in June and denounced his constitutional reform in October; 109 of the 121 Conservative deputies voted for the motion of censure, leaving only a small remnant of Conservative Gaullists under Valéry Giscard d'Estaing, the finance minister, to fight the 1962 election with Gaullist backing and provide the marginal votes which gave the Pompidou government its secure majority in the new parliament. While these Gaullists survived the election, the rest of the CNI went down to disastrous defeat—moderates like Paul Reynaud and Bertrand Motte as well as the sympathizers with the extreme Right. Of 101 deputies seeking re-election on an opposition platform only twenty-five were returned, and only four new ones were elected; most of the twenty-nine now rallied to Giscard's party of Independent Republicans, but a few affiliated to groups dominated by MRP or the old Radicals. Though it still claims the allegiance of many senators and local councillors, the CNI has never recovered from this debacle and its non-Gaullist moderates were absorbed, along with MRP, into the shaky structure of the Democratic Centre.

Their competitors on the extreme Right shared their rout. Whereas the Conservatives are a party of politicians with many voters but no active rank and file, extremist movements of the Right have always found activists easy to recruit but electoral support difficult.[1] The Algerian war gave a fillip to ultra-nationalist tendencies, which were stimulated by the army unrest that first carried de Gaulle to power and then threatened to unseat him. Defence of the patriotic cause in Algeria brought many Gaullists, Conservatives and Radicals and a few Socialist and MRP politicians to associate with men they would in normal times have repudiated, and when de Gaulle adopted the very policies they had expected him to prevent, Jacques Soustelle and Georges Bidault became his bitter enemies; both ended in exile. Other active politicians were mostly more cautious: many had mistakenly believed the defence of French rule in Algeria would prove a winning cause. But there were only some 1,200,000 votes cast for *Algérie française* at the referendum of January 1961 and only 1,800,000 at that of April 1962; so by that autumn, with peace restored, most of these politicians had returned to their old parties. All of them, the ex-Gaullists, ex-Radicals, CNI and Poujadists alike, went down to a common disaster at the election; and though the influx of refugees from North Africa offered them a new electoral clientele, their presidential candidate in December 1965, J. L. Tixier-Vignancour, scored only a disappointing $1\frac{1}{4}$ million votes. For most anti-Gaullist Conservatives and indeed many extreme right-wingers preferred a more respectable candidate with better prospects even though he came from the ranks of the Christian Democrats they so despised.[2]

---

[1] Pierre Poujade's $2\frac{1}{2}$ million votes in 1956 were a flash in the pan, and by no means all came from the far Right.

[2] See below, pp. 124-5.

The Christian Democrats
(*Mouvement Républicain Populaire, MRP*)

Year	Votes	Seats	Members
1946	5,000,000	167	200,000
1951	2,500,000	96	
1956	2,400,000	84	
1958	2,300,000	57 (64)	46,000
1962	1,600,000	36 (55)	40,000?
1967	in Democratic Centre		
1968	in Progress and Modern Democracy		

Of all the 'parties of yesterday' MRP was the least attached to the past. Christian Democrats had never formed a significant party before the second world war; the new movement, founded in 1944, enjoyed a mushroom growth at first because the old-fashioned Right was discredited by Vichy and de Gaulle was still holding himself aloof from the political struggle. As soon as these favourable factors disappeared it lost half its votes, but settled down as a respectable middle-sized party with a rather conservative voting base, a mildly progressive body of activist supporters and a leadership which steered between the two but frequently veered to starboard. With a solid foundation in the flourishing professional organizations around the Catholic Church, MRP recruited a younger and more active rank and file than the other parties of the Fourth Republic, but its gains were essentially in the rural areas; while it sank deep roots in the political soil of parts of the countryside, it was unable to attract any following in the big cities.

In 1958 Georges Bidault, the party's best-known leader, was the first leading politician to come out for de Gaulle as the man to keep Algeria French. Pierre Pflimlin, the premier who resigned to make way for the General, was a moderate over Algeria as over nearly everything else; and while a tiny fraction followed Bidault and became extreme champions of *Algérie française*, the majority of the party preferred Pflimlin's cautious and critical support of de Gaulle's policies. MRP ministers stayed in office throughout the Algerian war, and when Pompidou replaced Debré he strengthened their representation, bringing back Pflimlin himself (who had resigned for personal reasons at the end of 1958). But within a month all the MRP ministers were out, in protest against de Gaulle's sarcastic mockery of their European faith at his May 1962 press conference. The breach soon widened from foreign policy to other issues. The censure motion of October 1962 was voted by fifty of the fifty-seven MRP deputies, though Pflimlin (who was among the fifty) led the minority of one-fifth who wanted the party conference nevertheless to support direct election of the President. Instead they voted No for the first time at a referendum, and went down to the usual fate of parties which turned against the General after once supporting him, losing at the election a third of their 1958 vote instead of making the gains they had counted on a few months before. Most of their younger and more left-wing deputies lost their seats, and under a new secretary, Joseph Fontanet, the party machine swung to the Right.

They remained the most willing of all the old parties to envisage a far-reaching political realignment. A new party would avoid the polarization between Gaullists and Communists which they feared above all. It would allow them to capitalize on their central political position, and provide a moderate and attractive alternative to the regime which they badly needed, for their voters were dangerously tempted by Gaullism while their active supporters were growing increasingly hostile to it. Moreover, MRP had the vigorous rank and file which its rivals lacked, and these militants would play a large part in a new movement which might provide the new look that all parties wanted to achieve. From 1963, therefore, MRP officially proclaimed its eagerness to dissolve itself in a new and wider political formation. But it did not make clear whether this new movement of the Centre would be a little to the Left as the activists hoped, or a little to the Right as the voters probably preferred. The presidential campaign was to force them to abandon this position of prudent ambiguity.

The Radical Party

Year	Votes	Seats	Members
1946	2,100,000	43	
1951	2,000,000	76	
1956	2,400,000	75	20,000?
1958	1,800,000	25	
1962	1,400,000	41	
1967	in Left Federation		
1968	,, ,, ,,		

(These estimates are much more approximate than those for any other party, as the Radicals have less organization, more splits, and more electoral pacts with equally unorganized neighbours.)

The Radical party was the pivot of any coalition of the Centre—which without it could appeal only to the clerical sector of opinion, but with it would have strong links to the Socialists. For the Radical party shares with them a common devotion to the traditional Republican creed, though it has always repudiated their conception of a disciplined party voting unitedly for a single policy. Instead Radicals have prided themselves on allowing their members full freedom to interpret the extremely vague party principles in the way that best suited their personal convictions or constituency requirements. Where the Socialists were a solid organized party with an opportunist policy, the Radicals were an electoral cooperative of political individualists who covered the whole ideological and political spectrum. When Pierre Mendès-France tried in 1955 to take over the old machine and turn it into a modern party with a policy, he won new supporters from a younger generation repelled by old-style politics, but he alienated the old professional politicians who were the party's flesh and blood. Under the strain of the Algerian war his opponents left the party to move into association with the far Right; later he and his supporters went into the wilderness, ultimately to find a temporary and uneasy home in the PSU.

As the most traditionalist of all French parties it was not surprising that the Radicals were the most suspicious of Gaullism. Even in 1958 they supported the new constitution by only a three to two vote (the minority, the largest in any democratic party, being drawn from both the conventional conservatives and the Mendèsist Left). By 1960 they were opposing the government on everything: its treatment of parliament, its 'anti-European' foreign policy, its concessions to the church schools—and above all its Algerian policy where the party's left and right wings came together to decide by a two to one majority to advise a No vote at the referendum of January 1961. Next year the standard-bearer of the opposition to the constitutional reform—and to the unconstitutional procedure chosen—was the Radical President of the Senate, Gaston Monnerville. At the 1962 election the Radicals, like the Socialists, lost votes but gained seats by some tactical alliances with the Communists, based on a common republican vocabulary and common enemies rather than an identity of view on any subject; nevertheless they attracted some new deputies from the debris of the shattered Conservatives, and these newcomers reinforced their right wing. When the preparations for the presidential election forced them to take sides, the Radicals were split as usual. A few individuals either chose Gaullism or genuinely favoured left-wing policies; an important minority preferred to bury anticlericalism and work with the anti-Gaullist Conservatives and MRP for a moderate Centre policy, prudent at home and strongly European and Atlantic abroad; the majority, though thoroughly conservative in political outlook and in social and economic policy, opted for the old left-wing alliance because the party's anticlerical and Republican tradition still drew it towards the Socialists.

The Socialist Party (SFIO)

Year	Votes	Seats	Members
1946	3,400,000	105	354,000
1951	2,800,000	107	('52) 116,000
1956	3,200,000	99	120,000
1958	3,200,000	40	102,000
1962	2,300,000	65	89,000
1967	in Left Federation		
1968	,, ,, ,,		

The Socialists and the Radicals, separated in theory by deep doctrinal divergences over the economic organization of society, in practice had much in common. These two parties of the 'Old Left' were the surviving exponents of the Republican tradition, suspicious of and hostile to the old ruling classes, the Catholic Church, the army and (in theory) the bureaucracy. Based primarily on the small-town provincial lower middle class, they were both weak in and mistrustful of the biggest towns—above all of the capital.[1] Their tradition insisted that government was dangerous and the executive must be kept weak and submissive to legislative pressure. Yet like the Radicals before them, the Socialists became a government party in the Fourth Republic. They usually took office because without them no democratic majority at all could be found; this situation, which quite frequently obtained on the national level, was permanent in many provincial towns. Local government became their great stronghold. Providing many efficient and popular mayors, they developed in these local fortresses into a 'party of government'. Thus they attracted to their ranks prospective administrators, pragmatists and careerists who had only verbal sympathy for the traditional doctrine of opposition and protest. But the old outlook was given a fillip when the Socialists went out of office in Paris at the formal inauguration of the Fifth Republic in January 1959. They uneasily tolerated the Gaullist regime

---

[1] But unlike the Radicals the Socialists had a working-class following in some industrial areas.

while the Algerian war lasted. But when peace came and the presidential system developed in its full form, they (like most Radicals) reverted to their own tradition of republicanism and stood out as its strongest opponents, as ardent as (though less violent than) the extreme Right and far more hostile than the Communist party.

De Gaulle's advent split the Socialists, half their deputies voting for him as Premier on 1 June 1958 in order to avert an insurrection, while half refused to submit to military blackmail. But when he presented his new constitution in September the party conference approved it by a seven to three vote. De Gaulle was still the best bulwark against civil war; he had convinced the most important of his former critics, Gaston Defferre, that he meant to pursue a liberal policy in Algeria; and his constitution appeared to retain the foundations of the parliamentary system. Moreover, the country was in his favour: so that opposition would mean electoral catastrophe while support might enable the Socialists to hold the pivotal position, indispensable to every majority, which would enable them to dominate the new parliament. This last hope was swept away in the Gaullist tide, and when the General and his Conservative finance minister adopted a deflationary economic policy in December, the Socialists abandoned office for 'constructive opposition'. When the self-determination offer to Algeria set de Gaulle firmly on the road to decolonization, they were torn between their growing doubts over many of his policies and their approval of his actions on the issue which dominated all the rest—and where they knew he alone could hope for success where they had failed. They decided by a two to one majority to vote Yes in the referendum of January 1961 which approved the self-determination offer.[1]

During 1961 Socialist opposition stiffened. They still supported de Gaulle over Algeria but they deplored both his domestic and his foreign policy and they distrusted the way

---

[1] Those of the old minority who had violently criticized Mollet's Algerian policy left the party in 1958 to become the nucleus of the future PSU. Others, former close associates of Mollet who trusted de Gaulle less than he did, stayed within SFIO as a growing Left opposition which wanted to vote No at the 1961 referendum; so did the small extreme right wing of the party which still favoured *Algérie française.*

he worked his constitution. But they were too weak to oppose effectively on their own; if they were to break with the regime they would have to choose their allies—either conservative democrats whose economic and social policies they disliked, or Communists who had reviled them for years and whose democratic *bona fides* they deeply distrusted. In July 1960, still preaching 'constructive opposition' to Gaullism, they had warned that cooperation with the Communists might mean that Paris would suffer the fate of Prague twelve years before. By September 1961 they were far more hostile to Gaullism, extending their opposition now to the regime and not merely to Debré's government; they called upon 'all democrats, only democrats' to join them in fighting it. At the height of OAS terrorism in January 1962 they recognized that it might be necessary to unite with the Communists to oppose a fascist putsch, but would have no truck with them in less desperate circumstances. When de Gaulle announced his bill for direct election to the Presidency in September 1962, they joined the other old Fourth Republican parties in a 'Cartel des Non' to resist it—but in the spirit of their old alliance declared their continued opposition to 'totalitarians of Left and Right', the Gaullists and Communists they had resisted together in the old regime. It was therefore quite an unexpected shift when Guy Mollet, three days before the first ballot in the 1962 election, advised his followers that the UNR was the immediate danger and they should vote Communist on the second ballot where necessary to keep a Gaullist out. The Communists were delighted to reciprocate, and though the Socialists lost a quarter of their votes they emerged with twenty more members. Half their deputies now owed their election to Communist support. In December this most cautious, conservative, compromising political organization proclaimed itself yet again 'a revolutionary party of class struggle'.

But this apparent swing to the Left marked no fundamental change in the character of the SFIO. When Guy Mollet acquired the leadership in 1946 he was the intransigent leader of the militant Marxist wing of the party; he held it over twenty difficult years by tactical skill and sensitivity to the moods of the French people and the Socialist rank and file in particular. Generally lacking support in the most modern and prosperous parts of the country, tied to an outmoded conception of weak government, sympathetic to the claims of colonial rebels when it was in opposition but not when it was in power, the Socialist party acquired an unenviable reputation for opportunism and conservatism. Yet the most prominent of the leaders who took this path were old Marxists, who never lost their capacity to offer their followers left-wing slogans as a substitute for left-wing actions. They preserved the party's electoral base by flexibility of tactics, and the manœuvre of 1962 merely afforded them an extra option: cooperating with Conservatives at one election or in one area and with Communists at other times and places, they exploited their advantages of political position in an attempt to strengthen an army whose direction of march was never clear. They exemplified all the characteristics which had discredited the Fourth Republic and its politicians, and though their machine survived nationally and locally, they failed to recruit new members and their electoral following slowly ebbed away as impatient young radicals turned to other parties (PSU, MRP, even UNR) or away from politics altogether.

The Socialists were well aware of their declining strength and reputation and, except in a few areas where they had long been solidly entrenched, were deeply concerned by it. Most agreed that an effort must be made to regain the confidence they had lost and to bring the various independent little groups and movements of broadly socialist outlook, if not back into the party itself, at least into friendly instead of hostile relations with it. But while few openly rejected the idea of a new look, many wanted the transition to be carried out within the old framework and under the old management; if a change of tradition or leadership was necessary to broaden the party's appeal, they were not prepared to pay the price. Moreover, the modernizers themselves faced the dilemma which had hampered the party for so long: was their new-model party to become the partner of the Communists in a left-wing alliance, or was it to throw over its (purely nominal) Marxist creed in order to attract other progressive democrats, most of them Catholics, as Mollet's opponents had tried to do just after the war? Each course had its advocates who mistrusted the supporters of the alternative strategy, and their conflict offered the party leader plenty of scope for his tactical skills.

7

A NEW PARTY STRUCTURE?

The PSU (Unified Socialist Party)

Year	Votes	Seats	Members
1962	340,000 in 99 seats (2% of the total, 9% in seats fought; real strength in between)	2	20,000?
1967	500,000 in 120 seats (2% of the total)	4 (affil. to Federation)	11,500
1968	870,000 in 321 seats (4% of the total)	0	15,000

Long before the Fifth Republic, politicians in all parties, especially men of the younger generation, had grown increasingly frustrated by the calculations, compromises and manœuvres inherent in coalition politics. Disillusionment with the 'parties of yesterday' and their stalemate politics, exploited so successfully by the Gaullists in 1958, had already brought grist to the mill of such very different critics as Pierre Mendès-France and Pierre Poujade. To this general malaise was added, among a minority of Socialists and the Mendèsist Radicals, a special sense of shame and exasperation. Allied in the Republican Front to win the 1956 election on a policy of ending the Algerian war, their parties had then proceeded under Guy Mollet and Robert Lacoste to give the settlers priority over the Muslims, insist on military victory before political reforms, extend the fighting in Algeria and invade Egypt. (The shame and exasperation were all the greater

116

because these hard-line policies plainly won the approval of French public opinion.) De Gaulle's advent brought to a head the crisis within the non-Communist Left, and when their parties decided in September 1958 to support the General's constitution, the anti-war, anti-Gaullist minorities broke away. The Socialists resigned to form a new Parti socialiste autonome (PSA), the Mendèsists were expelled for fighting the November election as part of the Union des forces démocratiques (UFD), an ephemeral alliance including the PSA, into which most of them were soon absorbed.

These were not the first left-wing defections from the 'parties of yesterday'. From 1948 on a series of splinter groups had broken with SFIO and MRP, mostly because of anti-American neutralism. In 1956 there were dissensions in the rival camp as well, when Soviet repression in Hungary alienated many of the Communists' allies in the small Progressive party. In 1957 several minority groups came together to form the Union de la gauche socialiste (UGS), a conglomeration of neutralists, revolutionaries, Left Catholics and former fellow-travellers. The PSU (Parti socialiste unifié) was formed in 1960 by the fusion of the UGS with a tiny dissident Communist group and with the PSA, which was more than double the size of the other two together. More active and dynamic than their partners, the former UGS militants before long provided the bulk (though not the whole) of the leadership, and many of the refugees from the older parties soon resigned from the PSU. Young, active, strong in intellectual appeal and—unlike every other French left-wing party— largely Catholic, the PSU often took the lead against the war and the regime, filling the vacuum left by the sluggishness or timidity of their large rivals.

Relations with the Communists were the new party's dominant problem; they were determined not to be driven into systematic anti-Communism, yet the Party had no sympathy with them and indeed viewed them as a long-term threat. Early in its life the PSU voted by a fairly narrow majority (413 to 353) to vote No on the self-determination referendum of January 1961; most of the old Mendèsists and Socialists were in the minority which advocated abstention. At the next referendum on peace in Algeria, when the Communists decided to vote Yes, the PSU seized with delight the chance to distinguish itself by showing greater intransigence; by a three to two majority it called on its supporters to spoil their papers by writing on them 'Yes to peace, No to the Gaullist regime'. That summer the party voted by ten to one against political unity among the Common Market countries, and promptly shed many of its moderate supporters. Its most distinguished individual member, Pierre Mendès-France, for years played no part in its activities, was never invited to speak on its behalf at elections or referendums, and at the 1962 election fought as an independent, avoiding mention of his party like the plague.[1] At its 1963 conference, indeed, the PSU seemed near to disintegration; there were no less than six different factions within its meagre ranks (labelled alphabetically from A to F to avoid naming them after their leaders). This, however, was the party's low point; a year later there were only two groups, in effect the most left-wing of reformists and the traditional revolutionaries of a semi-anarchist kind. Neither had any significant popular following, and the only places where the PSU had any real electoral support were those where an old Socialist had brought over his local party and many of its voters. Many of these men, however, were as unable to accommodate themselves to their new associates as the PSU militants were to tolerate the compromises of electoral politics; consequently those few PSU members who ever won an election, whether as deputies or as mayors, were usually established politicians who quarrelled soon afterwards with the party—though at Grenoble, one of the fastest-growing towns in France, a PSU-organized team of young civic reformers won a startling victory at the 1965 municipal election.

Despite its negligible popular support, the PSU attracted active members (perhaps as many of these as the Socialist party had) and a good deal of sympathy in the trade unions and peasant organizations as well as among students. Its abler and younger leaders in their thorough commitment to modernizing policies and attitudes not infrequently found themselves on the same side as the Gaullists they condemned. While they called for left-wing unity and denounced Gaston Defferre for opportunist concessions to the Centre, they were

---

[1] In 1965 he was, however, approached to stand for the Presidency — but refused because he disapproved of the presidential system. In 1967 he was the PSU's television spokesman. He left the party in July 1968.

cordially detested by the party machines of the Left for much the same reasons as he; and when Socialists and Communists made a municipal pact in the Paris area in 1965 the PSU was virtually frozen out. Busily promoting intellectual discussions between socialists of all parties and none, it found itself excluded (often by its own choice) from most political manifestations of the left-wing unity it assiduously preached. In the 1967 election the PSU, after bitter bargaining, obtained Federation support for thirty of its candidates and elected four of these, including Mendès-France at Grenoble. But in eighty other seats where negotiations failed, it fought the Federation and was routed—the Communists profiting from the damage done to both contestants. In June the party voted by more than two to one against association with the Federation, changing its leadership and losing many of its remaining founding fathers as a result. Under Michel Rocard the PSU was now set on an increasingly intransigent course, criticising both the Federation and the PCF for their inadequacies of policy and opportunism of tactics, and emerging in May 1968 on the Communists' Left as the sole party supporting the revolutionaries. At the June election it trebled the number of its candidates but only doubled its vote, and all its seats were lost.

The new leadership believed that the Communist Party was incapable of adapting itself to the changes in French society, and the Socialist Party incapable of exploiting the opportunity thus opened to them. With leaders young enough to wait, the PSU therefore subordinated immediate electoral success to long-term strategy and regarded with much equanimity the damage its tactics did to the non-Communist Left as a whole. In electoral politics it consequently appeared as a mere irritant, able to split and wreck for its own sectarian ends, but hardly ever to win.[1] Intellectually, however, its independence of established electoral interests allowed this splinter party to play a fertilizing role of quite disproportionate importance, realistically analysing the situation and the needs of contemporary France where its rivals usually rested content with the allegiance of the declining social groups, and the inspiration of the ancient slogans, that had served them so well in the past.

---

[1] At least until Rocard's spectacular victory over Couve de Murville in a by-election in October 1969.

The problem of realignment

All the old parties—including the Communists—relied on the persistence of old-fashioned loyalties and voting habits centred on attitudes to the Church and the republican tradition of a strong parliament. These habits and loyalties were most effective when the voter was choosing within an established local framework rather than in a new-style national consultation. The modernizers of the extreme and moderate Left thus had a common and even occasionally a conscious interest with the Gaullists in disrupting the old habits and blowing up the old framework. To this end de Gaulle used his power of initiative with brilliant effect. The referendum of 1958 loosened the Communist party's hold on its voters, that of 1961 shook both Left and Right, that of October 1962 shattered the Right and Centre. After 1962 the impending presidential election was the lever with which the modernizers hoped to force the parties to adapt. But it was to be preceded by a municipal and followed by a parliamentary election, which would be fought out amidst traditional local, personal and ideological conflicts. In 1962 the voter, like an Englishman, had chosen a government; but some politicians preferred not to notice, and none could be sure he would do it again. The presidential election was therefore a less powerful lever than the modernizers hoped—at least while it was distant.

Modernizers in the opposition feared that de Gaulle might resign the Presidency and call an early election which would find them wholly unprepared. But they could use the danger to force their parties to face the new situation. Gaston Defferre's candidature was launched at the end of 1963 as an attempt to exploit the presidential election to lay the foundation of a new party of the democratic Left, which could compete with the UNR for a broad popular following and a stable parliamentary majority. He was thwarted by the established party machines and the reluctance of the hesitant to take risks when the prospect of defeating de Gaulle seemed impossibly remote. After his failure François Mitterrand and Jean Lecanuet embarked on less ambitious efforts to regroup different sections of the Centre forces by conciliating the existing machines instead of forcing their hand.

In any attempted realignment the decisive voice was that of the Socialist party. Without its help neither the Communists nor the anti-Gaullist Right and Centre were strong enough to look like a credible alternative government. Yet if the Socialists consistently aligned themselves with either of these forces they would divide their own ranks, alienate some of their voters, and endanger the parliamentary and local council seats which they held with the electoral support of the rejected partner. Guy Mollet hoped to preserve the party's strength (and his own leadership) by continuing his policy of masterly ambiguity, allowing each local branch to choose its allies but making no firm national commitment.[1] Since the presidential election was designed to make this familiar style of politics impossible, Mollet chose to ignore it—while Defferre stressed its importance. But both agreed that the party must build up its bargaining power—however it was to be used—and both therefore wished to win over those socialists who were outside the official party. All of these, however, distrusted Mollet as an opportunist while many of them feared that Defferre's presidential ambitions would lead him to make too many concessions to the Right. These doubts were felt widely in the Fabian-style political clubs, and universally in the PSU.

The Defferre episode

For where the PSU was to seek to outflank the Communists, Defferre had answered their hostility by attempting to force their hand. Instead of summoning the Left parties to the traditional tribal pow-wow out of which an agreed (if often meaningless) compromise programme would emerge, he put forward his candidature and his views and invited the parties to accept or reject them. Recognizing and capitalizing on public resentment against the old political system, he—like Mendès-France before him—counted on a new style to attract support among the citizenry, and discovered that it also provoked the violent hostility of the bosses he was trying to bypass.

His first supporters were the political clubs, which had sprung up since 1958 among progressive Frenchmen dis-illusioned with the old parties and seeking a new basis for cooperation among men of the Left in activities of a Fabian

---

[1] He himself at Arras was elected mayor with Catholic votes, and deputy with Communist ones.

Society type.[1] Largely composed of civil servants, teachers and other professional and technical men, and often (though not always) inspired by progressive Catholics, they had hitherto avoided direct participation in the political struggle. But in promoting Defferre's candidature they hoped to renovate the old Socialist party as Mendès-France, helped by some of the same people, had once tried to revive the Radicals. They gained many sympathizers, notably from Catholic trade union and peasant leaders who could not feel at home in the old SFIO. But to win their battle they had to open that highly conservative party to the winds of change, an operation in which Léon Blum himself had failed twenty years before. Ever since then the party had been declining throughout the country—though it had made progress in Defferre's own city of Marseilles. He warned his colleagues that the decline would go on, as Blum had predicted, unless they abandoned the traditions of the last century and adapted themselves to the modern world. Bogus Marxism and real anticlericalism prevented them appealing to progressive Catholics; revolutionary words and opportunist actions disillusioned the young; their preference for the old system of weak government was a fatal handicap (Defferre's critics rightly charged him with favouring 'Gaullism without de Gaulle'). The old Socialist party was discredited and only by a spectacular demonstration that its outlook and character had changed could it attract the new generation and become the nucleus of a party with a claim to govern the country, give a better deal to the poor— and persuade Communist workers not to waste their votes on a sterile party of protest.

Defferre was thus a threat to the Socialist leadership in the short run and to the Communists in the long run. Mollet counterattacked; he condemned any attempt to broaden the party into a *grande nébuleuse* without an ideological faith, preferring a small party, *agressif, pur et dur* (this did not prevent him promoting a federation with the Radicals two years later); and to stop any Socialist standing for the Presidency, he bizarrely suggested that all democrats should support a respected non-political candidate 'like Albert Schweitzer'.

[1] They proved so popular and advantageous that Right and Centre politicians tried to copy the formula, some —notably Giscard —with success.

This was not much of an alternative to Defferre's programme, which offered the hope of reviving the party's energy and appeal by making one of its leaders the standard-bearer of the whole democratic Left. Defferre's lever proved powerful enough to win the approval of the Socialist party conference for his candidature in February 1964, with no open opposition. But after this unexpected success he faced a more formidable obstacle: the Communist party.

Since Defferre's whole appeal lay in his independence of the discredited party machines, he was determined not to become dependent on the Communists and hoped instead to seize the initiative from them as he had from Mollet. At the presidential election only the top two candidates could contest the second ballot; thus if Defferre ran second to the Gaullist at the first round, the Communist would have to withdraw and could not bargain for a concession in return. Their threat to oppose Defferre at the first ballot might therefore turn out to be bluff, for they risked losing votes to both him and de Gaulle. The municipal elections allowed them (with Gaullist connivance) to escape from their dilemma by forcing Defferre to fight for his political life at Marseilles.[1] If he accepted their municipal alliance on their terms he was bound to them nationally; when he refused it, they incited a few ambitious local Socialists (anticlerical rather than notably left-wing) to split his party and join them.

Defferre won, but paid a price: the lost hope of being the candidate of the whole Left, the reduced chance of winning over the Communist voters, even the risk of running behind the Communist at the first ballot. He now had to move further to the Centre for votes, and to find a new method of persuading the public that he was not just the candidate of the old Socialist party but stood for a real reform of the party system. He therefore advocated a 'big federation' between all the various groups of the moderate Left and Centre—Socialists, 'New Left' groups, Radicals and satellites, and MRP (but not Conservatives)—to form the new would-be majority party he had wanted from the start. But the move towards the Centre alienated many left-wing modernizers, while the appeal to

---

[1] The Gaullists split the city into several electoral districts, drawn to weaken Defferre's chances —while proclaiming their ardent hope that a new leader would reorganize and revitalize the opposition.

MRP allowed his opponents in the Socialist machine to stir up against him an anticlerical as well as an old-fashioned Marxist appeal. The Communists were now his sworn enemies, and the prospect of anyone winning the presidential election against de Gaulle seemed so absurdly remote that no politician was willing to make any sacrifice for it. Nevertheless he aroused public interest, and no one wanted openly to wreck his attempt; astonishingly, both the Socialist and MRP party conferences endorsed his appeal. But when their leaders met in private to settle the terms, the negotiations quickly collapsed and Defferre, rather than remain as the candidate of the unreconstructed Socialist party, withdrew from the race in June 1965.

New combinations: the Democratic Centre

When political activity resumed in September, after the summer holidays, the election was only three months away. François Mitterrand, the left-wing politician most acceptable to the Communists, put forward his own candidature and was welcomed with relief by the bosses who had opposed Defferre: he was no more willing to subordinate his programme to their public approval, and his policies were no different, but he was not an immediate threat to their positions. Both Socialists and Communists hastened to offer him support, though the Radicals were split as usual and the PSU endorsed him only belatedly and with evident reluctance.

Defferre, especially after Marseilles, was a candidate acceptable to Centre leaders—and to their voters; no one had wanted to stand against him and risk damaging defections to him as well as to de Gaulle. Mitterrand had no such appeal in the Centre, and without a candidate of their own most of its voters—except only the left-wing Radicals—would swing either to the General or to the champion of the extreme Right, J. L. Tixier-Vignancour. A brilliant lawyer who had defended General Salan and the leading OAS assassins, he counted on the votes of the North African refugees and their sympathizers; to extend his appeal in the Centre, he tried to shake off his extremist past by announcing that he hoped to found a French equivalent of the British Conservative party (and even arranged a visit to an unwary Edward Heath, to make the claim look more plausible). But these concessions to democracy offended the open fascists among his associates, and when he polled only a meagre 5 per cent of the votes, his hopes vanished and his following split into three factions, none of which won a single seat at the next two general elections.[1]

Tixier's presidential chances were blighted by the belated emergence of a serious Centre candidate. The Conservatives, MRP and moderate Radicals had first tried hard to persuade Antoine Pinay to stand, but failed (despite public encouragement from Guy Mollet!). Several less well known figures were then approached, and finally they settled on the national chairman of MRP, Senator Jean Lecanuet, who promptly resigned his party post—for, like all the candidates, he shared Defferre's insistence on dissociation from the old organizations and his claim to stand for a new course. Emerging from his campaign as a national figure, Lecanuet founded a new party which he hoped would not only absorb MRP and the Conservatives but also attract political newcomers, especially the young technicians to whom all the modernizers tried to appeal. Mitterrand presided over a 'little federation' of the Left, which included the Socialists, most Radicals, and a 'Republican Convention' embracing a minority of the political clubs—but neither MRP nor PSU. Thus instead of Defferre's proposed new left-centre party, isolating the Conservatives and perhaps the MRP right wing, there were now two rival Centre groups between which the Radicals were split.[2]

If Defferre could ever have organized his 'big federation', that alliance—strong enough to look like a potential government—might have attracted some support both from Gaullist voters seeking a more progressive domestic policy and from Communists anxious not to waste their votes, thus carrying some bargaining power when he came to confront the Communists. Lecanuet and Mitterrand found their new organizations easier to create, since they divided broadly along the old

---

[1] They polled under 200,000 votes in 1967 and a mere 29,000 in 1968, when only 16 candidates (of 2,267) were classified as 'extreme Right'. By then Tixier was supporting de Gaulle.

[2] The most anti-Communist Radicals (and, privately, a few Socialists) preferred Lecanuet. But the left wing of MRP was attracted to the Federation; and Lecanuet's most right-wing followers would vote for anybody against a Gaullist. Defferre and even Mollet (recently so eager for a *pur et dur* Socialist party) now favoured the little federation.

anti-clerical watershed, but for the same reason more traditional and less appealing. Since neither could possibly aspire to win a parliamentary majority on his own, their power of attraction—and therefore independence of action—was much less. If they stood alone, without allies, they would be crushed. If they attempted local bargaining with different partners in different seats, they would seem to be continuing the bad old habits of the Fourth Republic; nor would this course be open to them if their better-disciplined potential allies, Communists and Gaullists, were to insist on national pacts or none at all. The Communists did so insist, and finally brought the Federation to agree to their terms; the Gaullists fielded a single candidate in every constituency; and Lecanuet thus found himself in a position of hopeless isolation and weakness.

His Democratic Centre (CD) was launched in April 1966, on the wave of his presidential success, aiming at a 'vast regrouping' with 'Communism as one boundary and unconditional Gaullism as the other'. It soon claimed 40,000 members of whom half had previously belonged to no party. But his Radical allies maintained the characteristic Radical posture, with one foot in his camp and the other in that of their old party; and the simple combination of MRP with anti-Gaullist Conservatives had little appeal to progressive voters and none to anticlericals. In fact, therefore, its electoral base was the same as the Gaullists'; and the consequences soon became apparent. First Lecanuet was abandoned by a third of the Centre deputies, mostly MRP members who had prudently supported the government and were now rewarded with the Gaullist ticket which ensured their safe re-election. Next the Federation's nationwide pact with the Communists deprived him of the hope of electing members by trading second-ballot endorsements with the Left, and so made his followers wholly dependent on Gaullist goodwill. Thus, unable to establish its credibility as an alternative government, the Centre lost potential voters to stronger rivals, Conservatives to the government and some MRP to the Federation, and went down to defeat. Lecanuet himself failed even to find a constituency to contest, his chief Conservative supporter, Bertrand Motte, was soundly defeated, and his leading Radical ally, Maurice Faure, saved his seat only by a humiliating last-minute switch to the Federation.

Reduced in numbers from forty-two deputies to twenty-seven, below the Assembly's minimum for an official party group, the Democratic Centre was forced to combine for parliamentary purposes with scattered moderate and Conservative remnants into a *groupe de convenance*, Progress and Modern Democracy (PDM), chaired by a former Radical, Jacques Duhamel. Too heterogeneous to maintain a coherent parliamentary line, PDM lapsed at almost every clash between government and opposition into the traditionally ambivalent three-way split of Centre coalitions. Lecanuet found himself struggling from outside the Assembly to build a party which had lost much of its separate identity within PDM, and in which defeat had revived old divisions. He urged the dissolution of the old constituent parties, CNI and MRP, leaving CD alone to attempt the regrouping of the centre; but despite all his efforts these plans hung fire, while support slowly ebbed. Caught more cruelly than ever between the Gaullists and the Left in the 1968 election, CD's fortunes slumped still further; Lecanuet himself was severely defeated, and only twelve of his supporters returned to the Assembly. The attempt to unify the Centre had apparently lost both its impetus and its electoral appeal.

Federation of the Left or New Socialist Party?

On the Left, Mitterrand at first profited more skilfully than Lecanuet from the wreckage of Defferre's enterprise. Strengthened by the prestige of his ten million votes at the second ballot of the presidential election, Mitterrand built up the Republican Convention as his own machine, hastened the creation of the 'little federation', and formed from it a 'shadow cabinet' full of familiar (and not particularly appealing) figures from the past. Now he confronted the same dilemma as Defferre: alliance with the Communists alienating Centre support, or a bitter quarrel with them. In the presidential campaign they had found it hard to stand out, but in the parliamentary contest they were at least as strong as the Federation, and had much less to lose. They demanded no alliance at all at the first ballot, insisting on contesting every seat, and a complete one at the second—refusing to countenance any truck with Lecanuet and his 'downright reactionaries' or with any Socialist or Radical who supported them, even locally.[1] After months of hesitation the Federation accepted almost all their terms, agreeing that both Left organizations should support at the second ballot the better-placed of their candidates at the first, wherever he could win. This meant voting for a Communist even in seats where his main rival was a Socialist who could have won with the aid of right-wing votes, even in those in which a Federation man might have beaten the Gaullist but a Communist could not. The Federation, rejecting a common programme, insisted only on retaining the right—hardly used in the event—to support a Centre candidate against a Gaullist where no left-winger had a chance. But it wholly renounced the traditional strategy of winning seats with Communist help in some areas and Centre help in others.

At the election both candidates and voters of the Federation showed quite unusual discipline. Hardly any defied the pact and stayed in the contest against a Communist who had run ahead of them, and dissidents (like Maurice Faure) were severely punished by the voters. Even Socialist deputies obediently conceded seats they might have held to their Communist rivals. The Communists requited Mitterrand for this fulfilment of the pact by a minor concession, withdrawing in favour of fifteen Federation candidates who were slightly behind them; nine won, including two of Mitterrand's closest associates. Had they extended this policy more generously there would have been no Gaullist majority. Making substantial progress in the industrial areas but losing many Radical votes to the Gaullists in the centre and south-west, the Federation ended with a net gain of half a million over the whole country, and 300,000 fewer votes than the Communist party. Its deputies—76 Socialists, 24 Radicals and 16 Convention—gave up their separate identities to form a single parliamentary group (which chose Defferre as chairman). But the Federation deputies of 1967, even more than the Socialists of 1962, owed their seats to Communist votes at the second ballot.

Mitterrand had now to struggle with the interlocking problems of consolidating his party's precarious unity and reaching some *modus vivendi* with the Communists. After protracted negotiations between the party and the Federation,

---

[1] See below, p. 140.

the two signed a common declaration which, for all its eloquent silences on foreign policy and its catalogue of agreements to differ, was the greatest measure of agreement the two sections of the Left had achieved since the collapse of *tripartisme* over twenty years earlier. A poll showed that 58 per cent of the Federation's voters favoured inclusion of Communists in a left-wing government—but 44 per cent also thought that once in the government the Communists would seek to take it over. And while the voters were less alarmed than before at the prospect of Communists in office, the politicians were increasingly concerned at the terms of cooperation with a more and more powerful partner. The delicate bridges between the Federation and the PCF, shaken by the Arab-Israeli war, were to be destroyed for the time being by the Soviet invasion of Czechoslovakia, despite the Communists' initial repudiation of the Russian action.

Contradictory hopes and fears within his own ranks over relations with the PCF were among the many pitfalls besetting Mitterrand in his attempt to consolidate the Federation. Unable to expand to include the PSU, Mitterrand also found difficulty in persuading the Federation's existing constituents to dissolve and allow the party to stand alone with its own direct membership. The Radicals, as always facing both ways, preferred a 'multiform' Federation to an outright fusion and characteristically named to the Federation's executive Maurice Faure and Félix Gaillard, their most prominent advocates of alliances with the Centre. Some Socialists were stirred by the threat of extinction to a revival of 'party patriotism', others hankered for Defferre's 'big federation', others again tried to set the fusion bandwagon rolling as a device for ousting Mollet. Only the Convention gave the plans for fusion firm support.

This fragile and limited progress towards a new party was shattered by the Events of May and the ensuing Gaullist triumph. Electoral defeat brought to the surface longstanding antagonism to Mitterrand personally. Real or imaginary, all the party's tactical errors in May were laid at his door, particularly his speech indicating readiness to fill the vacuum should the regime collapse. For a man whose position had rested not on numbers but on progress or the hope of progress this was fatal. Ailing before May, the Federation was moribund by the autumn. Recognizing his failure, Mitterrand joined those who called for a fresh start with the formation of a Democratic Socialist Party, and stood down, declaring with a parthian shot at Mollet that a new party must have new leaders.

The new party had a difficult birth. The PSU was contemptuous at its opportunism, the Radicals feared its discipline, the SFIO component was as faction-ridden as ever, and the Convention, resentful of their leader's downfall, was outraged at Defferre's attempt to use the new party for his catastrophic second bid for the Presidency. Nevertheless the new party began a fragile existence in July 1969 and chose the ablest of the newcomers, Alain Savary, as its general secretary. After sixty-four years the initials SFIO disappeared from the political scene; after twenty-three years Mollet was no longer at the helm. With his departure party realignment had its first real chance. Yet the new party still confronted, in a weaker posture than ever, the dilemma that had wrecked the old one: could it survive either in alliance with the Communists, or in opposition to them?

8

THE COMMUNISTS

Year	Votes	Seats	Nominal Membership
1946	5,400,000	183	800,000
1951	4,900,000	101	
1956	5,600,000	150	430,000
1958	3,900,000	10	425,000
1962	4,000,000	41	405,000
1967	5,000,000	73	426,000
1968	4,400,000	34	

Early defeats

A striking feature of the early Fifth Republic was the outward stagnation and inner ossification of the French Communist Party. That once formidable revolutionary movement had lost its élan well before the advent of de Gaulle; even in 1956 when it polled a record vote, its appeal to youth had gone, its intellectual prestige had waned, the enthusiasm of its followers was in decline and its revolutionary potential was spent: the great strikes of 1947 and 1948, or even the riotous demonstrations of 1950 and 1952 were things of the past. When the General came to power the Party was flourishing only in that political sector to which revolutionaries should have attached least importance: the electoral field.

The Fifth Republic dealt the Communists a massive blow even there. At the November election a third of its voters defected, perhaps half of them to other parties (mainly the Gaullists) while the rest stayed at home. Even of those who

131

remained some 650,000, or one in six, appear to have voted Yes at the September referendum. Yet this defeat, severe as it was, was still one from which a dynamic party should have recovered without undue difficulty. In November 1958 a national hero, trusted by the French people, seemed to offer the only hope of settling the Algerian problem and averting civil war. He promised an end to the dreary era of do-nothing governments against which Communist voters were protesting no less than against their economic and social lot; and his followers were willing to proclaim that the strong government of the new regime would introduce the social reforms the Fourth Republic had failed to achieve. Isolated in its denunciation of the new prospect which every other party in France was applauding, the Communists lost the confidence of some of their followers who seemed at last to have found a new hope. By 1962 these new hopes of the followers had vanished along with the isolation of the Party. Apart from the UNR themselves, every political group which had campaigned on a Gaullist ticket in 1958 had turned to denounce the General four years later. The Communists, having done so from the start, should surely have reaped some reward for their foresight. While in 1958 they were still treated as political lepers by other politicians, by 1962 their alliance was courted and Socialist and Radical leaders were competing to offer them certificates of republican respectability, which should have reassured some doubtful voters. Nor had the new regime delivered on its social promises. Speculative building for the rich went on apace, but cheap housing for the poor was falling behind even the Fourth Republic's provision. In education the Gaullists made a genuine effort, but could not keep pace with the swelling demand of a fast-growing school population. The Communist who had switched his vote in hope of reforms in 1958 had grounds for switching back four years later.

The Party gained little from these advantages. On the first ballot its poll was no higher than it had been in 1958, though on the second it seems, where a direct comparison can be made, to have increased by as much as 20 per cent. This would suggest that it regained perhaps 800,000 voters (or half the defectors of 1958) for the decisive ballot, even though they would not bother to turn out on the previous Sunday. Yet as early as March 1959, at the municipal elections, the Communist vote had recovered to this level. Even on the most favourable interpretation, therefore, the Party had made no electoral progress over three years. Meanwhile many other signs of decline were admitted by its own spokesmen. Even by its official figures (which probably inflate membership to 50 per cent above the real figure) the annual loss was about 30,000, and exceeded the intake in every year before 1962. The Party's organization secretary warned repeatedly against frightening away inactive members by expecting them to do too much—hardly a sign of militant vigour in the ranks. The circulation of Communist dailies fell to half the figure of ten years before, only a quarter of the 1945 level; and when in 1964 the fellow-travelling *Libération* suddenly closed, barely a quarter of its readers chose to take *L'Humanité* instead. At its low point in 1962 the French Communist Party seemed, like the German Social Democrats before 1914, to have degenerated from a powerful revolutionary movement into a comfortable electoral machine, huge, slow, timid and bureaucratic. Its revolutionary vocabulary concealed only indifferently the desire of its supporters and leaders alike for a quiet life, in which their total intellectual repudiation of the existing order compensated for their total inability to do anything practical to change it.

The Party leaders were largely responsible for this development. Ever since 1947, when they were denounced at the first Cominform meeting (especially by the Yugoslavs!) for their opportunistic parliamentary illusions, the French leaders had remained the most abjectly Stalinist of any western Communists. In 1956 they had attacked their Polish, Hungarian and Italian colleagues and found no Communist Party to praise except the Albanians. Not until 1961 did Maurice Thorez at last produce an explicit condemnation of Stalin's crimes (though not of Stalin himself); even then revisionism and opportunism were still decreed more dangerous than dogmatism. Only after the Cuban crisis did this perspective change. Now the Soviet-Chinese dispute was presented as involving 'not subtle doctrinal nuances for the initiated but fundamental political choices—socialist democracy or "barracks communism", internationalism or chauvinism, peace or war'.[1]

---

[1] Kanapa in *L'Humanité*, 5 August 1963, quoted by J. Ranger, 'Evolution du PCF', *Revue française de Science politique*, 13.4 (December 1963), p. 963.

But in breaking with the Chinese view the Stalinist leader-ship were continuing in their old tradition of uncon-ditional devotion to the Soviet Union's current line; and in the new position as in the old they were protecting them-selves against potential rebels from below who might question their own conduct. As long as they dared they clung to the concept of the infallible leader (so convenient for fallible leaders); when it became untenable they fell back on the safest position they could find—defence of the existing Soviet leadership against the upstart rebels of Peking or Rome, both dangerous because both advocated real debate among Com-munists.

The same timidity showed itself in their political decisions. Unwilling to risk offending the authorities—or some of their own race-prejudiced voters—they played a cautious and equivocal part during the Algerian war, constantly moderating those of their own militants, or of their fellow-travelling allies, who wanted at first unqualified support for Algerian inde-pendence, later active aid to the FLN in France. When French fascists and OAS terrorists were most active, there was no Communist counter-violence against them (though there were a few Communist physical attacks against Trot-skyites). Partly because of a temperamental affinity for bureaucrats as against gadflies, partly because of their per-manent anxiety lest weaker groups should exploit the great Communist organization for their own ends, the leaders showed a marked preference for dealing with their fellow machine-politicians of the official Socialist party, rather than with the smaller and more active groups further to the Left. Thus in 1960 the Party vigorously condemned the campaign of solidarity with young men who evaded call-up to protest against torture in Algeria—a campaign which at the time was sweeping intellectual and student circles, especially among Catholics. When the Students' Union decided to defy a police ban against an anti-war demonstration, the Party denounced them as provocateurs and adventurers who would bring about an anti-Communist repression (a fear which proved quite unjustified). Relations with the fellow-travellers, above all in the *Mouvement de la Paix,* became increasingly strained; one sign of this was the decision at thirty-six hours' notice to cut off the subsidy to *Libération* and so kill the only pro-Communist paper which gave the Party any hearing outside its own ranks. The Communist students, not surprisingly, became restive under this regime and came under rebel leadership for a time, but after a long struggle they were brought back into line in 1965 and were promptly merged into the 'young Communist league' as an insurance against a recurrence.[1]

Fear and hatred of the smaller extreme Left groups did not preclude ardent wooing of the Socialist Party from 1962 onwards. The old antagonism took some time to perish; in 1961 Guy Mollet was still denounced as a defender of monopolies, and social democracy still stigmatized as a form of class collaboration and defence of imperialism. But in the autumn of 1962 the tune changed. 'We have never been the Party of all or nothing', proclaimed Thorez solemnly on 3 October 1962. Six weeks later Etienne Fajon appealed to the Arras workers for 'no vote to be withheld from Comrade Guy Mollet' at the second ballot for the new Assembly. Half the new Socialist deputies were returned with Communist support, and on 15 December Thorez predicted that the Socialist Party would never be the same again, and declared that a Socialist-Communist alliance was not at all conditional on a repudiation of NATO. 'Some comrades', said the Communist leader from Mollet's own area in May 1964, 'say we can never reach agreement with the Socialist Party while it is led by Guy Mollet. But we must explain to these comrades that we have no right to interfere in the choice of a Socialist leader.' This United Front was to be from above, not from below — for both partners.

Nor were the Socialists the only beneficiaries of this moderation. In the 1962 election the Communists called repeatedly for an alliance of all 'true republicans' against the Gaullist regime. Among 'true republicans' they then counted not only MRP but Radicals of strongly conservative views and even prominent capitalists who were also Conservative politicians. In September 1962 the local Communists of Côte d'Or earned a rebuke from headquarters by failing to withdraw their

---

[1] When their journal wished to print Togliatti's 'testament', it was prevented by the eminently capitalist method of threatening the printers with the withdrawal of the Party's custom. The Party's treatment of the students was to prove costly in May 1968 — though later it recovered in the universities as the extreme Left splinter groups discredited themselves.

candidate for the Senate on the second ballot in favour of a Conservative, and so allowing a better known and more reactionary Conservative, Roger Duchet, to retain his shaky seat. Two months later, at the general election, the Party went to the limit of conciliation, supporting anti-Gaullists of all descriptions where its own men had no chance and even withdrawing in favour of some Socialists and Radicals who had fewer votes than the Communist at the first ballot but more chance of victory at the second. These conciliatory tactics lasted for a year, but well before the municipal elections of March 1965 they had been wholly abandoned: MRP, Conservatives and right-wing Radicals were once again branded as enemies with whom there could be no accommodation; and though Socialists and some Radicals remained acceptable partners, the Party insisted on exacting its full share of candidates, even when this meant open Communist preponderance and consequently almost certain defeat. Often the Communist proposals for alliance seemed designed to provoke a refusal which could be blamed on the other parties. Plainly they preferred a divided and dispersed opposition to a strong anti-Gaullist coalition from which they were excluded. But did they at this stage still want to overthrow, or even to embarrass, President de Gaulle?

Later ambivalence

The Communist attitude to the Fifth Republic has changed several times since 1958. Immediately after the General's return to power which they had so signally failed to impede, the Party continued to call for defence of the Fourth Republic against those who were trying to subvert it; and in July when Mendèsists and other independent left-wingers advocated a Constituent Assembly to draft a new constitution in a democratic way, the Communists rebuked them for hair-splitting when the regime was in danger. But it did not take long for them to realize that their troops were not prepared to follow them in this battle, and would no more vote than fight for the Fourth Republic. By September, therefore, the Party was echoing the critics it had despised, condemning equally the old regime and the new and in its turn demanding a Constituent Assembly. The switch no doubt reduced the damage de Gaulle was doing them; nevertheless the loss was severe, a third of their votes at the election and perhaps nearly half at the referendum. Some of the younger leaders like Marcel Servin were already urging (though this was not yet publicly known) that the Party should conserve what it could by moderating its attack on the regime.

Although this advice was not accepted and the official line remained one of all-out opposition, tactical adjustments became necessary before long. When de Gaulle promised self-determination for Algeria in September 1959 the Political Bureau denounced it as a demagogic slogan which would make it harder to arrive at a real solution, and which objectively made a long war likelier. Two months later Maurice Thorez, who had fortunately been absent from that meeting, reversed the policy and approved self-determination; Khrushchev's visit to Paris the following spring no doubt encouraged the Party's new and milder line. The referendum on self-determination in January 1961 was, however, to revive the Communists' embarrassment. Servin and Laurent Casanova, leading a group of prominent younger members, were removed from the Political Bureau and condemned for erroneously arguing that Communists should exploit the division between the agents of American imperialism and the 'national bourgeoisie' represented by de Gaulle. On the contrary, the leadership proclaimed, de Gaulle and his followers were a greater (because less obvious) danger to the interests of the French people than the open fascists of Algiers; and unless the Party fought him at the referendum, he would win 90 per cent of the votes and so encourage illusions among the French workers and make the next stage of the struggle harder. Fifteen months later the Algerian war ended and the President called another referendum; without even waiting for the question to be announced, the Communist Party declared it would vote Yes —and de Gaulle won 90 per cent of the votes, with consequences for the proletariat's illusions that can only be imagined. As so often in the history of Communist parties, the defeat of a dissident faction was swiftly followed by the adoption of its policies. But though the Party abandoned the struggle against de Gaulle over Algeria, it remained eager to conciliate other opponents of his domestic and foreign policies in the 1962 election campaign—coincidental with the Cuba crisis in which the President wholeheartedly supported the United States.

For several years thereafter the Communist Party displayed

a wholly uncharacteristic ambivalence towards the Gaullist regime. Their hesitations may have owed something to uncertain leadership (Thorez died in June 1964 and his successor, Waldeck Rochet, had far less personal authority) and may well have reflected the impact of the Vietnam war on the progress towards peaceful coexistence. But they were accentuated by problems inherent in the French party's situation. Its voters, traditional men of the Left, disliked the Gaullist regime for its conservative economic and social policies and for its constitutional style, and they always welcomed any move to break the Communists' isolation through a new Popular Front. But the activists were more disposed to resent unrequited concessions to other parties, and attached more importance to the General's foreign policy as it evolved increasingly to their satisfaction.

By March 1964 Thorez was already pointing with pride to the Party's support for self-determination, criticizing the Communist deputies for voting against the Algerian aid estimates 'solely on the pretext of opposing the government', and approving the Communist senators' correct decision to vote for these estimates along with the Gaullists—and with no one else. Under pressure from the people, he observed, Gaullist policies were developing positive aspects in many parts of the world besides Algeria—in the recognition of China, encouragement for neutralism in South-east Asia, support for Cuba and opposition to the United States in Latin America. Before long Gaullists and Communists were aligned against the rest of the Assembly in most foreign affairs debates, and in opposing an amnesty bill for minor OAS offenders. Just as in the Fourth Republic, they joined in angry denunciation of the Centre parties, and the Communists' tactics in the municipal elections suggested that objectively—and perhaps subjectively —they were now playing the General's game.

The hard line was ruthlessly pursued during the municipal campaign, and the ban on MRP and Radical 'downright reactionaries' (the 'true republicans' of 1962) was used to cut the Socialists off from their old associates and bind them exclusively to the Communist alliance. These tactics were particularly effective against Defferre, splitting his local party and threatening his survival as mayor of Marseilles. But they were not reserved for old antagonists of the Party, and were applied equally to men like Georges Dardel, a Socialist boss in the Paris suburbs who had been its ally for five years, and even to François Mitterrand, the one national leader who had insisted ever since 1958 that without an understanding with the Communists it was futile to oppose the regime. All three were re-elected as mayors, but Defferre had to move to the Right in the process and so became more vulnerable to his many enemies (especially in his own party). When he withdrew in June 1965 the opposition had no serious presidential candidate in the field.

In September, only three months before polling day, Mitterrand put himself forward. Within two weeks—though not without internal dissension—the Communists decided to support him even though he, like Defferre, presented them with a readymade (and very similar) programme instead of negotiating it with them as they demanded. But Mitterrand made more verbal concessions than Defferre and clearly showed that he did not present an immediate challenge to the party machines. By supporting him they could escape from their ghetto and strengthen their ties with the rest of the Left, whereas a Communist candidate running against him might well lose votes (to him as well as to de Gaulle) and so display the Party's weakness. And, like everyone else, they expected de Gaulle to win comfortably. They campaigned loyally for their candidate and delivered nearly their full vote.[1] Yet the conciliatory mood did not quite last out the campaign. Earlier on they had moderated their hostility to European unity, refrained from criticizing Mitterrand's foreign policy, and even had *L'Humanité* suppress a Tass communique praising the President's. But when Waldeck Rochet spoke on the subject on television between the two ballots he did so in blatantly nationalist and Gaullist tones.

With de Gaulle re-elected, the Communist tenderness for the opposition again evaporated. In parliament they treated the government with a moderation they had rarely shown in the Fourth Republic, frequently abstaining on or even voting for its minor bills and even, for the first time, refusing to vote a censure (against withdrawal from NATO). In the country they directed the weight of their attacks, not against the UNR,

---

[1] But the minuscule group of pro-Chinese dissidents split three ways on the second ballot—some for de Gaulle, some for Mitterrand and some for abstention.

but against Lecanuet's new Centre party. The Communists would do nothing to help these 'downright reactionaries' defeat a Gaullist, and they threatened to stay in the field at the second ballot to punish any Socialist or Radical who accepted Centre support or spoke for a Centre candidate in another seat.[1] By these tactics they might hope both to win more seats and to isolate the non-Communist Left from the Centre— securing themselves against the risk of abandonment by allies who were now dependent upon them. They would also ensure the re-election of a government whose foreign policy satisfied them.

But before the general election the Communists' tactics changed yet again. For the Federation finally agreed to a pact which conceded their principal objectives, allowing them to strengthen their parliamentary representation and agreeing to break off all its own links with the Centre parties.[2] Having committed themselves to left-wing unity, the Communists made the most of the theme in the election campaign, and they emerged as the chief beneficiaries with seventy-three seats and five million votes, 300,000 more than the Federation. While their percentage of the votes cast remained unchanged, this stability really represented Communist progress.[3]

This success was won by a party which seemed, since 1964, to be regaining much of its lost vitality and making itself a more acceptable political partner than it had been for a generation. Membership was gradually increasing,[4] the

---

[1] This threat was expressly directed—by Roland Leroy on 5 July 1966—against those Socialist deputies (half the total) who had had Communist support on the second ballot in 1962.

[2] See above, pp. 127–8.

[3] For the numbers going to the polls were rising sharply and the Communists gained their full share of this increased turnout: yet it was not the Communists but the Fourth Republic parties whose voters had stayed at home in 1962; see above, pp. 71–2. The Communist losses had occurred in 1958. As we have seen the 1959 municipal election and the 1962 second ballot suggested that perhaps half those losses were recoverable, and the 1967 gains suggest they were recovered—though no more: the 1967 second ballot showed no similar hidden reserve to that of 1962.

[4] The net loss 1958–61 was 30,000, the net gain 1962–66 50,000 (but these official Party figures do not square with the equally official membership figures given at the head of this chapter).

average age declining, and intellectual debate within the party livelier than it had been since the pre-Stalinist era. Cautiously and tentatively the Communists were giving themselves a new look: by their acceptance of the 'peaceful road to socialism' and (not without some equivocal reservations) of a multi-party system even in a socialist state; by their overtures for a friendly dialogue with Catholics (though these had been made before); above all perhaps by their cautious assertions of independence from Moscow, notably at the time of Khrushchev's fall and in Aragon's public protest against the trial of Siniavsky and Daniel.[1] Even over current political issues their discussions began to show the first faint signs of facing real problems instead of merely seeking to amass the maximum profit from electoral discontent.[2]

Meanwhile, the general unpopularity of the government's domestic policies, and de Gaulle's pursuit of a *rapprochement* with the Russians while baiting the Americans, had done much to make the Party's attitudes respectable. In the 1965 and 1967 election campaigns it had seemed at last on the way to escape from the ghetto to which it had been confined since 1947.

But despite the continuing appeal of de Gaulle's foreign policy, the Communists' best hope of consolidating the advantages he had brought them now lay in strengthening their influence among their potential allies on the Left, rather than through reinforcing a Gaullist party which might follow a quite different path once its leader had gone. The fragile, divided, and numerically weaker Federation was a partner they could reasonably hope to dominate. They were the more hopeful of succeeding in this because of their success in regaining members and vitality without sacrificing discipline. Yet, as the Party regained ground and became better integrated into French society, it had become, like its followers, less revolutionary. It held the allegiance of the bulk of the working class—yet in social origin, outlook and behaviour its leaders

---

[1] But their attitude to Israel cost them much goodwill on the Left.

[2] See on both sides of this question the articles of Jean Irigaray (agriculture), Robert Fossaert (economy) and Georges Lavau (strategy) in *Esprit*, October 1966.

and spokesmen were much more bourgeois than in the past.[1]

Inevitably there were some who rejected the evolution towards a more constitutional and reformist position, and denounced the leadership's 'revisionism'. Better than anyone, the Party knew how the old *ouvrièriste* and revolutionary traditions had gripped the imagination of the French worker; small wonder that with its innate hostility to being outflanked on its Left, it gave disproportionate attention to the less inhibited 'Chinese' and libertarian socialist groups which sought to project themselves as torchbearers of those traditions, or who expounded the heresy that the millennium would be attained not through the workers and their organized vanguard, but through the students with their mass spontaneity. Consequently the Party's initial reaction to the outbreak in May was to denounce more violently than ever the 'political adventurism' of the 'false revolutionaries' of the Sorbonne. Only when the force of the upheaval and the strength even within its own ranks of sympathy for the students became evident did the leadership swing abruptly behind the movement—finding themselves obliged to swallow temporarily the taunts of the revolutionaries and their own relegation (in keeping with other party politicians) to a humiliatingly modest position in their demonstrations. It was local union militants rather than the CGT's national leadership who spread the agitation from the universities to industry, and it was only when the strikes and occupation of factories were well under way that the Communists leapt on to the moving bandwagon — one hand reaching for the steering wheel and the other for the brakes. During the Grenelle negotiations with the government it was the CFDT which demanded major changes in the economic structure, and the largely Communist leadership of the CGT which pressed for an essentially orthodox package deal—and had to go back to the bargaining table and ask for more when the militants rejected the first agreement. When the regime was hovering on the apparent verge of collapse the Party chose to follow a 'constitutional' course

---

[1] On the social origins of its spokesmen see A. Kriegel (and M. Perrot). *Le Socialisme français et le Pouvoir* (Paris, 1966), pp. 205–9; on their conduct, cf. R. W. Johnson and A. R. Summers, 'The Communist Campaign in Asnières', *Parliamentary Affairs*, 20.3 (Summer 1967), pp. 239–41; on future perspectives, Lavau, *loc. cit.*, pp. 498–504.

rather than risk everything on a bid for power—and bitterly denounced the 'leftist opportunism' of the PSU and the revolutionaries, who had so much less to lose.

The Communists' choice of caution may have saved the regime, but it did not save them from being tarred unmercifully with the revolutionary brush by the Gaullists during the election. The Party lost 600,000 votes at the first ballot, and at the second found Federation and Centre voters unwilling to rally to it against the Gaullists. Yet the leadership was probably concerned more with the Party's position within the Left than with its reduced parliamentary representation. While some of the revolutionary groups had been outlawed, they reappeared hydra-headed, and the PSU seemed intent on installing itself permanently on the Communists' left. Although the Party itself appeared to have weathered May remarkably well, *L'Humanité* uncharacteristically admitted unresolved differences between the central committee and many Communist intellectuals, and there were signs of discord within the political bureau itself. Then came the invasion of Czechoslovakia—where the prospect of a more democratic and 'national' communism had awakened keen sympathy in the French party. Waldeck Rochet flew to Moscow in an attempt to dissuade the Russians. When they went ahead the PCF promptly denounced them, its first open repudiation of a Soviet action in its entire existence. This break with the *suivisme* of a lifetime was intolerable for some older comrades—among them Thorez's widow, who resigned her party offices—and the bold gesture was soon virtually cancelled out. The central committee had also to reprimand its most widely known theoretician, Roger Garaudy, for his repeated criticism of 'party dictatorship' and the 'relapse into Stalinism' of the Soviet Union. For all its hesitations, over Czechoslovakia the Party had gone further than ever before towards invalidating the taunt of being 'Moscow's parrot'. But the change was not lasting. Apparently it was set on preserving the new image which Rochet was cultivating since May 1968: that of a 'party of order and political wisdom'. But with a new generation of bureaucrats in control, it found difficulty in convincing Frenchmen that any real liberalization had taken place.

9

THE PRESSURE GROUPS AND SOCIAL ORGANIZATIONS

Group organization

It was not only the parties which had to grapple uncomfortably with fresh situations. The style and shape of government in the Fifth Republic, and the pace of change in economic and social life created a crisis of modernization for the interest groups too. Under the old system, with unstable governments, incoherent parliament and undisciplined parties on the Right and Centre, they had enjoyed exceptional opportunities for leverage. While the parties in a two-party system are usually reluctant to become too intimately linked with any sectional interest for fear of jeopardizing their wider appeal, under the Fourth Republic the summit of party ambition was to win a share of power rather than to exercise it outright. One way to achieve this was to outbid one's rival for the support of a clientele—Gaullists against Conservatives against MRP over the Catholic schools, Communists against Socialists against Radicals on behalf of secular education—and each against all for the favours of home distillers, ex-servicemen, peasants or small shopkeepers. In a parliament where no party ever had a majority there were ample opportunities for manœuvre and obstruction. Not only could any important group command a substantial following on the floor of the Assembly, but many of the specialized committees through which legislation was channelled—most notoriously those dealing with agriculture, shipping and fishing, and alcoholic drink—were firmly in the grip of the interests concerned. Legislation they disliked was almost inevitably doomed. Even the governmental machine suffered severe penetration: the Ministries of Agriculture and Ex-Servicemen were particularly notorious for their uncritical promotion of their clients' demands within the cabinet and administration. At its feeblest the Fourth Republic was exploited unmercifully by such determined unscrupulous groups as the 'alcohol' and 'North Africa' lobbies, which caused most governments to tremble and some to fall.

Yet the ascendancy of the groups was never unqualified. Even the alcohol and North Africa lobbies were sometimes resisted successfully, while a number of major decisions, such as French membership of the European Coal and Steel Community, were carried over the furious opposition of powerful interests. Many of the strongest groups were confronted by the countervailing pressure of opposing interests, which enhanced ministers' scope for manœuvre. Even the parliamentarians could not be driven too far; too flagrant a display of the arrogance of group power could stir them to defiance rather than submission. Moreover, the declining efficiency of parliament as a legislative machine, to which the groups contributed, meant that it became less useful to them as a channel for securing their own demands rather than simply blocking what others proposed. Governments turned increasingly to demanding powers to legislate by decree as a way of shoving through measures like the Laniel economic reforms of 1953 or the Mendès-France anti-alcohol measures of 1954, which the groups would have killed in parliament. The short-lived character of governments with its consequent blurring of responsibilities made it hard for the groups to ensure that the promises they had exacted were honoured, or that defectors were punished. Even when parliament and the cabinet had been overcome, the bureaucracy often had extensive and devious means of resisting the implementation of measures it disliked. Thus the groups were in the end less successful than was popularly believed. But regardless of the final outcome, the constant ruthless assertion of sectional demands and the resulting immobilism in policy contributed to the constriction and discredit of the Fourth Republic.

When the groups did achieve excessive influence, this was often due more to the chronic weakness of the political system than to their own inherent strength. French groups have generally been weak and divided. Ever since the Revolution overturned the countless féodalités of the ancien régime it has been sound republican doctrine to denounce intermediary bodies which come between the State and the citizen; France was the last major democracy to grant freedom of association.

This associational weakness was prolonged by the reluctance of the traditionally individualist Frenchman to be a 'joiner', and above all by the relatively slow emergence of big cities and large-scale industry. Even now the transition from essentially locally-based interests to unified national organizations is very recent or still incomplete. The groups still reflect and emphasize the splintered character of French society: typically each social and economic sector has a number of groups with low aggregate membership, competing with each other along the historical lines of social, political or religious cleavage— and thus perpetuating the fragmentation of society rather than knitting it together. As fragments of sectional interests, these groups' effectiveness is often impaired by mutual antagonisms and inadequate resources, which leave them incapable of maintaining organizations of the scale and calibre that their importance really requires.

Nevertheless, the rapid social and economic changes of the years since the second world war have forced the groups to adapt. Not surprisingly, the employers have been among the most effective in developing their national organization, the Conseil National du Patronat Français (CNPF). Normally a coordinator of industrial opinion rather than a policy leader or a national negotiating body, CNPF has always preferred discreet discussion to public demonstrations, knowing that the cause of big business is rarely likely to command mass sympathy. (Even more discreetly it continues to channel contributions to candidates and parties sympathetic to free enterprise.) It has understandably found the Fifth Republic's taste for private 'technical' discussions more congenial than have the workers' unions—particularly since CNPF and its constituent trade associations are so often represented at these by former civil servants, talking in terms of friendship or equality to their ex-colleagues after taking the traditional course of *pantouflage* into a career in industry. However, from the early sixties industry became increasingly restive at the *dirigiste* strain in Gaullist economic policy—the Vallon proposals for profit-sharing, the extensive intervention in prices and collective bargaining after the stabilization plan of September 1963 and in May 1968.[1] In the 1965 presidential election the weight of business support was behind Lecanuet

---

[1] Discussed in more detail below, pp. 298–308.

rather than de Gaulle, and relations remained uneasy right up to the General's retirement: then, however, businessmen rallied behind Pompidou rather than his Centrist opponent Poher.

Relations with Gaullism have exacerbated the long-standing differences within the employers' movement. The Confédération Générale des Petites et Moyennes Entreprises, PME (which is affiliated to CNPF), was founded at the Liberation to defend the interests of the small firm—almost as much against the big industrial interests which dominated CNPF as against encroachment by the State. Where CNPF has normally been cautious and discreetly conservative, PME has been aggressively militant and ideological, with its readiness to threaten a public outcry or direct action, its Fourth Republic flirtation with Poujadism, and its opposition to 'trusts', 'technocrats' and other malign influences in an extensive demonology. On the other hand, the younger and more modern-minded capitalists of the (largely Catholic) Centre des Jeunes Patrons—later renamed the Centre des Jeunes Dirigeants d'Entreprise—have been better disposed towards the reforming aspects of Gaullism. In 1965, in a mood of irritated frustration, CNPF published a fourteen-point charter outlining its philosophy of politico-economic relations—rock-ribbed economic liberalism tempered by nineteenth-century paternalism. Largely stimulated by skilful politicking by the PME wing, this uncharacteristically bold pronouncement was sourly received by the Jeunes Patrons (and the wider public). It led to a breach between CNPF and the young employers, who went on to give further offence by approving the government's mild bill on works committees,[1] and saying they believed in strong trade unions.

May 1968 crystallized the tensions within the *patronat* and threw CNPF into its worst crisis since the war. Some members complained that by negotiating the Grenelle agreements with the government and the unions the leadership had exceeded their mandate, and a few resigned. Others were as dismayed at the feeble and unimaginative response to the events. In reaction an independent Centre National des Dirigeants d'Entreprise was founded, largely by 'graduates' from the Jeunes Patrons and American business schools, to promote

---

[1] See below, pp. 303–4.

the viewpoint of the new generation of managers; this actually supported workers' participation. Then a group of the largest firms set up the Association des Grandes Entreprises Françaises to counter the excessive influence of PME on the Confederation. Within CNPF a ginger group of more dynamic firms brought about a shakeup in the leadership and pressed for changes to make it a more efficient and progressive spokesman for industry. Timid reforms were introduced in 1969; though they satisfied few, at least the dissidents agreed to stay under the formal umbrella of CNPF. But industry and commerce seemed no nearer solving their basic problem of representing their economic and ideological diversity without relapsing into immobilism.

If businessmen have been divided in their attitude towards economic modernization, the strains have been far greater among the farmers, whose organizations were even more sharply split by internal conflicts of interest. The chief of them, the Fédération Nationale des Syndicats d'Exploitants Agricoles (FNSEA), is a federation of departmental farmers' unions and a great number of producer organizations for wheat, wine, milk, eggs and so forth (many of them with long-standing internal tensions between regions or varieties). Since the war FNSEA has overshadowed both its rivals: CNMCCA, the companion organization of agricultural credit, cooperative and friendly society interests; and the Chambres d'Agriculture, public bodies elected by the farmers, which have become steadily less relevant to policy-making. Modernization of agriculture has produced an acute conflict of generations within FNSEA itself. Farm politics in France—like the farms themselves—were traditionally in the hands of the older generation, and the national farm organizations were run by large-scale operators from the north-east and the Paris basin—for the small men had neither time nor money for extensive involvement in union affairs. This comfortably situated middle-aged leadership had little taste for preparing the structural and technical transformation the industry needed. It clung to the traditional policy of campaigning primarily for higher prices, which spelled affluence to the big producer but only marginal relief to the struggling family farmer, thus preserving the two agricultural nations behind the sentimental myth of 'peasant unity'. In fact, there was an unbridgeable gulf between the 1,400,000 dairy farmers with

under twenty cows and the 30,000 with more, or the 13,000
producers of over fifty tons of grain and the 700,000 harvesting
less. The recurrent resort to violent protest by farmers under
both the Fourth and Fifth Republics owed much to the short-
sighted, selfish and technically uninstructed way their leaders
led them into dead-end policies.

During the fifties a new generation emerged, schooled in the
Catholic rural youth movement, ready to envisage radical
solutions. Welcoming this unusual interest by the 'young
men', the elders of FNSEA encouraged the development of
the Centre National des Jeunes Agriculteurs (CNJA), only to
find they were riding a tiger. By 1958 Michel Debatisse, the
foremost spokesman of the 'silent revolution' in the countryside, was with his followers in command of CNJA and laying
siege to FNSEA itself. Although CNJA members were active
in demonstrations against official farm policies in 1959–60,
they later developed a more fruitful relationship, first with
Debré and then with Pisani, who found a more imaginative
response from them than from the traditionalist FNSEA.[1]
During his five years at the ministry CNJA had a continuing
influence on the adoption of longer-term *dirigiste* policies,
until in 1966 Edgar Faure restored preferential relations with
FNSEA—which by now counted Debatisse and other CNJA
veterans in its leadership. But with the continuing drift from
the land, the widening gap between the farmers and the urban
workers, and the emergence of massive surpluses in France
and then throughout EEC, relations between the farmers and
the government could never really be easy. Nothing Pisani or
his successors could do would bring more than temporary
respite to the doomed marginal farmer. It needed only a
seasonal glut or a delay in increasing guaranteed prices for the
countryside to flare into direct action and for bitterness over
short-term crises to imperil solutions to the underlying
problems. As CNJA policies became orthodoxies in turn, their
contradictions and inadequacies were revealed. The cautiously
progressive and European FNSEA leadership found in the
later sixties that as a further radical revision of agricultural
policy became inescapable, it was flanked on its Right by
the conservative Chambres d'Agriculture and the Centre
d'Agriculture de l'Entreprise—a new and vocal exponent of

---

[1] Discussed more fully below, pp. 291–4.

large-scale 'industrial' farming—while on the Left there were renewed radical stirrings from the new generation in CNJA. Moreover, the recently formed Mouvement de Défense de l'Exploitation Familiale (MODEF), which had close affinities with the Communists, was drawing increasing support for a fresh rejection of change from the disgruntled farmers of the south-west, and attacking Debatisse and FNSEA for 'collusion' with the Gaullists: 'We are fed up with being represented at the Elysée and elsewhere by farmers' leaders with white hands.' While both FNSEA and the Ministry fought hard to avoid recognizing MODEF, the spur of its militant competition inevitably sharpened FNSEA's own dealings with the authorities.

Though its influence among the peasant organizations has been only limited and regional, the Communist Party has naturally held a far stronger position in the trade union movement. Yet this strength is only relative, for by international standards the French working-class movement is anaemic and splintered. No accurate figures exist, but it seems that at most three of the fifteen million employed workers are paid-up union members[1]—a maximum of 20 per cent, compared with about 40 per cent in Britain and 35 per cent in West Germany. Three major organizations and several smaller ones compete for their share of this inadequate cake. The Confédération Générale du Travail (CGT), founded in 1895, is the oldest and largest with about half the total members. Long under Communist leadership, the CGT has followed roughly the same evolutionary path towards reformism as the party itself—though with its substantial non-Communist membership it has long ceased to be merely the Communist Party's industrial instrument. It has also been less monolithic than the Party, particularly during the period in the fifties and early sixties, when one of its senior officials, Pierre Le Brun, led an active and intelligent minority which tried to push it into a more enterprising reformism, until Le Brun split with the CGT over its support for Mitterrand in 1965, and went on to complete his transition from crypto-

---

[1] In April 1968 *claimed* union memberships totalled over four million, but real membership was probably rather under three million. May 1968 gave an immediate fillip to membership (perhaps as much as 800,000); the long-term effects remain to be seen. Cf. *Le Nouvel Observateur*, 21 Oct. 1968 and *L'Express*, 18 Oct. 1968.

communism to crypto-gaullism. Officially the CGT remains committed to a Marxist view of capitalism, hostile to the EEC as a monopolists' plot, and opposed to participation in the preparation of the Plan on the ground that this would condone a doomed system. Yet when the general strike suddenly blew up in 1968, the CGT not only denounced leftist adventurers, but set its face against revolutionary behaviour and presented the employers with a conventional if costly list of demands which raised no fundamental challenge to the economic system.

Such basic challenge and new thinking as the trade union movement provides have tended to come instead from the Confédération Française Démocratique du Travail (CFDT), founded under another name in 1919, with about half a million members and its roots in the Catholic workers' movement. The most dynamic and ambitious of the workers' organizations, CFDT abandoned its former confessional basis in 1964 to broaden its appeal in competition with the CGT and Force Ouvrière. However, many of its leaders show the stamp of their upbringing in the Jeunesse Ouvrière Catholique in their preoccupation with social fundamentals and with many non-industrial issues like educational reform, housing and democratized planning. During and since the Algerian war the CFDT has shared most of the concerns of the intellectual Left. Although so often among the regime's most forceful critics, CFDT has been more prepared than the other union federations to attempt cooperation with it in planning and incomes policy—though invariably it has been disappointed by the outcome. Characteristically, it alone of the workers' organizations strongly sympathized with the students in 1968, and called for major changes in the structure of industrial relations rather than a conventional wages-and-hours package deal.

CFDT's radical critique contrasts sharply with the more muted position of Force Ouvrière, which was formed in 1947 as a breakaway against the Communist domination of the CGT, and has rather under half a million members. Although conventionally described as 'Socialist-inclined', the tenuousness of FO's links with the SFIO and the ideological indigence of the party rob the label of whatever significance it may once have had (though both FO and the SFIO draw their main support from public service workers). The chief intellectual

stock-in-trade of FO would seem to be anti-Communism—
though it contains a small anarcho-syndicalist minority.

Smaller still, the Confédération Générale des Cadres
(CGC), formed from independent unions of executives and
technicians in 1944, which stands rather apart from other
workers' organizations, is normally moderate and unmilitant.
There is also the Confédération Française des Travailleurs
Chrétiens, with under 100,000 members, which broke from
the CFDT over the dropping of its specific ties with the
Church in 1964, and whose principal *raison d'être* is to sustain a specifically Catholic witness in industry. Finally there
is a sprinkling of wholly unaffiliated unions, and the
quarter-million strong Fédération de l'Education Nationale
(FEN).

'Of the four workers' organizations, two issue from splits
over different conceptions of society', the president of CGC
commented in 1966. 'There exists a gulf between those who
believe in an ideal society on Marxist lines . . . and those who
put their confidence in progressive structural improvements,
and no longer look on employers as hereditary enemies.' He
made it clear that his organization would cooperate only with
the second type. While exaggerating the revolutionary character of the CGT today, his remark underlines the continuing
problem of French trade unionism: the way low membership
and disunity combine to limit both their industrial and
political effectiveness. Energies which could better be devoted
to influencing employers or ministers, must be devoted to
watching rivals. Joint action between the three major organizations has been limited to a few major crises—and even then
has usually taken the form of simultaneous rather than truly
joint activity. With its engrained hostility to the CGT, and its
apprehension of CFDT (which it believes—probably rightly—
to have ambitions to take it over), FO has been the most
reluctant to engage in joint action, preferring to negotiate
bilaterally. A substantial element in FEN remains virulently
anti-CFDT, seeing it as merely the latest façade for the time-
less clerical enemy. CGT, as the largest organization, tends to
be touchy about action originated by its rivals, and scornful of
the 'intellectualism' and 'dilettantism' of CFDT. A limited
agreement between CGT and CFDT in 1966 on joint action
marked a small but significant advance—but the paths of unity,
or even cooperation, remained difficult. However, despite the

unions' limitations, on occasions when they have had their members firmly behind them they have made a significant mark on the history of the Fifth Republic—most notably in the token general strike supporting the government during the generals' revolt in 1961, the miners' strike of 1963, and the great general strike of May 1968 when the leaders had to struggle to restrain the pressure from below.

One of the few sections where French unions have always had a powerful hold has been education—though this is also the extreme example of fragmentation. There remains the traditional division between opponents and supporters of State aid to religious schools—on the one side the militantly Catholic Association des Parents d'Elèves de l'Enseignement Libre, and on the other the Centre National d'Action Laïque and the Ligue Française de l'Enseignement. The state sector alone has four rival national associations of parents. Inevitably the lay teachers in the Church schools have their own unions, while most of those in the state system are grouped in the Fédération de l'Education Nationale, an umbrella organization of many independent sectional and specialized unions which, from the very diversity of its political and professional make-up, suffers chronic internal tensions. Even so, many unions at every level remain outside, preferring to affiliate to the main trade union federations or stay unattached—including three of the four unions of secondary technical school staffs and most of the university teachers' organizations. The tiny minority of students who belong to a national body are divided into the schismatically left-wing Union Nationale des Etudiants de France (UNEF) and its conservative rival, the Fédération Nationale des Etudiants de France with, once again, a scattering of unaffiliated and sectional bodies.[1] Thus discussion of educational policy has been bedevilled not only by the split over *laïcité* (now fading in the country but surviving most tenaciously within the teachers' unions), but even more by the intense corporatism which the group structure encourages and entrenches. In no section of society have the organized groups played a more important part in resisting necessary reforms—with consequences which became apparent in May 1968.

---

[1] See below, pp. 324–6.

Church, army and cause groups

The teachers' traditional enemy, the Roman Catholic Church, has had a better record of adaptation to the twentieth century. Catholic social doctrines have been among the most powerful influences on a whole generation, which has graduated through the Church's various youth movements and other Catholic Action organizations to wider responsibilities in CFDT, CNJA, UNEF and the Jeunes Patrons. Individual prelates have been active in a wide variety of political causes; at one extreme some identified themselves with the OAS, while others were active on the militant Left. Over the neglect of regions like Brittany, unemployment, low farm prices, redundancy, and the miners' strike of 1963, bishops have made outspoken comments which, to the government's irritation, frequently proved significant in changing the climate of opinion. However, the hierarchy has been at pains to avoid creating a confrontation between Church and State by committing itself in day-to-day political battles. Its public collective pronouncements have usually been appropriately muted and lofty declarations of general principle. During the 1959 struggle over the extension of State aid to Church schools, it was the parents' organization APEL, and the conservative politicians eager to outbid the Gaullists for Catholic support who made the running, rather than the hierarchy, which seemed to prefer a less total victory with a greater chance of long-term survival should the Left return to power. During the great moral controversies arising from the Algerian war, the public utterances of the assembly of Cardinals and Archbishops, while ethically impeccable, were again muted; the Protestants were often more outspoken. On these and other issues the Church made discreet interventions (which are said not to have been appreciated by the General). But apart from education, and formerly birth control, it is hard to identify any major correspondence between the Church's views and the policy of the regime.

The rise of left-wing Catholicism has undermined an alliance of social groups—Church and army—which had played a great part in French history. For it was the younger generation of Roman Catholics who took the lead not only in welcoming and adapting to social changes at home, but in opposing colonial wars abroad. Inevitably this made them the most outspoken critics of the army which, traditionally *la grande muette*, became increasingly involved in politics during and after the dying years of the Fourth Republic. In May 1958 its defection destroyed that regime, and despite his determination to restore civilian control, de Gaulle could not change the situation overnight. The army was fighting in Algeria, and running much of the civil administration there. Some of its officers had tasted political power and were reluctant to return to being mere disciplined fighting men — and they could point to de Gaulle's own magnificent dissent of 1940 as justification of patriotic disobedience. Many officers, particularly below the colonel level, had come to look on themselves as the guardians of patriotism and national honour, and to believe that setbacks in Indochina and Algeria were due to political corruption and the spinelessness of the civilians. Those who saw political intervention as a path to national salvation were supported up to a point by a section of the domestic Right, and by a variety of patriotic organizations and ex-service associations (as well as the old North Africa lobby). They implemented their own policies in Algeria and tried to force new ones on Paris; when that failed some of them turned to attempts to overturn the regime itself in 1960 and 1961, and a small minority went to the desperate lengths of terrorist action in the OAS. But the apolitical tradition remained strong, while the mass refusal of the conscripts to obey the rebel officers was fatal to the 1961 generals' putsch.

The failure of that revolt, the fratricidal struggle with OAS, the subsequent trials and retirements, and the abandonment of Algeria created scars which could only heal slowly. The military tended to withdraw in upon themselves to lick their wounds and close ranks. Countering this, de Gaulle restored morale gradually by throwing the forces into the new task of adaptation: from being a mainly colonial fighting machine living in dangerous isolation from the rest of the nation, the army was to become a European-based force with a global mission and a challenging range of new weapons. But when the fate of the system again hung in the balance in 1968, the services could not help but be a factor in the situation. De Gaulle was obliged to ascertain from his military leaders where their loyalties lay; apparently unanimously they indicated their readiness to support the legally constituted government —with an evident reluctance to be involved. On a smaller scale there were similar problems with the police. The disaffection of the police and the CRS (the semi-military mobile police controlled by the Ministry of the Interior) had been one of the fatal weaknesses of the Fourth Republic. As long as the Algerian war endured, and the police were having to cope with left-wing demonstrations and suffer murderous attacks from Algerian nationalists, the authorities never felt able to bring under effective check their penchant for clubbing (and sometimes even killing) demonstrators and Algerian suspects. In May 1968 the police were again out of political control at times, and again the authorities turned a blind eye—while the police unions gave warning that they would not be uncritically at the regime's disposal.

If the strong government of the Fifth Republic could not always be sure of its own armed forces, could it carry out its claims to stand above the interest groups and resist their pressures? In so far as it could, this was because the new strength of the State was supplemented by the continuing weakness of the groups. For, overall, group structure has altered relatively little during the Fifth Republic; consolidation in one area has been balanced by increased fragmentation elsewhere. The problems of low membership, inadequate staff and shortage of funds persist almost everywhere outside the industrial trade associations. Naturally cause groups have continued to come and go (though the Ligue des Droits de l'Homme survives as a perennial opponent of oppression). They have ranged from the bodies like Vérité-Liberté and the Comité Maurice Audin concerned with torture in Algeria to such typical groups of the later sixties as the Mouvement Contre l'Armement Atomique, the Mouvement Français pour-le Planning Familial, and Télé-Liberté (opposing governmental interference in television). Ephemeral and apparently ineffectual as many of these groups are, they have often made a significant impact on the intellectual climate, particularly over Algeria.

But, perhaps more significantly, the attitudes of the main groups towards their role in society have been changing. Quite apart from their response to the different political style and technique of the Fifth Republic, many have come to take a broader view of their role. This was most evident in the early years, when bodies like the CFDT, UNEF, the CGT and some teachers' unions campaigned against torture, demonstrated against government domination of ORTF, and rallied to the regime when it was threatened by insurrection in Algeria. This in part reflected the exceptional political instability of the time and the depth of the discredit of the traditional political parties. Although for a while the unions and clubs were widely hailed as 'the vital forces of the nation' from which political renewal would spring, they themselves rapidly realized how unsuited they were to fill the vacuum; there could be no substitute for a healthy party system. However, the sense of wider involvement persisted. To some degree this may be a byproduct of their participation in the Economic and Social Council and the Plan, where groups are regularly confronted with some of the broader implications of their activities, but it also reflects the deeper social concern and civic commitment of the younger generation, particularly those who have graduated to responsibilities in the groups by way of Catholic Action organizations. Paradoxically, while this extension of horizons from the narrow-minded defence of sectional interests is something Debré particularly had urged, the refusal of many groups to 'mind their own business' has been a source of repeated irritation to Fifth Republic leaders.

Governmental and parliamentary attitudes

With his essentially monarchical view of political relationships, de Gaulle seemed to look on the interest groups as one of the means by which the sovereign might apprise himself of his subjects' views, should he wish to do so—and in that qualification lay the seeds of many bitter political storms. Of course the groups were expected to know their place. De Gaulle was naturally unflinchingly hostile to having his autonomy of decision impaired by sectional interests—though, where necessary, he could deal with the groups as pragmatically as with other inconvenient political realities. However, where the parties were invariably stigmatized by the President and his followers as irredeemable and unrepresentative relics of the past, the groups were seen as having some kind of role to play in the expression of social and economic reality. With rare exceptions like the vindictive handling of UNEF,[1] groups were not exposed to the systematic attempts at disruption

---

[1] See below, pp. 323–6.

which were directed against the parties. Some of the Fifth Republic's reputation for hostility to the groups is more properly attributable to Debré personally. His 1957 pamphlet, *Ces princes qui nous gouvernent*, assailed the leaders of almost every important social, economic, religious and cultural group in the land, lumping them in a common anathema with the party politicians. He came to office deeply imbued with Rousseauist-Jacobin hostility to intermediary groups in general.

Taking its tone largely from Debré, at first the new regime's course seemed deliberately and aggressively aimed at bringing some of the noisiest and most demagogic groups to heel. The economic reforms of December 1958 angered the unions by raising social security charges, abolished many token pensions to ex-servicemen, and struck down the system of linking farm prices to costs which the farmers had just won after years of pressure. Later followed the abolition of the notoriously abused right of the *bouilleurs de cru* to distil tax-free alcohol,[1] and measures, infuriating the small shopkeepers, to prevent manufacturers withholding supplies from price-cutters. When the president of UNEF complained that the budget gave insufficient funds to education, de Gaulle icily told him that this was a matter for the government alone; protest demonstrations would be a waste of time. When the farmers persuaded a majority of deputies to request a special session of parliament in 1961, the President refused at the cost of minor mayhem to the constitution, and wrote to the president of the Assembly, 'however representative this group may be in regard to the particular interests it defends, it is nonetheless in law completely devoid of authority and political responsibility'. He left no doubt where authority and political responsibility now lay. Replying to protests over pensions from the ex-servicemen, he said in one of the Fifth Republic's most celebrated phrases: 'In matters where the national interest is involved, the State does not give way' (*le pouvoir ne recule pas*).

Thanks to such firmness the 1958 devaluation, almost alone of France's many devaluations, was not squandered in ensuing inflation. Yet even de Gaulle could not always stand firm. The 1958 austerity ordinances were later followed by concessions to ex-servicemen, farmers and social security

---

[1] Cf. Williams, *The French Parliament*, pp. 85–9.

beneficiaries, while the attack on the home distillers proved more difficult and protracted than expected. Sometimes defeat could be camouflaged, but at others (like the confrontation with the miners in 1963), the retreat was ignominious. One of the biggest pressure group coups of the Fifth Republic came during this early period of defiance. At the 1958 elections the Association des Parents d'Elèves de l'Enseignement Libre lined up pledges of support for greater aid to Church schools from two-thirds of the new Assembly. Under APEL pressure Debré set up an exploratory commission with the hope that it would realize his long-held desire to find a solution which would finally remove this festering issue from politics. Meanwhile, APEL's supporters pressured him into granting an increased subsidy on account. When the commission subsequently reported in favour of large subsidies combined with more rigorous controls, APEL's unwavering pressure for more aid without strings forced Debré to water down the system of control even at the cost of losing his Minister of Education in protest.

Thus even in Debré's time the government sometimes lost its battles. Moreover, even he was not in practice systematically antagonistic to all the groups. He collaborated fruitfully with the Young Farmers on the 1960 Agricultural Orientation Law[1] and accepted the place of the groups in the Economic and Social Council and, later, on the Regional Economic Development Councils. Then again, his new team lost its initial momentum as new teams do; and above all it was forced to realize that relations with the groups could not be compartmentalized neatly as a series of technical problems, for they interacted both with one another and with the wider political context—in which the search for an Algerian solution then took precedence over everything else. De Gaulle could risk neither a general disaffection undermining his support at a referendum, nor indignation in any major group becoming so intense that his Algerian opponents could channel its hostility against the regime itself—as nearly happened in a farmers' demonstration at Amiens in 1960. Thus the government found itself giving ground to a number of interests as the price of carrying its Algerian policy.

Debré's successors were not as disposed as he had initially

[1] See below, pp. 291–2.

been to teach the groups their place. Rather, as de Gaulle was freed from the Algerian incubus, the groups were seen as allies—or pawns—against the politicians. This found one expression in the mid-sixties vogue for 'concerted politics'— which in the minds of many Gaullists involved bringing the government and the relevant interests together round a table to reach decisions 'outside politics', thereby cutting out the parties.[1] These ideas also found more institutional expression. As early as 1946 de Gaulle had proposed extending and formalizing the role of the groups in an Economic Senate; he finally moved to put this into practice with his ill-fated proposals in 1969 for reform of the regions and the Upper House.[2] Debré, once more in the thick of the battle, now hailed the inclusion of the groups in regional councils and a reformed Senate as a major democratic advance, and castigated the parties for their opposition to sharing responsibility with sectional interests as further proof of their incurable conservatism.[3] The form of the attack was revealing; it was clear that the neo-corporatist streak in Gaullism owed more to hostility to the parties than to any real enthusiasm for the groups. Rather, they fitted conveniently into the unwearying struggle to disrupt, discredit and devalue the traditional parties.

Though courted at times by the leaders of the regime, the groups all found their standing and tactics affected by the

---

[1] The notion of *concertation* is neither specifically Gaullist, nor does it necessarily imply exclusion of the parties; in its wider form it stresses the interdependence of decision-making by government and interest groups in an interventionist mixed economy. Cf. J. E. S. Hayward, *Private Interests and Public Policy* (London, 1966), pp. 3–4.

[2] See below, pp. 165, 253–4, 344–6.

[3] 'Just one question is put to the voters, and it is this: "Is it now good for the State, for the nation, in a word for France and the French people, for representatives of unions and trade associations, economic bodies and social associations to have a useful part in administrative and political institutions?" One may answer no; that is to assert that in twentieth-century France . . . we must continue to live with groups of workers, managers, farm-owners, the liberal or commercial professions, seeking challenge, conflict and even violence to obtain satisfaction. . . . Let those who have a taste for destruction reject this attempt to adapt. . . . Everything which may serve the expansion of our economy and social peace disturbs their plans' (*Le Monde*, 4 April 1969).

redistribution of power within the system. All of them saw
their established channels of influence and access disturbed
by the advent of the Fifth Republic, with its changes in
political personnel, its concern for the authority of the State,
and its transformation of relations between parliament and the
executive, and within the executive itself. They could no
longer look to parliament as a ready bulwark against unwelcome measures, now that it was confined to shorter sessions,
limited to 'the domain of the law' and forbidden to propose
higher expenditure. Moreover, as during the Fourth Republic,
decisions which were going to infuriate powerful groups were
not infrequently enacted under special powers to avoid
parliamentary embarrassments, as with the suppression of the
'privilege' of the home distillers in 1960, and the economic
ordinances of 1967. Within the Assembly the nineteen
specialized committees which had been so readily dominated
by sectional interests gave way to six larger committees with
broader competence, which even skilful log-rollers found
harder to swing behind their schemes (though their debates
were often attended mainly by deputies with some special
cause to plead). Occasionally groups pressed for a bill to go
to an *ad hoc* committee, which they promptly tried to pack
with their sympathizers—as with the special committee on the
government's proposal for a levy on milk producers in 1961,
which issued a unanimously hostile report obliging the government to withdraw its bill and start again (successfully). But
even when a group rallied a committee behind it, the government now usually held the whip hand in debates. This did not
always prevent group sympathizers going through the familiar
motions with an eye to eventual electoral advantage: discussion
of the annual estimates for the Ministry for Ex-Servicemen
continued to give rise to all the traditional pleas for higher
pensions, and the occasional concession would be wrested
from the minister, but all this was a far cry from the days
when governments trembled annually as the debate
approached.

Yet at least sporadically parliament remained an effective
channel for sectional pressures. The reluctance of successive
governments to bring forward long overdue legislation to
reform local government owed much to the high proportion
of mayors and councillors among members of parliament of
every party. Bills to set up the Paris District, to establish

'urban communities' in the major conurbations, and to reform
the local taxation system all gave rise to protracted parliamentary battles in which the government had to give ground
to advocates for the local authorities. Occasionally there was a
complete debacle. On the Value-Added Tax Bill (TVA) in
1965 the government came under pressure from every party,
not least from the UNR, and the Assembly lobbies were
thronged with spokesmen for pressure groups as blatantly as
in the bad old days of Pierre Poujade. With a parliamentary
election approaching, the government made concession after
concession to shopkeepers, small businessmen, self-employed
craftsmen and farmers, totalling £130 million.[1] Again in 1968
long-overdue proposals to increase death duties roused such a
storm of protests from a wide range of groups and every party
from the Communists to the Gaullists, that even with the
largest parliamentary majority in the history of the Republic,
the government gave way. Other groups which won occasional
successes, either directly on the floor or through behind-the-
scenes agreements between the government and its supporters,
included the refugees from Algeria, country lawyers (over
alterations in land-transfer law), the farmers (on a number of
issues such as the Agricultural Orientation Law, TVA and
health insurance), and the taxi drivers (over social security).

Even so, few groups were more than a shadow of their
former parliamentary stature. Those which suffered most were
the ones with little support in either the important ministries
or the press, whose influence had always turned on their
parliamentary and electoral leverage, such as the home distillers, the ex-servicemen, or occupiers of rent-controlled
property. But it was the persistence of a conservative majority
in the Assembly, almost as much as the changes in the system,
which explained the weakness of the groups which attract
sympathy predominantly from the Left. During the Fourth
Republic the Assembly had been an important prop to the
farmers. Now their assessment of parliament's value declined
drastically, despite their occasional coups. And with the
decline in the importance of parliament to the groups went a
corresponding lessening of their traditional lobbying and
extracting of pledges at elections, though old habits often
continued from mere force of tradition.

---

[1] See Williams, *The French Parliament*, pp. 93–5.

Increasingly, therefore, the groups switched their main efforts from parliament to the executive. While nobody could regret the passing of times when shaky governments were regularly held to ransom by rapacious lobbies, the change was not pure gain. For even the Fourth Republic Assembly acted more than was appreciated as both a shock absorber and a channel of communication between governors and governed. As a shock absorber it often deferred or attenuated, and sometimes resisted, pressures from below, while the regular contact between deputies and the interests in their constituencies provided Paris with a useful early-warning system of political trouble brewing, and gave the groups some insight into political realities. But with governments now apparently uninterested in deputies' reports of constituency opinion, and generally discounting the importance of parliamentarians in return, deputies felt freer to act as undiluted advocates of group demands (particularly over the farmers' discontents in the early sixties). At other times the government's supporters welcomed its resort to the package vote or special powers (as notably over the 1967 economic ordinances) for relieving them of the embarrassment of responsibility. As parliament was listened to less, and was less prepared to play its true political role, its value as a shock absorber and communications channel also weakened. As a consequence, the regime often failed to detect impending trouble in time, finding itself all too often meeting groups in sudden, unexpected head-on conflicts.

Consultation and direct action

The Fifth Republic brought few formal alterations to the complex structure of executive-group relations inherited from the Fourth Republic. There was talk in 1958 of abolishing the entire range of consultative bodies with functions overlapping those of the Economic and Social Council, but ministries and groups alike successfully objected to their established relationships being disrupted. The network of some five thousand advisory councils, committees and commissions was broadly retained; though some either disappeared or fell into decay, like the Conseil Supérieur du Plan, others were created to meet fresh needs, like the Comité National de Conciliation set up to settle disputes arising from the new system of aid to

Church schools. Though here and there the system was pruned—most effectively in agriculture—its weakness remained the proliferation of overlapping committees with excessively narrow terms of reference, unable to see problems in their wider context. Another popular device maintained from the previous regime was the round-table of interested parties, called *ad hoc* to discuss such problems as farm prices, viticulture, union rights and education reform. Groups still served on such working parties as the 'article 24 commission' on agreements between doctors and the social security system. They continued to share in the operation of a wide range of public and semi-public bodies, from social security *caisses* to the Office National de la Navigation, and from the Sociétés d'Aménagement Foncier et d'Etablissement Rural (SAFER) to the Sociétés d'Intérêts Collectifs Agricoles (SICA)—both of which were major Fifth Republic additions to the large number of agricultural bodies supported by public subventions or parafiscal levies.

While the system of consultative administration has operated mechanically much as under the Fourth Republic, ministers have been more inclined to by-pass it as a luxury or an unnecessary formality when they were in a hurry or knew they would hear unwelcome advice. Thus in 1959 thirty-eight of the fifty members of the Conseil Supérieur de l'Education Nationale resigned after the government had sent the bill to aid Church schools to parliament without consulting them; earlier the same body refused to consider a bill on apprenticeship and vocational training brought before it with only a few hours notice. Yet although the committees were not infrequently treated casually, consultative administration was also criticized for operating against the public interest and perpetuating social divisions, by creating a privileged embrace between the executive and sectional interests. The closeness of relationships meant that if certain groups became 'domesticated', a ministry like Agriculture stayed as constant (if less uncritical) an advocate of its clients within the administration as it was in the Fourth Republic (and almost any other country).

Representation of interests has also remained a feature of the national Plan. About half the 3,137 members of the commissions, sub-commissions and working parties involved in preparing the Fourth Plan were taken from interest groups (though nominally they sat as individuals rather than as group spokesmen). The net was cast wider still for the Fifth Plan; typically eighteen of the seventy-three members of the Manpower Commission, and no fewer than fifty-five of the sixty on the Steel Commission came from the groups (the unions being consistently underrepresented in both places and chairmanships).[1]

At the peak of the advisory consultative structure is the Economic and Social Council. It seemed for a moment in 1958 that de Gaulle might press forward with his scheme for an Economic Senate including representatives of a broad range of interests, but the idea was shelved in the face of opposition from both politicians and the groups (chiefly the unions). The Council was retained for the time being as an advisory assembly with two hundred members (including forty-five from the unions, forty-one from business, forty from agriculture and fifteen from other groups), and given a number of indications of the regime's esteem for these spokesmen for the new, dynamic social and economic forces, in whom were placed greater hopes than in the old discredited parties. Debré was assiduous in seeking reports from the Council and studies with policy recommendations, even if he did not always take its advice. He and de Gaulle both praised its work. Pompidou was much less interested. He needed some nudging before he called on its expertise, and he circumscribed the Council's contribution to the Fifth Plan. (Though the ESC's critical report gave the opposition some useful ammunition, it had little influence on the government.) Nevertheless, the Council's investigations of such questions as immigrant labour, the economic cost of alcoholism, wages policy, housing and education, have had some influence on political and specialist opinion. But as long as de Gaulle was there the ESC's long-term future was in doubt; he returned to the Economic Senate idea in both 1963 and 1964 without result, before incorporating it in his 1969 referendum proposals. Not until their defeat, and his departure, could the ESC look forward to continuing its modestly influential role in security.

Much of the most significant business between the groups

---

[1] See below, pp. 246–7. A record level of group involvement in the preparation of the Sixth Plan for 1971–75 was announced in 1969; but numbers and influence are not necessarily to be equated.

and the executive is transacted outside the elaborate administrative-consultative structure in delegations to ministries, conferences on specific proposals or grievances, ministerial visits to group conferences and other less formal ways. The style of the Fifth Republic tends to favour in these encounters those whose bent and skill lie in mastery of technical presentation and discreet negotiation, rather than those whose strength rests more on a broad appeal to the public. Only the tip of this particular iceberg is ever visible: the French domestic appliance industry has had marked success in securing government support in Brussels for protection after the EEC tariff barriers came down; the finance ministry negotiates price control contracts with a wide range of firms and industries; vested interests not infrequently wield excessive influence in such fields as financial regulation or planning permission for major projects around Paris or on the Côte d'Azur. In other ways too, the regime has felt bound to respond to political pressures despite its contrary claims. The film of Diderot's *La Réligieuse* was banned after protests from convents in the minister's constituency, and despite repeated favourable votes by the official censorship advisory committee, which included representatives of Catholic family associations. The General's poor showing in the 1965 presidential election was followed by a shower of measures to placate the farmers. Twice, in 1959 and 1969, Ministers of Education announced reductions in school holidays—which are the longest in Europe—only to back down in the face of the teachers' reactions. After shopkeepers and independent craftsmen had taken direct action over their grievances in 1969, tax inspectors were secretly told to show particular leniency to small traders during the referendum campaign in terms going well beyond the injunction to discretion they traditionally receive at such periods.

Once the chill of the regime's early months was over few major groups found access a serious problem, though a few remained frozen out: the home distillers, cast permanently beyond the pale; the refractory UNEF which ministers were determined to bring to heel; the CGT, whose exclusion from full recognition (inherited from the Fourth Republic) endured until 1965; and, among later arrivals, MODEF. While cause groups rarely won regular entrée, the larger interests could therefore count on putting their views to 'their' minister, and the most important on seeing the finance minister or the Premier. Occasionally they would even be received in audience by the President himself; it was said that on one such occasion Edouard Leclerc successfully won the General's ear to stop manufacturers cutting off his supplies. Some ministers, particularly those with conventional political backgrounds, took the initiative in inviting groups to discuss their proposals. Pisani's relations with CNJA and Faure's with FNSEA are notable cases in point. Faure also preceded his 1968 university reforms with a strikingly diverse and intensive round of consultations.[1] The Ministry of Labour's 1966 bill on apprenticeship and retraining emerged from round-table discussion with substantial concessions to the views of both the CNPF and the unions, while on the 1966 bill creating 'urban communities' in the largest conurbations, the UNR rapporteur held hearings on the spot at which the local authorities gave evidence, and the measure was reshaped by the minister as a result of his consultations.

Though such constructive instances have not been infrequent, relations between the regime and the interest groups have been afflicted by an underlying malaise, of which the most tangible sign was the frequency with which groups stepped outside the conventional paths of negotiation and discussion. Strikes have been called not only by workers, but by milk producers (over prices), shopkeepers and independent craftsmen (over taxes), students (about overcrowding and visiting rights), butchers (on reform of the distributive system), Corsicans (about plans to close the island's railways or to cut the tax privileges granted them by Napoleon), doctors (over social security contracts), and mayors (sympathizing with redundant workers or angry winegrowers). Above all, almost every year has brought outbreaks of direct action in the countryside, whether over prices, gluts, sales of land to 'foreigners', competition from imports, freight rates or factory farming. This has taken a wide variety of forms, from courteously distributing peaches and pamphlets at the roadside to blocking roads or railways, felling telephone poles, destroying produce or ransacking industrialized piggeries, and to occupying prefectures and clashing with riot police. More extreme still were the street battles with students

---

[1] See below, pp. 327–9.

and the occupation of factories by workers in 1968, and the wrecking of tax offices followed by the theft of documents by irate shopkeepers in 1969. This ready resort to direct action has long been characteristic of French pressure group behaviour, with its tendency to arrogance, violence and ruthlessness, but it seems to have spread under the Fifth Republic.

Yet the frequent reliance on force rather than persuasion is more than a hangover from the tradition of *incivisme*. Nor is it merely a frustrated reflex by sectional interests against their political impotence, or a contagion from the tortures and *plasticages* of the Algerian war, or even the inescapable outcome of the tensions arising from rapid change within a fragmented and conservative society—though all these are elements in the explanation. Both the resort to such methods, and the widespread belief that 'only direct action pays', indicate a weakness within the system itself. With the weakening of parliament and the parties, the participation of the groups in the administrative and policy-making processes became more essential than ever, since no political system can dispense with its shock absorbers or rise superior to its channels of communication. The high public expectations placed in the groups were reflected in the 1962 survey in which 54 per cent of the public looked to groups to protect their interests, only 10 per cent to parliamentarians, and 8 per cent to the parties. But the groups were never able in practice to meet these expectations. Partly this was due to their various limitations: poverty, inadequate membership, internal divisions and demagogic leadership. But the regime was also to blame. While the authorities were usually ready to receive the groups and sometimes wooed them, even the most moderate group leaders felt they were more endured than welcomed, and that they were seen as hindrances to executive autonomy rather than as essential participants in the making of technically sound and socially palatable decisions. Far too often they emerged from such encounters frustrated and embittered.

The rulers of the Fifth Republic have paid dearly for their recurrent reluctance to listen, their disposition to outwit the groups rather than negotiate, and their fallacious expectation that technically correct decisions will also be politically acceptable. The wave of peasant violence in 1961 broke out when, despite repeated promises to the farmers,[1] the decrees implementing the agricultural orientation law had not been issued after ten months. The ignoring of rumblings in Brittany in 1963 led to direct action flaring up over a glut of early potatoes which could have been foreseen weeks earlier.

The humiliating capitulation to the miners in 1963 and the accumulation of frustrations which preceded the events of 1968 could have been avoided by ministers with an ear to the ground. Time and again ministers have forfeited political credit they could otherwise have won, by mistiming their decisions or neglecting to explain them to those affected. Such incidents were not fortuitous. The example came from on high, where de Gaulle so often presented his ministers with *faits accomplis*. Though he suffered relatively little pressure group incursion within his reserved domain of defence and foreign affairs, he was not beyond intervening outside it to impose a final decision in defiance of established procedures of consultation. Although de Gaulle boasted of the number of audiences he granted to group spokesmen, it is doubtful whether he ever negotiated or even engaged in a purposive dialogue with any of them.

Ministers who were not always consulted not surprisingly tended in turn to be careless of consultation on occasion. A Minister of Justice who had repeatedly lauded the virtues of 'dialogue' and occasionally practised it reformed the Cour de Cassation in 1967 without consulting the legal professions. Both Faure and Pisani took quite unilateral decisions at times.[2] The result of such experiences is that though the groups' relations with the authorities have always been extensive and frequently productive, their position has remained uncertain and precarious. The unpredictability and emptiness of so much formal consultation is one of the most common griev-. ances of the groups against the regime. For despite his proclaimed attachment to *concertation* and then *participation*,

---

[1] Cf. 'Every group in this country possesses a copious list of dishonoured promises and more or less fraudulent ruses, which the administration has been guilty of over many years. Hence the anger and, worse than anger, scorn': J.-M. Domenach, *Le Monde*, 11 Nov. 1969.

[2] In turn some groups refused to join in discussions. One of the teachers' unions 'broke off relations' with the regime in 1963: UNEF refused to participate in discussions of the 1968 university reforms.

the instinctive reaction of the Fifth Republic's founder was to command and assert rather than to listen and discuss. So long as such an attitude endures, all the formal extension of recognition to the groups is unlikely to produce a stable and fruitful relationship.

III

THE STATE RESTORED

10

'NO DYARCHY AT THE TOP'

The President's role

'A constitution is a conception, a set of institutions, and a manner of acting.'[1] By each of President de Gaulle's three standards, the constitution of the Fifth Republic is not single but dual: two different conceptions, two different groups of institutions, two different ways of acting.

It is dual in conception, for underlying it are two distinct interpretations of the nature of politics in general and French politics in particular. 'The higher interest of France [is] quite different from the immediate advantage of Frenchmen.'[2] The fundamental issues of the nation's future, the safeguarding of its unity, its continuity and its independence must be in the hands of a monarch—albeit, in the twentieth century, a republican monarch. Parliament may be a suitable forum for the day-to-day clashes of interests and factions, but it showed in the Third and Fourth Republics its incapacity to deal effectively and in time with the great problems of national defence and decolonization, and in major crises was repeatedly driven to abdicate its authority to a national saviour. Yet behind this distinction between 'noble Politics' and 'common politics' lies an implied assumption that Frenchmen think and act differently at different levels: they are quarrelsome and irreconcilable where their personal or group interests are engaged, but by heroic leadership they can be united and

[1] Press conference of 31 Jan. 1964. On this occasion, discussing the roles of President and Prime Minister, he remarked that 'it would be quite unacceptable to have a dyarchy at the top. And in fact there is not one.'

[2] C. de Gaulle, *Mémoires de Guerre*, III: *Le Salut* (Paris, 1959), p. 28.

brought to demonstrate a coherent general will when the nation's future is at stake. The legitimate leader of the nation must understand, express and crystallise this general will — which to the irreverent usually seems identical with the will of the General.

> For General de Gaulle, President of the Republic, the essence of the matter is what is useful for the French people, is to know what the French people want. I am conscious of having discerned this for the last quarter of a century. Since I still have the strength I am determined to continue to do so.[1]

The conception of the constitution, then, is dual because de Gaulle saw politics on two distinct levels. Its institutions are dual because the constitutional scheme he had outlined at Bayeux in 1946 (which itself was not a strictly presidential system) was adopted twelve years later, but with significant modifications. The details of the constitution of the Fifth Republic were worked out by Michel Debré and other Gaullists; but they acted in consultation with a few leading ministers who had all had distinguished careers in the Fourth. After years of constitutional conflict, political necessity now brought the party leaders to compromise a great deal, and even the Gaullists to make some concessions. The ministers could not now oppose the introduction of a strong presidency, but were anxious that the new constitution should guarantee that responsibility of the government to parliament which, to French democrats, had always been the test of legitimacy.[2] De Gaulle himself, deeply impressed with the need for a strong President to provide a centre of authority, was equally concerned that that authority be accepted by Frenchmen as legitimate. Moreover, he was quite willing to accept the retention of a responsible premier who would relieve him of

---

[1] *Le Monde*, 26 Sept. 1963.

[2] 'I insist: on the day a head of the government or the ministers in that government cease to be responsible to the elected representatives of the nation, on the day parliament can no longer supervise their acts in the name of the sovereign people, democracy [la République] is at an end': President Vincent Auriol at Quimper, 31 May 1948, attacking de Gaulle's RPF.

the burden of common politics. Reserving himself for 'arbitration' on the great issues, the President would preserve that aloofness from petty men and affairs which he had always believed necessary for true authority.[1] The invention of a Prime Minister would thus enhance and not detract from his monarchical status.

From the other side, Debré (and *a fortiori* his ex-Fourth Republican colleagues) thought far more than de Gaulle in terms of a traditional parliamentary regime, though they agreed on wanting a stronger government. It was the ex-premiers, and not Debré, who inserted into the constitution the dubious devices in which the latter years of the Fourth Republic had been so fertile: the package vote on bills, the censure motion on which only votes against the government were counted, the passage without a positive vote of bills which the government made a question of confidence (unless its opponents could carry a censure motion). Debré would have preferred governmental stability ensured, as in Britain, by the loyalty of a party majority. But he shared his colleagues' scepticism about the chances of finding a majority, in the short run at least, and saw constitutional rules as an inferior but necessary substitute for the missing majority. Above all the country's need for a strong executive could not be allowed to depend on that uncertain political prospect. In Debré's conception no less than de Gaulle's, a powerful and autonomous President was indispensable in case the effort to restore strong parliamentary government proved a failure. But they agreed that the President should govern only through ministers who, despite all the protective armoury of the constitution, were ultimately vulnerable to overthrow in the Assembly. 'There are in reality *two constitutions* in the text of 1958: one is that of a parliamentary regime restored to health, the other that of an organized substitute for a classical parliamentary regime become impossible.'[2]

In some respects the formal constitution bore a distinct resemblance to that of Great Britain, which Debré so much admired. Protected by the new barriers against parliamentary

---

[1] 'No authority without prestige, no prestige without remoteness': C. de Gaulle, *Le Fil de l'épeé*, 10: 18 edn. (Paris, 1962), p. 55.

[2] Léo Hamon, *De Gaulle dans la République* (Paris, 1958), p. 158; italics in original.

encroachment, the government was free to govern. Parliament was confined to its regular role of voting taxes, amending legislation proposed, on all major matters, by the government, and supervising the latter's activities. The Assembly was restrained from harrying ministries to death in the time-honoured manner, but could still overturn a cabinet which forfeited its confidence—but (as in Britain) normally at the price of its own dissolution so that a single ministry could usually count on lasting throughout the life of a single Assembly. The President would stand somewhat in the background, like an eighteenth-century British monarch. In normal times he would 'arbitrate' between the numerous parties and their factions, and was felt to have a special responsibility for external affairs; but in an emergency he might assume and exercise full power himself. Presidency and parliament thus provided two distinct institutional sources of legitimacy.

The formal arrangements soon turned out to be a façade. For under de Gaulle the constitution of the Fifth Republic, born of two conceptions and embodied in two sets of institutions, has been operated in two successive ways. In its first year or so the initial separation of powers was observed. But under the pressure of the Algerian crisis parliament itself often preferred to reinforce the power of the President rather than that of the Premier responsible to it. From 1960 the evolution proceeded rapidly until the day (31 January 1964) when de Gaulle could enunciate his breathtaking claim:

'It must of course be understood that the indivisible authority of the State is confided in its entirety to the President by the people who have elected him, that no other authority exists, neither ministerial nor civil nor military nor judicial, which is not conferred and maintained by him. . . .'

The President had emerged from his aloofness as the maker of major policies—at first, indeed, only in a few crucial sectors but those were chosen by him. The government fell gradually into the background as the more or less zealous executant of policies decided elsewhere. Parliament suffered even more: the government was as powerful as in Britain, the opposition was weak and disoriented, the new standing orders were designed to fortify the executive, and there was little in French parliamentary tradition to protect minorities. Parliament and cabinet thus lost prestige and power to the Presidency, though the shift came about with a truly British flexibility, by changing the practice rather than the law. The process was, however, recognized and accelerated in October 1962 by one major constitutional change: the election of future Presidents by direct popular vote. The new law probably made the trend to presidential government irreversible; by polling day in December 1965 every serious candidate for the Presidency was assuming that he would be making the nation's policy if he won.

Direct election of the President had been considered in 1958, but rejected for three reasons which had lost their importance four years later. Wanting a large majority at the referendum and underestimating their own appeal, the Gaullists feared in 1958 that a directly elected Presidency would incur the charge of Bonapartism and so lose votes. In the longer run they feared that left-wing candidates for the Presidency would be dominated by the Communist party, the strongest in France: its losses and their own gains greatly diminished this risk. Moreover, the President would also be President of the Community, not to mention Algeria: these territories could neither be denied their voice in electing him, nor allowed (as universal suffrage would have ensured) to determine who should govern in France herself. For these reasons a solution like that propounded by de Gaulle at Bayeux in 1946 was retained twelve years later: the President was to be elected by an electoral college, devised so as to weaken the political parties, in which nearly all the 80,000 voters were local councillors and the cities were underrepresented almost as flagrantly as Algeria and the states of the Community. Overwhelmingly elderly, masculine and rural, the electoral college enjoyed little prestige, and in the referendum which abolished it the Gaullist spokesman (Chaban-Delmas) made an effective appeal to women and young people by pointing to the weakness of the institution the Gaullist constitution-makers had so recently invented and so ardently defended.

De Gaulle himself explained the need to change the system in personal terms: future Presidents would require the 'explicit confidence of the Nation', which had not been the case in 1958 when 'historic events had already ensured that this need was met'.[1] Some observers rashly inferred from this argument that he would not stand again at the end of his first term, but in fact there were strong reasons independent of the personal factor. Negatively, the old grounds for fearing universal suffrage had gone: Algeria and Black Africa were independent; the Communists were weaker than in 1958; 'Bonapartism' did not seem such a dangerous charge (and in the event remarkably little was heard of it). Tactically and strategically, the new plan would help the Gaullists and weaken the old parties. Immediately, it forced the latter to fight on bad ground (refusing to the ordinary Frenchman the right to choose the head of his own government); in the longer term, it 'blew up the road back to the Fourth Republic'—for once the ordinary voter had this power he would not give it up, and once the President could claim popular legitimacy, it would be hard indeed to deprive him of executive authority in the future. But in addition to these political reasons there was another cause for the change: de Gaulle's experience of the presidential office.

In 1958 de Gaulle did not want the President of the Republic to take direct control of the executive: he feared both that routine business might swamp him, and that any pressures to amend his foreign policy would be the harder to resist if he were vulnerable at all points to parliamentary criticism. The Prime Minister would provide him with a useful screen against both the trivia of day-to-day business and the inconvenience of parliamentary attack. This conception of government reflected the General's determination to concentrate on strategic issues and avoid being diverted to 'quartermaster's business'. But it was tenable only in the situation de Gaulle had known in his previous spell in office, during and just after the war, when victory and economic reconstruction were objectives common to all political groups, however bitterly they might quarrel over their separate ideologies and interests. The circumstances after 1958 were quite different, and within four years he had found that the President, to be effective, must be the leader of a political majority rather than the non-political arbiter between factions.

The breakdown of *arbitrage* first became apparent over

[1] 20 Sept. 1962.

Algeria. Eight months after entering the Elysée the President announced, not an arbiter's verdict, but a policy-maker's decision: Algeria was to have self-determination. Four months later the army was still ruling Algeria as effectively as ever, until the barricades rising of January 1960 afforded it an opportunity to try to blackmail Paris into reversing the new policy. To impose that policy the President had to emerge from his place in the background, to determine personally (against the Premier's wishes) that the insurgents must be broken, and then to take over the execution of policy in order to keep the initiative he had regained. In Algeria, then, the full presidential authority was needed to overcome military and administrative resistance to a new course.

It was required in less dramatic matters also. The parties were poor transmission belts for communicating policy. The opposition were ineffective because they feared to hamper de Gaulle's handling of the Algerian crisis, while hoping to displace him and return to 'normal' once it was over. The government party, in these early days, lacked both cohesion and conviction: the President had to act without them and indeed against them. The interest groups found parliament and the parties ineffective mediators, and sought, whether by negotiation or by direct action, to influence ministers or the President directly. And as in the USA, without an effective party system there was no way of overcoming bureaucratic inertia or pressure group hostility unless, again, the President committed his own authority.

Neither in noble Politics nor in common politics, therefore, could the President in practice remain in his chosen role of aloof arbitration. But in addition the distinction between the spheres soon broke down: they were too closely connected. They were connected through the budget: since everything costs money, the limits of possible progress in domestic matters were set by the costs of external policies with their higher priority. They were connected also through the repercussions of discontent of all kinds on presidential authority. The monarch might prefer to ignore petty politics: those whose lives were affected by it were driven to attract his attention by agitation that might interrupt that 'regular functioning of the constitutional authorities' which he conceived it part of his duty to maintain. Thus without his intervention conflicts were likely to remain unresolved; but if they festered for too long they weakened his authority even in the spheres he really cared about. In February 1960 peasants protesting about farm prices rioted in Amiens amid shouts of *Vive Massu!*[1] In December 1965 Marcel Barbu, the 'underdog candidate' who sometimes expressed very effectively the views of very ordinary Frenchmen, appealed to the voters not to turn out the General but to force him to a second ballot so as to impress on him that they were not just 'raw material for history'. At each of the three referendums in between, de Gaulle himself had announced, despite the constitution which says the President is responsible to no one, that he would resign if his policy was repudiated. But if the President as supreme policy-maker must be responsible to the people, should he not be elected by them as Léon Blum had foreseen in his prophetic comment on the Bayeux speech?

> In this system the President of the Republic will be the effective chief of the government and administration, the Prime Minister being reduced to following a brief and acting as a trusted subordinate. . . . For a Chief Executive of this type an enlarged electoral college will not suffice. Since all sovereignty necessarily derives from the people, it will be necessary to go right to the source of sovereignty, and have the Chief Executive elected by universal suffrage.[2]

His constitutional powers

Direct election thus confirmed the President in his role of political leadership, rather than *arbitrage*.[3] It enhanced the prestige and authority of future Presidents and strengthened the likelihood that these would use their constitutional powers

---

[1] General Massu, who had played a vital role in bringing de Gaulle to power in 1958, had just been removed from Algiers after publicly wondering whether the army had made a mistake in doing so.

[2] Quoted by Jacques Fauvet, *Le Monde*, 5 Nov. 1965.

[3] Nevertheless in March 1967 an opinion poll found that while 62 per cent thought de Gaulle *had* acted as chief of a majority political group and only 17 per cent as a man outside political parties, only 21 per cent thought the President *should* act in the former role and 62 per cent in the latter: *Sondages* 1967, no. 4, p. 49.

to the full, as de Gaulle had, and would not allow them to slip back into the hands of the Premier. These constitutional powers are of three kinds. First, those enjoyed by the President as head of state are formally his, but require the counter-signature of a minister; under any other President than de Gaulle they would probably have quickly lapsed to the government. Secondly, the President has several 'prerogative' powers which he exercises personally, without counter-signature, but which in theory never allow him finally to decide a matter himself, only to refer it elsewhere for decision—to the Assembly, for nominations to the premiership and for presidential messages; to the Constitutional Council, for bills and treaties; to the people when the Assembly was dissolved or a referendum called. These 'prerogative' powers might in time, under a weak President, have drifted back to the government; a President directly elected by the people is unlikely to let them go. Lastly, under Article 16 the President has in a great emergency the supreme authority to take over all power himself. His discretion is unfettered but he is obliged to seek advice from several authorities confirming the reality of the emergency and from one, the Constitutional Council, concerning the measures he takes to meet it; moreover, parliament meets automatically and may not be dissolved. There are only two ways to remove a President: for incapacity, affirmed by the government and agreed by a majority of the membership of the Constitutional Council; and for high treason (an offence not defined in the penal code), by an impeachment motion voted publicly in both houses and tried before a High Court of twelve deputies and twelve senators.

The President's formal powers, subject to countersigna-ture, are much the same as in previous Republics and need no comment.[1] His 'prerogative' powers, not requiring counter-signature, fall to him as guarantor of the constitution and of the nation's integrity and independence. In the early days de Gaulle assumed a right to act without countersignature as President of the Community, a point on which the constitution was silent and which has disappeared with the Community itself. His remaining 'prerogative' powers are to nominate the Premier, address messages to parliament, refer matters to the

---

[1] But he is now empowered to negotiate treaties, not merely to ratify them.

Constitutional Council (see Chapter 13), dissolve the Assembly and decide on proposals for a referendum. All operate quite differently from the way the words of the constitution, traditionally interpreted, had suggested.

In theory the President nominates a Premier whom he cannot later dismiss (article 8).[1] The Premier (who was expected to be the leader of the parliamentary majority if one existed) then chooses and can later dismiss the ministers; appointments to other major posts are made in cabinet. The reality is, of course, quite different; as de Gaulle put it on 31 January 1964, 'the President chooses the Premier, appoints him and the other ministers, and is entitled to change him because he has completed the task the President assigned him or because he no longer has the President's approval'. Thus in 1958 the principal leader of the Gaullist majority was Jacques Soustelle; the President chose Michel Debré as Premier. After refusing several requests by Debré to resign, the President in April 1962 replaced him by Georges Pompidou who, unlike Debré, had never held any elective office and was not even a member of the UNR.[2] After the 1965 presidential election Pompidou resigned (in keeping with custom), was reappointed, and reshuffled his cabinet, making Debré Minister of Finance in place of the Independent Republican leader Giscard d'Estaing. But parliament was not called into special session. Until the regular session began three months later it had no opportunity of showing its confidence (or lack of it) in the new cabinet. Then Pompidou declared that he saw no need to seek the Assembly's approval for a simple continuation of the same majority with the same programme; the onus was on the opposition to challenge the government by a

---

[1] In answer to a question by Paul Reynaud, de Gaulle assured the Constitutional Consultative Committee that the Prime Minister could not be dismissed by the President who had chosen him: 'No! For if that were so he could not govern effectively. The Prime Minister is responsible to parliament and not to the Chief of State...'. *Avis et Débats du Comité Consultatif Constitutionnel* (Paris, 1960), sitting of 8 Aug. 1958, p. 118. It is not even clear that the President is entitled to refuse a Premier's resignation.

[2] After the censure vote of 4 Oct. 1962, Pompidou offered his resignation which de Gaulle refused. In a radio debate with Mendès-France during the 1965 presidential campaign, Debré loyally claimed he had resigned and not been dismissed in 1962.

censure motion. In 1966 his control of the Assembly was scarcely in doubt; but in 1967 he again faced the Assembly with a paper majority of one at most, to announce a substantially reshuffled cabinet and major changes in policy. Again he refused to seek the Assembly's confidence on the same grounds as in 1966.[1]

When Pompidou forgot his place and in turn lost the President's favour his 'resignation' followed much the same scenario as Debré's, and he, too, was followed by a man who had held no elective office until a few days earlier, and who was not a member of the UNR. Despite the massive Gaullist majority in the new Assembly Couve de Murville again refused to seek parliamentary endorsement of his policy. Where Debré had in 1959 expressly set the precedent of demonstrating his government's parliamentary support, it was now contended that a government enjoying the President's had no need to ask the Assembly's.[2]

As for the other ministers, in January 1959 'M. Michel Debré presented for the approval of General de Gaulle his conception of general policy and the names of those public figures who would, if it were so decided, become his colleagues in the Government'. Ministers who left in 1959 were officially announced to have 'resigned', those who did so in 1960, to have been 'replaced'; the dismissal of Pinay (who opposed Debré's domestic as well as de Gaulle's foreign policy) was officially a 'decision of the President on the Premier's proposal', that of Soustelle was formally 'approved' by de Gaulle.[3] On other appointments, too, the first President of the Fifth Republic, unlike those of the Fourth, used his traditional countersignature of nominations to establish a new and effective right of veto. But he concentrated his attention on particular men and posts rather than on the whole field of appointments. Four men with no parliamentary past were clearly presidential nominees: André Malraux and Maurice

---

[1] See below, p. 231n.

[2] This practice carried over into the new reign: Chaban-Delmas invoked Pompidou's argument in declining to seek the Assembly's endorsement in June 1969 —though he did seek it later, in September.

[3] P. Avril, *Le régime politique de la Ve République* (Paris, 1964), pp. 238–9; J. Raux in *Revue du droit public* 81.2, March-April 1965, pp. 239, 248.

Couve de Murville who sat in the cabinet from the start, Louis Joxe (from 1959) and Pierre Messmer (from 1960). But other appointments often seem to have been left to the Premier's discretion: in the reshuffle of August 1961 it was Debré, not de Gaulle, who insisted on removing Edmond Michelet and Robert Lecourt, while in that of January 1966 Pompidou seems to have had a fairly free hand, except over a few changes (notably the crucial one at Finance). After the 1967 election the Premier was able to bring in three ministers who had served on his own staff, one of them (François Ortoli) as Minister of Finance.[1] Couve de Murville also appointed a couple of friends and collaborators.

Articles 18 and 19 give the President the right, not subject to countersignature, to address formal messages to the nation or its representatives; in addition, of course, President de Gaulle expressed himself very frequently on television, in his provincial tours, in the solemn lectures to journalists which it suited his sense of humour to describe as press conferences, and in official communiqués from the Elysée. With so many means at his disposal the formal messages were rare: one to the nation and five to parliament. The former was delivered on 23 April 1961, as the constitution requires, when the President invoked article 16. Of the latter, two were official welcomes to newly elected Assemblies, which were thus offered 'evidence of my confidence' (15 January 1959) and adjured to 'deliberate with dignity, hammer out good laws, define political choices and clearly express them' (11 December 1962). (The Assemblies of 1967 and 1968 were apparently not welcome to the Chief of State.) Three messages were announcements of important events; but in no case was parliament the first audience to hear of these events and in each the announcement seemed designed to put the members in their place. On 25 April 1961, two days after the message to the nation, another message to parliament informed it that article 16 was in force—and that it must not legislate on matters covered by the President's new powers. On 20 March

---

[1] But in June 1968 René Capitant, who had violently attacked the Premier only nine days before for endangering the regime by his unprecedented incompetence, told journalists that he was entering the government 'on the orders of the Elysée, and there was nothing Pompidou could do about it': in the words of P. Rouanet, *Pompidou*, Paris, 1969, p. 270.

1962, two days after a presidential announcement on television, parliament learned officially of the referendum to be held on the bill approving the Evian settlement with the FLN and transferring sweeping powers to the President to bring it into force. Six months later, on television on 20 September, the nation heard from the President what a cabinet communiqué had revealed a week before, that the bill to elect the President by universal suffrage was to bypass parliament and go straight to referendum; the members were not told by message until 2 October. Many other major decisions were never the subject of messages: the referendum on self-determination for Algeria (announced by a cabinet communiqué); the ban on legislation during the special session while article 16 was in force (by a letter to the Premier); the ending of article 16 (by a communiqué); the exclusion of Algerian members from parliament when Algeria became independent, which contradicted a famous precedent set in 1871[1] (by an ordinance, made by the President under his special powers); de Gaulle's decision to stand for a second term (by a television statement); and the referendum proposed in May 1968 and eventually held in April 1969 (announced, postponed and revived on television respectively on 24 May, 30 May and 7 June 1968). The General was believed to dislike formal messages because they had to be read for him by the presidents of the two houses, when he wished, like the Queen of England, to read them himself.[2]

Parliament's subordination has been emphasized in more important ways. Article 29 prescribes the dates and length of ordinary sessions but allows special ones to be summoned either by the Premier or at the demand of a majority of the deputies. Under article 30 these special sessions are opened and closed by a presidential decree; in former constitutions (and in 1958) the same provision was always considered obligatory on the President once the conditions of article 29 were fulfilled. But in March 1960 the President successfully claimed under article 30 the right to refuse a special session to

---

[1] When Alsace and Lorraine were ceded to Germany their deputies remained in parliament because, in theory, they represented the whole nation and not just part of its territory.

[2] As he once complained to Guy Mollet. It was one of the rare occasions when de Gaulle was discomfited; Mollet asked whether he, like the Queen, would let the Premier write the messages!

a majority of members who had demanded one under article 29. There is no argument about the President's unfettered right to dissolve the Assembly at will; the one restriction is that this right cannot be used twice within twelve months. In the first parliament the deputies were made well aware that rejection of a major presidential policy would at once be met by dissolution (notably over the bill to establish a French nuclear deterrent in the autumn of 1960);[1] and when they censured Pompidou's government over the constitutional amendment of October 1962, they were in fact dissolved. Although the new house had a safe Gaullist majority, there was sometimes talk of dissolving it at a moment convenient to the government—after all, as Pompidou pointed out, a British cabinet can call a snap election at a time convenient to itself.[2] But there was a deterrent: if after a dissolution, the new Assembly had no majority or an unsatisfactory one, it could not be dissolved again for a year; after an election at the normal time, it could. The second parliament therefore survived to the end of its term. With the Gaullists' formal majority reduced to vanishing point its successor lived under almost permanent threat of dismissal. But again de Gaulle had to weigh the chances of the Gaullists improving their position against the problems of being saddled for a year with an immovable Assembly. With the government's popularity in the country uncertain, the gamble was not worth taking while it could retain control of the Assembly.[3] When he did dissolve the Assembly after fourteen months it was in response to the quite extra-parliamentary crisis of May 1968.

The Fifth Republic provides two forms of appeal to the people: the dissolution and the referendum. In theory the President alone can refuse a referendum but not initiate one. The question could arise either on a constitutional amendment proposed by the government,[4] under article 89, para. 3, or on certain ordinary bills, under article 11. Under article 89

---

[1] De Gaulle even considered using article 16 if this bill was rejected, according to L. Terrenoire (then a minister), *De Gaulle et l'Algérie* (Paris, 1964), p. 196.

[2] *Le Monde*, 9 Nov. 1963.

[3] See below, pp. 232–3.

[4] Or on one proposed by a private member? Apparently not.

the proposal, once voted by parliament, would normally go to referendum but the President could, as a substitute, call a joint session of the two houses (*congrès du parlement*) at which it would require a three-fifths majority to pass. Under article 11 the President could agree to or refuse a referendum on certain bills (those dealing with either the *'organisation des pouvoirs publics'*, or a treaty affecting them, or a Community Agreement), provided that the referendum was requested either by both houses of parliament (so that these would not be bypassed) or by the government during the parliamentary session (so that it could be censured).[1]

However, none of the three referendums of de Gaulle's first term was held in the circumstances envisaged in the constitution. The first, on allowing self-determination in Algeria, was promised by de Gaulle 'on my responsibility', as he stressed, in September 1959. When his policy was challenged on the Algiers barricades, he reacted vigorously: 'I have laid down a decision on the subject of Algeria. Let it be *everywhere* understood—let it be *thoroughly* understood— that I will not go back on it.'[2] The referendum itself, held on 8 January 1961, was foreshadowed by the President in a speech in October and a television broadcast in November. Three weeks later it was proposed by the government; parliament was still sitting, and on the last day of the session it was allowed to debate the subject; but the bill was not published till the first day of the recess. The Left protested bitterly that they were asked to give one reply to two questions (do you approve of self-determination *and* the bill setting up provisional institutions for Algeria?) with a third added later (are you willing to risk my resignation in the middle of the Algerian war?).

---

[1] The constitution (article 7, para. 4) made the President of the Senate acting president during a vacancy, but denied him the right to dissolve or decide on a referendum. Gaston Monnerville, who held the office, opened a bitter feud with the regime by his violent attack on the procedure used in October 1962 to alter the method of electing the President. The bill which did so also changed the arrangements during a presidential vacancy, giving the government the power to act in default of the President of the Senate, but ruling out any constitutional amendment bill or vote of confidence in or censure of the government during an interregnum.

[2] Broadcast of 29 Jan. 1960.

The second referendum in April 1962 again posed a double question: approval of the Evian agreements with the FLN *and* full powers to the President to bring them into force. A special session was called to approve this bill, which was passed without any vote because the government made it a matter of confidence and no censure motion was proposed. Algeria did not go to the polls owing to the OAS terror there, and was called on to vote only in July when the FLN were already installed: again this procedure, however practically necessary, was unauthorized by the constitution.[1] Only the extreme Right protested; silence in April weakened the opposition's case six months later. At the October referendum on direct election of the President, de Gaulle chose not to use article 89, which applied to constitutional amendments but required parliament to vote on them, but instead to invoke article 11 dealing with bills for the organization of public authorities.[2] The referendum was duly 'proposed' by the government (from which one minister resigned in protest) well after the President had announced it to them; the government was overthrown for making the 'proposal' but was at once reappointed and parliament dissolved. When critics complained that the procedure was unconstitutional, Gaullists asked them why they had never raised this objection over the earlier referendums. After more than five years without recourse to a referendum, the President called one in May 1968 but had to cancel it; that of 1969 was also announced by de Gaulle and subsequently proposed to him, and again bypassed parliament by resorting to article 11. Some non-Gaullists conceded that the 1962 vote had made the procedure permanently respectable, but the Conseil d'Etat held this referendum (like its predecessor) unconstitutional. Though the case was even more clearcut, its opinions were again ignored.

---

[1] For nothing in the constitution permitted a referendum in one part only of French territory: whether it was the subsequent self-determination vote in Algeria alone, approved in advance in January 1961, or the 'Evian' vote held everywhere except Algeria in April 1962. The Left, however, were not much concerned with legalisms either: in January 1961 they wanted a referendum on negotiations with the FLN, which was certainly unconstitutional.

[2] This term had been used in 1875 for the bill providing *inter alia* for the method of electing Presidents of the Third Republic.

But this time the sovereign people did not absolve the irregularity.

His emergency powers

Besides his formal and his prerogative rights, the President also holds the formidable emergency powers conferred by article 16, which he can invoke if two conditions are both fulfilled: first, there is a threat to the institutions of the Republic, the independence of the nation, the integrity of its territory or the fulfilment of its international obligations; and secondly, the regular functioning of the constitutional public authorities is interrupted. It was justified as a necessity in case of nuclear war, but also as a measure which in another 1940 would allow a President who went into exile to continue the struggle to do so as the unchallengeably legitimate representative of France. It has been used once, on 23 April 1961 when the four generals seized control of Algiers. The constitution required the President to ask (but not necessarily to take) the advice of the Premier, the presidents of both houses, and the Constitutional Council on the justification for invoking article 16 and of the latter body on the measures taken under it (the purpose of which must be to return as soon as possible to normal rule); the Council's opinion on the threat though not on the measures had to be published. After consultation which took thirty-six hours it found the conditions fulfilled, since the Algiers rebels had arrested a minister and the government's civil and military representatives, set up illegal courts, and aimed to seize power in France (a charge the generals denied). The 'regular functioning of the *constitutional* public authorities' was thus held to be interrupted even though government and parliament were meeting as usual, presumably because their decisions were not being carried out throughout French territory. This was a wider interpretation than had been expected in 1958, but at the time almost no one contested the applicability of article 16 to the putsch crisis.[1] The doubts arose later, when the putsch collapsed after four days, but the emergency powers were kept on for five months. For though the constitution-makers had carefully provided for the

---

[1] In a nation of *frondeurs* with an active and querulous legal profession, this was a remarkable indication of the strength and unanimity of feeling.

President to hear other opinions before using his discretion to invoke article 16, they had made no provision whatever for its termination. Indeed at an Elysée garden party on 29 June de Gaulle seems to have told some deputies that it would continue till the war was over; however, it led to unexpected difficulties with parliament and he renounced his full powers and declared the emergency at an end on 30 September.[1]

The powers were sweeping but their use was restrained; with the President already holding the special powers conferred by the bill of February 1960 and those he could wield in a state of emergency, the advantage of article 16 was mainly psychological. De Gaulle took eighteen measures (known as Decisions), eleven in the first two weeks and three to divest himself of his full powers; only four, therefore (all during June) were imposed during the period of 'phoney crisis'. Three of the eighteen Decisions (one to start and two to finish) were purely procedural; three set up special courts or gave powers to investigating magistrates; four dealt with arrests, internments, the suppression of certain newsletters, and the prolongation of the legal state of emergency (which normally would have needed parliamentary consent); seven allowed the government to purge the army, police and judiciary without the usual safeguards;[2] and one, mysteriously, provided for quicker promotion for brigadiers. Most of the Decisions incorporated an early time limit, the rest were to expire on 15 July 1962 (or earlier if parliament so chose; though under his 'Evian' powers de Gaulle extended most of them to 31 May 1963, and their effects of course continued, otherwise the rebel generals would have regained their titles and commands once the emergency ended). These Decisions were taken by the President in a legislative capacity and the Conseil d'Etat therefore held it had no jurisdiction over them. But it has examined the use made of these powers, notably in several cases of purged officers. In practice the dismissals were on very favourable financial terms, and most of them were for inefficiency, not for disloyalty. But one army officer purged for inefficiency won his case because his dismissal was not related to the events for which article 16 was invoked; and a number of policemen won (in a

---

[1] See below, p. 192.

[2] Including allowing it to post judges out of Algeria, despite article 64 which provides that judges are irremovable.

lower administrative court) because they had not been shown their personal files, because the authorities had not acted within the 'spirit and limits' of article 16, and because when the Decision was taken (8 June 1961) there were no special circumstances justifying such a drastic measure as allowing officers to be dismissed without the usual safeguards. The emergency over, the courts, as in other countries, have thus hastened to reclaim the ground ceded to the executive and even to challenge the propriety of the President's Decisions themselves.

The most unexpected problems, however, were posed by parliament. When article 16 is invoked it must meet and cannot be dissolved. April 23 was a Friday, four days before the ordinary summer session began. De Gaulle sent a message warning that the houses should not interfere with article 16 matters, and Debré would answer no questions on the President's use of his powers—though in the end he reluctantly acceded to a debate in both houses (having no way of stopping one in the Senate). At the end of their three-months' session the deputies showed no zeal to pass the summer in Paris just because article 16 was in force; they recessed but retained the right (or duty) to meet at any time. So when the peasant pressure groups urged the Assembly to reconvene, the President could not refuse as he had eighteen months before: crisis powers without a crisis were proving an embarrassment to the man who wielded them. Instead, therefore, de Gaulle wrote a letter to Debré saying that parliament, which met under article 16 only to help the President and government, could in these extraordinary sessions discuss nothing but article 16 questions. Both sides were now enmeshed in absurdity: the President had claimed in April that the deputies could discuss anything except article 16 questions, but now said in September that they could debate nothing else; the opposition wanted both to end article 16 and to hold the session which would have been impossible if their wish had been granted. When they met, the government said (truly) that its bills were not ready and those of private members were not constitutional; the Socialists put down a censure motion, and on 12 September all members but the Gaullists walked out of the house in protest. Debré wanted to allow the Assembly to debate the motion but de Gaulle would not;[1] the President

---

[1] P. Viansson-Ponté in *Le Monde*, 11 May 1962.

of the Assembly, Chaban-Delmas, had the embarrassing task of inventing a formula which would bar the motion of censure (to satisfy the President) without excessively exasperating the members. After a vain attempt to pass the buck to the Constitutional Council, who rightly declared themselves without competence, he evolved an argument which had no logical or juridicial merit but led to a politically tolerable compromise: no censure now but it could be moved in the ordinary session a month later.[1] De Gaulle's embarrassment was indeed acute: for if the opposition had been forbidden to propose a censure motion, the government could not have made the budget a matter of confidence, and might then have been unable to pass it; but now the government might soon be censured successfully and the President, unable to dissolve, would have to give way. Not surprisingly, de Gaulle announced on 20 September, the day Chaban-Delmas's ruling was published, that article 16 would cease to be in force at the end of the month.

The unchecked powers of article 16 were intended to ensure to the President the means of executing his duties in the realm of noble Politics, as defined in article 5: there he is made the guarantor of the country's national independence, fulfilment of her international obligations, and the regular functioning of her public authorities. This was the so-called 'reserved sector' for which de Gaulle felt special responsibility. The evolution of the regime, however, was soon to show that these high matters could not in practice be separated from the lowlier sphere of common politics, and that even within his preferred domain the President could not get his policy enforced merely by announcing it in public and expecting the government to carry it out. Especially but not only in Algeria, it became evident that it is often the execution rather than the original intention of a policy which determines its impact in practice. Even without a crisis of article 16 dimensions,

---

[1] He said: under article 5 the President may interpret the constitution (no: he must protect it); and can therefore decide how institutions operate while article 16 is in force (no: he must restore normal operation as soon as possible); consequently the presidential statements of April and September are authoritative, from which it follows (by a yet more dubious piece of reasoning) that a censure motion can be moved in an ordinary session but not when parliament is meeting at other times for article 16 purposes.

therefore, de Gaulle soon found that within the area that pre-occupied him he often had to short-circuit his own ministers and take direct control from the Elysée. But after 1962 everything changed. Already the original conception of a President responsible to no one, looming above the battle as the supreme arbiter, had given way in practice to that of a ruling President responsible to the people for the whole conduct of policy. Again, the end of the war allowed a broadening of de Gaulle's interests beyond the misnamed 'reserved sector' which had hitherto engaged his full attention; and indeed required it if the President was to maintain his political authority. This development was the easier because, with peace in Algeria and the departure of Debré, the cold war between President and Premier was ended and effective cooperation began. But there was no doubt which was the senior partner; more than once during the President's absence abroad the television news has blandly announced, 'In the absence of General de Gaulle there is no political news today'.

His officials, counsellors and ministers

The 'reserved sector'—foreign policy, defence, Community matters and Algeria—was first publicly defined by the President of the National Assembly, Jacques Chaban-Delmas, at the UNR's first conference at Bordeaux in November 1959. At the time everyone took it for granted that these were the areas where the President meant to lay down policy, leaving the government to act elsewhere. Later, however, Chaban-Delmas was to explain that he had meant something quite different: this external sector was 'reserved' not from the government and parliament but from the Gaullist politicians he was addressing, who were free to urge changes of policy on the government in other matters but expected to follow the President in these. In fact, however, even in these areas de Gaulle had a good deal of trouble imposing his authority on the governmental machine. In foreign affairs, where Couve de Murville never pretended to a mind of his own,[1] there was

---

[1] 'If only I were minister of foreign affairs', he is said to have remarked when de Gaulle, without having informed him, vetoed British entry into the Common Market.

notorious and prolonged resistance to the President's policies from the Quai d'Orsay which had for years been a preserve of ardent European federalists. Community problems provided matter for some bitter bureaucratic conflicts: MM. Lecourt, Jacquinot and Soustelle all claimed shares of authority in a field which interested the President, the Premier and, of course, the Ministry of Finance. Debré also sought to assert his primacy over the defence ministry, wresting from it control of the general staff: while on a lower level a ministry largely run by military officers had little sympathy for the President's changing Algerian policies and at times seems even to have sabotaged them.[1] Over Algeria, however, the resistance came from the top, since the Premier himself was plainly a most reluctant follower of his master. Rather than rely on such unwilling instruments, the 'paramount power' was driven in the end to give up 'indirect rule' and take direct control.

The decisive event was the barricades revolt in Algiers in January 1960. The President had laid down a general policy objective; the army and administration in Algeria accepted it on paper but counteracted it in practice; the European population resisted it openly and the official machine refused, until the President put forth the full weight of his personal prestige, to restore the authority of Paris over Algiers. Presidential *arbitrage*, until reinforced by presidential decision, spelt only impotence. Within a few weeks the major spheres of external policy—Algeria, the Community, defence—were each committed to a new organization, a presidential committee (*comité*) meeting at the Elysée with de Gaulle in the chair, and composed both of the relevant ministers and of the leading officials concerned, like the secretary-general of the Community or the chief of the general staff.[2] The only two

---

[1] No officers purged under article 16 were allowed to see their personal files—a manifest illegality which meant that the courts would reverse the dismissals. See Avril, *Le Régime politique*, pp. 227–9 on Debré and the defence ministry, 231–3 on the Community.

[2] There was also a committee for European affairs. When Algeria and the States of the Community became independent, the committees naturally lost most of their importance, but they still occasionally met. The defence committee, renamed council, was given the disposal of the French deterrent by a decree of 14 January 1964; the constitutionality of this arrangement was attacked by the opposition and defended by the Premier: *JO*, 24 April 1964.

ministers with any personal following in the country were dismissed, Soustelle for favouring the insurgents and Pinay, a little earlier, for opposing the General's foreign policy. In November the handling of Algerian affairs was removed from the Premier's office and put under a non-political minister, Louis Joxe, who was directly subordinate to the President. It was now Debré rather than de Gaulle who could express his distinctive view of Algerian policy only by occasional specific interventions rather than by continuous control.[1]

Under Debré the common politics of factions and interests impinged relatively infrequently on a President absorbed by the Algerian war and its repercussions abroad and in the armed forces. There were technician-ministers to carry out domestic policy, party leaders in the cabinet to broaden its support, and a Premier whose role sometimes seemed, as one Gaullist observer put it, to spare his master by serving as a whipping-boy, like the coachman of an eighteenth-century ambassador who had quarrelled with some other dignitary.[2] Consequently, as the *Canard Enchaîné* once put it, 'There's the President, and under him there's a vast void. And afterwards there is nothing. And below that, nothing. And then, nothing. But finally one stumbles over the government.' This was an exaggerated picture even during the war, and it soon changed in peacetime. The President always could take charge of anything he chose; even as early as February 1960 he set up a presidential committee on agricultural prices. With the end of the war domestic policy naturally came to command an increasing share of de Gaulle's attention. There never had been a 'reserved sector' from which the President was excluded, and after two years in office Pompidou could assure the National Assembly that neither was there any sector in which the government played no part.[3] Presidential *arbitrage*

---

[1] For example, the arrest and imprisonment in November 1962 of Abderrahmane Farès, one of de Gaulle's preferred intermediaries with the FLN and later head of the transitional government, on a charge of aiding the FLN to transfer funds from France to Algeria.

[2] L. Hamon in *Les Institutions politiques de la France* (Paris 1964: a discussion published, roneo'd, by the Association française de Science politique), p. 32.

[3] 24 April 1964.

gave way to a new system in which presidential government carried political responsibility. This new system brought about major changes in the presidential office, in the cabinet and in the Premier's role.

A ruling President needed a larger staff, and the Elysée came to house a team of assistants comparable to the White House staff in number, distribution of tasks,[1] and relations with the regular departments of state. Their total numbers (excluding secretaries and minor officials) rose from twenty-one in the Fourth Republic, when Coty succeeded Auriol, to thirty-six when de Gaulle still considered himself an arbiter of conflicts, and to fifty-two in 1964 when he had accepted his governing role. Their tasks changed too: in 1953 most dealt with matters of administration of protocol and only two with political questions; by 1959 the two had become thirteen and by 1964, twenty.[2] With the exception of three professors advising on educational and research matters, all were senior civil servants or diplomats. They digested the policy proposals put up by the Premier or the departments, followed ordinary administrative business, and prepared papers on any question in which he was taking an interest. It was not unknown for members of the presidential staff to be used almost as anti-ministers, preparing briefs and plans contrary to those of the ordinary department in order to provoke debate and enable the President to make an informed decision—as he did (in the department's favour) over Fouchet's educational reform. But this never became a systematic practice as it was over Algerian questions in the early days, and the President's staff probably wielded less personal power subsequently than they did during the war. In 1961 it was claimed that among the nine men to whom the President listened were only three ministers (one of them Debré) but four from the Elysée staff (one of them

---

[1] Except for the speech writer!

[2] There were also four political advisers dealing with the Community in 1959 (counted among the thirty-six); by 1964 this group was larger but outside the Elysée. (The President has a military staff of about ten officers.) The unofficial staff was about half as large again, making in 1966 a total of a hundred advisers: P. Viansson-Ponté in L'Evènement, 10 March 1966, p. 31. President Pompidou had twenty-two (civilians). We are also indebted to an unpublished paper by Nicholas Wahl.

Pompidou).[1] But over the years that staff, while increasing in numbers, changed in quality: many more were civil servants, fewer were old Gaullists, and most of the strongest and most independent-minded personalities left. The President disposed of more effective machinery for translating his policies into action, but that action took place through regular channels, not through a semi-occult rival government. Yet even in 1966 Pompidou seems to have thought Michel Debré less dangerous as the holder of the most powerful ministry than as an unofficial adviser with the ear of the President. Indeed, de Gaulle always reserved his real confidence to a small group of political counsellors who might or might not at any given time hold official posts on his staff or in his government.

There were also changes in the working of the cabinet. For many years the French cabinet has had two identities: the formal *Conseil des ministres* with the President of the Republic in the chair, and the informal *Conseil de cabinet* presided over by the Prime Minister, which dealt mainly with parliamentary business and political tactics. In the Fourth Republic two strong-willed Premiers—Pierre Mendès-France in 1954, and Charles de Gaulle in 1958—preferred to govern through the latter body under their own chairmanship rather than the former under someone else. But when de Gaulle became President and could no longer attend *Conseils de cabinet*, he showed less enthusiasm for them and the more dignified body became the effective organ of government.[2]

Accounts of cabinet meetings in the Fifth Republic show wide variations. Jacques Soustelle, who had never sat in a cabinet before and left after eighteen months to become a

---

[1] Eight of the nine (the ninth having become ambassador in London) were still among the twenty most influential advisers in 1966: *loc. cit.* Of the twenty, six were ministers, four present and six past members of the Elysée staff, and four politicians without governmental office. For 1961: P. Viansson-Ponté in *Le Monde*, 7 November. One was Jacques Foccart, secretary for African and Malagasy affairs: see below, p. 350n. It is said that he secured the dispatch of paratroops to Gabon in 1964 without even consulting the President. M. A. Burnier *et al, La Chute du Général* (Paris, 1969) p. 123.

[2] A *Conseil de cabinet* preceded all twenty of the *Conseils des ministres* held while the General was Premier, but only fifteen of the ninety-one held in the first two years of his Presidency: Avril, *Le Régime politique*, p. 242; F. Ridley and J. Blondel, *Public Administration in France* (London, 1964), p. 17.

bitter enemy of de Gaulle, has alleged that no discussion was allowed and ministers who wished to give their views were stopped from doing so. On the other hand Robert Buron, a minister with much longer and more varied experience, claims that cabinet debates on Algeria in the Fifth Republic were more vigorous than those on Tunisia or Indo-China in the Fourth, and that President de Gaulle was a more patient chairman than President Auriol; even more significantly, he records cases of ministers forming alliances within the cabinet in order to influence policy even over so burning a subject as Algeria. A President who chose to govern rather than to arbitrate would clearly have more need of a cabinet in which issues could be thrashed out; Pompidou is supposed to have managed his colleagues by tactfully checking verbose ministers and otiose discussions, but he has asserted that the President discussed every important question not only with him and the ministers directly concerned, but also in the full government. However, he has also admitted that the letter to President Johnson announcing France's withdrawal from NATO was seen beforehand only by the three ministers directly concerned.[1] All three, significantly, belonged to the little group of men with no parliamentary past whom de Gaulle preferred for the posts to which he attached most importance.

This group has markedly declined in recent years. Their peak came with the reshuffle of early 1960, just after the barricades affair when the President began to emerge from his arbitral role. Then men who had ever sat in parliament formed only half the cabinet; none of them (except the Premier) served on the new Algeria Committee; every major post—foreign affairs, defence, finance, the interior, Algeria—was held by their non-political colleagues; and every politician of weight in the country—Pflimlin, Mollet, Pinay, Soustelle—had left the government (as the *Canard Enchaîné* put it 'We too have a shadow cabinet, just like the British—only ours is in office'). But the politicians soon began a comeback, taking over the Ministry of the Interior in May 1961 and that of

[1] J. Soustelle, *L'Espérance trahie* (Paris, 1962), pp. 94-5, 97-8, 108; R. Buron, *Le Plus beau des métiers* (Paris, 1963), pp. 221-3, and *Carnets politiques de la guerre d'Algérie* (Paris, 1965) Part II, Ch. 1 and 11, especially pp. 119-20); Pompidou in *JO* 24 April 1964, p. 951 and 20 April 1966, p. 808. Over both the Middle East and Quebec the President's policies were highly personal.

Finance in January 1962. When Pompidou became Premier he compensated for his own lack of experience in parliament by bringing more of its members into the government: the proportion rose to three-quarters, and in the October election most ministers stood and won seats. The constitution obliged them to resign these seats to their substitutes in order to remain ministers but old habits did not change.[1] Ministers still thought of themselves as constituency members: Roger Frey published his Journal of the 12th Arrondissement and Robert Boulin, re-elected at Libourne at a by-election early in 1966 (his substitute had been killed in a car crash), publicly attributed his handsome majority in part to his constituents' gratitude for all he had done for the district since he became a minister.[2] By that time the non-political minister was a dying species and the few who remained were (apart from Malraux) required by de Gaulle to seek a parliamentary seat in the 1967 and 1968 elections.[3] The wheel had come full circle.

The officials had not always proved a great success as ministers, but essentially the change came about because the political circumstances had altered. In 1959 the political ministers belonged to parties which either had opposed de Gaulle in the past like MRP or CNI, or like most of the UNR professed both deep loyalty to de Gaulle and passionate views on Algeria where he intended to keep a free hand. He was obliged to turn to non-politicians to find men who could be relied on faithfully to execute his policies. But seven years later these policies constituted the governmental record on which a party could be built and electoral support could be sought. For much the same reasons, the second phase of the Fifth Republic saw the achievement in fact of that governmental stability which had been little more than a façade in the first phase. It was psychologically important that the same

[1] On substitutes see below, p. 208n.

[2] Similarly, in 1970 the Prime Minister, on the death of his substitute, stood again for his old seat—with a new substitute to whom he promptly relinquished it to keep his office.

[3] Jeanneney stood only in 1968, not in 1967. Couve and Messmer were beaten in 1967 but kept their posts, and won seats in 1968. Others who lost resigned.

Premier presided over the same government from January 1959 to April 1962; but in reality this apparent stability was misleading. The cabinet had no secure parliamentary majority, it was composed of parties which differed and factions which cut across party lines (on Church schools, for instance, as well as over Algeria). And in four and a half years, from de Gaulle's advent in June 1958 to the end of 1962, there were at least seven occasions when a Fourth Republican government would have fallen—about the same annual rate of crises as in the old days, though the symptoms of the disease had been successfully suppressed.[1] In the six leading posts (omitting the premiership and Algeria) the same number of men served as in the old days, though changing places rather less often;[2] and when in December 1962 the ninth Minister of Education was succeeded by the eighth Minister of Information he announced with pride that this marked no break in the stability and continuity so essential to the achievements of the new regime.

But after 1962 the stability was real, for the majority was solid and the cabinet united. There was little internal friction, except of course with the Minister of Finance (who did not belong to the UNR);[3] and only three changes before the presidential election, none of them for political reasons. When Pompidou at last fell, he had been Premier longer than any other Frenchman except Guizot. In the ten years of the Fifth Republic up to de Gaulle's retirement,

---

[1] The departure of the Socialists over economic policy in January 1959; of two senators over relations with parliament (though nominally on health grounds) in May; of the Minister of Education over the Church schools bill in December; of Pinay and Soustelle early in 1960; of three prominent ministers in August 1961; of MRP over Europe in May 1962; and of Sudreau over the constitutional clash of October 1962.

[2] Sixteen men were appointed to them in the first four years of the Fifth Republic, seventeen (on average) in four years of the Fourth; there were seventeen different appointments as against twenty-seven. The six posts were Finance, Foreign Affairs, Interior, Defence, Justice and Education.

[3] Under Couve in 1968 the usual feuding broke out again, with Debré and Marcellin (Interior) openly trying to block Edgar Faure's educational reforms.

three men filled the office; in eleven years of the Fourth, fourteen.[1]

His Prime Ministers

Above all the new Presidency meant a new relationship between Elysée and Matignon. The change from Michel Debré to Georges Pompidou helped this new relationship, for as de Gaulle remarked 'they acted with an evident effectiveness but each in his own way and their ways were not the same'. With a prodigious capacity for work and a large staff, at thirty-four equal in size if not quality to the President's, Debré could wield a dominant influence outside the 'reserved sector' and much even within it. Interested in everything, better informed on their own departmental problems than the ministers concerned, he prodded them constantly into action while insisting that they must communicate with the President only through him, and in some departments the 'super-ministers' on the Matignon staff acquired more real power than the minister officially in charge. Debré's influence thus steadily grew, whether in the choice of men, the organization of the government or the formation of policy. When the cabinet was reshuffled in August 1961 the decisions were his: Robert Lecourt was dismissed because of repeated conflicts with the Premier, Edgard Pisani was Debré's choice for Agriculture, Edmond Michelet was removed from Justice because he had dealt with FLN prisoners in a spirit closer to de Gaulle's Algerian policy than to Debré's, and Maurice Schumann was not brought in as the President had apparently hoped. The Prime Minister imposed his conceptions of military organization on a recalcitrant Ministry of Defence, and decided whether or not his ministers should appear before parliamentary committees which wished to hear them. He sometimes had his way even within the 'reserved sector'—the President once announced a shorter term of military service,

---

[1] From June 1958 to July 1968 de Gaulle's governments were reshuffled twenty-six times. From January 1959 when he became President, ninety-four men had served as his ministers. Five posts (including the premiership, the Foreign Office and Defence) had had three incumbents or fewer; fifteen had had from four to eight; Education eleven (one for four years, a record) and Information twelve.

which nevertheless did not come into force. He even imposed policies upon the Ministry of Finance, successfully insisting on increasing investments in backward areas. Indeed after Pinay's fall he was described as 'the real minister of finance and of social affairs'. An active and passionate reformer, he was both the instigator and the driving force behind the major administrative changes of the early years—in the government of the capital, the prefectoral system, regional development—and the main agent of progress in many sectors of policy: the Plan, scientific development, agricultural reform, public health. He also made a courageous attempt to settle the vexed and vexing problem of the Church schools.

His successor, totally different in temperament, dealt quite differently but no less capably with the President, with his ministers and with the problems of administration and government. Where Debré appears to have irritated the President by bringing huge piles of files on each of his irregular visits, Pompidou took no papers whatever with him on his daily calls at the Elysée—so that even their respective staffs had no idea what the two men had discussed and with what result. Where Debré would first seek instructions and then raise objections to them, Pompidou was said to try to anticipate de Gaulle's wishes and not to criticize his policies. On some questions, such as treatment of the North African refugees, the second Premier is believed to have won the President round to a different standpoint; and on the major issues he explained to the Assembly that 'I could not continue my task or bear my responsibilities unless I were and shall be in complete agreement on all the aspects of the policy which it is my job to carry out'.[1] It is believed that on a very few occasions he threatened to resign, and de Gaulle gave in. With his cabinet colleagues, too, relations were more regular and less stormy than under his predecessor. Cabinet committees,[2] with the Prime Minister in the chair, prepared the agenda for cabinet meetings at which there was genuine discussion. Unlike Debré, Pompidou did not try to prevent his colleagues appealing direct to the President. But naturally he endeavoured

---

[1] *JO* 24 April 1964, p. 951.

[2] Once called *conseils interministériels* to distinguish them from *comités* chaired by the President; later, confusingly, called *comités interministériels* while the President presided over *conseils*.

to save de Gaulle's time by bringing the rival ministers into agreement whenever possible, like the Sherman Adams of an active Eisenhower. In other words, as the President found that *arbitrage* was no substitute for direct decision at the summit, so the Premier, who influenced rather than made the major decisions, came instead to fulfil a useful role of *arbitrage* at a lower level.[1]

It was a role more suited to Pompidou's temperament than to Debré's. The latter is at once an ardent reformer and a determined defender of certain fundamental social principles, bringing the same passion to both kinds of cause; the former, more pragmatic, is as coolly sceptical about basic principles as he is about basic reforms.[2] Pompidou believed in letting his ministers run their own departments without excessive harrying from the Hôtel Matignon; unlike Debré he was neither keen on initiating new projects nor persistent in following up their progress and taking over direct control of them if necessary. Pompidou preferred to wait until inter-ministerial conflicts came before him to be resolved: *arbitrage* again. But this did not prevent him from extending his authority over large areas. Though his private office of twenty was much smaller than Debré's, its members served for a long period and often came to know their subjects quite as well as the ministers dealing with them. Moreover, their influence within the ministries was enhanced because support from the Prime Minister's office, if it can be won, is a valuable

---

[1] He also took over many of the President's ceremonial functions, 'opening the flower shows' on which de Gaulle said he had no intention of spending his time.

[2] Consequently Pompidou the sceptic was more willing than Debré, a defender of the sacred rights of property, to contemplate (say) municipalization of building land. On the contrast cf. P. Viansson-Ponté, *Les Gaullistes* (Paris, 1963), pp. 104–5 on Debré: 'His mission is clear: it consists in giving the regime its most harsh and unpleasant characteristics ... he takes on a mission of sacrifice, and he is fully aware of it'; and p. 169 on Pompidou: 'He knows that a political leader can be criticized for each of his acts, for all his decisions, for every reform, but that it is harder to complain against him for failing to reorganize the structure of the State or of the economy, for letting an awkward report slide quietly into the waste-paper basket. For him, reforms are like pears: when they are ripe they fall of their own accord.' For Debré's conservative side see below, pp. 252, 288–90.

and perhaps indispensable asset against the Ministry of Finance. Without that asset, the spending minister will quickly take the best compromise he can get; with it he will fight for his full claim. The Premier's *arbitrage* may thus sometimes be applied to a conflict he has had a quiet hand in promoting. Besides, some of the most important functions of government are not controlled by ministers but by senior officials, sometimes directly responsible to the Prime Minister: the Delegates for the Paris District and for regional planning (*Aménagement du Territoire*), or the Planning Commissioner, are quite as powerful as most ministers and more so than some.[1]

In their public attitudes, too, the two Premiers differed sharply. Debré paid more attention to parliament, partly because he had served there for years and believed strongly in its importance and partly because his majority in the Assembly was never secure. But his hold on it was weak, for in practice (though not in theory) he deeply resented criticism of acts and policies so patently justified and high-minded as his own. He was a bad party man, believing firmly that the administration should be kept (or rather made) free of political interference and that the UNR was entitled to no favours in return for its loyalty. And his public relations were appalling. Admirable in his Jacobin determination to resist all the pressure groups which had so often obstructed reform in the past, Debré characteristically reacted so excessively that he came positively to welcome his unpopularity as the one sure sign that he was right.

Pompidou, on the other hand, was sure in his early years of his parliamentary majority and could better afford, as he was more willing, to conciliate opinion outside; and his banking background and economic respectability made him more acceptable to business than the rigid Jacobin Debré had ever been. His one serious rival for the leadership of conservative opinion was Giscard d'Estaing, his able young Minister of Finance. But while businessmen condemned the government as a whole for interfering too much with the economy, they distinctly preferred the Premier's mild expansionism to the

---

[1] *The Times*, 2 Feb. 1966, on the career of M. Ortoli, newly appointed Planning Commissioner and later to become Minister of Finance.

finance minister's 'stabilization plan'. In parliament, too, the younger members of the majority and the former Left Gaullists criticized the cabinet and its head for being too cautious in social and too deflationary in economic policy. Michel Debré, once the UDT's *bête noire*, became with his critical speech on the Fifth Plan the virtual leader of this 'H.M. Opposition' until, in January 1966, he was appointed to succeed Giscard. Although at first he seemed almost a co-premier in *le ministère Pompidoublé* (as the *Canard Enchaîné* called it), the Ministry of Finance was no base from which to launch great reforms and the economic situation allowed only a limited shift in policy.

Despite minor frictions Pompidou's authority over the UNR grew remarkably during his premiership. At first his appointment was resented by a party of which he was not even a member. But he soon showed unexpected qualities. On television he was most effective, projecting the ordinary voter's favourite image of the sensible moderate conservative, balancing the budget, making cautious progress when the time was ripe, defending the currency, maintaining stable government and preserving peace. His mild and conciliatory manner, like that of an old-style Radical, mollified some of the wrath of dissatisfied strikers or farmers who would have been further enraged by Debré's intransigence. Pompidou proved equally skilful in parliament, winning approval among his opponents for such convincing performances as his defence of the government's controversial educational reforms. But he was no mere conciliator, and when he faced major political challenges in the Assembly he revealed himself a devastatingly aggressive debater, delighting his followers by routing even so formidable an opponent as François Mitterrand.

Pompidou's growing ascendancy was both affirmed and confirmed by hints that he was de Gaulle's preferred successor. Had the General chosen not to stand for re-election in 1965, few doubted that the Premier would have been the Gaullist candidate. But the choice was never officially made public, and from time to time de Gaulle took care to show that he retained his freedom of action—most notably when at the end of his Latin American tour in 1964 he at the last minute cancelled as quite unnecessary the final cabinet meeting Pompidou had been authorized to call in his absence. Pompidou showed no resentment at his somewhat uncomfortable situation, recognizing a dual responsibility: to the deputies who could remove him from office by a vote of censure, and to the President who could frustrate his tenure of it by refusing to sign any of his proposed decrees. But his influence in the government continued to grow, and in 1967 it was he who dominated the choice of parliamentary candidates and managed the election campaign. Early in 1968 opinion polls found him more popular, and in the crisis of May and June he seemed more effective, than the President himself.

That was unpardonable. In July he was dismissed and replaced by Couve de Murville. It had taken Pompidou over two years to establish his authority in the premiership; Couve held the office for less than a year, but this able civil servant and successful diplomat revealed none of the unexpected political talents of his predecessor, developed no style of his own, and never established his authority with the public, the party, parliament or his warring ministers.[1] The Gaullist party organization and parliamentary group were dominated by Pompidou men, and Couve had no personal following in either—though he became *ex officio* the rallying point of the President's ultraloyal followers against the open challenge of Giscard and the covert dissidence of the fallen Prime Minister. But with the General's departure it was Debré who became the recognized spokesmen of the ultras, and Couve vanished into the political void. His brief reign suggested that de Gaulle, hoping to find successful prime ministers in men with no political background, had been undeservedly lucky to pick a winner on his first try, and had, not surprisingly, drawn a blank on the second. At any event, President Pompidou went to the other extreme, choosing a professional politician of long experience, known guile, and proven acceptability to

---

[1] In *Les Gaullistes* (1963), Viansson-Ponté's list of 115 prominent personalities omitted the man who had then been Minister of Foreign Affairs for five years. After Couve had held the premiership for some months Claude Krief could write: 'The government scarcely exists as a centre of coordination and decision. Georges Pompidou had concentrated the reins of power at Matignon. Not a minister moved without his agreement. . . For almost six months now ministers have run wild, and the members of the government act in a quite uncoordinated way' (*Le Nouvel Observateur*, 16 Dec. 1968). Couve was perhaps further handicapped politically by a name which suggested (misleadingly) that he was an aristocrat by origin.

colleagues of other parties.[1] Bordeaux's deputy and mayor ever since 1947, Jacques Chaban-Delmas typified those Gaullists who had willingly settled for office under the Fourth Republic; his career suggested, and his appointments confirmed, that some old habits would now begin to creep back.[2] Whatever the new division of responsibility might turn out to be, Chaban-Delmas was unlikely to parallel exactly the role which Pompidou had been expected to play when, as de Gaulle had characteristically put it:

> Clearly it is the President alone who holds and delegates the authority of the State. But the very nature, the extent, the duration of his task imply that he be not absorbed without remission or limit by the political, parliamentary, economic and administrative round. That, on the contrary, is the lot, as complex and meritorious as it is essential, of the French Prime Minister.[3]

---

[1] 'He knows also that politics consists in relationships of force and that ... a politician counts only as much as the power-levers he can pull, the services he can provide and the trouble he can cause ... discreetly, without a fuss ... respecting the unwritten rules of the game' (Viansson-Ponté, p. 88, on Chaban-Delmas).

[2] He had thirty-nine ministers, eight more than the largest previous government in the Fifth Republic: de Gaulle began with twenty-four, Debré with twenty-seven, Pompidou began with twenty-nine and ended with twenty-nine, Couve de Murville had thirty-one. Chaban-Delmas, 13 years after the end of the Fourth Republic, had more ministers who had held office in that regime than any of his predecessors. His personal *cabinet* (private office) numbered eighty.

[3] Press conference of 31 Jan. 1964. In 1967 Pompidou, to save the Premier becoming bogged down in detailed management, appointed two more ministers of state (five in all).

A PARLIAMENT WITH A MAJORITY

Legal limitations

The Gaullists who came to power in 1958 believed that the overweening power of parliament was the basic cause of the weakness of the Third and Fourth Republics. France, in their view, needed above all a strong executive authority to meet international crises, combat disaffection in her empire, and carry out necessary reforms at home. Parliament was an obstructive and not a constructive force, incapable of throwing up effective or durable leadership and active only in defending established interests. The heart of the Gaullist programme had been, ever since the General's Bayeux speech in June 1946, the creation of a strong executive and the limitation of parliamentary omnipotence.

The President of the Republic, endowed with extensive powers at all times and unlimited authority in a great emergency, was to be chosen independently of parliament in a way devised to weaken the influence of the political parties. The Prime Minister was his choice, and ministers were not allowed to sit in parliament.[1] After the National Assembly had once given its approval to the composition and general policy of the cabinet, it could change its mind only by a formal vote of censure carried by a majority of its entire membership. The President could dissolve the Assembly whenever he chose, except during the twelve months following a dissolution (this limit ensured that he could defy a parliamentary majority but not the people, and that if he was disavowed at a general

---

[1] Every parliamentary candidate stood together with a running-mate or substitute (*remplaçant éventuel*) who took his seat if he died or accepted ministerial office. New ministers had to resign their seats within a month. A substitute could not contest his seat against his principal in the ensuing general election.

election, he had either to resign, or accept a government which could command a parliamentary majority). Parliament normally sat only for five and a half months in the year, for without the government's consent extra sessions were difficult to arrange in theory and impossible in practice. Subject to strict rules, parliament could question the ministers, who could make statements of policy to it—but (except on a censure motion) there could be no vote on these unless they agreed. Its standing orders needed the approval of the Constitutional Council, which prevented any escape from the new restrictions. It was no longer even the sole medium through which the sovereignty of the people was expressed, for during the session the President at the request of the government (or—improbable hypothesis—of parliament itself) could call for a referendum on certain bills. De Gaulle was to show that none of the safeguards prevented this formidable weapon being used to weaken the influence of the political parties.

These rules created and protected an executive authority which was still responsible to parliament, since in the last resort the deputies could remove it; but until that moment it could function without needing to seek their confidence, and it had alternative sources of political support in the Elysée and, it was expected, in the Senate. Ostensibly they established a constitution of separated powers, while allowing both executive and legislature the ultimate right to remove the other by dissolution and censure respectively. But the restrictions went much further, for they impinged on parliament's traditional prerogatives by organizing strict executive control over the programme of legislation. The most sweeping change of all, enshrined in article 34 of the constitution, prevented parliament passing laws on any subject not specifically enumerated there, and even on some of the enumerated matters permitted it only to lay down 'fundamental principles' and not detailed rules; everything outside this defined 'domain of the law' constituted a 'domain of regulations' where only the government could act and parliamentary encroachment was barred. While almost all areas of major importance were included within the domain of the law, the restriction was striking in principle and might occasionally have serious practical effects.

Another change, imported from Britain and embodied in article 40, denied members of parliament the right enjoyed by their predecessors to propose the expenditure of public money. Within the limits left to it, parliament's legislative authority was still further curtailed by the transformation of its procedure. Government business was now to have priority, except for question time once a week. Legislative committees, hitherto so influential in the law-making process, were reduced to six in each house and lost the privileged position they had hitherto enjoyed in debate. Entirely new machinery was devised for reconciling differences between the houses by means of a conference committee representing both: only the government could set one up or, if it failed, authorize the deputies to override the senators. In certain exceptional circumstances laws could be passed even without a positive vote by the deputies.[1]

These were drastic limitations on a parliament which had once predominated in the French State. But they were not entirely novel, for the Gaullist suspicion of parliament had long been shared in right-wing (and indeed some left-wing) political quarters, and even among the parties which ruled the Fourth Republic, leaders and ministers had gradually become convinced that some changes were needed to strengthen the stability and authority of the government. There were precedents for most of the legislative changes: for giving the administration a free hand on minor matters, for making it harder to upset the agenda, for allowing bills to be debated on the government's draft, for denying a separate vote on awkward details of legislation. Temporary delegations of legislative power to the government were frequent between 1934 and 1940 and after 1953. The upper house lost its power to obstruct in 1946. Parliamentary sessions were limited in length from 1954. The members' right to propose expenditure had gradually become so restricted that they were ready to give it up entirely even before the Fourth Republic fell. A new procedure, introduced in 1956, strictly limited the time taken in debating the budget. The new rules were thus in part the systemization of a process which had been going on in piecemeal form for a generation. But they went much further than this because of the outlook of their main author, Michel

---

[1] On these cases (emergency powers, confidence votes, referendums, etc.) see below, p. 229. The conference committee system was borrowed from Bonn.

Debré. He believed that a parliament could work efficiently only if, like the British, it was led and managed by the government; and that only formal rules, enshrined in the Constitution itself and rigidly enforced, could restrain the deputies from reverting to the bad old habits hallowed by the ancient tradition of parliamentary preponderance. This analysis rested on a political assumption: that France could never produce the disciplined majority parties which uphold governmental leadership in the House of Commons. The institutional checks, he declared, would be superfluous 'if only we had the possibility of calling into being tomorrow a clear and consistent majority'.[1]

Debré and his colleagues drew their new rules from many different sources: the Gaullist proposal for a strong President able to appeal to the people by referendum; the traditional conservative idea of allowing the executive to dissolve the Assembly; the procedural changes which had been accumulating in successive parliaments over thirty years; some weird devices, such as the package vote and the censure rules, which had been concocted by desperate governments in the decadent years of the Fourth Republic; the constitutional arrangements of Westminster and of Bonn. With all these varied weapons in their arsenal the Gaullists then acquired a loyal majority after all.

Deputies and senators: the first parliament

The new institutions showed at every point a deep-rooted suspicion of parliament and of the National Assembly in particular. The deputies, it was assumed, were incapable of disciplining themselves to sustain a government and were certain, unless restrained, to paralyse the executive in their efforts to control it. Minority parties, each indispensable to make up a majority, could therefore each wield a veto; in consequence obstructive tactics were facilitated and constructive action impeded. The Gaullists therefore weakened the Assembly by authorizing the referendum, creating the new Presidency, giving the government a dominant position in parliamentary proceedings, and bestowing greater prestige

---

[1] Debré, *La Nouvelle Constitution* (pamphlet, Paris, 1958), p. 10 (and *Revue Française de Science Politique*, 9.1, Mar. 1959, p. 17).

(though not power) on the Senate. The number of members in both houses was sharply reduced. France itself, with 20 per cent more inhabitants than twenty years before, had 130 fewer deputies and 50 fewer senators. There were 465 of the former and 255 of the latter (increased by five and four respectively in 1967 to allow for the growing population of the new departments around Paris). At first they sat with a strong contingent of members from overseas, but very few (17 and 19 in the two houses) remained after the 71 deputies and 34 senators from Algeria and the Sahara disappeared, by presidential fiat, two days after Algeria became independent on 1 July 1962.

The electoral law was, as we have seen, altered in 1958 with unexpected consequences.[1] It enabled the UNR to pre-empt a favourable position in the electoral centre, and to emerge as the strongest party by far in the first and third Assemblies, with very nearly a clear majority of the second, and a large overall majority of the fourth. Contrary to expectations, the new law did not protect sitting members against the wrath of the electorate; the 1958 Assembly contained a record proportion of newcomers, while in 1962 also a very large number of seats changed hands. The result was, as after other great French crises, a very substantial rejuvenation of parliamentary personnel.[2] In 1958, most unusually, there were more deputies under forty than over fifty, and in 1962 a fifth of the UNR members (but only a fifteenth of the others) were in their twenties or thirties. No other party had ever elected so many of its newcomers though many had put forward even younger men—for the UNR continued, sixteen years after the Liberation, to recruit nearly half its new deputies from the Resistance movement. Gaullist victories, however, hindered rather than helped a similar rejuvenation among the opposition which was forced back on the areas where its traditional strength lay, so that its younger men were hampered in finding winnable seats.

There were also significant changes in the occupational composition of the Assembly. The proportion of working-class

---

[1] Above, p. 67. It applied in France itself and in the overseas departments and territories (not in Algeria).
[2] Details in Williams, *The French Parliament*, pp. 32–4. Newcomers were much rarer in 1967 and 1968.

members was low at first, as Communist representation was sharply reduced by the electoral system (and by the electorate): in 1958 there were only seven worker deputies, the fewest since 1885. Peasant numbers were nominally reduced, but notoriously many 'peasant' deputies of past regimes had had only slender links with the soil, and many of those who replaced them were much more authentic farming types (especially the rural deputies from MRP, which for a time became the young farmers' party). Among the middle-class members who predominate in all legislatures, France had always had a remarkably high proportion of professional men and surprisingly few spokesmen of the great economic activities or of the administrative world. The great Gaullist incursion changed this picture, and brought in more businessmen, managers and administrators at the expense of the journalists, lawyers and teachers—though doctors flourished in the favourable soil of the single-member constituency.[1]

The new electoral law did not affect the Senate, which was renewed as a whole in April 1959, under a virtually unaltered electoral system which gave the decisive voice to local village councillors. The senatorial electoral college was adopted with little change for the Presidency of the Republic also (and a vacancy in that post was to be temporarily filled by the President of the Senate, now—after the President and the Premier —the third person in precedence in the Fifth Republic). For the constitution-makers of 1958 did not presume the senators to share the original parliamentary sin of the deputies, but rather regarded them as potential allies of the government. No doubt the main reason was that, having less expectation of office, senators had participated less feverishly in the struggle for it (to which Gaullists always attached exaggerated importance as a factor making for weak and unstable government). Moreover, Debré had been a senator for ten years, and on the issues which preoccupied him before 1958—first the struggle against the European army treaty, then the Algerian war— his colleagues with their permanent conservative and nationalist majority had taken up attitudes much more acceptable to

---

[1] Numbers for these seven groups in the 1967 (less Gaullist) Assembly were respectively: 50, 66, 30, 19, 47, 71, 51. There were 16 from other professions, 27 minor civil servants, 19 white-collar and 19 manual workers, 43 from agriculture and 26 miscellaneous.

him than the deputies. The Senate of 1958 was thus privileged in comparison with the Assembly.

These Gaullist expectations were very quickly disappointed. For, in the first place, the senatorial electors were those same traditional 'intermediaries' whose influence the Gaullists had so often deplored. They were predominantly rural: a majority of senators was returned by sixty-three departments which had only 40 per cent of the population between them, and a majority of senatorial electors came from the small communes (of under 2,500 inhabitants) which had less than 36 per cent. The towns of over 9,000, where the UNR was stronger, had 48 per cent of the population but less than half as many electors. Moreover, these local dignitaries were relatively immune to the popular mood, which in any case changed sharply between the November 1958 general election and the April 1959 vote for the upper house.[1] The new Senate therefore included few newcomers, few young members, and few Gaullists (never more than 40 out of 307). It at once emerged as the staunchest bastion of traditionalism in the whole political system.[2]

There were other reasons for senators' resentment against the regime. Unlike the deputies, they were not allowed to move a motion of censure on the government. Opposition critics were therefore more severely hampered than their colleagues in the Assembly when the Constitutional Council, more rigid even than Debré, ruled that the standing orders of the two houses must not allow any resolutions to be moved at all.[3] Before long the friction spread from matters of procedure to matters of substance. Senatorial conservatism over Algeria, which Debré had applauded in the past, became less welcome to him when with the utmost reluctance he himself followed de Gaulle along the winding path to self-determination and ultimate independence. Above all there was trouble

---

[1] Above, p. 68.

[2] But bills to reform its electoral system, introduced by both Gaullist and non-Gaullist senators towards the end of the General's term, were kept off the agenda by the government.

[3] Unless authorized by the constitution, like impeachment or censure motions in the Assembly, or internal to the house concerned (kitchen, library, etc.). Debré would have allowed resolutions to be moved but not voted on.

over agriculture. This was by far the most important domestic subject of legislation in the first parliament and the government's enlightened policy, though warmly approved by some of the younger peasant leaders, disappointed their elders.[1] The Senate has naturally always been susceptible to rural interests, because of its electoral system, and especially to the outlook of the older rural generation, because election by notables gave it a preponderance of old men.[2] There was a striking example in the debate on a bill to amnesty certain common-law offenders in 1966. Generously, they amended the bill to cover several offences omitted by the deputies: electoral fraud and corruption, spreading sedition in the army, insulting the President of the Republic, libelling ministers and foreign dignitaries. They removed from the amnesty one misdemeanour only: poaching.[3]

Besides being more predisposed to criticize than the Assembly, the Senate also had more effective opposition leadership. Some of the ablest opponents of the government lost their seats in the general election of 1958, but returned to parliament six months later as senators. They made of the upper house a better forum for debate than the turbulent, strident and intolerant Assembly, dominated by the raucous voices of the champions of victory at any cost in Algeria. But those deputies owed their self-confidence, if not their virulence, to their conviction that public opinion was with them. In this they were mistaken, for they had won their seats because the voters wrongly believed them to be loyal supporters of de Gaulle, the man who had saved France from civil war and could now settle the Algerian problem. When the President outraged the extremists by announcing self-determination for Algeria and then breaking the settler and military opposition to it, he earned their undying hatred but the gratitude of French public opinion; and, quite contrary to most expectations in 1958, seven-eighths of the UNR parliamentary party chose to follow de Gaulle, and the voters, rather than cling to the lost cause so many of their chief spokesmen had

---

[1] Below, pp. 291–4.

[2] Though at the time of the 1969 referendum its average age was just below that of the Assembly.

[3] *JO (Sénat)*, 24 May 1966, pp. 611–18.

once espoused. Moreover, though his right-wing opponents were willing to use any means and welcome any alliance to overthrow de Gaulle, his left-wing critics would not accept their overtures, fearing that if they won a victory in the Assembly and provoked a dissolution, the political crisis would encourage the army and its allies to strike.

There were in any case few issues on which the oppositions could agree: foreign policy, after the startling conversion of the extreme nationalist Right to friendship with the United States, was the principal one. But even on these few issues the government was secure against defeat until the end of the Algerian war. This was not because it was popular. Whatever their view of de Gaulle, most deputies detested Debré, who survived only because of the danger of military or political subversion. Their natural frustration was still further exacerbated by the rules so successfully devised to protect the government from the traditional forms of parliamentary harassing. The surprisingly large majority for the censure motion of October 1962—which had been expected to carry, but by nothing like forty votes—was a sign of the repressed resentment seizing its first opportunity to burst out.

Even the government's own followers were thoroughly disgruntled. The UNR deputies faced competition from the Conservatives, who appealed to much the same electoral clientele, not only over Algeria but on all domestic issues from the farmers' grievances to the problem of the Church schools. Although their rivals were well represented in the government and held the key finance ministry, the UNR found themselves deserted when distasteful responsibilities had to be faced, and the Debré government's first budget, drafted by a Conservative minister, was passed by UNR votes with more Conservatives against it than for it and more still not voting at all. Nor did the Conservatives ever clearly advise their followers to vote Yes in a referendum or support the government against mutiny and subversion from across the Mediterranean.[1] The brunt of defending unpopular government policies always fell on the UNR, and they had little encouragement in their task, since the austere Debré would not use government patronage

---

[1] Individual Conservatives of course did, but the party was split, and its general secretary (till 1961) led the anti-Gaullist wing (above, p.106).

in their favour and they had no certainty that President de Gaulle would give them any assistance at the polls. When the war ended in the spring of 1962, Debré was replaced by Pompidou and MRP was driven out by de Gaulle's sardonic mockery of their European faith at his press conference in May. The decision to introduce direct election to the Presidency, and to dispense with sending the bill to parliament, provoked all the various opposition groups to unite at last and censure the government.

The second parliament and the organization of the majority

The constitutional change aroused unexpectedly strong opposition among the deputies. But the senators were angrier still, for the government was violating the constitution in order to prevent them rejecting its bill. The opposition was therefore led by Gaston Monnerville, the coloured Radical from the West Indies who had presided over the upper house ever since 1947. In 1958 he had played an important part in smoothing the General's path to power; now he denounced de Gaulle's violation of the constitution and accused the Prime Minister—who bore the technical responsibility—of *forfaiture* (criminal dereliction of duty). This provoked a bitter feud with the President of the Republic, whose ministers thereafter appeared much less in the upper house to defend government legislation, often leaving that task to a junior colleague. Social relations were broken off between the Luxembourg and the Elysée, and it was now the senators' turn to feel insulted and aggrieved. They were restrained by their natural conservatism (and by fear of a constitutional referendum directed against them) from all-out and systematic opposition to the government, but in the second parliament it was fairly rare for them to vote a major controversial bill. The government therefore came to take their hostility for granted and to carry its measures over their heads.

Fortunately for the ministers, while the senators were making more difficulties for them, the deputies were making fewer. The Gaullists went into the electoral battle in 1962 expecting to be badly beaten, and only as it progressed did they gradually realize that their record of fidelity to the President and his government might prove profitable at the polls. Emerging with sixty extra seats, the UNR in the second parliament had a new motive for continued loyalty. The government set itself to consolidate this support. Pompidou was a less austere and a more conciliatory Premier than Debré. He flattered his followers by choosing his new ministers from their ranks; helped them to build support in their constituencies; and took pains to maintain close links with them by organizing the parliamentary party far more thoroughly than in the past.

The exclusion of ministers from parliament soon became something of a sham. At first many ministers had been 'technicians', and after 1960 those with parliamentary experience were second rank men in second rank posts. But Debré himself had halted this trend, and Pompidou now reversed it. After 1962 parliament again became the nursery of ministerial talent (though a very few new ministers still came from outside it). Members of the government behaved as representatives of their former and future constituencies as though article 23 had never been. They and their followers benefited outside parliament from the patronage which had been denied in the puritanical Debré era. And in the Assembly the UNR, taking over almost all the key committee posts, could ensure a hearing for its views on all legislation, so that the minority of ministers who unwisely omitted to consult the party in advance were likely to meet with difficulties on the floor of the house.

While the UNR members continued, like a British majority party, to vote loyally and usually solidly for the government, its rapporteurs by no means used their privileged position in debate to echo the official point of view. Louis Vallon on the budget and J. M. Poirier on the education estimates made more effective criticisms than the official opposition spokesmen; so from a back bench did Michel Debré on the Plan. Besides the open debates on the floor, the weekly party meeting offered an opportunity for vigorous if not always enlightened criticism—allowing Debré, for example, to launch a strong offensive against the bill to recognize conscientious objection, and to oblige the cabinet to dilute still further a proposal never marked by an excess of liberality.[1] The most effective influence of all was (again as in Britain) exerted in private. To bring a neglected topic to the government's attention, a UNR

[1] Below, pp. 288–91.

member could raise it through his 'subject group': some of these party committees existed only nominally but others were very active, notably the agriculture and labour groups (though the latter, dominated by Left Gaullists, was often out of line with the party as a whole). Through these or through the party leaders, a measure could be urged upon the government, or even taken up by the party as a whole and presented as a private member's bill with its official backing: both courses were sometimes adopted successfully. These party committees and the party meeting could be used as well as the official machinery of the house to block or modify an unpopular measure. If the minister would not make concessions, and if feeling was strong among UNR members, the critic could take the matter up with the party's *bureau politique*. If the criticism came from all benches it was expressed most readily, and with least recrimination between government and party, if it found expression through defections among the Independent Republicans—the thirty Conservative Gaullists whose votes were necessary to give the UNR a majority.

In these ways the UNR could exercise a discreet but effective influence on the government. It was able to get bills introduced, or modified before their introduction, or amended in the house itself, or postponed, or withdrawn and improved, or cancelled. This influence was not always successful and ministers sometimes behaved inconsiderately to their followers.[1] As such actions were public, while party pressure was generally exerted behind the scenes—and much more effective when it was—the public did not realize that it existed and sadly underestimated the importance of parliament in the new system; only when a major public row occurred, as over the value-added tax in December 1965 where electoral panic in the majority forced a major government retreat, did commentators observe (only to deplore) that the deputies still counted for a good deal.[2] At other times the UNR's 'unconditional' obedience was a subject of mocking misunderstanding. Gaullists, however, were justifiably proud of the

---

[1] For example by misusing their control of the timetable to rush bills through without proper committee discussion, and by abuse of the package vote (below, pp. 224, 226, cf. 243).

[2] Williams, *The French Parliament*, pp. 93–5. Much the same happened over death duties in 1968, though there was a big Gaullist majority and no election imminent.

responsibility and discipline with which they supported their leaders throughout the second parliament, of the impressive legislative programme they had enacted, and of the governmental stability which so clearly found favour with the electorate. For from 1962 to 1967 ministerial changes were few, and the government owed its security neither to paper defences nor to the fear of an explosion in the country, but to a real majority which saw its political future guaranteed by its loyal support.

These developments narrowed both the gap between members and ministers and that between ministers and the President. Satisfied now that he could count on parliamentary support in a normal situation, de Gaulle no longer needed the special powers and referendum appeals which, throughout the Algerian crisis, had maintained his authority at the price of demonstrating at every turn that the elected representatives of the people played no useful part in the regime. But the same changes left the opposition more frustrated than ever. They now had no chance of defeating the government, no rationalization of public duty to excuse their inaction and impotence, and no shred of hope that opinion would soon turn back to them: for although the President's popularity was brought to its lowest point by the mishandled miners' strike of 1963, it soon recovered and was shared, for the first time, by his ministers too. Opposition leaders therefore neglected the second parliament more than its predecessor. There were nine motions of censure and seven votes of confidence in the 1958 Assembly, two and none respectively in the 1962–67 parliament.[1] The deputies' obsession with making and unmaking governments had been successfully overcome, but some of them failed to find any other interest in parliamentary life.

Ineffective criticism

Gaullists did not often recognize that a high price had been paid for the genuine gains the new institutions brought, and that the discontent of the minority was not always—though it

---

[1] The figures for the 1967–68 parliament were to be respectively six and three; in the first four sessions of the fourth parliament there were one censure motion and one vote of confidence.

was often—mere nostalgic regret for the past. Some leaders of the old parties were still hoping for an impossible return to the old order of parliamentary supremacy and unstable governments, or still cherished Vincent Auriol's improbable conviction that 'where there are no cabinet crises there is no liberty'.[1] But this was not true of them all, and the defect of the new system was that it offered no useful role for the opposition, whether moderate or total. This was largely because the opportunity for constructive or damaging criticism was denied them by strict enforcement of the rules intended to protect the government from the harassing tactics of the past. When a majority of the deputies called for a special session of parliament in March 1960, in response to the clamour of the farming pressure groups, the President claimed that article 30 of the constitution entitled him to refuse.[2] When the government made policy statements to parliament, it always denied a vote and sometimes even a debate.[3] In October 1961, when the Paris police were accused of throwing dozens of Algerian demonstrators into the Seine to drown, the government staved off a senatorial inquiry by setting up a judicial one;[4] and made a statement to the Assembly to which the only reply allowed was given by one of its own supporters. In June 1962, 293 deputies—a clear majority of the membership—were driven to sign a declaration of support for the European policy which the government seemed to be repudiating, because they could not affirm that support by a vote in the house.[5]

---

[1] *L'Année politique*, 1959, p. 137.

[2] Article 29 provides that a majority of deputies (or the Premier) may call for a special session, and article 30 that the President signs the decree opening and closing it. These provisions were inherited from previous Republics but no one, before or in 1958, had ever suggested that they gave the President a veto. Cf. Debré, *La Nouvelle Constitution,* p. 5 and *RFSP,* 9.1, Mar. 1959, p. 11.

[3] Except on declarations of *general* policy: above, p. 208.

[4] Under an organic law, the second precludes the first. Its verdict, if ever pronounced, was never published.

[5] They could have moved a censure motion—but that would have provoked a dissolution which, three months after peace in Algeria, would not have served the cause of united Europe or the careers of its defenders. If the government had allowed a vote but threatened to dissolve on defeat, it would certainly not have had 293 opponents.

Debré had intended question day to be the occasion on which the opposition could express its criticisms, though not press them to a vote, in short debates rather like adjournment debates in the House of Commons. It wholly failed to fulfil this function—though the fault was on both sides. The vast majority of questions, from members of every party, were about limited and local or individual grievances. They were heard on Fridays, a constituency day for most members, and might be answered by a minister who was not himself responsible but merely read his colleague's departmental brief; in 1963 an attempt to stop these abuses was made by UNR members themselves, but was frustrated by the Constitutional Council.[1] In the Senate, which had more time and better opposition leadership than the first Assembly, and in the second Assembly when some experienced critics regained their seats, question day was more frequently used for debating matters of national policy. But though opposition questions were generally answered in the end, and sometimes very quickly when this suited the government's convenience, they could not be pressed at the moment when their authors felt that a debate would most embarrass the government. For the choice of which questions to call, and when, was in the hands of a business committee of party leaders, the Presidents' Conference; and while it sometimes stood up to ministers on behalf of the Assembly as a whole, in the last resort it reflected the majority in the house. It had, therefore, no reason to favour and every reason to frustrate the opposition's tactical manœuvres. Thus in 1963 questions on the wine-growers' grievances, put down before a by-election in a wine-growing area, were debated at length only after the election was over. In 1964 a debate on the government's control of television was allotted much less time than the sponsors wanted. In 1966, after the Djibouti riots, François Mitterrand put down a question asking why his question of three years earlier had never been called. Question day was an unduly neglected and potentially a moderately useful outlet, but the opposition could not control its timing, which in political warfare is often decisive. The only way the opposition could enforce a debate, at its chosen moment and with a vote at the end, was by a motion of censure. Yet when they did so in 1964, in response

---

[1] For details see Williams, *The French Parliament*, pp. 46–50.

to a direct challenge from a minister, Pompidou reproached them for using 'the supreme weapon' as a 'mere squib'.[1]

The new rules and the new majority had rendered it unnecessary for the government to make concessions even to those critics who shared most of its aims while regretting some of its methods. They made it difficult for other opponents, who had no hope of persuading ministers to use parliament effectively as a sounding-board for appealing to public opinion. As a result they fostered disillusionment, low morale and persistent absenteeism, which in turn further reduced the esteem in which parliament was held in the country.

Legislative efficiency

The opposition was discouraged because it felt impotent, and this feeling has not been assuaged by the working of the new legislative machinery. Here, however, the majority members at least could play a useful and an influential role, and effective government leadership and majority support allowed useful work to be done which was rarely possible amid the shifting combinations of Fourth Republican parties. Consequently the new parliament proved much more successful than the old as a legislative machine. The government could now get its business through with reasonable speed without stifling discussion (though it did try to avoid damaging votes, and the budget was usually rushed).[2] Minor government bills quite often passed the second Assembly unanimously, even the Communists abstaining or supporting them. Controversial measures could be carried without undue delay, though not without reasonable debate, even against the resistance of the upper house. The second parliament was thus able to build up an impressive record of legislation, which was continued in the third parliament during its short life. Though the achievements of the 1968 Assembly were fairly modest in its first four sessions, considering its huge Gaullist majority, this was due to the political hesitancy of the executive before and after

---

[1] P. Avril, *Le Régime politique de la Ve République* (2nd edn, Paris, 1967), p. 395.

[2] But frequently after bills had passed through parliament their implementation was long delayed by the government's own failure to publish the necessary decrees, e.g. below, pp. 292 and 311–12.

the General's departure rather than to any impairment of the legislative machine.

One of the main changes was in the timetable arrangements. The programme had, till 1958, been controlled by the house itself, acting with notable inefficiency through the Presidents' Conference. Now the government acquired the right to bring up its bills for debate at a time of its own choosing. This gave an opportunity for much better organization, but it also allowed the government, well protected by the rules, to display the same carelessness and inconsiderateness which once characterized the deputies. In the Fifth Republic as in the Fourth, both houses—especially the Senate—were still always slack at the start of a session and overwhelmed at the end.

With government legislation taking up nearly all the time of the houses, opportunities for private members were sharply curtailed: and were further diminished by the elimination of their right to propose expenditure, and by the restriction of parliament to a specified 'domain of the law'. But the deprivation was not unduly severe, for even in the past the financial limits were already strict and private members' bills were usually trivial, often intended for constituency propaganda rather than legislative result.[1] Most of these now fell outside the domain of the law, and the few that passed needed—as in the House of Commons—the government's goodwill or at least tolerance. Article 34 also eliminated much minor government legislation, and mainly because of it the number of laws enacted was halved after 1958.[2] This was sheer gain, for though these bills were usually uncontentious and took little time in the house itself, they did require the attention of rapporteurs and committees. In general article 34 was not interpreted unduly restrictively by the Constitutional Council.[3] In liberating parliament from a mass of trivial detail it enabled members to concentrate on the subjects that mattered, and rarely prevented them acting on any question of importance. Certainly it was far less damaging to parliament's work (or its

---

[1] Williams, *Crisis and Compromise*, pp. 261–6.

[2] The average in 1955–57 was 175; in 1959–65 it was 80. Of fifty-two laws enacted in 1959, only one had begun as a private member's bill; but in 1965 15 per cent had, and in 1967 22 per cent. In 1962–67 6 per cent of private members' bills became law.

[3] Williams, *The French Parliament*, pp. 58–60.

reputation) than the repeated abdication of responsibility by which in the past members had to authorize the government to legislate on any difficult and far-reaching problem; though such delegations of legislative power could still take place, they appeared—until 1967—to have become abnormal instead of commonplace.[1]

The discussion of bills was also more efficient than it had been, though much less so than it might be. Contrary to early expectations, few bills went to *ad hoc* committees set up specially; these proved unpredictable and subject to packing by pressure groups, though on some complex technical measures they worked well, especially in the Senate. Most bills went to the ordinary standing committees, of which the constitution allows only six in each house. Every member still served, so they were far larger than in the past;[2] in the Assembly four of sixty members and two of 120, in the Senate from thirty-five to sixty-eight. But members came only when interested in a particular bill, and the number of working members was not large (it never had been). Committee chairmen and (except by accident) rapporteurs on bills always came from the majority and usually from the UNR; their point of view often differed from that of the minister in detail and occasionally in substance. Opposition amendments were often accepted in committee, and on non-political measures of some social importance like the reform of the adoption law, the minister, the UNR and the opposition might work together amicably in improving a measure in a wholly non-partisan way.[3] But where the matter was one of serious political controversy, the Gaullist deputies steered a

---

[1] In de Gaulle's reign there were eight: two arising from the Algerian war; three (two of which were not applied at all and the third only twice) to allow the adjustment of French law to Common Market requirements; one (also not applied) on evacuating the Somali Coast if it chose independence; and only two which recalled the abuses of the past. These were the law against 'social scourges' (alcoholism) in July 1960 (cf. Williams, *The French Parliament*, pp. 85–9) and the socio-economic programme of 1967 (on which see below, pp. 231–2).

[2] Though the intolerant first Assembly ingeniously contrived to exclude Communists.

[3] Williams, *The French Parliament*, pp. 95–6. Not all ministers were so cooperative.

careful course—like British MPs of the government party—in trying to press criticisms on ministers without defeating them and damaging their prestige. As in Britain again, the ministers more readily made concessions in the privacy of a preliminary talk or a committee discussion rather than in the glare of public debate: hence the false impression that majority members were obedient sheep without views of their own. But the more effectively the government's supporters pressed their views in private, the less chance had its opponents of making an impact by their criticisms in the house.

The minister now piloted his own bill through the Assembly (but private members' bills were still introduced by the rapporteur in the form in which the committee redrafted them). Though the minister was entitled to rule new amendments out of order, he normally allowed them to be freely moved from the floor, and sometimes debates degenerated into a disorder recalling the bad old days, to the detriment of good drafting. One devastating weapon, the package vote, permitted the minister to refuse a separate vote on any politically dangerous clauses or amendments, and to settle their fate in a single vote on the entire measure cast in the form in which he was prepared to accept it. This enabled him to protect his own supporters against demagogic (or reasonable) opposition amendments which he was determined to resist. Intransigent opponents lost little by it, for they usually attacked controversial measures in principle rather than in detail, but it frustrated and exasperated moderate critics like the MRP leaders, who wanted to modify rather than to reverse official policy. For, whenever their criticisms found an echo in the ranks of the majority, the minister could keep his supporters solid by insisting that the bill could not be altered in detail but must be accepted or rejected as a whole. It is symptomatic of the spirit of the new regime that this powerful and dangerous weapon was wielded much more freely by Pompidou, whose majority was loyal and secure, than by Debré whose support in the Assembly was always somewhat artificial and precarious.[1] Had the Gaullist leaders really wanted an effective parliament with a real opposition, the political situation in the second parliament allowed them to encourage it by permitting amendments to their bills to be

---

[1] *Ibid.*, pp. 66–7.

freely moved and voted on. Instead they imposed much tighter limits, and insisted more strictly on minimizing the number of votes, than their predecessors who had some excuse for falling back on this protection. Invented as a substitute for the missing majority, the rules were enforced even more rigorously when a majority was found after all.

Whatever the frustrations of opposition deputies, those of the senators were worse still. New machinery for settling disputes between the houses was devised to strengthen ministers, who could let the Senate block bills they did not want but could support the Assembly in insisting on those they favoured. In the first parliament each house usually chose its seven conference committee representatives according to party strengths; as there were few Gaullist senators (forty was the maximum) and many opposition deputies, government supporters were in a minority. In the second parliament, therefore, the Assembly (though not as a rule the Senate) took to choosing its conferees exclusively from the majority parties. Even so, conference committees and both houses reached agreement on a compromise draft surprisingly often: forty-five out of seventy-eight times up to September 1968. But as irritation between the houses grew, these compromises became less usual and, even when achieved, were increasingly frequently rejected, especially in the Senate. Then, or if the conference committee had failed to agree, the government could call on the faithful UNR deputies to pass the bill without regard to the Senate. The proportion of bills carried in this way was only 1 per cent in the first parliament[1] but rose to 6 per cent at the beginning of the second and 16 per cent at its end: and they were, of course, the most controversial, and so usually the most important bills.[2] The draft

---

[1] In the Fourth Republic also the upper house was overridden on 1 per cent of bills passed into law.

[2] Of 829 bills voted up to September 1968, 751 were agreed without a conference committee, forty-five through that procedure, and thirty-three by the Assembly alone. In nine of the thirty-three the Senate opposed only a few clauses of a generally acceptable bill; on twelve it was obliged by a package vote to accept or reject a bill as a whole; on three the Assembly carried the measure only on a vote of confidence under article 49 (below, p. 229). The Senate, as its conference committee record showed, was more conciliatory than the government, and when ministers showed it ordinary courtesy it sometimes voted their bills.

submitted by ministers to the Assembly for a final decision might be the conference committee version, amended only with the ministers' consent;[1] they used this clause in a few exceptional cases, notably on the broadcasting and television law, to impose their own amendments on the deputies through a package vote and then force these into law against the wishes of the senators.[2] On non-political legislation, conference committees worked excellently to reconcile the views of the two houses and reach a satisfactory compromise without undue delay. Always they worked much more rapidly than devices used for the same purpose in the past. But on controversial measures their real function was usually to allow the government and its obedient majority to carry legislation quickly against the Senate, and occasionally to allow ministers to impose their own terms on the majority in both houses.[3]

The French budget had always been at once the great event of the legislative year, and the chief occasion for criticising government policy and administration. Consequently, until the procedural reform of 1956, it absorbed an enormous proportion of parliamentary time. That reform was replaced in 1958 by a new system, which gave much less scope to the finance committees of the two houses and tightened the time limits imposed on parliamentary debate. In practice the new rules, as one Gaullist critic commented, were applied to secure 'only one objective—speed'.[4] There were constant complaints of rushed and inadequate discussion, not least from Gaullist rapporteurs—met by official apologists by the reiteration of Debré's bizarre belief that the House of Commons disposes of the budget in one afternoon.[5] The spirit in which the government treated parliament is indicated by its decision in 1964 to present the budget on television before parliament had discussed it. Nevertheless the Gaullist

---

[1] It might also be the draft originally voted by the Assembly (with or without senatorial amendments).

[2] See Williams, *The French Parliament*, pp. 91–3.

[3] Article 49 provided a more spectacular device with the same object: below, p. 229.

[4] L. Hamon (and C. Emeri) in *Revue du droit public*, 80.1, January 1964, p. 81.

[5] *JO (Sénat)* 21 Dec. 1959, p. 1923.

rapporteurs were no tame creatures of the ministers, and budget debates were often very vigorous. The government, too, made concessions and accepted many amendments on fiscal matters, especially from the Assembly's finance committee.[1] The budgetary procedure of the Fifth Republic was much preferable to the chaos which sometimes reigned in the Fourth, though not to the reformed system invented in 1956.

Finally, in some exceptional cases laws could be made without the specific consent even of the deputies: first, if a bill was sent direct to referendum under article 11; secondly, if the President assumed unlimited emergency powers under article 16; thirdly, if parliament itself delegated authority to the government under article 38, to act during a fixed period on matters normally within the domain of the law; fourthly, under article 47, if parliament failed to reach a decision on the budget (hitherto an inordinate consumer of parliamentary time) within seventy sitting days, when the government could bring it into force by ordinance; fifthly, under article 49, if the government made a bill a matter of confidence, in which case it passed automatically unless a clear majority of deputies voted a motion of censure.[2] During de Gaulle's presidency 157 'laws' came into force without a parliamentary vote in one or other of these ways, while 884 were voted in the ordinary way. Of the exceptions, 70 per cent arose out of the Algerian war.

Missed opportunities

The new parliament sat for too short a period of the year to fulfil all its tasks adequately.[3] But the time at its disposal was greatly extended by its relief from three major burdens—the frequent government crises, the excessively long budgetary debates, and the load of petty legislation on matters of purely local or trivial importance. Yet because of the new rules, the spirit in which they were worked, and the opposition's discouragement and failure to adapt, parliament ceased

---

[1] P. Lalumière, *Le Monde*, 27–28 Oct. 1963.

[2] Article 49 was used seven times in the first parliament (in 1959 on the budget, and six times to force acceptance of a nuclear striking force), but only three times since—in 1967, on passing the government's social and economic programme by ordinances.

[3] In 1967 the sitting time was only 551 hours.

altogether to focus public attention and its members lost much of their status in the eyes of the citizen—or the administration. Morale was lower than ever before, and absenteeism worse. For, by protecting the government against the harassing operations of its opponents, the new rules had also insulated it from any effective criticism, so that neither senators nor opposition deputies could feel they were playing any worthwhile role in public life. The traditional politicians were slow to adapt themselves to the new conditions which so severely limited their opportunities. Those public men who differed from the government used the press and the platform much more than the tribune to express their criticisms. The pressure groups often turned their attention elsewhere (though they continued to operate in parliament much more than had seemed likely in the Algerian war period).

Ministerial supporters had the opportunity to press their views on the government and to persuade it, usually in private but occasionally by a public demonstration, to modify its proposals. But while they enjoyed about as much influence, and felt about as much frustration, as ministerial backbenchers in the House of Commons, their opponents were very differently placed. Like the opposition in Britain, they could rarely hope to convince the government; unlike it, they were usually foiled when they tried to use parliament to demonstrate the grounds of their opposition to the country. The package vote on bills and the restrictions on motions and questions prevented them forcing a vote, or even sometimes a debate, which would record their criticisms in the most effective way. The traditional methods of parliamentary operation were no longer available, and the new ones were strictly limited: no doubt the senior leaders of the opposition parties were remarkably slow to adapt, but it is surely significant that hardly a single newcomer from these parties made a parliamentary name for himself in the Fifth Republic. Several UNR deputies did, but even their reputation was limited to a narrow political circle, for the general public paid no attention to parliament at all. Its debates got little space in the press, members' prestige declined, and the people, who had once deplored the old 'bullfights', now ignored the prosaic activities of the new order.

But the government also failed to adapt, and its fault was the more reprehensible. For the new situation, more favourable—especially in the second Assembly—than the Gaullists

had ever expected, made it possible to test the reality of their
belief in a genuine parliament offering effective criticism. The
cabinet was secure against old-fashioned harassing tactics and
could carry its legislation smoothly and rapidly. These were
precisely the circumstances which Debré (believing them
unattainable in France) had said would make the procedural
rules superfluous. But instead of exploiting its formal advantages less, the government used them even more than before.
Against a feeble and sluggish opposition, the Gaullist leaders
displayed neither magnanimity nor statesmanship.

Yet the determined preparations by all parties for the 1967
election gave a clear indication that parliament still occupied a
key position. Outright victory for the opposition could have
paralysed the President himself, forcing him either to change
his government and his policies or to double his stake by a
dissolution—imperilling his own position if he lost. Even
limited progress by the opposition would hamper a Gaullist
government by endangering its legislation. On the other hand,
a third Gaullist triumph would install the regime for five
more years, and at last compel the old parties to adapt or
perish. The ambiguous outcome left the Gaullists with a
majority so insecure that they were tempted to lean more
heavily than ever on their procedural advantages. Pompidou
opened the new parliament by refusing to put his support to
the test of a vote on the statement of government policy.[1]
Next day he called on the Assembly for a delegation of powers
under article 38 to legislate by ordinance for a wide range of
social and economic matters—most of which had been
postponed until after the election to avoid losing votes, but
were now held to be of such compelling urgency that there
was no time for parliamentary debate. This resort to special
powers both put parliament firmly in its place and freed the
government from the need to fight one unpopular measure
after another through the Assembly on a wafer-thin majority;

---

[1] This broke the convention introduced by Debré in 1959 and
confirmed by Pompidou himself in 1962. Pompidou was sure of
surviving a censure motion which requires an absolute majority to
unseat the government, but he might have lost a motion to approve
his policy, where a simple plurality prevails. Owing to inept drafting
of the organic law, when Pompidou met parliament the Gaullists
were twenty-five votes below strength because neither the ministers
nor the substitutes who would replace them in the Assembly could
vote during the first month.

it was also a relief to Gaullist backbenchers, who were only too happy to let the entire odium fall on ministers—and a personal rebuff to Giscard, who had argued that parliament should have more say and now had to vote to give it less.[1]

Electoral success and the prospect of having the Gaullists in difficulties revived the opposition's interest in the Assembly. It returned to launch its most sustained debating attack on the government for several years, and at last showed interest in exploring the few procedural devices that standing orders left it for embarrassing the government. But it gained at best only modest fleeting satisfaction from minor coups like electing a hostile rapporteur for a government bill or rejecting the Assembly's supplementary agenda. Opposition enthusiasm waned with the realization that the public were unimpressed and that the government was far stronger than it appeared because of the reluctance of the Centrists to break with it. In the six censure motions during the fourteen months of the parliament, Pompidou was never closer than seven votes to defeat. Freed from so many potentially delicate votes by its resort to ordinances, the government put through its remaining legislation with little difficulty. Its few minor setbacks on the budget were rapidly cancelled by the package vote, though it was defeated on its bill to amnesty crimes committed in relation to the Algerian war—the sole issue to produce any significant breach in its supporters' discipline.[2] This easy

---

[1] Although the bill was sent to parliament under the urgency procedure on 27 April, the government did not bring it up for debate until 18 May and it finally passed on 16 June after two rejections by the Senate and three unsuccessful censure motions in the Assembly. Despite this leisurely 'urgency' procedure, the government was not ready with its ordinances: of the thirty-five taken before the law expired on 31 October, only four were issued during the first month. As under the Third and Fourth Republics civil servants seized the opportunity to push through a shoal of minor measures which had been gathering dust in ministerial pigeonholes. Despite government promises, the ordinances were not submitted for parliamentary ratification until the fourth Assembly, with its safe majority.

[2] The government found it far less difficult to muster its full vote than it should have done because the provisions requiring deputies to vote in person had fallen into disuse, and party whips freely pressed the electronic voting buttons on behalf of their absent followers. Even on the final censure motion against 'special powers' in 1967, eighty-one of 237 votes against the government were cast on behalf of deputies who were officially too unwell to vote personally.

passage also reflected the divisions and tactical ineptitude of the opposition, and with Centre support the government's followers who had at best a majority of one on committees, retained their near-monopoly of committee offices and all the posts of rapporteur for the budget. Mechanically at least the new procedures proved themselves in just the kind of circumstances for which they had been designed. But with so small a majority, the preoccupation of both sides with tactical sparring produced an atmosphere in which a more constructive parliamentary spirit could scarcely flourish. Finally the events of May brought the Assembly the double humiliation of being ignored as irrelevant by the processions of demonstrators, and prematurely dismissed by de Gaulle with the contemptuous valediction that it had been born with a 'vocation to be dissolved'.[1]

The 1968 electoral triumph offered a further opportunity to build a constructive relationship with the security of a safe majority. But the early sessions were overshadowed by uncertainty about both the regime and parliament itself. Although Monnerville was succeeded by the more conciliatory Poher as President of the Senate, de Gaulle would not now be swayed in his resolve to abolish the upper house in its existing form, with all the consequential upheaval in legislative procedure. Only after the rejection of Senate reform and the departure of de Gaulle did hope revive of 'normalizing' relations between the senators and the regime. Meanwhile, following Pompidou, Couve de Murville refused to seek the new Assembly's endorsement. The real struggle now lay once more within the UDR rather than between the majority and its scattered, demoralized opponents. The victorious but anxious

---

[1] Broadcast interview, 7 June 1968. Referring to 'the terrible crisis which occurred outside the National Assembly and is being resolved outside it', de Gaulle was almost as bitter about the government's supporters as about the official opposition. The Assembly 'had within it what was called a majority, but which in fact was not one at all . . . even when in censure motions it received the slender and vacillating assistance of a few groups or grouplets. And this majority was internally impeded by three-, four- or five-handed games of persons or factions which, as I say, constantly hampered it. As for the others, who were not the majority . . . they were absolutely incapable of getting together any sort of majority to form any sort of policy and, *a fortiori*, to support a policy which would not have been disastrous for the country.'

Gaullists were impatient for a greater voice in policy-making. Instead they had to accept the brusque deposition of Pompidou and imposition of Couve and to swallow the harsh budgetary backwash from May and unpalatable university and trade union reforms. No parliamentarian, the austere and unbending Couve could never arouse his supporters' spontaneous enthusiasm. Even with their huge nominal majority, ministers fell back on the package vote to carry an increase in death duties (emasculated by backbench pressure), and to reform the building permit system (opposed by an imposing crossbench syndicate of mayor-deputies). Though major measures were passed during Couve de Murville's brief premiership, bearing the detailed imprint of backbench amendments, this never produced a constructive understanding between ministers and their frustrated backbenchers. But Couve's successor as Prime Minister had served for a decade as President of the Assembly, pondering problems of executive–legislative relations from the members' side, and had repeatedly uttered discreet and ineffectual pleas for parliament to have more say. This may therefore prove to be an area on which President Pompidou's reign improves on that of his illustrious predecessor.[1]

Under de Gaulle, however, instead of a parliament which dominated the government and denied itself executive leadership, France had one which was subjugated by the government and provided little effective criticism. As usual in her history, the reaction against past abuses brought equal and opposite abuses in their place. It was legitimate before 1962, and perhaps understandable in 1967–1968, that new rules which protected the government against all imaginable dangers, should seem a necessary insurance against a return to the old vices. But from 1962 to 1967 and again after 1968 the security of the cabinet was fully guaranteed by a loyal majority, and it had a chance to work the new system in the most favourable conditions. It would have run no substantial risk, though it might have suffered some tactical inconvenience, in allowing freer votes and more effective criticism in the Assembly and even in the Senate.

---

[1] An opinion poll by SOFRES in November 1969 found parliament's prestige much higher than in the Fourth Republic (or than expected) with 52 per cent (as against 36 per cent then) finding it 'very' or 'fairly' useful, 15 per cent (against 27 per cent) harmful.

During the General's reign the opportunity was lost. In parliament, as elsewhere, the Gaullists preferred the short-term advantage of their party in power to the long-term objective of consolidating the Fifth Republic by making it acceptable to those sections of French opinion which had so far mistrusted both the regime and the men who made it. In so acting they behaved no worse than most politicians, French or foreign, would have done in their place. This would hardly be a matter for reproach, did they not claim for themselves, more smugly, more stridently and more frequently than any other party in the democratic world, a standard of political morality and public duty immeasurably superior to that of their rivals.

235

12

A TECHNOCRAT'S PARADISE?

The Central Government Machine

'The government has the administration and the armed forces at its disposal' (art. 20). The terms in which the drafters of 1958 referred to the administrative machine for the first time in any French constitution were clear recognition of the importance that the leaders of the Fifth Republic attached to it and their determination that henceforth it would be the instrument of the political masters. It was a brave assertion in both the context of the Algiers insurrection and the longer historical perspective of relations between the politicians and the civil and military servants of the State. Long before France had democratic institutions she had developed an exceptionally capable, self-confident, powerful and centralized bureaucracy, exercising great responsibilities and attracting many of her ablest men to the service of the State. Bound together by similar background and training, they developed an intense *esprit de corps*, which flourished particularly in the prestigious *grands corps de l'Etat* which formed the administrative elite.

Such a powerful machine was not readily controlled by ministers clinging precariously to political survival. The bureaucracy became accustomed to accommodating itself to chronically weak political leadership, devising procedures which enabled the business of the State to continue, and at times resisting by bureaucratic sabotage encroachments which they considered improper—and by filling the policy vacuum on their own initiative, both for better (as over European integration and economic planning) and for worse (as with some of the most disastrous episodes in colonial policy). Long years of such conditions enhanced the civil servants' sense that they alone upheld the national interest amid weak and incompetent ministers, rapacious interest groups and quarrelsome parties; and encouraged an attitude that decisions were best left to a disinterested elite of experts, insulated as far as possible from political pressures.

Yet even the best-staffed bureaucratic machine cannot survive decades of political upheaval and unstable government unscathed. Fitful leadership was far more a frustration than an opportunity to civil servants concerned with efficiency and modernization. With ministers living largely for the short term, and parliament shrinking from the larger issues and steadily becoming less and less efficient, proposals for reform (particularly administrative reform) gathered dust in the pigeon-holes—a few escaping to be rushed through when ministers held special powers to legislate by decree. The preoccupation of so many politicians with trivia produced fragmentary legislation and disrupted orderly administration. The integrity of the administration itself was breached by the penetration of interest groups into ministries like Agriculture, undermining the traditional commitment to the national interest. Other ministries like Justice, War and Education became hermetic baronies committed to the corporate interests they were supposed to regulate.

Even in 1964 the higher administration was described as 'suffering from sclerosis, lacking in suppleness and homogeneity, its senior members disenchanted and sometimes bitter'. While the competition was as keen as ever for entry to a higher civil service career through the prestigious Ecole Nationale d'Administration, there were problems of recruitment to other senior posts.[1] The waning morale of the service arose partly from the simple failure to offer competitive salaries and partly from the policies and methods of the Fifth Republic itself, but there were also specifically administrative concerns. The 1946 civil service reforms, which had unified the civil service up to the middle ranks, had left its upper reaches splintered. Not only were the *grands corps* left intact,

---

[1] Quotation from A. Passeron, *Le Monde*, 11 March 1964. In 1962, out of 110 competitions for posts in category A (roughly equivalent to the British administrative class), thirty-nine attracted fewer candidates than there were vacancies, and for only twenty-eight was there significant competition.

but the new *administrateurs civils* who were intended to form a single *corps* had split into no fewer than twenty-two—the Ministry of Finance alone having five and Public Works three.[1] This typically French fragmentation hindered career prospects, hamstrung transfers between ministries, and perpetuated a maldistribution of administrative talent which produced chronic under-administration in certain ministries: while Finance attracted some 200 *administrateurs civils* over fifteen years, the inbred Ministry of Agriculture had only four. Particularism flourished within departments as much as between them: Education and Agriculture were so rigidly compartmentalized that their political heads presided over unruly confederations of sub-ministries.

Particularly since the end of the Algerian war administrative reform has been one of the regime's most recurring preoccupations and substantial achievements—with the aim of creating a machine which was at once more efficient and more firmly the instrument of the leadership's political will. There was a need, said Louis Joxe (Minister for Administrative Reform, 1962–68) 'to adapt, to simplify, and to coordinate; to eliminate duplication and to reorganize the excessive number of divisions'. Creation of a unified and potentially more mobile body of *administrateurs civils* improved the homogeneity and efficiency of the higher civil service. Most of the major ministries—Finance, Defence, Education, Labour and Public Health—underwent major reorganizations (though a much heralded 'merged' Social Affairs ministry lasted under a year).

The chain of command from ministries down through the prefects to the communes was both lightened and tightened, and a number of decisions were 'deconcentrated' from Paris.[2] Reorganization of the external services of most ministries brought with it, for example, reduction in departmental directors handling health matters from 376 to ninety-four. Since 1963 a standing committee on the efficiency of public

---

[1] *Administrateurs civils* are graduates of the Ecole Nationale d'Administration who do not pass out well enough for the glittering rewards of a career in the *grands corps*; this disparity in the prospects of the elite and their poorer relations has led to ENA being criticized as a 'lottery'.

[2] Cf. below, pp. 249–51.

services has accelerated the introduction of Organization and Methods techniques.

The attempt to increase homogeneity was important not only in terms of efficiency but also as a precondition of effective policy-making, particularly in ministries like Education, which had for decades been an assemblage of autonomous factions (primary, secondary, technical and higher education) ruthlessly defending sectional professional interests and chronically deficient in basic administrative skills. Employing too many officials to deal with too many *administrés*, it was further handicapped because 'coordination between branches does not exist and, worse still, it is impossible'. The ministry was incapable of planning an integrated educational reform.[1] Reorganization at the Liberation was abortive: the stranglehold of internal and external sectional interests was intensified under supine political control. Even under the Fifth Republic only the most determined efforts have breached its entrenched corporatism. First, in 1959, the ministry was pruned by creating Malraux's new Ministry of Cultural Affairs and a Commissariat for Youth and Sport. Though now more homogeneous, it required partial reorganization again in 1960, yet again in 1961 and, since there was still inadequate unity of outlook, still again in 1963–64, when a secretary-general was appointed as its permanent head to impose a unified policy. This resort to a single civil service head recruited from outside the ministry was in double breach of administrative traditions; it showed up the gravity of the problem—and was deeply resented. But the battle was even now not won. It was not until the upheaval of May 1968 and the arrival of Edgar Faure that the ministry was jolted into preparing a thoroughgoing educational reform—which owed far more to the minister and his *cabinet* than to the permanent officials. Faure abolished the new secretary-general but improved ministerial control; nevertheless the routine administration seems wholly unreconstructed, addicted to submerging schools in a constant stream of detailed instructions which inhibit all initiative, yet even mismanaging such basic functions as the timely

---

[1] G. Caplat, *L'Administration de l'Education nationale et la Réforme administrative* (Paris, 1960), p. 92. Cf. W. R. Fraser, *Education and Society in Modern France* (London, 1963), ch. 3.

payment of teachers or the organization of half-term holidays.[1] Education is perhaps the extreme case, an all but ungovernable ministry coping with an unprecedented expansion; by 1969 some 50,000 officials were responsible for almost 700,000 teachers and nearly 11,000,000 people in full-time education. But there are other examples like Agriculture where successive ministers have had to battle constantly against the vested interests and narrow conservatism of rival divisions and technical *corps*.

Cumulatively the Fifth Republic has an impressive record of administrative reorganization. The machine is today more responsive and efficient, though much still needs to be done to reform the *grandes écoles*, which are the gateway to the administrative elite, to improve the calibre of the lower and middle ranks, and to achieve a significant degree of decentralization. But it is easier to alter structures than attitudes. Despite the inventive pragmatism of the younger technocrats, the engrained vices of the French bureaucratic spirit have not been eliminated: legalism, mistrust, resistance to change. Far too many administrative reforms have foundered on the hostility of middle and lower-rank officials, whose natural tendency to resist has been encouraged by the political traditions of the civil service rank and file (often Socialist sympathizers), and further intensified by the repeated imposition of changes without either consultation or adequate explanation. The French conceive of authority as absolute, anonymous and monarchic yet egalitarian. This conception inhibits initiative and imagination at the lower levels, produces impersonality, suspicion and unhelpfulness in relations with the public, and can turn simple administrative transactions into a nightmare of form-filling and frustration. There are cases on record of registration officials who, unimaginatively enforcing Napoleonic legislation limiting the range of permissible given names, have driven parents to petition the courts for a ruling that it would not be 'contrary to French

---

[1] In January 1967 the ministry issued circulars to schools at the rate of three per day. At a time when the minister was trying to encourage schools to organize more sporting and cultural outings the department issued instructions on the administration of such outings. These required that whenever any group of pupils was taken out, the headmaster must approve, beforehand, a detailed proposal specifying times, routes and means of transport; that the person in

public order' to call their children Daphne or Marjorie.[1]
Yet at its best the system can rise superbly to the occasion—as
over the rapid resettlement of the unforeseen tidal wave of
800,000 refugees from Algeria in 1962–1963. The intractable
problem of narrowing the gulf between the best and the worst
is that the system suffers not only from the vices of all bureau-
cracies, but also from the specific weaknesses of French
society generally and of the Gaullist style of rule in particular.

Few occasions have been missed to bring the machinery of
State more firmly under political control. Initially, the issue
was one of sheer survival against soldiers and civil administrators in Algiers accustomed to acting as a law unto themselves. But at least the passing of French Algeria freed France
from the era of unmanageable colonial administrators which
reached back over more than a century, though occasional
scandals still show that tradition dies hard in the few remaining
overseas possessions. Domestically, the civil service *statut* was
revised in 1959, tightening discipline and reducing the
influence of the unions, whose grip on the network of joint
committees had been a major cause of paralysis in personnel
and organizational matters. Later legislation removed the
right of several groups of State employees to strike and outlawed lightning strikes in the public sector. Ministerial control
of nationalized industries was also tightened, on Debré's
principle that 'this new State must not grow up outside the
old State'.
    While the closer subordination of the administrative
machine to ministers' policies has alleviated some problems,
like bureaucratic sabotage, it has emphasized others. Government domination of broadcasting, formerly mitigated by the
need to consider the susceptibilities of all partners in multi-
party coalitions, has been exacerbated by unsentimental
exploitation on behalf of the single dominant party. Again,

---

charge must be armed with a nominal roll of all pupils, listing home
addresses and telephone numbers, and that he must have the telephone numbers of the school and the appropriate hospital. *Le Monde*,
12–13 January 1969.

[1] Even the courts have balked at Sheila and some of the Celtic names
favoured by Breton nationalist parents. Consequently some children
have gone for years with no legal existence for (e.g.) educational,
social security and income tax purposes.

though the prefect has long been considered the advocate within his department of the government of the day, he has usually operated within the restraints of a pluralistic party system. Now prefects intervene in elections and referendums on behalf of a single party to a degree unrivalled in recent decades—even chairing Gaullist meetings and contributing to party journals; in 1967 the UNR circularized branches to enlist their prefects' help in making up invitation lists to the party's conference.[1] Prefects have always been quasi-political animals, but since 1958 there has been a striking increase in the employment of other senior administrators in important and often politically sensitive tasks. While consistent with the emphasis on depoliticizing policy-making, this also reflects the naively cynical hope that the findings of disciplined civil servants will be received by the public as the work of disinterested labourers in the national interest.[2] In the end this politicizes the civil service rather than depoliticizing the issues. Within the administration itself, some anti-Gaullists found their promotion prospects dimmed, and a handful were dismissed for intolerable disloyalty over Algeria. But the civil service was never purged and a sizeable fraction of it showed continuing hostility to the regime with impunity. On the other hand not a few ambitious young civil servants in the same period achieved spectacular administrative careers by partisan loyalty. Moreover, a number of jobs which would once have gone to junior ministers were undertaken by civil servants, and all de Gaulle's governments included administrators recruited directly without election to parliament—notably Couve de Murville, an *inspecteur des finances*, brought from his embassy in Bonn to serve as foreign minister for a decade, and winning election to parliament only days before his appointment as Prime Minister.

This blurring of the traditional demarcation between the permanent and political elements of the executive contrasts sharply with the strict separation of the domains of parliament

[1] On the other hand the administrative reforms of the Fifth Republic have given the prefect more interesting and important 'non-political' functions, particularly in economic matters, than his predecessors ever had.

[2] Notable examples have been committees on wages policy (below p. 298), profit-sharing (pp. 303, 305) and the future of the nationalized industries.

and the government—in turn only one facet of the wider restructuring of executive-legislative relations from which the permanent administrators have benefited perhaps more even than their political masters. Civil servants are now unworried by parliamentary questions, intrusive private members' bills or awkward debates in an Assembly which meets less than half the year. Measures they draft which would have once been ignored, mangled or rejected by the Assembly have now a better chance of passing parliament unscathed or of by-passing it altogether by decree. And while the conventional administrator in his ministry still predominates, there is also the growing army of specialists dispatched to run the national-ized industries and the vast penumbra of parapublic bodies, to keep the ORTF docile, or to serve in ministerial *cabinets* or the influential entourages of Matignon and Elysée—vantage points from which, as the voice of their master or the gateway to him, they may wield great influence.[1] Thus the Fifth Republic, with its belief in hierarchy and depoliticization, its indifference to meaningful consultation, and its elimination of so many of the former constraints and interferences, has given many of its technocrats exceptional opportunities. The presence of the distinctly untechnocratic de Gaulle ensured that the regime could not be labelled neatly a 'bureaucracy' or 'technocracy'. But in the celebrated phrase it is better to know a single *inspecteur des finances* than ten deputies.

Yet while many administrators have responded enthusi-astically others have been less wholehearted. For if the civil service has been a beneficiary, it has also been a victim,

---

[1] In recent years an increasing number of senior posts have been held by graduates of ENA—of which Michel Debré was co-founder at the Liberation. A 1967 analysis of ENA's graduates showed that they formed 126 members of the Cour des Comptes, 115 of the 250 members of the Conseil d'Etat, 143 of 250 *inspecteurs des finances*, and 870 of about 3,000 *administrateurs civils*. Fifteen of twenty-nine *directeurs de cabinets ministériels* at the time came from ENA (but only seven prefects and two ambassadors). In 1968 the new minister for the civil service was himself an ENA graduate.

Both inside and outside the civil service there are critics of this trend to 'Enarchy' and of the training ENA provides. Most dis-quieting for the government was the widespread questioning of the school's training and of traditional French administrative values among ENA students after 1968. *Contestation* among the future administrative elite persisted even after moderate reforms.

whether of the General's penchant for sudden Olympian fiats, or of the habit of ramming through reforms without consultation. High officials have been well placed to observe the exploitation of the State machine for partisan ends, the excessive rewards to politicized careerists and the readiness to ride roughshod over such niceties as the constitution—all as offensive to professional ethics as to any personal political views.[1] Some have found that the ascendancy of Matignon and Elysée have left them further from the centre of decision-making than ever. It was said of Christian Fouchet, Minister of Education in the difficult circumstances previously described, that he ran his ministry as he did the delegation-general in Algeria in the days when it was invested by the FLN and the OAS; he went a whole year without a meeting with his directors-general. Other energetic administrators have been disappointed by the preference of so strong a regime for meretricious prestige projects, by its irresolute capitulations to vested interests, and by the timidity of so many of its reforms.

Even among the technician ministers, some of whom (like Couve de Murville and Messmer) have served long and faithfully, others (such as Cornut-Gentille and Boulloche) have reached their personal breaking-point and gone (subsequently to enter that 'futile' body, the National Assembly). Although few senior officials (outside Algeria) have actually resigned, the opposition counts such impeccable technocrats as Robert Marjolin (formerly of the Plan and the European Commission), Etienne Hirsch (ex-Commissioner-General of the Plan, former president of Euratom), and the secretary-general of the PSU, Michel Rocard (an *inspecteur des finances* who had served with the ministry's forecasting committee). Providing a more circumspect outlet for many senior civil servants, who form a high percentage of its active membership, the Club Jean Moulin has maintained a steady flow of influential studies of public issues over recent years. 'The best way I know of getting my senior civil servants to work over-time', de Gaulle indulgently called it. But it is also a notable break in the tradition of confining frank discussion within a

---

[1] The two ministers who resigned in protest against unconstitutional behaviour by the government, Pierre Sudreau in 1962 and Edgard Pisani in 1967, both came from official rather than political careers.

small, socially homogeneous elite. The insistence on reform, democratization and popular participation which runs through the Club's publications represents a recognition by some of the country's ablest technocrats that in a modern democracy technocratic efficiency is not enough.[1]

Planners dispose . . .

One field where the themes of technocracy, politicization and participation have combined controversially is planning. No administrative innovation of the Fourth Republic has been more widely admired and emulated than the Plan. Although its impact on the economy cannot be proved, much less quantified, there is no disputing the significance of its psychological impact in the postwar transformation of French economic attitudes. The Commissariat-Général au Plan was built up by Jean Monnet in the forties as a small devoted economic brains trust and planning staff to the government as a whole, co-ordinating and conceiving development plans rather than administering them as a conventional ministry, committed to the view that the State has an active role to play in directing the economy. In no bureaucracy will such a body carry intrinsic political weight. It was Monnet's great achievement to win the respect of ministries suspicious of interlopers and the major interest groups and then, exploiting to the full the freedom that political instability allowed him, to hold the ear of his political masters and enhance the political influence of the Plan beyond its inherent due.

Even without the advent of the Fifth Republic planning would have met new problems in the sixties—victim, in part, of its own success. Earlier plans, dominated by reconstruction and the development of basic industry, had limited objectives determined largely by circumstances. As prosperity increased priorities became less self-evident, while the scope of the Plan expanded into areas where choices are more complex and more controversial. This became obvious with the publication of the Fourth Plan in 1960, with its transparent intellectual debt to Galbraith. In attempting to formulate a path for the French

---

[1] At Neuilly in 1965 the voters at one polling station, nearly all senior civil servants and their families, were far more hostile to de Gaulle than in the rest of that bourgeois suburb.

economy which postulated not simply a certain rate of growth but a particular pattern of growth, the planners rejected the 'affluent society' in favour of priority for social investment and the less favoured sections of the community. They were, in fact, moving from narrow technical preoccupations to the basic issues of social policy.

This inevitable politicization has been enhanced by the natural desire of the Fifth Republic's more stable governments to subject the Plan to their own priorities and make it the centrepiece of economic policy.[1] Recent Commissioners-General have been more conventional civil servants than their predecessors, to the detriment of their personal standing and reputation for political neutrality. The able Pierre Massé (1959–66) was used as a trouble-shooter in a number of contentious issues, and also appeared in the compromising role of 'professional' defender of the government's controversial decisions over the content and handling of the Fifth Plan before the Economic and Social Council and the Assembly. His two immediate successors were both appointed straight from Pompidou's entourage. One ex-commissioner-general (Ortoli) became a minister; another from an earlier period (Hirsch) spokesman on planning for the shadow-government. Yet the success and prestige of the Plan have lain less in its technical virtues than in its psychological effect, which owed much to the ability to command support even from political opponents of the government of the day by its eclecticism and reputation for standing slightly apart from the government, while wholly loyal to it. Though perhaps inescapable, politicization has weakened the Plan's wider appeal.

As the Plan's implications expanded, so 'democratic planning' became a major political theme. Formally an impressive

---

[1] Although de Gaulle called the Fourth Plan a 'burning obligation', it is indicative, not mandatory. Pisani even claimed once that 'excessive rigour in carrying out the Plan's programme is scarcely desirable'. It is not easy to evaluate the Plan's performance fully because of the inadequacy and imprecision of its reports. However, the Fourth Plan was 'corrected' by Giscard d'Estaing's 1963 stabilization programme and the Fifth Plan, which was already behind schedule in May 1968, required further correction to deal with the consequences of the Events and subsequent settlements. The tendency for the scope of the Plan to outrun available techniques and data has tended to make 'accurate' planning increasingly difficult.

network for consultation has always been provided through a network of commissions and working parties for specific areas of economic activity, the work of the Economic and Social Council (ESC) and since 1964, the Commissions de Développement Économique Régional (CODER) set up for the Fifth Plan.[1] The number of civil servants, outside experts and spokesmen for interests involved in this consultative structure now runs into several thousands. But there is more to consultative democracy than elaborate machinery. Up to and including the Fourth Plan the system operated reasonably well despite the drawbacks of inadequate union representation. The planners learned from the flow of specific expert comment, and could in turn reach and influence a significant element in industrial opinion. Through the commissions and the ESC the groups felt that there was a genuine dialogue in which they had some influence, without the integrity of the Plan being undermined by corporatism. But this relationship was impaired by repeated *faits accomplis* over the Fifth Plan. Pompidou would not let the ESC's Planning Commission undertake preliminary studies as Debré had done to good effect over the Fourth Plan, and would not pass on to it the calculated alternative Plans which would have enabled a full examination of the real range of policy options. Later the ESC had only a month to report on the Plan's major policy objectives—and almost no account was taken of its labours. The final Plan was published without waiting for the principal commissions to present their reports—necessitating some embarrassing recalculations when the Manpower Commission discovered some of the Plan's figures were wrong. Similarly the CODER were given only a few weeks to carry out their studies of the regional implications of the Plan, and were in turn left feeling little notice had been taken of their views.

Ironically, ministers justified rushing these consultative stages by the need for more time for democratic debate in parliament. The relationship between parliament and the Plan was generally admitted to be unsatisfactory. The First and Third Plans were never debated, the Second Plan was discussed only when it was more than half way through, and the Fourth Plan (1962–65) was debated at length several months after coming into effect—too late for parliament to

---

[1] See below, pp. 251–3.

have more than a minor impact. However, Pompidou promised to associate parliament closely with the conception and execution of future Plans. He hailed the 1964 debate on the main policy directives for the Fifth Plan (1966–70) as 'the first time in history that parliament has been consulted over the main options', citing this as proof of the 'fundamental collaboration between the executive and the legislature'. But parliament was simply called on to endorse or reject a brief motion approving the Commissioner-General's report, with no possibility of amendment. Several growth rates were mentioned as possibilities, but only the one the government favoured was worked through in detail—curtailing the chances of an informed debate about the range of options open to the country. Although the Fifth Plan was the first to receive parliamentary approval before coming into force, parliament's influence on the final draft was minimal: it passed without amendment under the package vote procedure. The weakening of the influence of the country's economic representatives in the ESC had been compensated by no more effective participation by its political representatives.[1] The reality of quiet if limited influence by the groups had been superseded by an illusory appearance of wider consultation. A senior official of the Plan, who has also served on the ESC, criticized discussion of the Plan for 'its non-credible and useless character in which dialogue is reduced to shadow-boxing'. The call for 'democratic planning' has everywhere proved peculiarly difficult to translate into reality, but the handling of the Fifth Plan marked a narrowing of the effective debate at the very moment when the Plan's social significance was broadening. Unless ways can be found of making the dialogue more meaningful, the enthusiastic involvement of the interest groups must be in doubt. Even in technocratic terms, little has been gained by transforming a process which tried to promote wider consensus about the country's economic goals into a simple assertion of political authority.

---

[1] While Pompidou's boast can reasonably be set against the reality, this implies no illusion about the amendments deputies would have voted given the chance: parish pumpery dominated the debates, and few attempted an overview or sustained critique. Constructive parliamentary participation in the Plan is in fact far more difficult than either Pompidou or his critics allowed.

Regionalism and democracy

Nowhere has the challenge to rethink and innovate been greater than in the relationship between Paris and the provinces and local government. Here reform not only meets the inevitable resistance of established authorities but runs up against fundamentally differing conceptions of authority and the State. The ninety departments inherited by the Fifth Republic were with minor exceptions as the Constituent Assembly created them in 1790. The map of the communes was much as it had been laid out in the Restoration of 1814— which generally reproduced the parish organization of the eighteenth-century Church—and the rules by which they were administered dated back to the early years of the Third Republic.

Traditionally the system has rested on the prefect in his department and the mayor in his commune. The prefect, established by Napoleon and successor of the *intendants* of the *ancien régime*, personifies the tradition of a strong central power controlling and invigorating the provinces. He represents both the authority of the State and the political will of the government of the day, the middle link in the chain of supervision of local authorities which stretches from the Ministry of the Interior down to the commune, and also the chief executive of local government within each department. The mayor, elected by his fellow councillors for six years, both acts as chief executive in communal affairs, and represents the State, serving as its agent in the numerous functions for which the commune is an instrument of the central power.

Even in its own terms, the traditional department-commune framework has long since ceased to function satisfactorily. Within the department the prefect's theoretical pre-eminence was eroded by the incurable centralizing tendencies of Paris, and by the proliferation for each ministry of provincial offices which communicated directly with Paris and the communes, bypassing the prefect. The outcome was contradictory policy-making and confusion, ministries clogged with trivial decisions and chronic delays: in 1963 40 per cent of new primary school places were being opened a year or more late because of administrative timelags.

Change was essential, and restoring the prefect's primacy

249

fully accorded with the administrative philosophy of the Fifth Republic: that a strong central power with its local agents well in hand can give them broad competence without danger. In 1962 an experiment was conducted in four departments to see whether the prefect really could be placed in effective charge of all the services in his department. This subsequently became one of the pillars of the 1964 administrative reforms. The prefect was now made the 'animator' and coordinator of almost all central government operations within the department. Though he was encouraged to delegate to the ministries' local directors, their authority was now held from him rather than from Paris. The ministries' external services and the prefectures were reorganized to bring them into harmony with the new structure. 'Deconcentrate' was the fashionable slogan, and a number of decisions on investment, school building, water supplies and rural electrification were transferred from the capital to the prefects. The aim, said Joxe, was to 'bring the administration closer to the administered, and bring authority and responsibility down to the provinces'.

However, the propensity of Paris to intervene dies hard. When the 1966 educational reforms were introduced, the accompanying circulars were said to 'bristle with prohibitions, rigid instructions and insistence on obtaining permission from Paris'. Despite the doctrine of giving local administrators more elbow room, 'the central authority ties them up in a straitjacket . . . which makes it impossible for them to act effectively unless they turn a blind eye to most of these orders'.[1] Changing *organigrammes* is one thing; altering the engrained attitudes of decades is quite another. Nevertheless, in 1968 further reforms allowed more decisions to be taken by prefects or communes without reference to Paris: the minister's permission is no longer needed to appoint an assistant lock-keeper or name a village street. Apparently even such modest changes alarmed some provincial civil servants, who preferred to be 'covered' by Paris. Then Edgar Faure's university reforms shook the grip on higher education of the most rigidly centralizing ministry of all, by extending a substantial measure of financial autonomy to the reorganized universities. However, in a country where the full cabinet still gravely deliberates on the summer holiday dates for every

---

[1] *Le Monde*, 14 Jan. 1965.

State school in the land, the need and the scope for still further decentralization are far from exhausted.

The triptych Paris–department–commune is challenged from still another direction. For over half a century the departments have had their critics. Too often they are too small for efficient policy-making and administration and too numerous (there are ninety-five) for effective control from Paris. Regionalism began developing under both Vichy and the Fourth Republic (which established eight regional coordinating prefects for emergencies and set up economic planning 'programme regions'). By 1958 almost every ministry had its regional network, a confusing patchwork ranging from the three air navigation regions to the nineteen educational *académies* and agriculture's forty *eaux et forêts* regions. Local initiative, notably in Brittany, gave birth to a number of regional committees for economic expansion, until the State felt itself compelled to intervene. In the growing debate about regionalism which followed, the issue lay between those who thought with Frey and Debré that the region would be primarily a device for more efficient administration, and those who saw in it a chance for broader participation in decision-making and for tilting the balance from Paris towards the provinces.

The inspiration of the first regional reorganizations of 1960–64 was unmistakably centralist. The country was divided into twenty-one planning regions, each with its regional prefect (doubling as prefect of a constituent department), responsible for economic coordination and certain decisions on public investment. Assisting him were a small brains trust of bright young technocrats, a coordinating Regional Administrative Conference of departmental prefects, and a Regional Economic Development Commission (CODER) —a sort of local Economic and Social Council, made up half of spokesmen for interest groups and a quarter each of government nominees and local councillors, giving its views on the Plan and public investment as they affected the region. Despite these strictly limited functions, the government was so apprehensive of the CODER exceeding their set role that it at first refused them funds of their own and put their meetings completely in the regional prefect's hands.

The change satisfied neither administrators nor democratizers. Regional prefects found their combined regional and departmental responsibilities onerous, while departmental prefects were suspicious of this new echelon cutting across their traditional direct access to Paris. The ambitious young men recruited for the 'brains trust' felt isolated and impotent. The twenty-one planning regions were widely criticized for being too numerous and illogically laid out. With only a quarter of the CODER members holding popularly elected office, many local politicians suspected that the government's aim was to use them to circumvent the democratically elected departmental councils, none of which were controlled by the Gaullists. CODER members complained that they were consulted very belatedly over the Fifth Plan, were forced to rush their reports, and then found little notice was taken of them. Though they were promised their own small secretariats and research budgets, and a greater say in future, even the moderate ex-premier René Pleven warned that without a thoroughgoing reform the CODER could have little future.

Though realizing that the 1964 reforms were incomplete the government was also aware of the suspicions of local politicians and of the bureaucrats' dislike of the disruption of established channels. It was also internally divided—like the opposition.[1] A thoroughgoing reform inevitably meant something more than a rejigging of the classic Napoleonic structure. To a traditional Jacobin like Debré any move towards strong regions was anathema: 'Those who wish to humble the nation seek first to humble Paris.' At the least regionalism would increase the antagonism between rich and poor areas; at the worst it could set up federalist or even secessionist tendencies which could imperil the unity of the entire nation. Debré had been arguing ever since the Liberation for scrapping the existing departments in favour of forty or so department-regions which could be controlled more efficiently from Paris —though they would be quite inappropriate for regional economic planning. But as so often he was eventually over-ruled by de Gaulle, who announced early in 1968 that 'the centuries-old effort of centralization which was so long

---

[1] However, perhaps because the opposition was relatively strong in the departments and isolated from power in Paris, the traditional Jacobinism of the Left had to a striking degree given way to recognition of the virtues of local initiative. The PSU and the clubs campaigned for 'decolonization of the provinces' and Mitterrand backed 'authentic regional authorities which will carry weight in the preparation of the Plan'.

necessary to achieve and maintain [national] unity . . . is now no longer indispensable'.

With the promise of greater 'participation' after May, regional reform was thrust suddenly into prominence. The government took the exceptional procedure of inviting some hundreds of local councillors, pressure groups, academics, cultural bodies, even clergy to make their views known through the CODER—producing a sort of monster national seminar on regionalism throughout the autumn. (This hopeful initiative was marred by the small account the government eventually took of the CODER views, and its resort to legislating by referendum, which ruled out fruitful discussion and improvement of its proposals.) The final scheme was much what might have been predicted before May. It rejected both Debré's forty department-regions, and the planners' proposals for eight to twelve regions based on existing departments; the existing regional map was retained intact (apart from splitting off Corsica as a separate region). The regional prefects gained a few new powers. New regional councils were to take over the advisory functions of the CODER and to be allowed to settle a number of matters hitherto decided in Paris —chiefly in town and country planning and investment in education, transport and communications, health services and tourism (though the lists bristled with exceptions). The councils were to be made up of roughly 60 per cent deputies and indirectly elected local councillors (in numbers depending on the region's population), and 40 per cent 'socio-professional councillors' (chosen by bodies representing farmers, industrial and white-collar workers, liberal professions, industry and commerce, families and higher education). This scheme rejected the ambitious proposals of the regionalists for independent regional executives and/or directly elected regional assemblies with the right to levy taxes. It added up to a cautious and strictly limited scheme of devolution, which was by no means as derisory as regionalist critics alleged, but did little to broaden 'participation' and roused little enthusiasm.

The problem, Couve de Murville said, was to 'put an end to the centralism which, carried to the excessive degree we have now, paralyses initiative, dilutes responsibility and puts a brake on development'.[1] But the protracted debate showed

---

[1] *Le Monde*, 25 March 1969.

how hard it would be to overcome both the traditions of centuries and the practical obstacles to extensive devolution. With the rejection of the proposals at the 1969 referendum, the problem went back into the melting pot once more. Apart from honouring one of Pompidou's election pledges by making Corsica a separate region, the new government's approach was slow and cautious: a fresh round of interdepartmental committees, then proposals for a limited experiment in regionalism from 1971. But with Pompidou showing little interest, and emphasizing decentralization rather than regionalism, the new regime's plans seemed to be more modest even than the 1969 proposals.

The local government tangle

Meanwhile, at the level of the communes, it has long been hard to dispute the unsuitability of a structure which reflects an age when France was still a peasant society. The problems have progressively deepened as the demands on local government have increased and become more complex, with industrialization, urbanization and the drift from the countryside. History has provided France with a system of communes which are too numerous, too weak and too inefficient to cope with modern conditions. With 38,000 communes, France has more basic local government units than all her five European Community partners and Switzerland combined, and the average population per commune of 1,276 is the lowest in western Europe. Only 32 communes had over 100,000 inhabitants in 1968, 50 more had between 50,000 and 100,000, while 35,000 had under 2,000 inhabitants (of which 24,000 had fewer than 500, and 3,500 under 100—all with their own mayor and *conseil municipal*). Rural depopulation continues to lengthen this 'tail' of deserted communes which nevertheless retain full powers and responsibilities. The system brings great benefits in civic involvement; over 400,000 people serve on local councils, and turnout in local elections is often higher in villages and small towns (but not in big ones) than in parliamentary contests. Practically and psychologically the *mairie* looms larger in the Frenchman's life than a British or American town or city hall. The determined defence of the tiny communes is more than a blinkered resistance by vested interests; it reflects the depth of the commune's appeal to loyalties and affections.

Yet, despite its closeness to the citizen, the small commune cannot meet even his most immediate needs. On the calculations of the Ministry of the Interior in 1964, more than nine communes in ten—containing a third of the population—lacked the financial and administrative resources to run adequate programmes of social investment efficiently. The 24,000 communes with under 500 inhabitants and annual budgets in the range £1,500–£3,500 were judged incapable of running even basic services satisfactorily. Traditionally the mayors of these communes have called on the village schoolteacher to act as part-time 'town clerk', but as rural schools close the mayor has to resort to retired postmen or *gardes-champêtres* to help meet his constituents' demands and discharge the many duties for which he acts as agent of the central government. In drawing up his annual budget he will often have to turn to the local tax-collector or the sub-prefect for advice. With little or no communal 'staff' for anything other than routine items he will have to seek the help of the central government's officials in the department. Yet theoretically the rights and responsibilities of the most impoverished hamlet in the Massif Central differ little from those of a wealthy metropolis like Marseilles.[1] The inability of the tiny communes to keep pace thus becomes a brake on progress generally, and not in the countryside alone, constantly impairing the efficiency and coherence of local administration and sustaining the tendency for national government to intervene.

As conurbations have sprawled across communal boundaries—there are 2,000 communes in the Paris region alone—difficulties of planning and coordination have intensified. While the demands on local government were becoming more exacting and complex the prestige and professional competence of their staff languished, for only a few large authorities could offer adequate training or careers comparable with the higher prestige and prospects of the central government service (transfers between local authorities being almost

---

[1] Practically the larger authorities have greater budgetary freedom. They also have their own trained staffs and carry greater political weight in Paris—though within their own departmental council they will usually be swamped by small rural communes.

unknown). Even the biggest authorities tended to be in financial straits as they struggled with the investment implications of the postwar 'baby boom', the relatively late emergence of urban growth, and an antiquated local taxation system dating back to the first world war (and a strongly entrenched tradition that local money should simply top off the shortfall in subventions extracted from Paris). The proportion of local authority income arising from local taxation was the lowest in western Europe.

By the fifties the local government system was not merely alarmingly anachronistic and a drag on social and economic change, but was actually undermining the very freedoms it was supposed to defend. The paucity and mediocrity of local administration had led to more and more matters being transferred to national government control, and was also invoked to justify the maintenance of detailed tutelage by the State over much of what remained. Moreover, the nominal margin of autonomy of the smaller communes was still further diminished by their close dependence on administrative assistance from the State even on minor matters. If the defence of local liberties was ever again to be more than a sentimental rallying cry it could be achieved only by creating local authorities with the financial, administrative, political and intellectual resources to conduct a dialogue with Paris.

Local government reform has thus been one of the Fifth Republic's continuing problems. Among its earliest measures was a 1958 decree (inherited from the Fourth Republic and originating in the civil service) authorizing the establishment in the conurbations of *districts urbains*—new multi-purpose joint boards of representatives of constituent communes, set up to handle specified lists of problems like housing, planning and public transport. This set the pattern for later approaches to the problem by superimposing a new structure without either superseding or abolishing the old one. In 1961 the Debré government moved on to tackle the problems of the Paris region—against strong political opposition. As Paris exploded outwards existing local government boundaries had ceased to reflect practical realities; the multiplicity of authorities was increasingly hampering the operation of existing services, while meaningful planning and development were all but impossible, as no single body could take the initiative. Drawing again on its Fourth Republic legacy the Debré government applied the *district* formula to the Paris area. However, the new *district de la région de Paris*, covering three departments with eight million inhabitants and responsible mainly for planning and development (again additional to the existing authorities) was perhaps not properly speaking an organ of local government at all. Although the District's board was drawn from members of local authorities in the region (half nominated by the government, ensuring Gaullist ascendancy), its chief executive was a delegate-general appointed by the government and directly responsible to the Prime Minister. Dealing with the graver and thornier problem of the small communes, the Debré government set its face against abolishing any existing entity, and opted instead for greater financial incentives for communes to merge voluntarily or form intercommunal syndicates to carry out specific functions.

None of these initial measures matched the extent of the problem, though the voluntary 'regrouping' of communes gathered sufficient momentum to involve one commune in four by 1968 (either in *districts*, intercommunal syndicates affecting nearly 9,000, or outright merger of almost 300 tiny communes). With the Algerian war over the Pompidou government returned to the problem. In 1964 it imposed a major reorganization of the government and administration of the Paris region and the District. The existing authorities were not consulted at all, doubtless because the Seine departmental council had an opposition majority and one of the unavowed aims of the changes was to weaken this hostile bastion. Effective from 1968, the reform created five additional departments, tracing their boundaries with manifest care to curb the political effectiveness of the Communist Party, and replacing the existing two-tier system of municipal and departmental councils in the department of Paris with a single elected assembly. This produced a considerable structural simplification and more efficient administration of the region, but did nothing to lessen the close control through the prefecture which has traditionally curtailed the effective self-government of the capital on the ground that the capital's special status as the seat of government and administration justifies a limitation of democracy.

Meanwhile the inadequacy of the *districts urbains* was increasingly obvious. Local fears, rivalries and jealousies were so intense that only a handful had been established and these found their effectiveness impaired by the difficulties of getting wholehearted cooperation. Consequently in 1966 *communautés urbaines* were created for Lyons, Bordeaux, Strasbourg, Lille, and optionally for any city of 100,000. Superseding the *districts* these were administered by 'super councils' elected by the existing *conseils municipaux*, and controlled most major questions, leaving the lesser ones with the communes. Inevitably the smaller communes, at the prospect of domination by their local 'metropolis', raised cries of alarm which were readily echoed by parliamentary conservatives of every hue. Less committed critics noted that the *communautés* were given no new sources of revenue. Yet the Plan was proposing an 80 per cent rise in local authority investment during 1966–70 for an increase in national income of only 27·5 per cent. No amount of shuffling of the organizational pack could succeed without local taxation reform. But though the existing system was universally considered inequitable and inadequate, all suggested changes were fiercely controversial. Reform, first promised in 1959 by the Debré government, was repeatedly delayed until the end of 1967, when Pisani's ambitious but politically hazardous schemes were rejected in favour of a cautious remodelling of the existing structure. Though useful beginnings were made with equalization measures for the poorer communes and dormitory areas, these only mildly alleviated the chronic financial anaemia of most communes. In 1968 the number of local authorities permitted to introduce their budget without the prefect's prior approval was raised from 646 to 3,083 (all over 2,000 inhabitants), thus removing a long-criticized brake on local initiative. Greater autonomy and heavier legal responsibility were given to mayors—to the annoyance of councillors jealous of the mayor's prestige. Overdue measures to improve the training and career prospects of local government officials were also introduced. Though insufficient in themselves, together these changes were a modest useful step in the direction of more effective local autonomy.

However, the problem of the tiny commune remained. Ministers had always resisted the urgings of the intellectual (and largely Parisian) Left to adopt a policy of compulsory amalgamations. The conservatism and political hypersensitivity of local political interests was such that ministers moved cautiously. It was only in March 1969, after lengthy consultations and airing of trial balloons, that a draft reform was published. This followed through the implications of earlier measures by consolidating a two-tier structure. Each department was to have its 'intercommunal cooperation plan', drawn up in consultation with the communes and the departmental council, dividing its area into *secteurs de coopération intercommunale* with a population in the area of 5–10,000. (This foreshadowed the disappearance of the *canton*, which was now of little but electoral importance.) All subsequent regroupings would have to conform to the new geographical outlines, to prevent the creation of 'unnatural' groupings or communes being frozen into impotent isolation on political grounds. The *secteurs* would have automatic jurisdiction over certain questions plus whatever the communes agreed to delegate to them. But the commune would remain to deal with minor matters and administration. The councils of the *secteurs* would be elected by the *conseils municipaux* in proportion to population. This paved the way for the emergence of 'super-communes', with the old communes either merging or lingering on as rather glorified parish councils, overturning the traditional commune–department basis on which so many local political power positions have traditionally rested. But for the transformation of local government to be complete, there would have to be at least a further reorganization of its financial structure—and this was promised only for the mid-seventies. However, with de Gaulle's departure the idea of a systematic revision of the local government map was shelved. The emphasis shifted back to financial incentives for voluntary reorganization and to allowing greater autonomy to the more viable authorities. The nettle of financial reform had still to be grasped. With elections in prospect for 1971, 1973 and 1976 the government was picking its way delicately. In the Fifth Republic, as elsewhere, modernizing local government is proving as intractable as it is politically thankless.

13

THE TRIBULATIONS
OF JUSTICE

Politics, subversion and the judiciary

Although the problems of the judiciary were overshadowed by more controversial issues in the constitutional debates of 1958, the Fifth Republic's heritage was as unenviable there as in the executive and legislative branches. The geographical distribution of the courts had scarcely altered since Napoleon's day. Judges were poorly trained and chronically underpaid, their career structure was tortuous, and recruitment was drying up year by year.[1] Harassed and unstable governments were incapable of tackling the long-term problems, and the circumstances in which the Fourth Republic decayed and collapsed had undermined the prestige of the judiciary still further.

In the new constitution the former 'judicial power' had become the 'judicial authority'. Though unnoticed by the general public the implied demotion was to rankle among the judges. In keeping with the general elevation of the President's status (but ironically in the light of later events), article 64 declared him the 'guarantor of the independence of the judiciary'. The High Council of the Judiciary was also transformed. Established in 1946 to oversee judicial promotions and discipline, the Council had had some success in reducing political influence

[1] The judiciary comprises both judges who sit on the bench (*magistrats du siège*) and the state prosecutors and examining magistrates (*parquet*). Some 4,100 strong, the judiciary is a separate profession with its own training and career structure. It is not recruited from among practising lawyers as in Britain and the United States. In 1956 even senior judges had salaries in the range £550–£2,200. The courts were notoriously ill-equipped; one judge was reported as relying on impounded typewriters to get his letters typed, and so many examining magistrates arrived at investigations late, on foot or by bicycle, that the Ministry of the Interior issued a circular to police suggesting that they might offer them lifts in police cars.

over judges' careers—even if, as sometimes alleged, professional sycophancy played an undue part in promotions instead. The reconstituted Council of eleven (instead of fourteen) now included the President of the Republic and the Minister of Justice, and nine others appointed by the President—two at his complete discretion, six from twelve nominees of the Cour de Cassation, and one from three proposed by the Conseil d'Etat. (Hitherto the judges had chosen four members and the National Assembly six.) While previously the Council had in effect appointed and promoted all judges, now it submits proposals for senior posts to the President for decision, and simply gives its opinion on the Minister of Justice's nominations to lesser positions. Presidential appointment was supposed to enhance the profession's prestige, but in practice political influence over promotions has increased under the Fifth Republic—most strikingly in the middle and lower grades.

One further constitutional innovation was article 66's proclamation that 'nobody may be detained arbitrarily'. Debré hoped that this would blossom into something akin to *habeas corpus*, but the necessary legislation was never introduced. Even after massive internments in Algeria had ended, suspects could still be held *incommunicado* for up to forty-eight hours (and sometimes longer), and once accused they might languish in prison awaiting trial for disgracefully long periods. Irregularities remained as hard to check as ever.

Hard on the heels of these constitutional changes followed a transformation of the judicial map. The 2,918 *juges de paix* were replaced by 454 *tribunaux d'instance*; above them, of 351 *tribunaux de première instance* only 176 survived as *tribunaux de grande instance*.[1] There remained 94 *cours d'assises*, one in each department outside the capital, 28 regional *cours d'appel*, and the Cour de Cassation in Paris. From hundreds of somnolent country courts judges were reallocated to the overworked urban tribunals; rural politicians were furious, but Debré promulgated the reform by ordinance and stood firm. He also improved the judges' pay, career structure and prospects to check the decline in recruitment. A Centre National d'Etudes Judiciaires was established, modelled on ENA, to improve the profession's competence and status—a hope

---

[1] These are civil courts. The corresponding criminal courts are *tribunaux de police* and *tribunaux correctionnels*.

disappointed as much by the 'exiling' of the CNEJ to Bordeaux as by its ill-adapted curriculum. There was also reform of the auxiliary professions associated with the courts, an enlightened extension of juvenile courts, and less liberal (but also less effective) changes in the penal code.

While they were.digesting this reorganization the courts also faced the graver problems of maintaining judicial standards in wartime. Colonial justice had long tended to turn a blind eye to irregularities. But from 1955 more and more Muslims on the mainland as well as Algeria recanted in court confessions allegedly extracted under torture. Although accusations of torture soon became standard FLN tactics, by 1957 (at the latest) few judges could have been unaware that there were grave presumptions that arbitrary internment, police brutality, torture and even summary executions were prevalent and spreading. Yet in trial after trial they listened impatiently to complaints of torture and police denials, then gave their verdict as if nothing untoward had been said. This contrasted with the patient search for truth in some 'civilian' cases (like the *cause célèbre* which culminated in the acquittal of Marie Besnard twelve years and three trials after her original arrest for murder).

By 1958 proceedings in Algeria were dominated by military justice—which, Clemenceau said, is to justice what military music is to music. On the mainland an increasing proportion of cases relating to the war came before military tribunals. When the judges were soldiers with comrades out in the *bled* fighting a viciously anti-French enemy, a guilty verdict became almost an operational necessity. Defence counsel vainly resorted to procedural technicalities which infuriated soldiers like Colonel Broizat, who believed that during the battle of Algiers 'true justice was done in 90 per cent of cases even if the parachutists did commit excesses in 80 per cent'. Colonel Argoud (himself to be a victim of irregular practices) boasted at the barricades trial that he had shot suspects in public after a drumhead court-martial.[1] Faced with the soldiers' tendency

---

[1] 'I would have felt I was failing in my job if I had applied legal justice', he said. Argoud alleged on oath that he acted with the full knowledge of his superiors, the cooperation of the *police judiciaire*, and the complicity of the Vice-President of the Cour de Cassation, who was also chairman of a commission to investigate allegations of torture. Cf. Comité Maurice Audin, *Sans Commentaire*, Paris, 1961.

to take the law into their own hands, the Debré government hoped to improve its control by compromising with them. It extended the jurisdiction of the military courts to all crimes directly or indirectly related to events in Algeria, accelerated trial procedures, lengthened the period before suspects need be brought before a magistrate (facilitating extended interrogations), and circumscribed rights of appeal over irregularities in the pre-trial stage, in the vain hope that the soldiers would agree to follow the new procedures.

However, the government tried to confront the torture issue. De Gaulle obliquely declared that it must end; Michelet denounced it; Malraux promised it had stopped. The government took up such notorious cases as Djamila Boupacha's. Many believed she had been tortured before conviction for complicity in terrorist bomb attacks. When the enquiry opened the military refused to transport her to the mainland, saying they had no funds. When the money had been found from private sources, systematic obstruction continued in other ways. Medical examination confirmed that Djamila Boupacha had been tortured, and the investigation suggested her conviction had been secured with the aid of perjured evidence, but it came to a dead end over the refusal of the Algiers military prosecutor (on express orders from the C-in-C Algeria) to produce either witnesses or documents.

Later, after a long struggle between the Ministry of Justice and the army, three conscript officers were brought to trial for torturing and executing two Algerians. But as soldiers they were tried by court martial, and although they admitted the facts they were acquitted; the military hierarchy was telling the civilians to keep off. Having failed twice, the attempt to stand up to it was now abandoned. Thus, although the murderers of Maurice Audin in an Algiers prison were known, they were never brought to trial. Later, on the mainland, fearing the police would go the way of the army the government did its own covering up. When the bodies of some seventy Algerians were fished out of the Seine after a demonstration in October 1961 the Minister of the Interior, Frey, saw to it that no official enquiry ever answered the public outcry.[1] Nobody was charged. Neither the executive nor the judiciary

---

[1] See above, p. 221.

could or would cope with repeated massive violations of proper procedures.

As Algerian policy took a more liberal direction, the courts had to cope with rebel officers and OAS terrorists. The system which had developed over the years for dealing speedily and incuriously with the crimes of the colonized was thrown into disarray when called on to try 'patriotic' Frenchmen. As early as 1958 the ringleader of an extremist gang which attacked the C-in-C Algeria with a bazooka was transferred to hospital, and predictably escaped to Spain. Similarly at the 'barricades' trial in 1960, the military court released the accused from custody and five promptly fled to Spain. These were the only ones found guilty; all those present went scot free. In the early trials of Algerian nationalists the judges had sternly refused to permit any examination of motives, but with the barricades trial and the Jeanson trial of FLN supporters, skilled counsel were allowed to give primacy to motives over deeds. Brilliantly unscrupulous defenders transformed the barricades trial into a sustained attack on de Gaulle's 'betrayal' of the army and the Europeans in Algeria. Both intellectual opponents of torture and later the OAS were thus able to turn trials against the government into an appeal to the wider public—with some success. Judges increasingly found that 'extenuating circumstances' justified leniency—though not for FLN sympathizers.

Following the 1961 generals' revolt, therefore, de Gaulle was determined to meet threats to the State with summary justice, even at the cost of infringing traditional safeguards. Acting under article 16 he authorized arrest without warrant and detention *incommunicado* for a fortnight, and even suspended the constitutional guarantee of 'immovability' for judges in Algeria, where some judges were notoriously partial towards the activists.[1] Determined to have no repetition of the barricades trial fiasco, the President set up a special High Military Tribunal to try such cases, composed of four senior civilian judges and five generals selected by himself. Procedures before the Tribunal were accelerated, the rights of the accused were limited, and there was to be no appeal from its decisions.

---

[1] The High Council of the Judiciary was at this time using posting to Algeria as a disciplinary measure. Protests by judges over the suspension of the constitutional guarantees were muted by their awareness of some of their colleagues' activities there.

The new procedure ran like clockwork from the trying and sentencing of ex-Generals Challe and Zeller within three days in June to the death sentence on the OAS second-in-command, ex-General Jouhaud, the following April. But in May 1962 skilful defenders turned the trial of the OAS chief Salan into an inquest on eight years of Algerian policy, and Salan was spared the death penalty because of 'extenuating circumstances'.[1] Forty-eight hours later the Tribunal was abolished by de Gaulle, having tried sixteen cases. In its place a Military Court of Justice was established by ordinance, with substantially the same jurisdiction. Under the Ministry of the Armed Forces (rather than Justice), it had a membership of five officers and five non-commissioned officers, none of them necessarily having legal experience. Its procedures were even more summary than the Tribunal's. People could now be tried within 48 hours of being charged (possibly after being held *incommunicado* for a fortnight); its president had greater powers to control the trial and decide whether evidence could be published—and no appeal from its verdicts was possible. France has a long and unhappy experience of special courts for political crimes, and disquiet mounted—especially in September when accelerated trial procedures and restrictions to rights of appeal were introduced in the regular courts for almost every crime in the penal code, again by ordinance, and against the advice of the Conseil d'Etat.

The Military Court of Justice began under a cloud with the suicide of its president. In its sixth case it sentenced the OAS treasurer André Canal to death for organizing plastic bomb attacks; he appealed to the Conseil d'Etat, which audaciously struck down de Gaulle's ordinance creating the Court on the ground that the situation did not justify a composition and procedure violating the basic principles of law guaranteed by the constitution. The government retorted that the Conseil

---

[1] An outraged de Gaulle was determined that Jouhaud at least should pay the supreme penalty, despite the incongruity of executing the subordinate while sparing the chief. Believing the execution would be a political blunder, Pompidou colluded with the Minister of Justice, Foyer, in inspiring an appeal which was transparently futile in law but forestalled the firing squad de Gaulle had ordered out. De Gaulle insisted he had personally created the Tribunal, and therefore knew there were to be no appeals. After a fortnight of grisly uncertainty, with Pompidou threatening resignation, de Gaulle capitulated and reprieved Jouhaud.

d'Etat was exceeding its proper role and encouraging subversion, and that its judgment was 'worthless'. It asked
parliament to approve the creation of a permanent Court of
State Security to deal with crimes against the State. Although
the new court of three senior judges and two generals had
better procedures and allowed appeals, its principle was
furiously attacked. De Gaulle, said Mitterrand, had '*his*
television, *his* government, *his* majority, *his* referendum, *his*
nuclear strike force ... now it seems he wants *his* justice'.
But Mitterrand proposed no convincing alternative.[1]

The bill included a clause retroactively validating the
ordinance establishing the Military Court of Justice, which the
Conseil d'Etat had annulled. Reluctant government supporters
accepted this as an essential piece of unimportant bureaucratic
tidying up—but once it was safely adopted the government
sent the authors of the Petit Clamart attempt to assassinate
the President before the resuscitated Military Court of Justice
rather than the new court from which they could have appealed.
Defence counsel attempted procedural obstruction until the
old Court's life expired, but the government rushed a fresh
bill through parliament prolonging its life until it finished
current business: the revivified Court did its duty, and the
chief conspirator was shot without a chance to appeal—the
fourth and last of the OAS executions. By now the OAS was
a spent force, its chiefs in exile or prison. The only major
row associated with the new State Security Court was over
ex-Colonel Argoud, an OAS leader previously convicted *in
absentia*, who was kidnapped by French special agents in
Germany and dumped for civilian police to collect in Paris,
to the annoyance of the Germans and in defiance of international law. Subsequently the Court worked its way through
the remaining 350 or so lesser fry in a series of uneventful
trials, and has since been employed mainly to try spies, and
autonomists from the overseas departments. Even in quieter
times, though, it has not wholly dispelled the fears which
attended its birth.

It is scarcely surprising that the Algerian war and its sequels
were an unhappy period for French justice. It is easy enough
to maintain the independence and integrity of the courts
when they are dealing with drunks and housebreakers,

infinitely harder in cases arising from the central issue dividing society and threatening the State's very survival, bringing exceptional pressures both on the judges and within their own minds. As *procureur-général* Besson said during the Challe-Zeller trial, 'I am fed up to the teeth with people talking as if soldiers are the only people with crises of conscience. Do these professors of virtue really believe that we are immune from them?'[1] Inevitably too there is rarely agreement over the criteria and procedures to apply to specifically political crimes. The unhappy handling of certain political cases by British and American courts during and since the war is a reminder that the problem is not peculiarly French. Nor was responsibility for the failings of justice during the Algerian war solely the judges'. It rested with the President, that 'guarantor of the independence of the judiciary' who made and unmade courts at his pleasure; with the executive which failed to support the judiciary against military obstruction and itself repeatedly interfered with the course of justice;[2] with the bar which failed either to oppose energetically the hampering and harrying of defence lawyers by the authorities or to curb the discreditable excesses of the committed advocates of FLN and OAS defendents, who cost all accused persons a restriction of their rights; with the press and the public for their initial indifference which allowed abuses to become established, and for their partisan condonation of injustice when inflicted on opponents.

Police and administrative abuses

Undoubtedly the judiciary's isolation contributed to its

---

[1] Besson in fact later resigned as the government's chief legal adviser in 1962 when procedures in the *cours d'assises* in OAS cases were changed by ordinance, refusing to 'cover by my silence a doctrine in which debate appears to be robbed of the place of honour due to it in a democracy'.

[2] One small instance: M. Rousselet, first president of the Paris Cour d'Appel, reprimanded the police for their behaviour in the Palais de Justice during the Salan trial. The Prefect of Police protested, but M. Rousselet refused to resign. Thereupon a decree reduced the retiring age for judges from 70 to 67, with immediate application to judges over 68½. M. Rousselet was just 68½. The decree was promulgated 'in the interests of public order' under special powers granted by referendum to implement peace in Algeria.

unhappy showing. So, too, did a long-standing weakness in the system—its inability to devise adequate remedies for irregular *actes de police judiciaire* at the pre-trial stages. During the Algerian war several members of the *parquet* became specialists in FLN and OAS cases, and some were notorious for their blindness to the physical conditions of those they were questioning.[1] Complaints over the conditions of interrogation and detention in political cases had availed little from the 1948 trial of Malagasy nationalists onwards. When, exceptionally, three policemen who admitted using electrical torture on Algerians were tried (*in camera*) in 1961, they were fined a mere ten pounds apiece. Again, newspapers were repeatedly seized and formally charged with either 'sedition' or 'demoralizing the army' after they had published material embarrassing to the government. Such charges were almost invariably pigeonholed, leaving publishers arbitrarily fined by the loss of an entire issue without even a chance of their day in court. Only when the war had been over for several years was partial redress found for this deliberate and systematic abuse of the machinery of justice—and then by the Conseil d'Etat rather than the ordinary courts. With only rare exceptions the courts failed almost completely to grant effective redress or even to sound the alarm over widespread violations of basic rights.

Even after the Algerian war the courts dealt with police misconduct with surprising leniency. A policeman convicted in 1966 of faking evidence against a man accused of murder (who had had to wait three years in jail to be tried) was granted 'extenuating circumstances' and given a suspended sentence with a small fine. In the Ben Barka Affair of 1965–66 a Moroccan exile politician was kidnapped and presumably murdered in Paris just at the start of the presidential election campaign; for more than two months, illegally but on government orders, senior police officials concealed from the examining magistrate how quickly they had discovered that

---

[1] The unhealthy close relationship between police and examining magistrates is a long-standing general criticism of the French system. However, in political cases the authorities have ways of influencing the selection of a particular examining magistrate, who will know where his 'duty' (or promotion prospect) lies, and they can get cases sent to certain courts which specialize in specific types of case, and which are composed of 'reliable' men.

two of their subordinates were implicated.[1] Police violence at demonstrations is virtually never punished—or even publicly regretted—no matter how gratuitous. Such incidents nurture the uncertain image of justice and the antagonism to the police which derive from both underlying French attitudes to authority and unfortunate historical experience.

Possibly judges reason that in political cases trial and sentence are rarely the end of the story. Pardon and amnesty are traditional epilogues. Very few FLN and OAS prisoners were executed. All the FLN prisoners were released in 1962 under the Evian agreements, and when, after a series of amnesties and presidential pardons, the final remnant of OAS prisoners were released in 1968, none had served more than eight years, and most substantially less. Those who had evaded arrest escaped scot free. Again in 1968 normal procedures were brushed aside when those arrested in the riots were released on government orders or immediately amnestied. While this political expediency very roughly compensated for the arbitrary violence of the riot police (also covered by amnesty), it neither lessened the temptation for policemen to beat up prisoners just to make sure, nor enhanced the prestige of the judicial system.[2]

During the sixties the malaise in the judiciary deepened. Recruitment dropped from 380 candidates in 1953 to 98 in 1964, well below the danger mark for the future vitality of the profession. The traditionally circumspect Union Fédérale des Magistrats (UFM), which had spoken of the 'disintegration' of the system in 1964, grew steadily more forceful in its protests. Even so a new Syndicat de la Magistrature was formed in 1968 to press more vigorously still for reforms. An unprecedented meeting of all sections of the Paris judiciary

---

[1] Cf. P. M. Williams, *Wars, Plots and Scandals in Post-War France* (Cambridge, 1970), ch. VI. His kidnappers may also have been Argoud's.

[2] Customarily the authorities reject or ignore even the most circumstantial corroborated complaints of police excesses, but in May 1968 the Paris Prefect of Police admitted in a memorandum not intended for publication that demonstrators had been beaten up at police stations. But no disciplinary action was taken, and he confessed that even his mild admonition might be 'taken badly'. In 1969 he happily announced that there had been 'only' nine clashes between police and journalists during the year.

unanimously endorsed a stern warning to the authorities about 'a moral and material crisis graver than anything they have known'. There was even recurrent talk of a strike. In 1969 UFM's president warned that 'too many Frenchmen have ceased to believe in justice', while a senior member of the *parquet* said that staffing was so inadequate that 'every day we are on the brink of catastrophe', and the first president of the Cour de Cassation (France's senior judge) declared solemnly in the presence of M. Pompidou that in civil matters 'the law is so antiquated that despite fragmentary tinkering here and there, the image of justice, the credibility of justice, the notion of justice itself have become dangerously obscured over the years'.[1] This massive discontent arose partly from the profession's low salaries, understaffing and limited career prospects, and partly from repeated failures to consult them about law reform. But the deepest anxieties arose over delays in reform and threats to the independence of the judiciary. The UFM complained in 1964 that apart from senior posts 'the executive now has almost complete discretion over promotions', and was showing 'undue favour' in a number of cases. In 1969 it was still complaining over the accelerated promotion of men 'whose lack of seniority is compensated only by qualifications notoriously unrelated to the exercise of their functions'.[2] This was only one of several deeply resented encroachments by the executive on the judges' nominal independence.[3]

---

[1] *Le Monde*, 4 Oct. 1969.

[2] Cf. *Le Monde*, 10 Nov. 1964 and 7 Feb. 1969. The UFM had in mind instances like the promotion of a member of the *parquet* from *substitut* right up the ladder to *procureur-général* in six years, during which he was detached to ORTF and exercised no legal functions at all. In 1969 the Minister of Justice admitted that there had been 'a very few promotions' which 'did not arise from the application of strictly professional criteria' (*Le Monde*, 16 Oct. 1969).

[3] In 1969 the UFM and the Syndicat de la Magistrature jointly complained at 'the inadequacy of the statutory guarantees extended to members of the judiciary, which fall short even of those accorded to civil servants' (*Le Monde*, 19 June 1969). The system by which the *parquet* and *magistrats du siège* are jointly administered means that annual reports, and consequently promotion prospects, depend partly on the local *procureur-général*'s view of the individual magistrate. See also C. Laroche-Flavin, *La Machine Judiciaire* (Paris, 1968), ch. 5.

With its reforms of 1958–59, the reorganization of the Cour de Cassation in 1967, and a number of major codifying acts, the Fifth Republic has in fact made many technical improvements in the law. However, in 1965 the Minister of Justice agreed that earlier reforms had been badly executed or overtaken by events, and that the judicial system no longer met legitimate expectations. His successor, René Capitant, promised 'the entire structure must and will be reshaped'. However, in 1969 a new minister, René Pleven, was still admitting that the Justice estimates were inadequate, and confessing that 'our country has neglected the modernization of its judicial apparatus to the point where the situation has become intolerable'.[1] He campaigned strenuously for increased estimates, and carried modest bills to improve recruitment and provide better safeguards for people in custody. Plans were under way to reorganize the distribution of courts, reform the Centre National des Etudes Judiciaires, improve the rewards and prospects of judges, and modernize the other legal professions. Though Pleven was apparently a determined reformer, he would clearly be a cautious one. But the test of the new government's determination and liberalism lay less in technical reforms than in its response to the demand for greater guarantees for the independence of both the *parquet* and the *magistrats du siège*, which entailed reforms of promotion and disciplinary procedures and thus a recasting of the High Council of the Judiciary itself. These were resisted by de Gaulle to the end; but without them the malaise of the judiciary seemed unlikely to disappear.

Institutional reform and political upheavals have left less imprint on the administrative courts. The Conseil d'Etat has continued to serve as the government's expert adviser on drafting legislation and decrees, and to deal with disputes between citizens and officials or between contending public bodies—while releasing many of its members for special tasks in the ministries, public corporations or (as with Michel Debré) for a political career. While the bulk of the administrative courts' judgments have been concerned with those minor acts of slipshod or arbitrary administration common to

---

[1] Cf. *Le Monde*, 19 May 1965 (Foyer), 29 Oct. 1968 (Capitant), 16 Oct. 1969 (Pleven).

all regimes, friction between the Conseil d'Etat and the rulers of the Fifth Republic was probably inevitable. Traditionally the Council holds a balance between the necessary authority of the State and the freedom of the citizen—an inevitably controversial matter in such circumstances as the Algerian war. The whole philosophy of the Council and the President was at variance. For the President, 'it must of course be understood that the entire indivisible authority of the State is confided to the President . . . that no other authority exists, neither ministerial nor civil nor military nor judicial, which is not conferred and sustained by him'; while, as *commissaire du gouvernement* Henry put it in the Canal case, 'The constitution of 1958 remains . . . the constitution of a parliamentary system. . . . This regime knows no sovereign power superior by its essence to all other powers. On the contrary, no power is ever absolute and each power always has limits.'

Early disagreements were in a fairly minor key. The Council opposed the procedure employed for revising the constitutional provisions relating to the Community in 1960, the 1960 and 1961 ordinances extending the powers of the military courts, and a number of other measures it considered unduly infringed personal freedom. But since these were purely advisory opinions the government suffered no more than annoyance and a little odium. Then in 1962 the Council ruled against the government twice in quick succession. It advised unanimously less one vote that article 11 of the constitution did not allow de Gaulle to put his bill for electing the President by universal suffrage direct to referendum (but he ignored its views); and by striking down the Military Court of Justice in the Canal case, it both administered a stinging rebuff and affected the President's plans for dealing with subversion. It was said that the Council had forgotten its underlying duty to the survival of the State, and broken tradition by intervening directly in a major political controversy. Privately it was whispered that an unsavoury coalition of unforgiving Vichyites, extremist supporters of *Algérie française* and left-wingers on the Council had ganged up on the government. Yet while some councillors may have had political motives, there was genuine widespread concern at political interference with the judiciary, and scarcely a jurist of standing believed that de Gaulle's amendment procedure was constitutional. Audacious though the Council's decision in the Canal case was in the light of its traditional reluctance to thwart a major governmental policy decision, it has long held that though governments must be given exceptional latitude in major crises, such powers should be used as briefly as possible and brought back within a structure of appropriate safeguards at the first possible moment. While prepared to accept special courts to deal with subversion the Council plainly believed that with the Algerian war ended and the main OAS leaders behind bars, such grave encroachments on due process as removal of the right of appeal were no longer justified. De Gaulle's anger at the decision was understandable only weeks after he had escaped death at OAS hands by inches, but the essential cause of his frustration was his propensity to substitute personal convenience for the rule of law.

Far from hampering governments during the Algerian war, the administrative courts had erred towards timidity, particularly over internment and press seizures. However, the Canal decision suddenly aroused the government to the 'problem' of the Conseil d'Etat. A committee to study its reform was promptly established—in part, it was said, to divert de Gaulle from a summary attack on the Council's jurisdiction. It suggested changing the rules of retirement and allowing the government to bring matters for accelerated decision by the Council's Bureau alone. Widely criticized, the reform was implemented shorn of its more contentious aspects, improving the Council's internal organization and its functioning, and promoting exchanges of members between its administrative and judicial sides. Since then there have inevitably been differences between the Council and the government —such as its adverse opinion on de Gaulle's broad and vague proposals for a referendum in 1968 and its ruling that the 1969 referendum was also unconstitutional—but nothing approaching the storm of 1962. Although the machinery of the administrative courts—despite its major reorganization in 1953—sometimes grinds so slowly that justice delayed becomes justice denied, the Council has retained and strengthened its reputation as one of the few French institutions respected and envied both at home and abroad.

The Constitutional Council

Unfortunately the same cannot be said of the Constitutional

Council, one of the 1958 constitution's few major institutional innovations. Though decked with the trappings of a judicial body, the Council (which strictly is part of the executive) was created in a far from judicial spirit. It was one of Debré's devices for moralizing politics and protecting the national interest from the depredations of partisan passions: insulated from political pressures, it was to help the President and cabinet resist attempts by parliament to regain its lost prerogatives, though it was also given the task of supervising referendums and national elections and ruling on election petitions.

Besides its narrow jurisdiction, the restricted access to it has made the Council an inherently limited body—though some of its decisions have had considerable constitutional importance. Only four people can refer matters to it: the President, Prime Minister, and the presidents of the two assemblies. The Council has no independent initiative. Debré argued that for individuals to have access would be contrary to the French tradition and parliamentary government; he refused even to allow the right to one-third of the Assembly—leaving the parliamentary majority unfettered to flout the constitution with impunity unless the minority can enlist the support of one of the four. In practice, however, the president of the Senate has so far provided a channel of access for dissidents.

The Council is automatically called on to decide the constitutionality of organic laws and of new standing orders for the assemblies before they can come into force.[1] When asked by one of the four authorities it considers whether any bill, amendment, or treaty is in keeping with the constitution and whether the government can by decree amend laws whose provisions are 'executive' rather than 'legislative' in the sense defined in article 34 of the constitution. Here, as elsewhere, its decisions are enforced automatically and are subject to no appeal. In addition to being guardian of the 'domain of the law', the Council is consulted if the President wishes to invoke article 16 (its opinion is published but not binding) and on measures he takes under it (these decisions are not published).

---

[1] See above, p. 209. The Council meets *in camera* and decides on the basis of documents without hearing argument, by a majority of its membership. Cases are normally decided within a month, or a week if urgent. No concurring or dissenting opinion is published.

Organic laws amplify and supplement the constitution.

It may also be called on to declare the presidency vacant on the grounds of the President's incapacity.

The Council was conceived of as a prestigious and respected body. Protocol assigns a lofty place to its nine members, appointed for nine years—three each by the presidents of the two assemblies and the President of the Republic, who also selects its president from among their number. (In addition former Presidents of the Republic are members ex-officio.) Yet the Council is an unloved body. Up to 1969 a majority of its members were appointed by de Gaulle and Chaban-Delmas, perpetuating suspicions of it as a partisan body. The first two presidents, Léon Noël and Gaston Palewski, both had long service as Gaullist politicians; Georges Pompidou was de Gaulle's *directeur de cabinet* before joining the Council, and his Prime Minister shortly after leaving it, while Edmond Michelet joined it after being Minister of Justice and left to re-enter the Assembly as a UNR deputy in 1967. Under a deliberate policy of including men with wide and varied experience in executive-legislative matters, some members have had little or no legal training, but appointments have also included eminent legal figures like Marcel Waline, a constitutional lawyer of Gaullist leanings, and René Cassin, a former Vice-President of the Conseil d'Etat. With one or two exceptions the level has been respectable to impressive.

Whatever its calibre, though, the Council is almost bound to be unpopular. Its time is spent policing the boundary within which parliament can legislate. If the constitution is violated elsewhere it is impotent. Resentment at this one-eyed watchdog role inevitably turns on the enforcement body itself. Almost from birth the Council was widely dismissed as merely the General's poodle. This was unduly harsh. The bulk of its constitutional decisions have related to article 34, which distinguishes between those matters on which parliament may lay down 'detailed rules' and those where it is confined to 'basic principles'. The Council's fifty or so rather laconic opinions do not as yet add up to a wholly consistent body of jurisprudence; while at times it has seemed unduly restrictive, it has not infrequently gone against the government with extensive interpretations.[1]

---

[1] The government's references to the Council are normally screened by its legal advisers; otherwise it would probably succeed less often.

The Council's unhappy reputation rests mainly on a few incidents, particularly its initial decisions on the standing orders of the two assemblies in 1959, which breathed an unmistakeable resolve to keep parliament strictly within the role laid down in the constitution. Subsequent rulings on minor revisions have shown no weakening. Then in 1961, to the annoyance of pressure groups and parties, the Council upheld against M. Monnerville the Prime Minister's contention that the detailed weighting of the system for fixing farm prices was not within parliament's competence. In two other disputes the Council was seen by the opposition as a broken reed. In September 1961 the Council perfectly properly held itself incompetent in the dispute over whether parliament could constitutionally censure the government while article 16 was in force. Then in 1962, after a five-hour debate, the Council first gave an adverse advisory opinion on de Gaulle's resort to article 11 in the constitutional referendum; but when M. Monnerville challenged the law after its adoption, the Council decided by six to four that it was not competent because the referendum had been a 'direct expression of national sovereignty'—thus the constituent power of universal suffrage was considered to have eradicated any prior irregularities. This led to the final withdrawal of a former President of the Republic, Vincent Auriol, from the Council's activities. In 1968, when the opposition again looked hopefully to the Council in a controversy over introduction of brand name advertising on ORTF, a sadly muffled and ambiguous ruling (reflecting the Council's internal divisions) allowed the government to act by decree. This did nothing to enhance respect for the Council.

The Council's creation did at least end one scandal of the old system by removing electoral disputes from parliament. Unfortunately, the electoral law is so outdated and disregarded that a large fraction of the Assembly would be unseated if it were enforced. The consequence is that at each election it unseats a handful of deputies for irregularities which might

---

In the 1962–67 parliament the government sought twenty-three rulings. It won ten, lost three completely and eight partly; on two the Council declared itself not competent. However, a ruling against the government usually means only that it must let parliament legislate on a matter it wanted to keep to itself; a ruling against parliament means that the members lose all competence in the matter.

have ensured their victory; the victims utter cries of outrage at this 'discrimination', and their electors promptly return them with increased majorities. Although the Council's decisions are by general consent superior to the unseemly controversies of the Fourth Republic, it has yet to establish itself as above suspicion. After the 1967 election Mitterrand termed it a body which 'fails in its duty as a high judge and is subject to the most shocking pressures from those in power'. He was particularly annoyed over two general rulings—on which the Gaullists' control of the Assembly hung. The opposition had challenged a group of UNR victories on the grounds that the candidatures were invalid under a badly drafted clause of the electoral code: preferring a commonsensical to a literal interpretation, the Council rejected all the petitions. The election of a further group of UNR deputies was challenged on the ground that the outcome had been swayed by de Gaulle's TV broadcast after the official closure of the campaign. The Council dismissed these petitions with the argument that the President's actions could only be challenged before the High Court of Justice (on impeachment for high treason!), and consequently the Council was not competent to consider whether his speech had violated electoral law. Thus neither imagination nor initiative has characterized the Council's electoral jurisdiction, and suspicion of partisanship is not yet dispelled.[1] It has usefully drawn attention to the widespread abuses of postal voting—particularly in Corsica, the Wild West of French politics—but it has yet to grapple effectively with either the serious irregularities which persist in many overseas constituencies, or the problems arising from newer and subtler ways of improperly swaying elections. In referendums and presidential elections too its powers of supervision and investigation have not yet developed adequately.

But the most serious weakness of the Constitutional Council is its continuing failure to establish its moral authority. It is inevitable that it appears less than impartial so long as none of its major decisions have gone in favour of the opposition, and it so plainly leans over backwards not to disavow the

---

[1] The record of invalidations has been: 1958, four deputies unseated (of whom one was UNR); 1962, seven (one UNR and one Independent Republican); 1967 five (one UNR); 1968 one (no UNR). Two of the three UNR invalidations were in Corsica.

President. Not surprisingly the opposition has promised reform—but the hope for the Council is that it does not threaten abolition. The Council therefore may yet have the opportunity to establish itself with broader jurisdiction as the constitutional court which the Fifth Republic has shown to be more than ever desirable.

IV

THE FIFTH REPUBLIC
IN ACTION

14

CASE STUDIES

Of the twelve case studies which follow, three illustrate Gaullist reactions to some of the problems of subversion and military indiscipline which troubled the Fifth Republic's early years. Five show the handling of a range of the social and economic issues which preoccupied successive governments—though they rarely attracted the sustained attention of de Gaulle himself. Finally, three show on both a tiny and a major scale how ministers dealt with questions concerning intellectuals: for the offhand contempt with which these were treated at first, the regime was to pay a high price.

All these cases, except those involving defence and security, offer examples of how pressure groups have operated under the Fifth Republic: sometimes by more or less successful direct action, sometimes by reluctant or uncomprehending dialogue or mild obstruction, sometimes even by active and constructive collaboration. Parliament, despite its presumed unimportance, played a significant part in about half the cases —and even when that part was backward-looking and illiberal it was still an important factor in the equation. Though in some instances the role of parliament was largely formal or rushed, in others it was able to compel the government to attend to neglected problems or aspects of problems, or to cooperate effectively with a skilful minister. But the outstanding impression of these cases is of the sharply varying attitudes of the executive, at times neglectful or contemptuous of other opinions in or out of parliament, at times anxious to exploit or cooperate with suitable partners but, in striking contrast with previous French regimes, more often than not determining the outcome of the dispute—even if it only contributed by its own follies to a result it had never foreseen, still less desired.

Problems of Subversion and Dissent

The Bomb Damage Bill, 1961

This case shows the UNR putting pressure on ministers, and using the committee system as the channel to express its grievances, with the Finance Committee, as in past regimes, standing midway between the government and the specialist committee and working for compromise. It also shows that the financial rules can be bent in practice, and that there are still resources of procedural obstruction available to a determined deputy.

The bomb damage in question was the work of right-wing terrorist sympathizers with the Europeans of Algeria. As de Gaulle's policy veered towards accepting independence, they began in the autumn of 1961 to use plastic bombs against the houses of their enemies in France itself—often left-wingers, still more frequently UNR members. There were some tragic injuries and one or two deaths, but the main damage was to property, and this was extensive. The government brought in a bill to provide that all building insurance should automatically cover this risk and the premium should be increased to compensate. The Finançe Committee, through its UNR rapporteur, was willing to accept this solution if the Committee on General Legislation and Administration did so too. But its rapporteur, André Fanton, a young and active UNR member from Paris, argued instead that the State should pay the cost. He urged that the bill be sent back to committee for amendment. The government agreed provided it was voted before the recess in a week's time, and made some concessions. The bill was to operate from the new year; the State was to pay for damage done during 1961 (but not earlier) to persons not covered by insurance policies, and it would contribute to the insurance fund if this proved necessary. This satisfied the Finance Committee but not the Legislation Committee: welcoming the progress made, Fanton said it was not enough, for the State should pay the whole cost. The government invoked article 40 against a private member demanding public expenditure—but the *rapporteur-général* of the Finance Committee ruled that it did not apply. Led by Fanton, the Assembly then proceeded to reshape the bill in happy disregard of the rule against new amendments from the floor.

After a confused discussion it emerged, in the words of another UNR deputy, as 'a monster which satisfies no one', could not work and was full of contradictions. The government used its right to seek a second discussion so that the committee could examine the new clauses, but then withdrew this request so that no one knew what was to happen to the bill.

On the last day of the session Fanton protested that it had not been reintroduced, and was told the government had withdrawn it from the agenda: there would be a new bill next session, several months later, and meanwhile the government would act by regulations. With the bomb outrages spreading fast, this did not satisfy the UNR; Fanton moved the rejection of the day's agenda—except for an opposition motion to censure the government—and won by a large majority. The Presidents' Conference met to consider the new situation and there the minister promised that the government would pay a substantial share of the cost (between £250,000 and £400,000) with which its critics were satisfied. Even on a financial issue the house had asserted its determination and got its way—by harassing the minister into proposing public expenditure he had not intended.

The State Security Court Bill, 1963, and its sequel

Even on a matter of the most bitter political controversy, opposition criticism can find an echo within the majority, which can communicate its uneasiness to the government without open defiance (in this instance through the RIs and through the conference committee) and thus make an impression on the result—while on a closely allied subject, when battle lines are tightly drawn, the government can nevertheless call on the loyalty of the majority and override all its critics.

One of the least happy aspects of Gaullist government was the handling of subversion cases. When they first came to power Michel Debré proclaimed that perhaps the chief and certainly the least noticed merit of the new constitution was that it guaranteed habeas corpus, for there could be no excuse for keeping a man in prison more than twenty-four hours without his going before a magistrate. But when the Gaullists themselves became the targets of the subversive activities they had so cheerfully organized against previous governments, their attitude changed abruptly. After the first offensive of the ultras, the barricades crisis of January 1960, the government took extra powers under which it authorized suspects to be held incommunicado (*garde à vue*) for four days—though it promised these powers would not be used to set up special courts. The second offensive, the generals' putsch of April 1961, led de Gaulle to invoke his emergency powers under article 16, and to create a special military court to try subversion cases—arising both from the putsch and from the OAS terrorism which followed it. This court sentenced to death some killers and also one of their nominal leaders, General Jouhaud, but (allegedly by one vote after a change of personnel) it found unspecified 'extenuating circumstances' for the chief rebel leader, General Salan, and gave him only life imprisonment. By then article 16 was no longer in operation but the President still enjoyed special powers given him by referendum to bring the Evian peace treaty into operation: he used these at once to abolish the military court and set up a new one, from which there was no appeal.[1] This court also pronounced death sentences, one of which was executed, but one of the condemned men, André Canal, took the case to the Conseil d'Etat on the ground that the establishment of a court without right of appeal was *ultra vires* the enabling act. The Conseil d'Etat found in his favour and this *arrêt Canal* undermined the legal basis for the special court.

Many Frenchmen with no sympathy whatever for the terrorists felt that courts with handpicked judges, which could be abolished and replaced when their verdicts displeased the authorities, were a profoundly shocking device. To meet this feeling the government brought in a new measure intended to be permanent. It set up a new State Security Court with drastic powers, which was to be appointed by the cabinet and would include two senior officers among its five members. The proposal was opposed by some critics root and branch and by others in detail: François Mitterrand was the chief spokesman for the first view, René Pleven for the second. The first point of contention was the scope of the bill, which originally applied to offences against the 'authority' of the

---

[1] 'Appeal' is used here as the nearest British equivalent of *recours en cassation*.

State. In committee on the bill 'security' was substituted for 'authority' and its scope and the number of offences coming before the court were thus substantially narrowed; this change brought Pleven and the moderate opposition to accept it in principle. When it came before the house in January 1963, in a special session called for the purpose, Mitterrand tried to restore the traditional type of French court for political cases, one elected by and from among the deputies; he failed and Pleven and his friends then set about amending the bill in detail. There were four main issues: the treatment of minors (many of the lesser offenders were students), the period of *garde à vue*, the right of appeal, and the court's independence: the minister made concessions on three points and was beaten on the fourth (the right of appeal) when Capitant, the committee chairman, indignantly told him 'We are not robots'. He agreed to a ten-day *garde à vue* instead of fifteen (Pleven had wanted five and Mitterrand two) and to a two-year term for the judges (instead of one, as he had first proposed, or three as the critics wanted). But then he called for a package vote—which drove MRP into opposition—and the bill, now split in two (one to set up the court and the other on its working), went through by 240–188 and 233–190.[1] Incorporated in it was an amendment by Capitant giving legal validity to all the ordinances made under the special powers conferred by the Evian bill; this parliamentary ratification gave them the status of law and not of regulations and removed them from the jurisdiction of the Conseil d'Etat, thus overriding the *arrêt Canal*.

The Senate did not miss the opportunity to strike a blow for liberty and against Gaullism (and for *Algérie française?*). It reshaped the bills completely, reducing the number of offences covered, eliminating minors entirely, limiting the *garde à vue* to the twenty-four hours allowed in ordinary cases, changing the procedure, and removing the military judges; having turned the measures completely inside out it then voted them by 125–109 and 129–109, MRP now rejoining the majority. This truculence might have been expected to provoke corresponding intransigence in the Assembly. Instead the majority deputies signified to the government

---

[1] The government's majority often fell well below normal, especially on the *garde à vue*.

their distaste for the bill and their demand for concessions by appointing among their conferees two opposition members —Pleven and a Socialist—and an RI deputy who had abstained from voting the bill. Such a conference committee was naturally disposed to compromise. In its agreed draft, some offences were cut out, for instance interference with traffic—a popular OAS propaganda stunt at the time—would not come before the court unless carried out under arms; some minors were excluded; the government got its ten days' *garde à vue* but a magistrate had to see the prisoner three times during it; the military judges were restored. The Minister of Justice, it was suspected, had little enthusiasm for the bill and was perhaps not sorry to have his hand forced; at any rate instead of using his powers to restore the government's proposals as amendments and then call for a package vote, he accepted the compromise and succeeded in the Assembly, 263–186 and 263–184, and in the Senate, 121–111 and 129–109. It was the first notable triumph for the conference committee procedure as a means of reconciling the two houses.

The sequel was less happy. Five days after parliament voted an agreed solution to the subversion problem, the government decided not to send the outstanding subversion case—the trial of the men who had tried to assassinate de Gaulle at Petit Clamart the previous August—to the new court. Instead they were committed to the old one, first set up under the 'Evian' powers, then disallowed by the Conseil d'Etat, but now restored to life—by parliament's acceptance of Capitant's amendment. Whether the object was to deprive the accused of a right of appeal or simply to put the Conseil d'Etat in its place, the decision seemed to confirm all the critics' doubts about the way the government would use its powers. The defence lawyers exploited this unexpected chance to attract sympathy for their clients and set out to obstruct proceedings until the new court came into being and the old one lapsed.

To defeat these tactics the government introduced a new bill prolonging the jurisdiction of the old military court until it had completed all cases that were before it. The RI disliked this move very much, there were protests from the UNR, and enough Gaullists were absent from the committee on the bill to allow Mitterrand to be chosen as rapporteur—and to throw the debate into confusion by resigning this position when the bill came to the floor. But now the government made it clear that it was determined to break the obstructionists and adamant against any compromise. The majority supported it in a series of most bitter debates, in which the Gaullists claimed that opponents of the bill were aiming their blows at the regime and taking the side of the assassins. A leading MRP deputy and a Conservative senator both tried to introduce a right of appeal from the special court, but were blocked by the minister demanding a package vote. It had become a straightforward conflict between the parties and the houses. The Assembly voted the new bill 271–170, the Senate rejected it 181–40, and the conference committee reached deadlock, rejecting an amendment by 7–7 and the bill itself by 7–7 also. On 19 February the last stages of the ritual were performed: in the morning the deputies approved the bill again, 271–171; in the afternoon the senators rejected it again, 155–39; and in the evening it finally passed through the Assembly, and into law, by 274 to 172.

Thus the two measures showed quite different political attitudes at work. On the permanent bill the opposition's criticisms caused widespread uneasiness among government supporters, and the majority carefully hoisted a series of warning signals indicating to the government that they would not follow it unless substantial concessions were made. With no overt humiliation of the ministers, a compromise was successfully worked out and the minister, refraining from waving his stick, accepted it gracefully. But when counsel for de Gaulle's would-be assassins tried to exploit the new bill the government treated it as a matter of confidence in which no defection would be tolerated, refused any concession and overrode all opposition—at the price of much tension but with no difficulty.

The Conscientious Objection Bill, 1963

This was a somewhat unusual case (at least in the second parliament) of a bill in which President de Gaulle was personally interested, which was approved by the opposition and deplored by most (not all) of the UNR and by almost all their Conservative allies. It shows the possibilities of procedural obstruction; the use of the package vote against the deputies of the majority; the use of regulatory powers to avoid a political difficulty; the main channels of conservative pressure —the UNR party meeting, the Defence Committee (always a stronghold of nationalist feeling), and the Senate; and the use and abuse of conference committees.

France has never been tender to conscientious objection: the Catholic tradition is less sympathetic than the Protestant, the Republican Left was long imbued with fiery Jacobin nationalism and regarded universal conscription as a symbol of equality, and a precarious geographical situation gave Frenchmen a more favourable attitude to their army than Englishmen or Americans to theirs. Before the Algerian war, conscientious objectors were very rare (from fifty to a hundred a year) and the great majority were Jehovah's Witnesses. The authorities used cat-and-mouse tactics with them, calling them up again as soon as their prison sentences had been served and sending them back to prison; their plight attracted little public sympathy. But the Algerian war drew attention to the problem, for protests against the methods used spread rapidly, notably among students: the objectors, sometimes from well-known families, were more numerous, more articulate and better-connected than ever before. One of de Gaulle's very first acts on coming to power was to order the release of those who had served ten years in prison, and by 1962 it was usual though not obligatory for them to be released after spending in prison twice the current term of military service. The President himself had assured Louis Lecoin (an elderly anarchist of some renown) that there would be a bill to deal with the problem, and after Lecoin went on hunger strike, he further promised it would be introduced forthwith. But the government laid it so late that it could not be debated without a special session. The Defence Committee wanted to kill it altogether and moved the previous question, but accepted the Legislation Committee's proposed compromise that the bill be referred back to committee. This was carried against MRP and left-wing opposition and there the bill languished untouched for a full year.

The government reinforced the impression that it had little real interest in the bill by reintroducing it again at the very end of the session. The Defence Committee, with its RI chairman, was again one centre of resistance, but now there was a second: Michel Debré had just been elected deputy for Réunion and celebrated his appearance in the Assembly by mobilizing opposition in the UNR parliamentary party. The Prime Minister himself had to assure the UNR party meeting that the government really did want the bill passed, while René Capitant, the Left Gaullist chairman of the Legislation Committee, reminded them during the debate that the President was its real sponsor; Moynet, Defence Committee chairman, tried the same tactics as the previous year and moved the reference back on the ground that a general reform of military service was due shortly (it was passed in the end in 1965). Capitant opposed him but showed some willingness to make concessions, and the reference back was heavily defeated, 358 to 94, with the opposition supporting the government. Before an unusually large house the debate proceeded on the bill, to which seventy-six amendments had been put down. But the minister now called for a package vote on a new draft of the measure, and the amendments which he was prepared to accept transformed its character drastically. In protest against the new version the opposition parties, Communists included, decided to withdraw from the debate and leave the government to fight out the issue with its majority.

The debate on the right-wing amendments continued. Two, which limited the bill to philosophic or religious objectors, and denied them any right to deferment of their alternative service, were accepted by the minister (but were eventually dropped). Another forbade propaganda or 'any form of publicity whatever' for conscientious objection (but only the ban on propaganda survived in the final version). Objectors were to serve twice as long as soldiers, instead of half as long again—Debré insisting that this was the minimum he would accept. Above all the government brought in a new clause as another compromise with Debré. The ex-Premier had an amendment down to exclude objectors from any form of public employment, any responsible post in a nationalized industry and any elective position national or local. Messmer, the minister, proposed instead their exclusion from certain positions of public importance—which he would determine by regulation.[1] The entire opposition abstained from voting on the bill as a protest against this abdication of its functions by

---

[1] When he told a questioner he was thinking of highly responsible positions or those connected with defence, UNR deputies chorused 'What about education?'

parliament, and it was carried by reluctant UNR members voting against their Conservative allies.[1] In the Senate the situation was stranger still, for the Conservatives and the few UNR senators disliked the bill, while the Socialists and MRP opposed the amendments Debré had forced into it: all but four clauses were rejected, and in the end the whole bill was defeated by 127 to 0 with the entire opposition again abstaining.

Next session the government brought in a new bill. Objectors were to be allowed deferment, but still had to serve double the soldier's term and were still excluded from some posts. After moving three amendments and accepting another from the Legislation Committee, the minister called for a package vote. The Defence Committee was again hostile, wanting the bill referred back, but after a debate of only fifty minutes it passed on a show of hands by about three to one, with the Conservatives hostile and the Left (on whose liberalizing amendments no vote was allowed) abstaining yet again. In the Senate as in the Assembly, the critics were led by the Defence Committee; after the usual protests against the package vote procedure, the upper house rejected the new bill by 140 to 12 (only 7 of the UNR senators voted for it). The government called for a conference committee, which had Moynet as chairman and duly reported by 9 votes to 4 in favour of referring the bill back to committee — a course he had always advocated, but a proposal outside the competence of a conference committee, whose report must take the form of a draft bill. Moynet's solution was generally condemned, rejected by 405 to 48 in the Assembly, and lost by show of hands in the Senate. By the third round members were resigned to a reluctant acceptance of the bill. Almost without debate, the deputies voted it by 238 to 71; the senators rejected clause 1 by 129 to 20 (with fifty nominal government supporters in the majority) and the rest without discussion or vote. At the fourth and final reading Moynet tried once again to get the bill referred back in accordance with the conference committee's report, but the Legislation Committee again opposed him. He made a last emotional appeal ('when you vote, think of the ex-servicemen and the fallen') but was beaten by

---

[1] By 204 to 32 with 197 abstentions. Of 233 UNR, 199 voted for, and of 34 RI, 24 voted against. For this debate there was an unusually large attendance.

344 to 94 and the bill went through on a show of hands. The government, bringing forward a measure for which perhaps the ministers and certainly the majority had no liking, found wholehearted support only from the opposition and from a handful of left-wing Gaullists. But it alienated opposition support by the concessions it made to criticism from its own followers, so that the real debate on the bill took place almost wholly in the lobbies, between the minister and Debré's rebel group; once the limits of concession had been defined there, new proposals came before the house in a package which neither liberal nor conservative critics were allowed to touch. Mathematically the government could no doubt have found a majority for a more liberal bill; politically, however, it could have done so only by relying on its opponents to overcome its friends. However regrettable the results in the particular case, the choice of the cabinet does not suggest that it regarded its parliamentary following as a negligible quantity.

Social Conflict and Conciliation

The Young Farmers and the Agricultural Orientation Programme, 1960–1962

When Michel Debré turned his attention to agricultural problems early in his premiership, he rapidly found the briefs presented by FNSEA delegations depressingly unimaginative and technically inept. They reflected the Federation's failure to confront the industry's long-term problems, and its traditional concentration on higher prices—which benefited the big farmers who ran the organization more than the army of small men who made up its ordinary membership. The conservative-minded farm leaders were disoriented by losing the entrenched position in the political process they had enjoyed under the Fourth Republic, and wavered between ineffectual resort to traditional pressures and furious diatribes against city-dwelling technocrats. A round table conference of civil servants, economists and farmers' spokesmen, which was called in 1960 to draft an 'agricultural charter', foundered in irreconcilable disagreement.

Mistrusting the Ministry of Agriculture as merely a lacklustre echo of FNSEA, Debré confided the drafting of his farm policy bill to his own staff. The young, aggressive, practical men at Matignon looked around for someone in the farming world who spoke their own language—if only, as cynics alleged, so that they could produce some group to quote as proof of authentic peasant support for their own policies. They noticed that FNSEA delegations included one or two younger men from the affiliated Centre National des Jeunes Agriculteurs, who seemed more interested in workable solutions than in either ideology or traditional demagogy, and who grasped more rapidly than their elders the implications of the swing in power from parliament to the executive. Even though many of the CNJA leaders had recently figured prominently in demonstrations against the unvarnished economic liberalism of the Debré government's early farm policies, a working relationship developed between the young farmers and the policymakers at Matignon. This not only proved mutually educative, it resulted in the young farmers' movement acquiring opportunities and resources which strengthened their position in the countryside. Though the government preserved its contacts with the traditional farmers' organizations through advisory committees and delegations, it was CNJA which increasingly had the ear of ministers. When Debré brought in his agricultural orientation bill in 1960, it was fought tooth and nail by FNSEA and the Chambers of Agriculture, echoed by rural deputies and senators, whose notion of defending their constituents was, almost to a man, to adopt the conservative FNSEA line. CNJA took no part in the outcry, realizing that by breaking with the strictly short-term and neo-liberal solutions practised hitherto, Debré had accepted some of its own ideas, even if in diluted form.

But the orientation law was simply a framework, requiring some thirty decrees to flesh it out fully. Despite repeated promises only two of these appeared over the next ten months. Aware of the hostility to the law of many senior officials of the Ministry of Agriculture, the young farmers blamed the delay on the old game of bureaucratic sabotage by inertia. Their anger contributed to the *jacquerie* which swept across rural France in May 1961, once again forcing the government to concede to violence what it could have granted to reasoned argument months earlier. The Minister was swept away and replaced by the ambitious, energetic and iconoclastic Edgard Pisani. Pisani was a man in a hurry with visions of vast horizons. Instead of publishing the outstanding decrees he set out to produce a supplementary orientation bill. At first the farmers were suspicious of the resulting delay, particularly since Pisani did not formally consult them over his first draft (though he had many private conversations with individual leaders). However, when the draft was strategically leaked to *Le Monde*, its great debt to the CNJA's ideas was immediately evident, though the FNSEA also found it acceptable. The first draft was then discussed in detail with the farmers' representatives, who had come round to trusting and supporting Pisani, though several of Pisani's ministerial colleagues were furious at his failure to consult them and over some of his specific proposals. However, the earlier leak had provided him with such an impressive display of support from the farmers that ministers hesitated to provoke an explosion by making drastic changes in cabinet. Even so, several important amendments were imposed on Pisani, to the farmers' fury.

The bill now went to parliament. Deputies and senators found it hard to forgive the introduction of such a major piece of legislation at the very end of the session under the urgency procedure, or the barrage of minatory communiques, delegations and messages from the farm organizations which accompanied it. There was the unusual spectacle of ministers and groups arrayed against members of parliament, whose attitude to agricultural problems remained obstinately conservative. Pisani had asked for much more than he expected to get in the bill to allow himself room for compromise. During the debates the bill was watered down at a number of points. But this in turn produced threats by the farmers to stiffen Pisani's backbone by taking to the roads with their tractors. The Minister apparently regained their confidence with the promise that the implementing decrees would be published rapidly and in close consultation with them. Finally the bill was passed in a rather weakened form. But the main structure survived to receive a muted welcome from CNJA.

This experience of the parliamentarians' hostility and timidity was a major reason for CNJA's subsequent refusal to join the Left, the student organizations and the industrial unions in opposing de Gaulle in the 1962 constitutional referendum and election. Though critical of the regime's autocratic style, the young farmers had come to feel that only a continuation of Gaullist leadership provided a hope of the new policies being seen through successfully. The supplementary orientation law probably marked the peak of understanding between Pisani and CNJA, though as long as he remained at the Ministry the CNJA was a significant continuing influence on farm policy. But this episode, in marked contrast with so much of the regime's relationship with the farmers, showed that direct action was not the only fruitful style; productive compromise through discussion was possible even with this most awkward of sectional groups.

The price of milk : three confrontations

'The price of milk' was the very phrase which de Gaulle once chose to sum up in contemptuous dismissal the entire range of mundane trivia which were beneath his attention. But equally it summed up just those everyday issues which a government neglects at its peril. For on the one hand there are almost 1,500,000 producers, many dependent for economic survival on the daily churn or two sent to the dairies, on the other every family budget in the land. Consequently the milk price has always been a highly sensitive political issue. Agreement on a national producer price has rarely been easy. In the Fifth Republic, as in the Fourth, threats of direct action, and sometimes worse, have been staple ingredients in the 'dialogue' between the dairymen and Paris. But the unfolding and outcome of these confrontations has varied strikingly.

(a) *Brinkmanship in 1963.* The summer price was due to be set by 1 April. Shortly beforehand the dairymen's union, the Fédération Nationale des Producteurs du Lait (FNPL, affiliated to FNSEA), sent a delegation to the man who really held the purse strings—the Minister of Finance. They wanted a 13 per cent rise to bring them into line with other EEC producers. The minister countered with arguments about mounting inflationary pressures and the dangers of overproduction. Privately the government also felt the need to reassert itself in the wake of its recent humiliation by the miners. Finding Giscard unreceptive, FNSEA turned to the less influential but more pliable Minister of Agriculture. The outcome was deadlock at ministerial level. Not until 30 March could the cabinet agree on a new price of 35·7 centimes per litre plus a 'collection allowance' in remote areas—well below the producers' demand for 39·7 centimes everywhere. FNSEA warned that the consequences of this disappointment would be dire, but the cabinet calculated that after a hard winter the farmers had neither time nor money to make trouble; it could get away with a firm line.

Privately FNPL and FNSEA leaders concurred with this assessment. But feeling in the countryside was running higher than anyone thought. In nine departments farmers defied the government by continuing to invoice milk at the higher winter price. Sensing the rot setting in, ministers hastily authorized maintenance of the old price for another three weeks 'where local conditions justify it'. Inevitably the concession was countrywide within hours; inevitably too it was denounced by FNPL as a half measure. Round one to direct action.

The Easter weekend brought renewed threats of demonstrations at farmers' meetings. Fearing that its branches were escaping its control FNSEA stepped up its own tone. By now UNR deputies from dairying constituencies were anxiously pressing Pompidou and Pisani for a face-saving way of giving an increase. Intensifying its pressure FNSEA set a deadline of 1 May for direct action. Concessions were now inevitable, but the finance ministry was still fighting a rearguard action for economic rectitude. 1 May brought feverish activity. After the finance minister had been summoned to talks with the President and Prime Minister, the farmers' leaders were hastily brought to Paris to hear the proposals which were to be put to the cabinet: a package deal conceding a record increase to 37·2 centimes per litre plus 'collection allowance' in return for a change to annual rather than semi-annual price reviews and a new 'absorption tax' to mop up surpluses. FNSEA and FNPL promptly accepted the higher prices and repudiated the tax. After two more days of wrangling Pisani capitulated and the attempt to get the dairymen to shoulder some of the responsibility for overproduction was quietly buried. Direct action had paid again. Even so the settlement was only hesitantly accepted in the countryside. It was no surprise when on 15 September FNPL denounced the May settlement and demanded a fresh rise to 38·5 centimes. But now they were overtaken by Giscard's stabilization programme with its general price freeze on goods and services. In this chillier economic and political climate the dairymen failed completely and without a struggle.

(*b*) *The Great Milk Strike of 1964.* The hot, dry summer of 1964 was ideal for holiday-makers, disastrous for dairymen. Talk of a possible milk strike began early in August in central France. Anxious to head off trouble at lowest cost, the Ministers of Finance and Agriculture reacted within hours to talk of direct action by authorizing local price increases in drought-stricken areas. But this success of direct action rallied all other producers in militant mood behind a demand to raise prices from 37·2 centimes per litre to 44·0 centimes. By mid-September there were scattered strikes against milk deliveries in the Marseilles, Avignon and Nîmes areas. In Paris the FNSEA Council resolved to back the demands with a national strike of milk deliveries for domestic consumption; disappointed with the government's firm line on cereal prices, the 'big' farmers of the Paris basin who dominated FNSEA calculated that the 'small men' of the dairy industry would serve as a battering ram against the price stabilization programme. But the government also knew that concessions on milk would unleash a deluge of other claims, wrecking its economic programme. Moreover, President de Gaulle had gone off on a Latin American tour with strict instructions not to back down. So the strike continued. Within days the larger cities were without fresh milk, though the sick and infants were supplied. Rural deputies pressed for concessions and aired proposals for a 'quality bonus', but they made no impression.

This time ministers had assessed the situation accurately. By early October the small farmers in areas remote from butter and milk-powder factories were being forced to call a halt; the strike began eroding in the smaller towns, then moved rapidly towards collapse. When south-western farmers tried to invoice milk at the higher price the government promptly threatened to prosecute any shopkeeper who bought it. Although the farmers won a momentary fillip from a parliamentary debate in which Gaullist deputies urged their leaders to be generous, the strike was increasingly unpopular and the small producers were at the end of their tether. On 18 October FNSEA called the strike off. This time direct action had failed completely.

(*c*) *A 'European' price, 1968.* By 1968 the development of EEC agricultural policy made the price of milk a matter for Brussels rather than the familiar ministries in Paris. At first the transition went smoothly, as French prices gradually rose to the higher levels of the EEC partners. But by 1968 concern was mounting at the emergence of vast surpluses of dairy products and the exorbitant costs of price supports and storage. When the time came to settle the first 'European' milk price on 1 April 1968, the Commission resolved (after a sharp internal debate over the political wisdom of such action) to challenge the high price/high support policy—beginning with milk. It proposed pegging milk prices for three years at 49·51 centimes per litre instead of the 50.85 centimes previously agreed by the EEC Council of Ministers. Though this was an increase on the 48·14 centimes then being paid in France, producers everwhere were furious. They reacted in both new and traditional ways. Angry FNPL and FNSEA delegations visited the finance and agriculture ministers in Paris. Michel Debatisse, secretary-general of FNSEA, declared that any pegging of the milk price would produce unprecedented violence among the peasantry. FNPL delegates joined with dairymen's delegations from throughout the Six in lobbying the Commission and Council of Ministers in Brussels itself. Even without such pressures ministers recoiled from the political and social implications of Mansholt's proposals. Edgar Faure, now Minister of Agriculture, assured dairymen there was no question of cutting prices.

Deadlock between the Council of Ministers and the EEC Commission was now delaying the entry into force of the new prices. (FNPL claimed compensation from Paris for the delay—without success.) Yet Mansholt's insistence that if nothing were done subsidies for dairy products would rapidly climb from £400 million per year to £900 million hit home. Ministers were caught between their farmers' pressure and the unacceptable financial implications of letting matters go on. As negotiations reopened there were scattered signs of agitation in the countryside and six thousand farmers thronged to Brussels under the auspices of COPA—the organization of farmers' unions of the Six.

By now the issue had become a grave affair of State. France threatened that unless agreement was reached on 1 July the full implementation of the common market for industrial products would be held up. With such forceful diplomacy the French won the day. The Council of Ministers agreed to the 'original' price of 50·85 centimes, and found the way to foot the increased bill for dairy products in the device the dairymen had proposed—a tax on margarine. But the farmers' victory probably owed more to the national self-assertion of Gaullist diplomacy than either to the favour their arguments might have found in Paris or Brussels or to threats of political upheaval.

First steps towards an incomes policy

One of the major preoccupations of most western European governments in the sixties has been the search for a workable and acceptable incomes policy.[1] In France a climate of opinion favourable to such a policy developed gradually during the late fifties and early sixties, until by 1963 it had become a matter of conventional wisdom, though there was little notion about how it might be achieved. However, it was recognized from the beginning that there would have to be extensive discussion with the main interested groups. Possibly stirred by the outcome of the disastrous miners' strike in the spring of 1963, in October of that year the government took its first major initiatives, by establishing an Enquiry into Incomes Policy under the chairmanship of Pierre Massé, Commissioner-General of the Plan, and a committee of three members of the Conseil d'Etat headed by M. Toutée to enquire into procedures for wage negotiations in the public sector.

The Enquiry conference had forty members, made up of twenty-seven representatives of interest groups (two each from CGT, FO, CFDT and CGC for the unions; two each from CNPF, CGPME, Chambres de Commerce and Chambres de Métiers plus one Young Employer; two each from FNSEA, CNJA, Chambres d'Agriculture and CNMCCA; two from UNAF), with the remainder civil servants, planners and members of ministerial *cabinets*. The aim of the Enquiry, in Massé's words, was to allow a 'multilateral dialogue' on the prospects and problems of an incomes policy. The moment the government had chosen could scarcely have been less auspicious for a calm scrutiny of long-term considerations. Most of the groups were alarmed or resentful

---

[1] This section draws on a much fuller account in J. E. S. Hayward, 'Interest groups and incomes policy in France', *British Journal of Industrial Relations*, 4 (1966), pp. 137–53.

at the deflationary stabilization plan introduced by the government a month or so earlier, while the unions were still annoyed over a law to circumscribe the right to strike in the public services which had been pushed through against their opposition during the summer.[1]

Yet despite the unpromising circumstances, thanks to Massé's diplomatic skills the Enquiry had a measure of success. At the very least it had allowed a full airing of group attitudes, and permitted the reactions of the various interests to be gauged. This showed that CGT was unremittingly hostile, and was joined by FO in the fear that an incomes policy would be merely a disguised form of wage restraint. CFDT, with its long-standing support for 'democratic planning', took a more sophisticated attitude in advocating a contractual policy in which in return for restraint the unions received certain guarantees, a viewpoint broadly shared by CGC, which was worried about the incidence on differentials. While the union spokesmen made no secret of their views, most of the employers' spokesmen were reticent. The CNPF, usually a coordinating rather than a policy-making body, did not even submit a general statement of its position. Though plainly many businessmen were concerned at the danger of increased governmental intervention, only the PME spokesmen spoke out strongly—as intransigent in the liberal direction as CGT had been on the Left. Only the Young Employers' spokesman spoke up timidly for the notion of an incomes policy. As for the farmers, they were divided between and within themselves, though both CNJA and FNSEA favoured an incomes policy as a means of achieving the 'parity' with other workers which was their main aim.

While the Conference cleared the air, Massé's report got a very chilly reception, particularly his proposal for an independent body modelled on the shortlived British National Incomes Commission, to rule on wage increases in relation to a stated norm. Only CGC and UNAF showed any degree of support, although Massé's own goodwill was not challenged. To some extent this was because the Enquiry had been a 'dialogue of the deaf' with the strong groups trusting to their own bargaining power, and the weaker ones hoping that an incomes policy would bring the government to their aid. But

---

[1] Cf. above, pp. 44–5.

mainly it was because all groups were increasingly irritated at the growing tendency of the government to notify them of decisions taken without engaging in genuine prior discussion. The problem was emphasized by the publication early in 1964 of the Toutée report on procedures for settling wages in the public sector. Pointing to the underlying 'absence of dialogue', the report recorded that 'the feeling of the union spokesmen is almost unanimous; their relations with the authorities, as far as wages are concerned, seem in their minds to be a tale of exhausted patience, misplaced confidence, dishonoured contracts and broken promises'. M. Toutée proposed a system by which the government would fix the total wage bill for each public corporation annually, in accordance with the national Plan, leaving the allocation of this sum to a joint committee of workers and management under an independent chairman. The unions were uniformly hostile: this spelled wages police rather than wages policy. Their antagonism deepened when the government ignored those of Toutée's recommendations which aimed at achieving a better negotiating balance between the two sides, and announced without any discussion with them in May 1964 that the system had been adopted in a most restrictive form. The very way in which the change was effected reduced the slender hope of clearing the climate of mistrust on which M. Toutée had commented.

Meanwhile, the wider debate on incomes policy continued in the Economic and Social Council. In discussing the policy directives of the Fifth Plan, union spokesmen on the ESC were outspokenly critical of the general framework of the government's economic policy, which they considered a wholly unacceptable background to the introduction of a wages policy—though at the final vote a coalition of farmers and employers prevailed over their objections. But in the main debate on wages policy business spokesmen also showed their hostility, fearing it would spell increased governmental intervention and a tendency for political criteria to take precedence over economic considerations in fixing wages. CGT, FO and CGC were all afraid that the proposals before them would be used chiefly for the narrower end of imposing wage restraint, while CFDT, as always taking a more nuanced stand, argued that the unions were not being offered enough in return for accepting an incomes policy. The clear conclusion of the debate was that neither industry nor labour was prepared to trust the government with the preparation and implementation of an incomes policy—though plainly their *arrières-pensées* were rather different.

Emphasizing the fact that it was travelling in the opposite direction from the government, early in 1965 CNPF came out with a highly doctrinaire manifesto wholeheartedly espousing economic liberalism, and particularly attacking intervention in employers' prerogatives by the State. It went on to make an independent agreement with the most amenable of the workers' organizations, FO, reflecting the union's own hostility to enforced incomes restraint. However, the unions were at this moment rather a spent force after two brief but bitter token general strikes had divided and confused the public. Sensing the moment for action, de Gaulle publicly endorsed the incomes policy concept at his February 'press conference'. The government brought pressure (through price controls) on private sector employers not to pay increases in excess of the norm and pressed forward to implement wage settlements in the nationalized industries under the Toutée procedure, even though union representatives had almost completely withdrawn. In the years which followed the *commissions de constatation* were all boycotted in whole or part by their union members—though here and there CFDT, FO and independent unions participated in the hope of turning the system to their profit. But the Toutée procedure never produced the dialogue that had been its object: the unions never tired of recalling the occasion in 1965 when a minister sat right through the discussions only to read to the participants at the end the decisions which had been in his pocket all the time.

With the unions invincibly suspicious of the government, and the employers committed to economic liberalism, the flight of the groups from the formulation of an incomes policy was complete. Experience had confirmed M. Toutée's own disillusioned comment in presenting his report in 1964: 'France is not ready for a body to take decisions on such disagreements, neither on the side of the unions nor on the side of the government.' Not that the attempt had failed completely; however imperfectly, the Toutée procedure had brought new concepts and a greater rigour into discussions of wages in the nationalized sector. But clearly '*concertation*' had broken down. It was left to the government to try more authoritarian approaches. The reaction of the workers to this new approach was to be seen in May 1968. And one of the provisions of the Grenelle agreement which emerged from the strikes was the final interment of the Toutée system—and the promise to seek, with the unions, a new system for discussing wages.

'Associating' the workers

Ideologically Gaullism has always travelled light. Freedom from encumbering doctrine was a major aid to the General's pragmatic rule, and to his ability to seem as many things as possible to as many Frenchmen as possible. Yet a few key general ideas formed familiar recurrent themes in his vision of the world: the well-aired notions of the Nation, the State, the international system, that 'certain idea' of France with which his Memoirs open, and a single point of social policy—the hope of finding a third way between capitalism and communism which would transform social relations. As early as 1945 his provisional government published an ordinance (suggested by René Capitant) requiring firms to set up consultative works committees. Later the RPF produced the more grandiloquent notion of Association Capital-Travail. It is somehow typical of Gaullism that over two decades later the content of this doctrine still remained nebulous. Consequently it was often dismissed as nothing more than the attempt of an economically conservative regime to give itself progressive trappings—and the timing of its recurrent airings did nothing to discourage such cynicism. And yet the Association seems to have been more than window dressing, for de Gaulle returned to the theme—under a variety of guises—despite repeated rebuffs and the indifference or hostility of so many of his otherwise loyal supporters.

Almost immediately he returned from the wilderness de Gaulle set his Minister of Labour, Paul Bacon, to preparing proposals to 'promote the association or involvement of workers in the firm'. Bacon, a leftish member of MRP, showed no great enthusiasm, while unions and employers alike suspiciously scented a threat to their prerogatives. All that emerged was an ordinance refurbishing Fourth Republic legislation, providing a limited voluntary scheme by which workers could benefit from higher profits or productivity through deferred stock or cash distributions. Despite its taxation incentives, by 1965 its provisions were benefiting under 1·5 per cent of industrial workers.

In 1960, when the Gaullists were again preoccupied with their 'social' image, their workers' wing pressed Debré for more rapid progress with Association Capital-Travail. Though the unenthusiastic Premier turned a deaf ear, Michelet the Minister of Justice assured the party that 'measures will be taken which will show that the General has not forgotten his promises'. Michelet's forthcoming companies' bill was to concentrate on enacting Association—but it had made no progress when Debré successfully claimed his head because of Michelet's concern with standards of justice during the Algerian war. Instead Debré set up a Commission de l'Intéressement, with members from both industry and labour, under M. Masselin of the Cour des Comptes. From this emerged proposals to overcome the technical limitations of the 1959 ordinance with the help of greater incentives to both firms and workers. A bill was sent to the Assembly in 1962, but languished there in an *ad hoc* committee, neglected by the parliamentarians, the pressure groups and Pompidou, until it perished at the dissolution.

For almost three years the matter rested with no more than ritual gestures towards Association, while relations between the regime and both sides of industry deteriorated. The unions were increasingly restive at wages policy and the stabilization plan. The *patronat*, which had been growing increasingly uneasy since the departure of Baumgartner (a former Governor of the Bank of France) from the Ministry of Finance in 1962, particularly disliked the regime's technocratic streak and resented de Gaulle's tendency to needle them with hints of greater *dirigisme*. Despite reassurances by the more emollient Pompidou, the *patronat* was retreating into a neo-Poujadist phase, which reached its paroxysm in the defiant liberalism of its 1965 manifesto.

It had long been clear that the 1945 ordinance on works committees was as good as a dead letter; of some 25,000 firms coming within its terms, only 6,000 had even nominally established a committee. De Gaulle ordered his Left Gaullist labour minister, Gilbert Grandval, to prepare a reform. After months of negotiations with unions and employers Grandval found the two sides so far apart that he went ahead in early 1965 with a mild bill slightly strengthening works committees and making them compulsory by 1968, and extending the workers' right to know the state of their firms' affairs. Despite the bill's reference to 'maintaining the authority of management intact', CNPF greeted its modest extension of the unions' role as a threat to employers' power to be masters in their own house. They were particularly outraged at the provision for an elected union official (*délégué syndical*) to sit on the committee, and for larger firms to grant him five hours weekly allowance for union work. CNPF launched a sustained attack privately and through the Economic and Social Council, where it rallied the support of nationalized industry representatives (over union protests) for an emasculated bill. For the unions, Grandval's proposals did not go far enough even in securing their right to be informed, still less in guaranteeing more fundamental rights. The employers were adamant that 'we will never admit union penetration of companies. It will have to be imposed on us forcibly'. CNPF expelled the Jeunes Patrons from its *bureau* for taking a more twentieth-century line. But with de Gaulle's backing Grandval maintained his original bill. Few deputies could raise any enthusiasm, and it was criticized from both the majority and opposition benches—echoing the criticisms of the two sides of industry. Faced with 128 amendments Grandval rapidly resorted to the package vote, irritating some of his reluctant supporters still further. The bill was carried by the apparently imposing majority of 381 to 3. But while the Communists had abstained, and the Federation had voted solidly for the government, only sixteen of the thirty-five Independent Republicans supported the bill and a dozen UNR abstained.

Hoping to sweeten industry's temper the government now introduced a companies bill incorporating tax concessions to shareholders and corporations. But Louis Vallon, the Left Gaullist *rapporteur-général* of the Assembly's Finance Committee, instantly seized his opportunity, and submitted an amendment committing the government to introduce a bill to 'lay down ways by which the right of workers to a share in the growth of the share value of the company accruing from self-financing is to be recognized and guaranteed'. The Vallon amendment was carried almost without debate. Yet even in the Gaullist ranks it had few wholehearted supporters. For the CGT it was a plot to entangle the workers in capitalism; FO believed it was aimed at undermining the workers' militancy and possibly leading to the emergence of company unions; only the CFDT pragmatically thought the plan might lead eventually to workers gaining a greater share in running their firms. This threat had not escaped the employers. While Pompidou was privately doing his best to soothe their fears, Vallon and Capitant were publicly depicting the amendment as the key to a fundamental change in the economic system. This over-dramatization of an essentially modest measure, following so soon on the reform of works committees, hardened the resolve of much of the *patronat* to support Lecanuet in the presidential campaign.

In 1966, after the presidential election, it fell to Debré to restore relations with business. Prudently he referred the Vallon amendment to yet another committee (again under a member of the Cour des Comptes, with eight employers to two from the unions), removing any interest the unions might have had in the outcome by instructing it not to involve itself in company reform. Some months later the Mathey committee duly reported that the Vallon amendment would be extremely difficult to implement, and recommended that any new scheme should be purely voluntary—and thus, on 1959 experience, ineffectual. But de Gaulle was not to be thwarted. From his warship in the South Pacific, where he was touring French possessions, came a message to prepare proposals for his return.

The long-rumbling dissent within the Gaullist camp broke into open conflict. Capitant accused Debré and Pompidou of trying to bury the whole thing, while on the eve of de Gaulle's press conference Debré dismissed the Vallon amendment as a 'diabolical myth', and Chalandon alleged it would lead to a 'people's Republic' (since the workers might eventually acquire a controlling shareholding). With the employers and unions antagonistic and his own supporters divided, de Gaulle announced that action was postponed until after the 1967 general election. But he made the employers' flesh creep by underlining the need for company reform and asserting that 'the conditions of the century lead us, without repudiating the spirit of enterprise, to practise an increasing degree of governmental intervention'.

When the Pompidou government emerged shaken from the

election, tucked away in its request for special powers was a provision—inserted at the General's request—for measures 'to ensure that the workers share the fruits of industrial expansion'. De Gaulle insisted that if the workers were to lend their full support to the necessary transformation of France, they must 'participate in an organic fashion in the development of expansion'. Though the task of preparing the new measure would normally fall either on the finance or social affairs ministers, Pompidou insisted on taking personal responsibility. Not surprisingly, the Vallon amendment was dismissed as unpopular and overcomplicated. Instead, the Masselin scheme for profit-sharing, based on the modest 1959 ordinance (itself harking back to the Fourth Republic), was rescued from its five-year limbo and used as a basis for new proposals. On hearing what was proposed Vallon, Capitant and other Left Gaullists sent an indignant memorandum to the Elysée—but de Gaulle countersigned Pompidou's ordinance.

When the ordinance was published in August 1967, it was understandable why even the chronically suspicious CNPF was reassured, and Debré considered the 'diabolical myth' had been exorcised.[1] The new scheme applied only to firms with over one hundred workers which were earning a return of over 10 per cent on their capital. It provided a share of profits after tax to be distributed to workers in proportion to their wages by various forms of bonus which would be frozen for five years. Firms investing in new plant a sum equal to what they allocated to *intéressement* bonuses would win fully compensating tax rebates. Workers were to be entitled to fuller information and consultation, but there was no question of the scheme bringing them a greater say in running the company. In short, the taxpayer was to finance a regressive redistribution of income of about 2 per cent to no more than one industrial worker in seven. Any firm which was maintaining a high rate of investment would actually be in pocket.

The scheme was greeted with indifference by the unions

---

[1] One of the rare employers enthusiastic about profit-sharing described the ordinance as 'derisory from every viewpoint but that of principles', and criticized 'the resistance of employers and the complicity of certain ministers—among others those who steered the Mathey commission, and thus dug the trap into which the Chief of State was to fall' (*Le Monde*, 22 August 1969).

and sardonic irony by the opposition, which considered that de Gaulle had been out-manœuvred by his own supporters. (It was even less surprising that this step towards implementing Gaullism's sole distinctive social policy should be enacted without parliamentary debate.) Soon after, de Gaulle learned to his anger that although the deadline for establishing works committees had passed, fewer than 10,000 of the 25,000 eligible firms had met their legal obligations. He was forced to a public admission that 'where these committees exist and operate properly—which is far, far, from being the case everywhere—there are contacts already. But these contacts touch the workers as a whole little or not at all.'

In May 1968 the old vision of Association merged with the new nostrum of participation. But as always the unions were more concerned with basic rights. For them the measure of the regime's sincerity about participation would be the way it fulfilled the pledge they won in May in the Grenelle agreements to introduce a charter of union rights. The government kept its word. After long discussions with both sides Maurice Schumann guided through the next session of the Assembly, by 438 to 4, a bill which was only slightly diluted by the government's more conservative supporters and the Senate. It seemed to grant the unions the legal recognition and effective rights to organize for which they had been pressing for years. Though branded 'catastrophic' by PME, the bill was welcomed by the Young Employers and the Catholic Employers, and after initial reservations, greeted by the CGT as 'the most important legal advance won by the union movement since 1884'.

There remained the problem of participation. The two chief saboteurs of *intéressement* were now on the economic sidelines, Debré at the foreign office and Pompidou in the 'reserve of the Republic': Capitant, now Minister of Justice, promptly proposed a tripartite company structure, with management accountable to both the shareholders and a workers' cooperative. Unions and employers alike reacted with predictable outrage. A *diversion mystificatrice* to the CGT, for the CNPF it would be 'the ruin of the national economy', though the organization of professional managers reacted less antagonistically. But to de Gaulle participation meant essentially that workers should be entitled to fuller information and the right to have their say in discussion of the company's problems;

management was for the managers. 'Discussion is a matter for several; action for one', he said. Despite the indifference or hostility of almost every organized interest and a majority of his own supporters de Gaulle would not accept defeat. He was still looking to the day when 'association will little by little replace the spirit and fact of the class struggle, as created by the "iron law" of capitalism and as nourished even now to a certain extent by the present conditions of the workers'. Instructions came down from the Elysée to press forward with operating the 1967 ordinance on profit sharing, to begin implementing the Vallon amendment fully, and to draft a bill on 'participation' in the factories (the first draft of which was rejected by de Gaulle as too timid). But nothing further had been achieved by the time the General departed. Association had remained to the end part of de Gaulle's vision. But it had never been one of those great causes for which he was prepared to fight single-mindedly. The slender achievements during the General's eleven-year reign showed that even under the nominally 'personal rule' of the Fifth Republic this was politically not enough.[1]

Health insurance and the self-employed

Fifth Republic ministers are often criticized for acting without consultations. But this case shows that even well-intentioned consultation may not produce viable policies. The problem goes back to the Fourth Republic. The 1946 social security law, with its ideal of 'national solidarity', was intended to embrace the entire working population. But the Comité National des Classes Moyennes (CNCM), inspired by Gingembre of PME, fought with a massive refusal of contributions against being lumped in with the ordinary wage-earners. In 1948 parliament capitulated to the social particularism of the self-employed groups by an amending act allowing them to run their own voluntary schemes of private insurance. However, doubts about the wisdom of this sturdy individualism grew during the fifties, particularly among the 'small men', who were both the most vulnerable and the least likely to have adequate cover. When the farmers won their own privileged State system in 1961, pressure for similar

[1] As he admitted: below, p. 343.

improvements grew rapidly among the self-employed. In June 1961 the Confédération Générale de l'Artisanat Français (CGAF) put proposals for compulsory health insurance cover for artisans to Jeanneney, the Minister of Industry. He promptly set up a committee of representatives from the ministries of Industry and Labour and the groups to study the matter.

But negotiating an agreement with a category as disparate as the self-employed was far from easy: over four million small businessmen, shopkeepers, craftsmen and members of the liberal professions were represented by a large number of groups of varying membership and competence. Together with most of the political Left, groups like the Centre des Jeunes Artisans and the Confédération de l'Artisanat et des Petites Entreprises du Bâtiment (CAPEB), favoured bringing the self-employed into the social security general system. But a majority of the groups, and their allies on the Centre and Right, advocated a new autonomous system offering more limited (and thus cheaper) cover than the general system.

Towards the end of 1962 the Left Gaullist Minister of Labour, Grandval, came out in favour of integration in the general system. Faced with this 'threat', the groups now joined under the auspices of CNCM in the search for a common front. After a year's discussion they agreed on a draft bill proposing compulsory health insurance organized in several autonomous occupational schemes, with subscribers choosing the cover they wanted (or could afford). Parliamentary interest was also stirring. The Communists, Conservatives and Socialists all presented bills during 1963, and the Assembly's Social Affairs Committee set up a special study group. In June 1964 a number of government supporters brought forward a bill reflecting CNCM's line; within a fortnight several more UNR members countered with another bill, reportedly inspired by Grandval himself, to integrate the self-employed in the general system. (In all, eight private members' bills were introduced; all were stifled in committee.) Meanwhile, the groups had persuaded Giscard d'Estaing that their proposals would cost the taxpayer less than integration in the general system. With Labour and Finance Ministers in disagreement, the groups pressed Pompidou to 'arbitrate' in their favour—but urgent preoccupations with the battle against TVA,[1] and the presidential elections deferred any decision.

In the new cabinet Debré was Minister of Finance, and his friend and political ally Jeanneney was at the new Ministry of Social Affairs. Both gave sympathetic assurances to CNCM delegations. In March 1966 CGAF tried to force the pace with a dinner-debate in Paris at which the authors of all the private members' bills outlined their proposals. In fact the government was now drafting its proposals in consultation with the groups. The crucial problem was the range of risk to cover compulsorily. The better the cover the higher the subscriptions—and the greater the burden on the small man. There was no more 'solidarity' between the groups than there had been earlier between the self-employed and the wage-earners. The CNCM wanted the range of cover to be wholly at the individual's discretion (which was least helpful to the vulnerable small man); Jeanneney wanted to come as close as possible to the level of the general system (with the danger of subjecting the economically marginal craftsman to highly regressive levies). Eventually all groups agreed to compulsory insurance of so-called 'major risks'.

In April Jeanneney both met the groups again and met the Assembly's Social Affairs Committee for a preliminary discussion of his proposals. Drafting was completed in May. Jeanneney proposed a series of autonomous schemes of compulsory cover for 'major risks', with additional cover available to those who could afford it. The government's supporters on the Social Affairs Committee were kept briefed on progress, and the UNR member who had been sitting on the private members' bills was already at work as rapporteur—though he was not officially elected by the committee until 25 May. Consequently his report, prepared in collaboration with the ministry, was published almost simultaneously with the bill itself.

But while the minister kept his supporters closely informed, parliament was not so well served. Summoned to hear Jeanneney's defence of the bill on 31 May, the Social Affairs Committee discussed it on 2 June so hurriedly that duplicated copies had to be borrowed from the ministry. Without inviting the views of the Economic and Social Council, the government

[1] See Williams, *The French Parliament*, pp. 93-5.

formally laid the bill on 3 June; on 9 June the bill passed through the Assembly at a single sitting. The opposition's predictable protests at this 'parliamentary gallop' were echoed by Dr Hébert, the Gaullist author of a private member's bill, who complained that the procedure was 'the negation of the true role of parliament', and showed 'how little account the government takes of our work'. Jeanneney justified the breakneck pace with the remark that 'when a matter has dragged on for so long there comes a moment when speed is essential'. In fact, the end of the session was at hand, a general election was in the offing, and Jeanneney may well have hoped that sheer speed would enable him to push an electorally popular measure through without any repetition of the previous year's fiasco over TVA. Indeed some two hundred amendments were submitted—many directly inspired by the groups and presented by the Gaullist chairman of the parliamentary Groupe d'Étude des Problèmes de l'Artisanat. Though spirited efforts were made by spokesmen for the lawyers and taxi-drivers to exempt them, most amendments were set aside either by article 40 or the package vote—though Jeanneney accepted amendments improving provision for widows and the elderly. The bill passed 359–0 with Socialists and Communists abstaining.

The Senate also dispatched the measure in a single sitting by a show of hands, though voting against Jeanneney for concessions to the lawyers and taxi-drivers. The conference committee worked so rapidly and smoothly (finding for the taxi-drivers but thwarting the lawyers) that the bill passed through both houses again with little further discussion by 29 June, hailed by Jeanneney as a fine example of cooperation between the two chambers and between parliament and the executive. On 13 July 1966 the bill became law, and Jeanneney promised to publish the implementing decrees by the end of 1966.

But in the apparently wasted words of the Assembly debate were some which foreshadowed the problems to come. Dr Hébert's onslaught on the bill had been so ferocious that he was applauded by the opposition alone. Attacking the 'balkanization' of the social security system, he challenged the claim of the groups that their members had no need of disability and death cover. He suggested that experience with the farmers' scheme showed that where conditions were less favourable than the general system pressure invariably mounted for benefits to be improved—without increasing contributions. The inadequacies of the new system, and the anomalies it created, bore the seeds of future discord. Jeanneney had proudly replied, 'this bill is not the product of a technocratic outlook, but springs directly from the opinions expressed by the interested parties'. But just how representative had Jeanneney's interlocutors been? Another UNR deputy reported his shopkeeper and *artisan* constituents as feeling 'that some of their organizations speak more for their leaders than for their members'. And although Jeanneney wrapped himself in group support, the law was coolly received by many of the groups, who knew that its vague phraseology had left most of the thorny problems to be resolved by the implementing decrees.

Jeanneney's deadline came and went, but not until December 1967 was the Caisse Nationale d'Assurance Maladie installed with temporary administrators drawn from the self-employed groups, to work out the final details. The CAPEB roundly declared the scheme 'quite unsuited to the needs of the *artisans*', and refused to serve. But it was only in November 1968 that decrees were finally published, introducing the scheme from 1 April 1969 and fixing contributions. Only then did the ordinary shopkeepers and craftsmen seem to wake up and realize what had been done in their name. Irritated already by tax grievances, TVA, supermarket competition and increased retirement insurance contributions, they now found they would have to pay more for less cover than they had been led to expect. Their annoyance was fanned further by the complete failure of the administrators to explain the scheme to its beneficiaries, the delay of four months between contributions falling due and benefits becoming payable, the demand for two quarterly instalments at once, and the discovery of retired people that up to 30 per cent of their pension was to be clawed back in sickness contributions.

The initial protests were orthodox—representations to Couve de Murville and a day of demonstrations and delegations to prefects. The government replied that change at this stage was impossible. But beginning in December in Isère (ironically, on the boundary of Jeanneney's own constituency), a grass roots revolt against the new scheme rapidly spread through the country. New 'defence' groups sprang up to

oppose the national group leadership as well as the government, in a neo-Poujadist revolt of small men, furiously and
instinctively rejecting a system they could neither understand
nor control. They were to take direct action further even than
Poujade himself. The following months brought plastic bomb
attacks, assaults on officials, ransacking of official buildings,
clashes with the police, and the seizure of thousands of tax
files as 'hostage' for their arrested leader. PME, which had
initially defended the scheme, climbed on the bandwagon to
demand its rejection and lead a further series of demonstrations and shopkeeper strikes.

With the referendum approaching, the failing regime was
ill placed to make a firm stand. First the date for initial
contributions was put back, then a fortnight before the
referendum the government agreed to subsidize the system
(having previously insisted that if the self-employed rejected
State control they had no claim to State aid). Pompidou
promised further concessions in his presidential campaign, but
the agitation continued. But if the mood of the activist
minority was clear, their demands were not. In August Boulin,
the Minister of Health, held a round table with both the
established and the unofficial groups which produced a head-
on clash between six irreconcilable solutions. The Vice-
President of PME threw up his hands in a complete confession
of failure and suggested a referendum to discover what his
members really thought. At a later round table, the choice
narrowed to either improving the 1966 scheme or integration
in the general system. The second course was now flatly
opposed by both CNPF and the trade unions. Most of the
groups now favoured the first—calling for increased State aid
in the name of the very 'national solidarity' their system was
designed to escape. Again the government gave ground. Amid
continued uncertainty about whether any scheme could win
general acceptance, it agreed to extend benefits and double the
State subsidy. This time it consulted the Economic and Social
Council, but although the new proposals won a majority, the
spokesmen for the shopkeepers and craftsmen were not part
of it. Amid their cries of discontent and sporadic direct action,
M. Boulin brought his bill to the Assembly in December
1969. There it was again exposed to a barrage of amendments
intended to accommodate a wide range of special interests and
droits acquis. After an exceptionally confused debate the bill

emerged incorporating still more concessions. Even so the organizations of the self-employed declared their dissatisfaction, and demanded even more generous terms. A fresh round of direct action flared up over the whole range of the small men's grievances, organized by the militant breakaway organizations. But this time the dissenters were divided and confused and the government's response was firmer. Though they won some minor concessions, their leader was jailed and the Prime Minister refused to meet their spokesmen. However, the militants won almost a quarter of the seats in the councils to administer the new system when it went into operation in 1970. Moreover, Boulin's proposals were not presented as any 'final solution' to the problem, but as a holding operation until a permanent scheme could be worked out. Thus after four years of acrimony only two things seemed really clear: that the fight was not yet over, and that the splintered and warring groups were no closer to playing effectively the role they demanded.

Parliament and the 1968 budget

In France, as in Britain, the parliamentary stage is the most visible but least decisive in the budgetary process. When Debré presented his 1968 budget to the Assembly's Finance Committee on 13 September 1967 most of the issues had already been settled in the relative obscurity of the ministries. He had had to prepare his budget against mounting evidence of economic stagnation: flattening growth, rising prices and unemployment, and a deteriorating balance of trade. It was apparently Debré himself who decided to diverge from Giscard's orthodox liberal budgeting, and to adopt the more Keynesian approach of selective tax cuts, expenditure outrunning expected growth in GNP, and an avowed planned deficit after three years of nominally balanced budgets.

With expenditure rising 7 per cent in real terms over 1967, the customary wrangling between Finance and the spending ministries had been less agonizing than usual. There were no angry cries and tactical leaks to the press, like those of 1963 and 1964 when Giscard was forcing through his cuts in public investment programmes, nor were there highly publicized intercessions with de Gaulle like Edgar Faure's in 1968. Debré had to fight hard with Construction, which pressed strongly to be granted sufficient funds to fulfil the Plan's target for the house-building programme; he succeeded in curbing the voracious appetite of the education budget without too great anguish; there were the customary angry arguments over whether Paris transport fares should rise or be subsidized further, which Debré won. Health and Justice as always had their hopes of building more hospitals and modern courts disappointed. But most of these disputes were settled bilaterally between Finance and the other ministries. Only a handful of irreconcilable differences remained to be decided by Pompidou's 'arbitration' in early July. The main lines of the budget were agreed before the summer break.

Mindful of the government's slender majority, Debré set out to prepare the ground with its supporters by a lunch for UNR and RI members of the Assembly's Finance Committee, at which he outlined his proposals and solicited their comments before even receiving final cabinet approval for them. The Centrist leaders were also received in audience; their votes would be crucial. As soon as his bill was approved by the cabinet, Debré met the full Finance Committee for two long and mildly critical sessions.

For the next four weeks the Finance Committee was considering the entire bill while the five other committees were preparing their advisory reports on particular estimates. When the Finance Committee began its general discussion a fortnight later Debré's general economic strategy was challenged not only by senior members of the opposition like Mendès-France and Gaillard, but firmly questioned from within the majority by Chalandon and Giscard d'Estaing (now out of office and chairman of the committee). This long, serious and semi-private debate was to provide the most searching and coherent examination the budget received. As always, discontent was crystallizing around a few secondary but politically sensitive questions which were to dominate the problems of steering the bill through parliament: the level of Value-Added Tax (TVA) and its extension to agriculture, the rate of farmers' contributions for old-age benefits, and an axle-weight tax on heavy vehicles. On all these the committee voted amendments against the government by large majorities, some on opposition instigation, but others on proposals from the Gaullists themselves.

UNR and RI Finance Committee members now met

Pompidou and Debré to discuss these differences. But Debré was in no mood to compromise; brushing aside customary courtesies he rebuked the committee in a press statement for cutting revenue by £105 million. He stood by his original proposals, with only minor concessions on TVA and vehicle taxes. The committee promptly rejected his advice by large majorities. But mostly the various committees discussed the departmental estimates placidly, adopting many without a formal vote. As always there were exceptions: the Gaullist rapporteur of the Ex-Servicemen's estimates resigned his report to the Social Affairs Committee in sympathy with the claims of wartime political deportees, and the Finance Committee rejected the Public Health estimates to protest at the inadequate hospital building programme.

Debré opened the Assembly's general budgetary debate on 11 October with an optimistic survey of the condition and prospects of the economy—followed by a muted but loyal critique from the Gaullist rapporteur. Then the Communists attacked with a motion to send the bill back to committee. Though this was swept away, a blocking move by PDM failed by only three votes. The Centrists never really intended to prevent debate, but they wanted to warn the government not to take them for granted, despite their disunity in a censure motion the previous day. In the detailed scrutiny of the bill they soon rubbed the point home, aided by Gaullist defections, by carrying against the government an amendment to link income tax rates to the price index.

Debré was now faced with either resort to the package vote or a long guerrilla battle in which the Centrists could score political points with impunity. Deferring discussion of the litigious clauses, he called a meeting at Matignon between government backbenchers, Pompidou and himself at which agreement was reached on compromises on some of the main thorny issues—TVA, farmers' contributions, axle-tax and taxes in Corsica (where the islanders are perennially prepared to take direct action to defend their fiscal privileges). The Matignon agreement rallied the majority. It promptly threw out an amendment to curb pursuit of tax evaders which was strongly supported in the UNR ranks. But just before the debate on the deferred clauses, Giscard d'Estaing suddenly laid a fresh amendment on the application of TVA to the farmers. Though he claimed his amendment was strictly technical, to Debré it was a betrayal of the whole Matignon compromise which jeopardized the principle of striking bargains outside the chamber in order to avoid resort to the package vote. Debré immediately laid the full story before the UNR and RI deputies. But although some of Giscard's chief lieutenants repudiated him, and the Assembly twice suspended its sitting while the search for agreement continued in the corridors, the government was defeated by two votes—with two of its supporters defecting. Debré railed bitterly at 'the incomprehension of the electronic vote'; many whose votes had been cast against him had never heard his masterly defence of his policy, but had gone to bed leaving their voting keys with colleagues. The government lost again over the farmers' contributions before the remainder of the Matignon compromise was carried.

The examination of the individual ministries' estimates which began on 19 October offered the main annual parliamentary opportunity for airing grievances and exposing shortcomings. Technical or less fashionable departments were rapidly dispatched after subdued and sparsely attended debates. As always estimates like Tourism, Merchant Marine and Overseas Territories gave deputies a chance to champion constituency issues or to press for concessions on such matters as the claim of flying clubs for concessionary fuel. More substantial questions were raised; during the Justice estimates the minister was pressed for reform of the system of remands in custody; the Youth and Sports debate brought searching criticism of the cost of the Grenoble winter Olympics, and the PTT debate produced the annual denunciation of the telephone system. On the Health estimates four rapporteurs from the majority led sixty speakers in deploring the many inadequacies of the public health services—and were only partly mollified by the minister's promise of a hospital building bill. The Minister of Justice warded off some predictable attacks by announcing an amnesty bill, but the criticisms of the Gaullist chairman of the Defence Committee extracted a reluctant minister's pledge to report on the progress of the weapons programme during the next session. While ministers were criticized as strongly by their own supporters as by opponents on matters like health or education, other debates produced confrontations with the opposition. Mitterrand and Pierre Cot used the normally uncontroversial discussion of the

Scientific Research budget for an onslaught on nuclear policy. The Foreign Affairs vote was a peg for criticisms on European and Atlantic policies, and attacks by the Right on aid to Algeria and by the Left on relations with the Greek colonels. Yet once issues had been aired, and assurances had been sought (and sometimes received), all but a few estimates were allowed to carry on a simple show of hands.

But as always a handful of issues produced stormy confrontations. On the Interior estimates Fouchet was assailed by speakers from every party who echoed the discontent of the police and prefecture officials and the grievances of the Algerian refugees. Nothing he said could overcome the fact that the funds at his disposal were inadequate or non-existent. The majority's discipline broke momentarily; the estimates for the police and prefecture officials were rejected by five votes, and those for the refugees by fourteen. In the second vote there were three Gaullist rebels from constituencies with high refugee resettlement. In the first, the twenty-nine defectors, mostly from the Paris region, included three former general secretaries of the UNR and five ex-ministers. This vote was partly the product of skilful lobbying by the prefecture officials (whom deputies meet regularly during their work), partly a reaction to a threat by police unions to demonstrate outside the Palais Bourbon. It also obliquely expressed the hostility of some Gaullists to M. Delouvrier's running of the Paris District. (At the next party meeting their provincial colleagues gave them a frosty reception for embarrassing the government with their feud.) Both votes were essentially a public warning to Fouchet to change his ways.

In the traditionally perilous Agriculture debate, which ranged from the state of world commodity markets to the effects of a cement factory on the vineyards of Beaune, Edgar Faure produced tactfully timed announcements of aid for rural electrification and water supplies. Even so he was unable to ward off defeat over the application of TVA to agriculture. The Ex-Servicemen's estimates as always produced minor drama; the Gaullist rapporteur stated he had resigned 'to help the minister in the task he has set himself of reconciling the ex-servicemen with the government', while the UNR president of the interparty Amicale Parlementaire des Anciens Déportés et Internés pleaded for the minister to honour promises allegedly given by his predecessor. When finally the procession of deputies pleading for a variety of concessions had ended, the minister announced two small amendments which placated the Assembly enough for the estimates to squeeze through by seven votes. As discussion of the departmental estimates drew to a close there was a sudden flare up over Information, heralding the battle ahead over introduction of brand-name publicity on ORTF. By 244 to 235 ORTF was refused permission to levy licence fees during the year ahead.

Meanwhile, the farmers' unions had become so aroused over TVA that the government felt obliged to make further concessions. Accordingly Pompidou met UNR and RI parliamentary leaders and agreed with them a compromise satisfying the farmers' main grievances over the extension of TVA. At the close of discussion of departmental estimates on 10 November Pompidou called for a package vote on the entire budget, embodying the few concessions made by the government but restoring all the estimates previously rejected. With the majority's ranks intact, and support from unaffiliated deputies, the budget carried by 252 to 234.

The Senate now had only a fortnight to cover the same ground. It was to sit early and late right through the week, but inevitably its discussions were hasty and sketchy at times. To emphasize the Senate's secondary status and its poor relations with the regime, the estimates were mainly defended by junior ministers, and Debré himself did not appear before it at all. (Ministers like Joxe and Messmer who did appear had a noticeably easier passage.) After spending only a single day in general discussion, the senators showed their disagreement with the government by moving token reductions. However, when they did this on the Foreign Affairs estimate—as a protest against the Gaullist line on Israel, Algeria and NATO —the minister countered by demanding a package vote; the irritated senators promptly rejected the entire estimate 160 to 69. Senators complained bitterly that the government was trying to provoke them by package votes into blackening their own reputation by unreconstructed opposition. But the government did not resort to the ploy again.

In fact, despite the Senate's reputation, many departmental estimates passed easily, sometimes unanimously. During the Transport debate the senators even obligingly struck out an amendment on internal airlines which Pleven had carried against the government in the Assembly. Occasional token reductions were voted, over the rights of local authorities, forest protection, or the closure of a branch line. But there were very few direct and determined attacks. When the budget was carried 173 to 82 (Socialists and Communists) on 30 November, the Foreign Affairs and Algerian refugee budgets had been rejected, the extension of TVA to agriculture had been defeated, and the refusal to let ORTF levy licences had been repeated. Altogether, the Senate had amputated nearly £200 million from the Assembly's version of the bill. But at least it had voted the budget (which it refused to do in 1965), had carried the Education estimates without amendment, and had accepted the estimates for the nuclear strike force for the first time. The senators at least were impressed by their moderation.

The conference committee quickly agreed (if only because all the Assembly delegates came from the majority, and the Senate's proportionally selected delegation included a Gaullist). On 5 December the Assembly was asked to vote its 'first reading' text with a few minor Senate amendments and twelve new ones from the government. In the brief debate well-worn arguments over the familiar controversial points were rehearsed once more. A thirteenth amendment appeared unexpectedly on the rate of TVA for wholesale fish merchants at ports. Backed by four Gaullists from coastal constituencies, it was opposed by other Gaullists from inland seats and readily defeated. The Assembly then adopted the new text on a package vote 245 to 235—with three Gaullists complaining that someone had cast their votes against the government in their absence.

Feeling was running high in the Senate over the purely 'platonic satisfactions' the upper house had obtained in the conference committee, and over the government's subsequent introduction of amendments. In an angry reflex the bill was rejected 197 to 41. Accordingly it had to return to the Assembly on the 7th, where it acquired a few more small government amendments, and a final unsuccessful attempt was made to cut axle-taxes. Back the bill went to the Senate for the last time, with the minister complaining that the government's concessions in the conference committee had been 'rewarded with sarcasm and insults', and the *rapporteur-général* alleging that the procedure adopted had 'virtually robbed the Senate of any hope of influencing the budget'.

After the Senate had rejected the budget again 180 to 49, the Assembly had the last word 249 to 233 on 9 December.

Thus the government emerged with its proposals almost intact despite its narrow majority in the Assembly. In a budget of nearly £10,000 million the cost of the various concessions amounted to only some £6 million. But the deputies and senators had not in fact been solely or even primarily concerned with transforming the budget. The debates were also a chance to press constituency questions, to seek promises of legislation or assurances on policy or administration, to ginger up ministerial colleagues, pillory opponents or (for Giscardians particularly) jockey for position within the majority. Thus the budget debates were not simply about taxes and expenditure, but provided one of the major skirmishes in the continuing political battle between and within the parties. Moreover, by March government measures to reflate the economy were to entail a conventional supplementary budget bill which raised the deficit a further £275 million. Then a second supplementary budget was required to cope with the fall-out from May—£550 million in expenditure and £190 million in new taxes and a deficit of £770 million. The government had proposed, but ultimately it was the rioters and strikers who disposed of the 1968 budget.

Friction with Intellectuals

The Cinémathèque affair

For some time the Ministry of Cultural Affairs had been brooding over the problem of Henri Langlois, founder and director of the Cinémathèque française. A man with a consuming passion for the cinema, who had rescued innumerable films from destruction for posterity, Langlois had been the mentor of an entire generation of French *cinéastes*, and had become a legend among film-makers and serious students of the cinema throughout the world. But his running of the Cinémathèque was intensely personal, even wayward. Impatient of auditors and safety regulations, Langlois himself admitted to being a disorganized administrator. He was not a man whose dealings with the conventional civil servants from the ministry could ever be wholly smooth. Early in 1968 it was decided he must go. The first thought was simply to cut off the Cinémathèque's state subsidy. This was abandoned as likely to cause a storm. The next was to stage a coup (as Malraux had done at least twice already to rid himself of awkward administrators elsewhere). The civil servants holding half the seats on the managing board received their orders. Without any notice at the next meeting (and apparently in the absence of Langlois himself), Langlois was brusquely dismissed and replaced by M. Pierre Barbin, founder of the Tours Short Film Festival. Immediately he was appointed Barbin declared all the Cinémathèque's sixty employees dismissed on the spot and rushed posthaste to the building, which was closed, to change all its locks so that Langlois would be unable to re-enter his office. But in their hurry the workmen overlooked an elderly colleague of Langlois's who was working alone in the building; her hammering to be released brought the coup to light prematurely.

Within hours the storm had broken. Godard, Truffaut, Resnais, Marker and Varda, leading the younger generation, were rapidly joined by more senior figures like Bresson and Renoir, and even such old guard directors as René Clair. Then protests came pouring in from all over the world, from figures as diverse as Chaplin and Bardot, Elia Kazan and Orson Welles. Director after director announced that if Langlois went he would refuse to allow his films to be shown at the Cinémathèque. In Paris producers, actors and directors —many of them sworn professional and personal enemies— held protest demonstrations (which were naturally violently broken up by the police), and picketed the cinema, now prudently closed for 'stocktaking'. Malraux, who should have understood if anyone could that men like Langlois will not function bureaucratically, issued a lengthy attack on Langlois's failings as a curator, and parties of selected journalists were led on conducted tours of Langlois's storerooms to witness the disorder and the deterioration of the prints. But the attack backfired, for Langlois had been pressing the ministry for better storage facilities for years. With criticism being voiced even among the government's supporters, scarcely a voice was raised publicly to justify Malraux's action.

From demonstrations, Langlois's supporters passed to organization. They established themselves as the Cinémathèque Defence Committee and succeeded in forcing an extraordinary meeting of the Cinémathèque's members. By now the publicity was becoming an embarrassment to the government, and it was increasingly unlikely that the Cinémathèque could function since so many films were either owned by Langlois, stored only he knew where, or embargoed by their producers. The coup had backfired. The minister had no choice but to give ground. On the eve of the special general meeting the ministry agreed to grant the Cinémathèque independence from State control, though on rather stringent financial terms. The unfortunate Barbin was dispatched elsewhere as suddenly as he had appeared, and Langlois was reinstated. Collective action by one of the most individualist of professions had prevailed.

The government and the students

Relations between Fifth Republic governments and the Union Nationale des Etudiants de France have always been uneasy, sometimes disastrous—and never cordial. There was a certain inevitability about this hostility. Here was a student generation stirred to heightened political awareness by the Algerian war, feeling drawn by the discredit into which the older parties had fallen into taking responsibilities broader than those normally assumed by pressure groups. Opposing them were ministers who resented both UNEF's youthful brashness and its intervention in matters outside normal student concerns, and who saw it as a body—unlike many they had to negotiate and compromise with—which could be put firmly in its place with impunity.

Things went wrong from the very beginning. When UNEF complained over 'neglect' of higher education in the 1959 budget, back came an icy reply from de Gaulle saying that this was a matter for the government, and the students should mind their own business. Yet governments do need teaching their business at times: the following year when the system of deferments from military service was revised without consultation with UNEF, it contained so many ambiguities and inequities that UNEF threatened action in the Conseil d'Etat with every hope of success. The scheme had to be withdrawn and rewritten. UNEF had shown that the specialist knowledge of an interest group has its uses to government—but had scarcely endeared itself to ministers. When it showed a mature and conciliatory approach, as when the great divisive issue of subsidies to Church schools flared up again in 1959–60, it received little credit for behaving better than many of the professional politicians. But the real bone of contention was Algeria. UNEF was among the first to denounce torture, and maintained contacts with the illegal Algerian students' organization. When a joint meeting of UNEF and Algerian students in Switzerland called for self-determination in Algeria, this was the last straw for the unhappy and frustrated Debré. UNEF's official subsidy was promptly cut off. Undeterred, UNEF called for a demonstration for a ceasefire and negotiations. The government banned it. From then until the end of the war UNEF outdoor meetings or demonstrations were invariably banned; those who demonstrated regardless were beaten or locked up by the police. But UNEF persisted in siding with opponents of the war and asserting its belief in Algerian independence. Ministers resorted to an all-out attack on UNEF's representative status, and even its very existence. In June 1961 government agents collaborated in the creation of an anti-UNEF, the Fédération Nationale des Etudiants de France. Even before FNEF had been fully set up and had held elections, the government granted it the subsidies withdrawn from UNEF and gave it half UNEF's seats on the Conseil National des Oeuvres Universitaires. Ironically enough FNEF was to become the main platform for student supporters of *Algérie française*. UNEF challenged the government's action in the administrative courts and won. At about this time the UNEF president was turned away from sitting the entrance exams to the Ecole Nationale d'Administration. Though he successfully challenged the ban before the Conseil d'Etat, this spiteful act of harassment cost him a year.

Peace in Algeria did not end UNEF's troubles. It was left deeply divided between all-out opponents of Gaullism and those prepared to negotiate with the regime. Moreover, the campaign for a greater say in student life brought it into conflict with former allies like the teachers' unions. (UNEF had no seat on the Commission on Reform of Higher Education, was given only half an hour in which to present its oral evidence, and told to limit its written evidence to two sheets of typescript.) Torn by internal crises and resignations, its membership sagging dramatically, UNEF was now in grave financial trouble. The Minister of Education persistently refused to meet UNEF delegations until March 1963. He then promised to restore the subsidy, but fresh bones of contention arose. UNEF was sharply critical of educational priorities, resentful of a reorganization of the Conseil National des Oeuvres Universitaires, viewing this with good reason as an attempt to pack the Conseil with a tame majority, and active in organizing strikes over working conditions in the universities which infuriated ministers and Gaullist deputies. Making it clear that UNEF would get no subsidy until its political line changed, the minister cancelled a grant he had promised for an international youth festival.

UNEF was in fact beginning to change—not because students were 'coming to heel' but because constituent associations were sick of the internal warfare, interminable sterile ideological debates, and administrative confusion into which the Union had fallen. The Union prudently kept out of the presidential campaign. It was now moving noticeably towards a more moderate line. Recognizing this, the minister agreed early in 1966 to meet the student leaders for the first time in over two years. He again announced the forthcoming restoration of the subsidy, agreed to support a cultural festival sponsored by UNEF, and confirmed its representative status —then withdrew one of its seats on the Conseil National des Oeuvres Universitaires in favour of the much smaller FNEF. The Union's leaders were now concentrating their attention more on strictly educational issues and grappling with their increasingly desperate internal difficulties. In 1967, after seven years, the government restored UNEF's subsidy and even paid some of its debts.

But the long years of mutual hostility and mistrust had left their mark. Ministers still found it difficult to open any constructive dialogue with the student leaders, whose influence with the ministry remained minimal. Under a PSU leadership from 1967, the Union was again racked by factional disputes and esoteric ideological quarrels. Its membership had sunk from the 1961 peak of over 100,000 to under 50,000 in a far larger student population. As the expansion of higher education and the failure to reform the university system created fresh tensions, UNEF had ceased to interest the great majority of students. Small extremist groups vied feverishly for their allegiance. Finally came the explosion. The conflagration of May 1968 was in some degree the price the regime paid for its long war of attrition against the Union. In their attempt to destroy it ministers had deprived themselves of any means of ensuring either an early warning of impending trouble or an opportunity for consultation with potentially reasonable student opinion. By nurturing a situation in which moderates despaired and were discredited while extremism took root, they nurtured their own grave-diggers as fatally as a Marxian bourgeoisie.

While the May outbreak was not of UNEF's doing, student solidarity brought the Union a resurgence of membership and vitality. The leadership swung far to the Left in support of the student revolt, vying for the initiative with the 'wild men'. They allied themselves with the forces pressing for the overthrow of the system and attempted to continue the fight well after it was plain that the moment had passed. Then they threw themselves into furious opposition to Edgar Faure's reforms. When these passed they embarked on a policy of systematic non-cooperation, boycotting the ensuing university elections and causing fresh deep splits within the Union's ranks. Membership sank back once more, and the fragmentation of the student movement intensified. Although both Faure and his successor, Guichard, were now prepared to consult and had abandoned the sanctions policy, relations between UNEF and the regime relapsed once more into a sterile confrontation.

The University Orientation Law, 1968

It was the barricades of the Latin Quarter in May 1968 which finally gave the impetus for the long overdue reform of French higher education. Within a month de Gaulle had announced that 'the university must be completely reconstructed ... with the participation of all its teachers and all its students'. To carry through this major reform he turned to Edgar Faure, a quintessential Fourth Republic figure who possessed in exceptional measure those much-scorned political skills to which the Fifth Republic was ready enough to resort in delicate situations.

The need for reform was no longer seriously challenged; higher education could never return to the *status quo*. But educational and political passions were inevitably running high. Extremist student groups were still clashing violently; UNEF was calling for the overthrow of the entire social order, and the Syndicat National de l'Enseignement Supérieur

(SNESup, the noisiest of the university teachers' unions), had declared it 'no longer recognized the government'. In the wake of the Gaullist electoral victory, the Conservatives more confidently and insistently demanded strong measures to restore order. Faure immediately set about lowering the temperature. In a speech of rare distinction during the Assembly's July debate on higher education, he extended an olive branch to the radical reformers by abandoning selection for university entrance, due to be introduced in October[1], and he offered 'to receive anyone with something to say' about his forthcoming *loi-cadre* on the universities. The reticence of many Gaullist deputies during his speech, and their hectoring of the one or two Left Gaullists who displayed any sympathetic understanding of the student revolt, showed that Faure would have to steer a difficult way between the disaffected radicals outside the chamber and the conservatism of the government's own supporters.

With parliament in recess Faure settled down to prepare the bill. A long procession of educational groups passed through his office day by day: teachers, administrators, candidates preparing the *agrégation* and others opposing it, deputations from provincial universities, and a number of student organizations. Ministerial envoys, more or less official, toured the universities. Together with the Minister of Social Affairs Faure organized a special forum on medical education which brought together a further two hundred group representatives to discuss reform. UNEF denounced the whole enterprise and boycotted consultation but SNESup, after initially rejecting the 'traditional ministerial audience', put its views to Faure, and precipitated the first major storm with its militant communique disclosing that he had agreed to political discussions being allowed on university premises. The rival conservative Syndicat Autonome des Facultés de Lettres declared it was 'thunderstruck', and accused Faure of a 'policy of capitulation which is handing over the university to subversion'; and was joined by that archetypal vested academic interest, the Société des Agrégés, in accusing Faure of siding with the wild men.

In early September Faure outlined his ideas to the

---

[1] Anyone who has passed the *baccalauréat* can go to university in France — though not for quite all courses.

Assembly's Cultural Affairs Committee at a four hour meeting at which the deep doubts within the Gaullist ranks crystallized round selection, political discussion in the universities, and the abolition of compulsory Latin during the first two years of secondary education. Then the UDR executive, with Couve de Murville, Debré and Pompidou present, voted its 'total and unanimous' disapproval of political activities within university precincts. Meanwhile, the extremist student groups were doing their best to frustrate moderate reform by trying to boycott, break up or discredit the September examinations.

Against this angry background Faure was drafting his bill with the aid of a handpicked working party, drawn largely from outside the ministry. On 10 September he brought his proposals to the Elysée, for a tête-à-tête with de Gaulle followed by a *conseil restreint* of the President, Prime Minister, Faure, and his junior minister, Trorial. There he won approval for his bill to be put to the full cabinet, but with its provisions on political activity toned down—though they were still too generous for many suspicious Gaullist backbenchers. The cabinet discussion the following day was long and hard. Of the dozen ministers who spoke, Debré and Marcellin, the RI Minister of the Interior, emerged as Faure's strongest critics, insisting on a tougher disciplinary line in the universities. With neither de Gaulle nor Couve de Murville throwing their weight behind him, Faure had to give ground on a number of important details and (a rare occurrence under de Gaulle) a final decision was held over until the following week, and it was admitted publicly that the cabinet was divided.

Faure now had to face Gaullist deputies and senators in conference at La Baule to explain his bill (which reorganized the universities, granted them a degree of financial autonomy, and introduced a system of student participation). As both a reformer and a 'relic' of the Fourth Republic whose Gaullism was widely suspect, he met suspicion and hostility. It needed a moderating speech by Robert Poujade, the party's secretary-general (who had earlier seemed a strong critic), and all Pompidou's emollient talents to keep the temperature down and postpone a final decision for a further week. However, Faure now had the satisfaction of seeing the bill approved with only minor qualifications by two consultative bodies, the Conseil Supérieur de l'Education Nationale and the Conseil de l'Enseignement Supérieur. At his next meeting with the Gaullist parliamentarians, which was less frigid than the encounter at La Baule, he rallied support with a promise to try to avoid resort to the package vote during the Assembly's debate.

The Assembly's Cultural Affairs Committee began its preparations for consideration of the bill with a series of hearings of leading educationists. Faure also prepared his ground in the upper house with a preliminary meeting with the Senate Cultural Affairs Committee. But now that he had to face his cabinet colleagues again, Debré was once more in the forefront of the opposition, doubly hostile as both a centralizer and Minister of Finance to granting financial autonomy. Together with Jeanneney (Minister of State) he fought the bill clause by clause. After two hours, de Gaulle's patience ran out. He tartly told the critics that Faure was not the fool they seemed to make him, and came down decisively on Faure's side, with particular insistence on the need for 'participation' and autonomy.

The bill was sent to the Assembly on 20 September, with a preface prepared by Faure himself. The Assembly Cultural Affairs Committee appointed as rapporteur Jean Capelle, formerly both a university rector and a senior administrator at the Ministry of Education, now a Gaullist deputy. Capelle, while approving university autonomy, was known as an advocate of selection and an opponent of political activity within the universities. He had already 'reported' the draft bill to the La Baule conference on behalf of the party's education working party. Under this moderate critic the committee proposed many amendments, generally limiting or diluting Faure's proposals, notably opposing staff-student parity in the new *conseils d'établissement* and making student participation in the voting for them compulsory. During its debates Independent Republicans and the opposition joined with one or two Left Gaullists in defending the government's proposals against the Gaullist majority.

During the Assembly's general debate on 4 October Faure was most warmly praised by his former Radical colleague, Billères, while his own 'supporters' applauded him only once—for a tribute to Pompidou. Watching the opposition warming to the measure, one hard-line Gaullist wondered dismally whether 'we have not got a bomb under our feet which will wipe out' the June electoral victory. Even the Communists granted that the reform was a step forward. However, relations with the bulk of the Gaullist group had improved since La Baule. Faure now knew he had de Gaulle's backing and used it unsparingly as a shield against his frustrated Gaullist critics, whose divisions he exploited with exceptional skill. Aware that the Gaullists would, however grudgingly, swing into line, he was now determined to rally as massive support as possible behind the bill. This meant he would be well advised to give some ground. In meeting the Gaullist deputies privately he reached agreement on compulsory voting, and compromises on this and several other outstanding issues were agreed with the Cultural Affairs Committee.

Even with Faure's careful back-stage preparation, the clause-by-clause discussion in the Assembly was long, complicated and at times confused. However, Faure not only won over many Gaullists by his explanations and readiness to make concessions, but also accepted a number of opposition amendments. Practically every article was altered in the end. While Faure could fairly claim his basic principles emerged unscathed, and that he had kept his word by avoiding the package vote, cumulatively the amendments had substantially diluted the original draft. Faure's reward was to carry the bill by a margin unprecedented for a major measure: 441 to 0 with six irreducible Gaullists (three of them former ministers) abstaining, together with the thirty-three Communists, who objected to 'reactionary' amendments.

Faure went on now to dazzle the upper house, shifting many of the senators from an initial scepticism. Here again a number of minor amendments were carried—sometimes restoring Faure's original draft over the Assembly's modifications. Faure even accepted a Communist amendment— though here the senators refused to follow him. However, in the Senate as in the Assembly, not one amendment was carried against his opposition. After a full rehearsal of the familiar arguments the bill carried 260 to 0 with 18 abstentions. The conference committee rapidly agreed a final version of the bill, and in early November it became law without further incident.

Thus the ill-considered parliament had shown that it could after all attain a high standard of illuminating debate reaching down to the real issues, and also that there could be a constructive relationship between a minister and both houses. By a rare exercise in political skill Faure had turned a government bill into a solemn national commitment binding on majority and opposition alike. It was a welcome asset in the greater problems lying ahead—those of implementing the reform against the converging opposition of revolutionaries and reactionaries in an unpromising climate of financial stringency.

Conclusion

It would take more than a dozen brief vignettes to convey fully the range and flavour of decision-making in the Fifth Republic. The light has inevitably fallen more fully on the public aspects of policy-making than on the private deliberations of ministers and the bureaucracy, or the lonely, sovereign decisions by the General within his reserved sector. Yet collectively these studies do convey both the untidiness of almost any government seen at close quarters, and also the strength and limits of executive authority in the Fifth Republic. The government could promote its incomes policy by peaceful persuasion, but could not carry it through on failing to win the consent of the pressure groups concerned (while the later attempt to enforce the policy by fiat was to shake the regime itself). On comparatively minor matters it could be compelled to heed the grievances of its own supporters (as over bomb damage) or even of an aggrieved though unorganized group of intellectuals (as over the Cinémathèque). Even on a major problem like subversion it might come under successful pressure from its own parliamentary followers, and though it could get its way if it really insisted, it must not do so too often. General de Gaulle himself was to discover the limited influence of his personal interests in trying to impose on a recalcitrant parliament concessions to conscientious objectors, and in trying to get unenthusiastic ministers to implement his views on workers' rights in their firms. Despite his constant brooding presence, de Gaulle's impact on these decisions outside his reserved sector was strikingly occasional and peripheral.

In favourable circumstances determined pressure groups could sometimes impose their demands with the use of direct action, but they might be crushed if they miscalculated their moment: in very different ways the milk producers and the students offer examples of success and failure—though the government was to pay a price for its victories. But these instances show relations at their worst. A capable minister like Pisani or Faure, willing to work with a modern-minded pressure group like CNJA or the more progressive education-alists, could often cooperate to their mutual advantage. But even a well-intentioned minister might find the groups—like those claiming to represent the self-employed—incapable of engaging in meaningful dialogue. The new structure and longevity of the regime gave great opportunities for construc-tive policy-making. But if ministers (or even the President) tried to use their new strength as a substitute for political discussion and to impose their own views without consulting interested parties, they were liable to arouse resistance which could frustrate their plans and even threaten their hold on power.

V

REPUBLICAN MONARCHY—
AND BEYOND

15

LEGITIMACY UNDER CHALLENGE

The consequences of May

'Amid so many countries which are being shaken by so many upheavals, our own country will continue to offer an example of effectiveness in the conduct of its affairs.' That confident prophecy in the President's New Year message for 1968 crumbled to dust within weeks amid the strikes and barricades of the May Events. His dismissal of the likelihood of France ever again being 'paralysed by crises of the kind from which we used to suffer so much' now turned to mock him. Neither the General's remarkable reassertion of his leadership at the end of May nor his supporters' subsequent electoral triumph could eradicate completely the memory of those days when the founder of the regime was so cruelly exposed, like some latter-day Wizard of Oz, as a querulous old man, caught in a situation beyond his grasp, and tugging desperately at unresponsive controls. His personal authority, which had been eroding imperceptibly for several years, had suffered a body blow.[1] In a sense, de Gaulle was the most illustrious of all May's casualties, and everything that followed was simply an epilogue to his decade of ascendancy. But the problem during the twilight of his reign was no longer the length of time the General would survive. It was whether the Fifth Republic would outlive him.

Although by the summer of 1968 France had outwardly

---

[1] However, de Gaulle's support remained impressive by most conventional standards. During his last year his popularity in the opinion polls never dropped back to the nadir it reached during the 1963 miners' strike. Those 'satisfied' with him were 61 per cent in April 1968, and 53 per cent in April 1969; the 'dissatisfied' were, respectively, 31 per cent and 33 per cent, having risen briefly to 38 per cent in February 1969. (*Sondages*, 1969, 1 and 2, pp. 18–19).

recovered from her brush with revolution, the shadow of May stretched over, and beyond, de Gaulle's closing months. In such areas as the family, the Church, industrial relations and political socialization the subtler reverberations of the upheaval could only be surmised in the immediate wake of events. Elsewhere they were sometimes rapid and unequivocal. In the university, where conservatism sought to restore its positions once the storm had passed, a persistent revolutionary remnant battled on in the hope of re-enacting May and overthrowing the system — or at least discrediting moderate reform. As it painfully grappled with both continuing rapid expansion and the reorganizations resulting from the Faure reforms, higher education remained a fertile field for those intent on exploiting grievances. Two years after the initial outbreak the universities were still being disrupted sporadically by strikes and clashes between rival extremist bands of students, or between students and the police, and the contagion was affecting some of the larger lycées. But although the universities remained potentially explosive, there could be no new May without the workers, and the workers were for the time being relatively quiescent in the wake of the Grenelle agreements and the resurgence in the economy.[1]

However, the 'spirit of May' now spread to other groups. The shopkeepers and independent craftsmen, bulwarks of law and order in May, now turned to widespread direct action to enforce their demands. Although few others went as far in flamboyant disruption, most sections of society were affected by the mood of *contestation* — a mixture of impatient self-criticism, old-style *incivisme*, and fashionable challenge to authority, which sometimes reflected resistance to change, but more often sprang from frustration at the slow pace of reform. The civil service, the judiciary, the professions, the employers' organizations, the arts, the Church, even the staid Bibliothèque Nationale were caught up in the groundswell of irritable

---

[1] Most workers won wage awards large enough not to be wholly eroded by inflation for some 12–18 months, while they could be expected to derive indirect benefits from the improved guarantees of union rights. However, public opinion polls suggested that the industrial workers were more pessimistic about the outcome of May than managers, white collar workers, or professional men — though less gloomy than the retired, employers, farmers or shopkeepers (cf. *Sondages*, 1969, 1 and 2, p. 8).

iconoclasm. Sometimes there was a positive outcome; more often when the mood dissipated things remained much as they had been. 'France', de Gaulle had said, 'reforms only in the wake of revolution.' And May was not a revolution. Although the Events emphasized the gulf in many social institutions between the need for change and the capacity for achieving it, they neither provided a catharsis for pent-up frustrations nor impaired the authority of entrenched hierarchies gravely enough to make major reform inescapable. France, in short, was experiencing a good many of the disadvantages of revolution with none of the benefits.

The malaise naturally extended to the politicians and the political system. As so often before the chief casualty of an upheaval was progress towards political modernization. Reduced to parliamentary insignificance, the Centre was now less than ever a coherent political force but rather a heterogeneous assemblage of survivors. Some, like Pleven, looked hopefully for a chance of reconciliation with the majority; others, like Lecanuet, still dreamed of launching a new, distinctive Centre party. But, shaken by the magnitude of their defeat and the spectre of disorder, they sank into prudent immobilism, hanging together in the hope of recovering their old pivotal role at the succession. On the Left, the frail chances of turning the Federation into a broad-based modern Social Democratic party were disrupted in rapid sequence by the May Events, electoral defeat and the invasion of Czechoslovakia. The clubs' insistence that the old parties must dissolve themselves to create the new one offended those who controlled the Radical and Socialist apparatus. The Radicals rapidly decided to stand aloof, their traditional dislike of a permanent commitment to the Left heightened by May and developments in Prague. Swollen by an influx of student militants, the PSU would also have nothing to do with the new party. From its new station on the Communists' Left, it tirelessly proclaimed the cause of left-wing unity while assailing every potential ally. Mitterrand's personal influence was at an end. Long distrusted by the traditional party leaders, he was now the scapegoat for all the failings of the Left in May and for the ensuing debacle at the polls. Announcing that he would not take office in the new party, he declared that its only hope of success lay through dropping the old guard—a patent hit at his old enemy and ally Mollet. And when, with a

337

heavy heart, the SFIO did agree to dissolve itself and join with a handful of Radicals and the rump of the clubs in a new Socialist Party, Mollet at last stood down after twenty-three years as general secretary. But despite the reforming intentions of the new secretary, Alain Savary, it remained to be seen whether the party could break the grip of the apparatchiks, or whether it would be simply a repainted SFIO.

Meanwhile, the invasion of Czechoslovakia had left the Communists once more outcasts within the system. The Party was as tireless as ever in calling for left-wing unity, but its determined efforts to bury the Czech issue and avert its gaze from 'normalization's' sinister progress in Prague continued to poison relations with all its prospective partners. The Party had also been jolted internally. For every Garaudy who broke over the issue there were several traditionalists who were angry and upset at the unprecedented breach in half a century of disciplined loyalty. Garaudy's highly-publicized dissent reached its inevitable culmination in his expulsion by the 1970 congress. Perhaps in hopes of demonstrating its democratization the Party allowed him a hearing both in its press and at the congress itself. But then tradition reasserted itself: he was excluded without a single publicly dissenting voice or vote within the Party—though there were signs that even in the higher reaches his viewpoint had some sympathy.[1] In the absence of the ailing Waldeck Rochet control of the Party now passed into the sure hands of its new assistant general-secretary, Georges Marchais. An unimaginative party bureaucrat with a notably unheroic war record, Marchais was very much a Moscow man. Under him the Party would be held in line, but at the cost of further bureaucratization and devitalization. Confident of a survival based on a massive working class vote, the Party would weather the storms over Garaudy and the later expulsion of Charles Tillon, one of the most prominent surviving Resistance leaders. But if the future was to hold more than survival it must also beat off the challenge from its Left. The student movement had largely degenerated into noisily warring factions, and violent Leftists who scorned the Party's moderation now proclaimed themselves the heirs to the revolutionary tradition. But if the

---

[1] Moreover, there was an unprecedented protest from thirty prominent ex-members.

activists were few, the PSU and the CFDT were also constant irritants, as they challenged the Party's claim to be the authentic vanguard of the Left and vied with it in the appeal to youth.

Even the Gaullists had internal preoccupations, despite their massive electoral victory. They were far from having regained confidence in either their leaders or themselves. The fruits of electoral victory remained frustratingly elusive. With 294 of the Assembly's 485 seats, the UDR was expecting ministers to be more attentive to its views. Instead, after swallowing the abrupt imposition of Couve de Murville as Premier in place of Pompidou it found him and his colleagues even less accessible and disposed to accept its advice than their predecessors. Elected on a somewhat summary platform of anticommunism and a return to law and order, many Gaullist backbenchers still saw the May Events as just an extremist conspiracy. Thinking more readily of repression than reform, they were baffled and distressed to see ministers courting the recent rebels rather than their own parliamentary supporters. They found themselves not only grappling thanklessly and impotently with unpopular austerity measures, but voting for unpalatable reforms tailored to placate the students and workers.

There was also the deeper uncertainty about the survival of the regime, and the anguishing thought that the succession might be snatched away from the faithful by some opportunist such as Faure or Giscard. With its large influx of new recruits, the UDR was now less homogeneous and less instinctively inclined to loyalty (though the rebellions over industrial and educational reforms were in fact led by senior and influential figures), while the cabinet was prone to technical and political errors. The morale of the backbenchers sank steadily, and their chairman formally protested to Couve at the way their views were ignored or brushed aside. But the Premier bluntly told his restive followers that without the government they could do nothing. Not surprisingly their mood was 'melancholy, neurasthenic and morose', in Couve's own words. Some of this frustration nurtured the constant tension between the UDR and their RI 'allies'. Giscard himself, evicted from the chairmanship of the Assembly's Finance Committee and shunned by the cameras of ORTF, was acting increasingly as the Pretender to the succession, carefully marking his distance from the UDR by a series of gestures which culminated in his party's subscribing to Jean Monnet's Action Committee for the United States of Europe.

As the Gaullists' irritation and gloom deepened, the clearest sign of the erosion of authority since May came at the close of the year. Despite de Gaulle's known backing for the university reform, a section of hard-line Gaullists branded it a 'bluff, a fiasco, and a dangerous time-bomb which will blow up not only the regime but also our civilization'. Faure, without reference to the General, promptly retorted in an article in *Le Monde* that the attack revealed the characteristic inspiration and methods of incipient fascism. The General made known his displeasure, but Faure remained in the government.[1]

One cause of low morale was that since Pompidou's abrupt relegation to the sidelines, the UDR was uncertain to whom it should look for day-to-day leadership.[2] Couve de Murville was scarcely the man to soothe their bruised spirits. Chilly, aloof and not one of the Gaullist family, his decade as a loyal subordinate in foreign affairs had scarcely prepared him for the premiership at a moment when internal problems were pre-eminent.[3] Couve never managed to weld his government into a coherent team. In addition to the personal tensions which were heightened by Pompidou's dismissal and the imminence of the succession, there were disagreements between economic expansionists and supporters of austerity,

---

[1] Cf. *Le Monde*, 30 Dec. 1968 and 3 Jan. 1969.

[2] The general secretary of the UDR gave this embarrassed reply when asked 'Who is the chief of the majority?': 'This is a difficult notion to isolate. Who directs the majority? Who directs the country? I think that in the last analysis the person who gives the majority its orientation is the person who constantly guides the country in its major choices. Thus it is the President of the Republic. . . . But I think that the Prime Minister is also, *ex officio*, a quite natural guide for the majority, and it is inconceivable that he should not have privileged relations with it.' M. Pompidou, he said, 'occupies a very special place within our movement—but he is not the only one to do so' (*Le Monde*, 25 Jan. 1969).

[3] Although Couve failed to impress the political class, his standing in the opinion polls was on a par with Pompidou's as Prime Minister. While he was considered to be cold he was also judged intelligent, sincere, loyal and able. In short he inspired respect if not affection (*Sondages*, 1969, 1 and 2).

and between advocates of the 'stick' and the 'carrot' in dealing with the consequences of May. Couve lacked the authority to impose a consistent line, and the General intervened only intermittently. The government was noticeably lacking in political skills. Couve himself thought that 'a Minister of Finance should be more of a technocrat than a politician', and a sizeable fraction of his cabinet had a primarily administrative background. Throughout, both Couve and his finance minister, Ortoli, paid inadequate attention to the political aspects of their offices—yet their problem was not to find technically ingenious solutions but to win acceptance for what they knew needed doing. It was no accident that the sole major political triumph of the final year was won by that most professional of Fourth Republic figures, Edgar Faure.

The feeling of political drift and indecision, and the deterioration of the financial situation, were largely a consequence of the government's political anaemia and the resulting gulf between what it wished to do and what it felt able to do without provoking a fresh May. Although both the Premier and finance minister were *inspecteurs des finances*, their handling of the economy was a further cause of low Gaullist morale. Their greatest gaffe was the simultaneous announcement of the raising of exchange controls and of higher death duties—which raised such an outcry from every group in the Assembly that the government was forced to give ground, and further aggravated the plight of the ailing franc. Funds began leaving the country in the traditional suitcases to Geneva and through more sophisticated escape routes. The mishandling of austerity measures in October and de Gaulle's dismissal of devaluation as the 'worst of absurdities', like the repeated denials from British Chancellors, roused the very anxieties they were intended to dispel. In the climate of general international monetary instability, the slow erosion of the strength of the franc (which had been discernible for two years), turned into a galloping crisis. Devaluation seemed inevitable. But when all arrangements had been made, in the last of his great acts of defiance de Gaulle decreed that the parity should be maintained. Fresh austerity measures were rushed into force, entailing both a recasting of the budget only hours after the Assembly had approved it, and a humiliating lapse into the quintessential Fourth Republic stratagem of stopping the parliamentary clock to honour the letter of the constitutional timetable.[1] For the moment devaluation was staved off, but this could not disguise the fact that within just six months the regime's proudest claims—to have solved the problem of political authority and produced a strong franc— had been cruelly devalued. Couve de Murville described the crisis as essentially international, and de Gaulle attributed it to the 'moral, economic and social shock of May', but many economists saw it as symptomatic of more serious maladjustment. The General had bought time, but his regime was now too weak to remedy the underlying disequilibrium, and he bequeathed a devaluation to his successor (who was to recall that he had considered it inevitable as early as July 1968).

Not surprisingly, the May Events proved a convenient explanation for many more deeply rooted shortcomings, with even the Gaullists finding in them the equivalent of the 'wasted years' with which governments seek to shift blame to their predecessors. But what had caused May? While opponents professed to see it as the inevitable outcome of Gaullist rule, the regime's supporters more readily attributed it to a handful of agitators or put the blame on the bureaucracy, in which they now discerned the failings to which academic critics had been pointing for years.[2]

The General's explanations varied. At first he found the events 'impossible to grasp'. Later, 'this explosion was provoked by a few groups ... which are in revolt against modern society, against the consumer society, against mechanical society, whether it be communist in the East or capitalist in the West. . . . By contagion, the same thing happened in a number of factories and, naturally, there again among the

---

[1] Under article 47, the Assembly must complete its first consideration of the budget bill within forty days, and the budget should be finally voted on within seventy days.

[2] Cf. Couve (above, p. 253) and, later, Chaban (below, p. 382). Also the explanation by Nouvelle Frontière—a Gaullist equivalent to the Club Jean Moulin: 'The centralized administrative apparatus of the State has, by its continuous, diffuse yet unceasing presence, provoked considerable frustration throughout society to a degree which has not always been fully realized. . . . This phenomenon has been accentuated during the past twenty years, and particularly during the last decade' (quoted in M. A. Burnier, *La Chute du Général*, p. 160).

young'.[1] In September he spoke of a crisis provoked by anarchy in the universities which became grave owing to 'that kind of vertigo frequently experienced here in France in the face of a rapid transformation, with all the blemishes, routinism and vested interests which this brings to light, thanks to the conditioning of public opinion by the press; ... the state of mind of certain intellectual circles ... the passivity of the masses'.[2] But by the end of the year he discerned more than a simple crisis of growth. 'The origin of this perturbation is the saddening and irritating feeling experienced by men of the present time at being seized and dragged into an economic and social machine over which they have no control, and which turns them into instruments.'[3] It was the closest he ever came to accepting that the Events might in part be the product of a style of authority which he himself had nurtured.

The End of the Reign

The nostrum was 'participation', which de Gaulle had preached if not practised well before May.[4] His initial response to the Events had been to propose a referendum on 'participation' in education, industry and the regions. Though he was forced to abandon this plan, the referendum remained necessary to him even after the UDR's parliamentary victory. He was not a man to be readily frustrated, and was aware of the restiveness of many of his followers; above all he needed to confirm his personal popular mandate. With the urgent university reform already confided to Faure, Capitant urged de Gaulle to make his referendum topic participation in industry. But despite his long-declared hope of finding a third way

---

[1] *Le Monde*, 9–10 June 1968.

[2] *Le Monde*, 11 Sept. 1968.

[3] *Le Monde*, 2 Jan. 1969.

[4] 'Participation' was qualified by the insistence that 'many may discuss, but only one can decide'. He admitted that 'nobody, myself included, can carry through such a reform single-handed. It requires a certain degree of consent and suitable circumstances. Thus it is true that although I have made a few steps in that direction, so far our structures and the social groups concerned, particularly labour, have resisted that change' (*Le Monde*, 9–10 June 1968). Cf. above, pp. 302–8.

between capitalism and communism, de Gaulle declined to fight on measures he knew to be unacceptable to management, the unions and a large fraction of his own supporters. Instead he decided on a spring referendum on regional reform, which he had already endorsed in March and which in one form or other had the blessing of most of the parties. He coupled with this the reform of the Senate, partly because his hopes of integrating interest groups into regional institutions were logically linked with his long-standing notion of an Economic Senate, and partly as a settlement of his bitter feud with the upper house.

In the face of this new threat Monnerville stepped down as president of the Senate after twenty-one years. His successor, Alain Poher, was a Christian Democrat who was best known as president of the European Parliament in Strasbourg. Although Poher presented himself as 'a man of union and conciliation' and the Senate broke into fervent protestations of self-reforming zeal, de Gaulle would not be swayed. Preparations for the referendum went ahead under first Guichard and then Jeanneney. Much of the gestation of the reform was conducted in secret, although some of its broad outlines were revealed in a memorandum from de Gaulle in August. A massive 'consultation' of local groups and notables held during the autumn was presented as a practical experiment in participation, but proved to be chiefly a public relations exercise providing statistics which ministers were to manipulate to demonstrate public support for their proposals. The real debate was confined to a very restricted circle; even a number of ministers were unaware quite what was afoot until a draft leaked to *Le Monde* two months before the referendum was due. It then became clear that the drafters of the regional reform had opted for caution; there was to be no redrawing of the regional map, only limited decentralization, and the new regional councils were to have nominated rather than elected members. No real attack was launched on the rural bias from which the existing regional institutions suffered, nor was there any significant renewal of elites. While the timidity of the reform roused the derision of the opposition, it nevertheless went too far for centralizers like Debré, who secured further restrictions on the powers of the new regional councils before the final publication of the bill a month later. Owing to the General's insistence on the bill's being complete in itself the final text ran to sixty-nine articles and fourteen pages of close print.[1] Given the uncertainty and improvisation surrounding the drafting it was scarcely surprising that, in addition to finding it unconstitutional, the Conseil d'Etat gave a severe drubbing to its detailed provisions.

The political climate was by now increasingly unpromising. Socially, sporadic unrest continued in the universities, and the shopkeepers and independent craftsmen resorted to strikes and ill-tempered disruption; relations with the unions were also tense as they attempted to hold the gains they had made at Grenelle in June against the rising inflation. Abroad, the invasion of Czechoslovakia had dealt a heavy blow to de Gaulle's East European policy, and he had dismayed many of his followers at the turn of the year by decreeing a total embargo on the shipment of arms to Israel, following a retaliation raid with Alouette helicopters on Beirut airport. In domestic politics the main change was Pompidou's announcement in January that he would be a candidate for the presidency when there was a vacancy. Since his eviction from the premiership Pompidou had remained an unofficial leader of the majority, despite attempts by enemies in the party's establishment to freeze him out and discredit him; now his hat was unequivocally in the ring for the succession, and the voters could meet the choice of 'de Gaulle or the unknown' confident that a known and tried successor was in reserve.[2]

---

[1] In addition to the regional reform and the creation of the new Senate, which entailed considerable consequential changes in legislative procedure and the disappearance of the Economic and Social Council, the proposed reform altered the rules governing vacancies in the presidency and constitutional revision procedures. Where the presidency fell vacant before the end of the normal term, the President's place would be taken by the Prime Minister (instead of the President of the Senate) or, failing him, by the next most senior minister. Constitutional revision under article 89 would have required henceforth approval by an absolute majority of the Assembly (after the Senate had given its views), followed by a referendum. Alternatively, instead of the referendum, after three months the President could submit the revision to the Assembly for a second vote, requiring a two-thirds majority.

[2] Although professional politicians treated de Gaulle's dismissal of Pompidou to 'the reserve of the Republic' as final, a July 1968 poll showed 67 per cent of voters believing that de Gaulle intended to prepare the way for Pompidou to succeed him (*Sondages*, 1969, 1 and 2, p. 20).

De Gaulle's supporters therefore viewed the campaign with apprehension. Having failed to persuade him to defer it, some of them urged him to put two questions, one on Senate reform and the other on the regions. He refused, because he at least believed the proposals formed a logical whole, and because splitting the referendum in two meant both abandoning the unpopular Senate reform and robbing the outcome of the plebiscitary element he needed.[1] In insisting that the referendum must go ahead with a single question, he was well aware of the risk of defeat. He was taking on the Senate, the provincial notables, all the established parties except the Gaullists, and almost every group which expressed itself on the question. Though he had fought alone before, never had he sent his supporters into battle with less enthusiasm or understanding of the cause. Yet whatever the outcome he could turn it to some advantage. Victorious, de Gaulle would reaffirm his special relationship with the people and confound the political class yet again; defeated, he would be able to withdraw with honour and dignity without being overtaken by a fresh collapse or 'the shipwreck of old age'.

The early stages of the lack-lustre campaign confirmed that the regional reform, though regarded as timid, was generally welcome. But few had a good word for the transformation of the upper house. It was never made clear why such importance was attached to the fusion of two assemblies, neither of which had played a really significant role in the political process. Zero plus zero, it was unkindly said, still equalled zero. It took de Gaulle's declaration that once again the choice lay between 'progress and disorder' to crystallize the issue by personalizing it. But while the Gaullists were fearful of the outcome, the opposition, more Gaullist than the General's own supporters, could not believe that he would

---

[1] Even before the detailed proposals were known 59 per cent favoured the creation of regional councils, but only 38 per cent the Economic Senate. Support for both subsequently declined, but the regional reform always had more supporters than opponents and the new Senate more opponents than supporters. Even among UDR voters, in mid-March 74 per cent favoured regional reform but only 47 per cent Senate reform. In another poll in November 1968 36 per cent wanted the Senate to have a more important role in future, and only 4 per cent a less important one (*Sondages*, 1969, 1 and 2, p. 34).

fail to outwit them yet again.[1] Only in the closing days of the campaign did they begin at last to scent victory—though de Gaulle himself had already realised that he had reached the end of the road. In his final appeal he promised that if successful he would definitely retire in 1972, and sketched out the doom which lay ahead if he were disavowed: 'How would the situation resulting from the negative victory of all these diverse, disparate and discordant oppositions be brought under control, with the inevitable return to a situation where ambitions, illusions, deals and betrayals would have full play amid the shock to the nation provoked by such a rupture?'[2] It was a curious valediction from the man who had moulded the Fifth Republic for better and worse for over a decade. Some of his supporters went still further in their glimpses of impending doom. If Couve and Pompidou spoke simply of unspecified disturbances, Schumann talked of 'the fascination of the abyss', Robert Poujade of a 'brutal crisis', Debré of 'a communist regime', and Marcellin of 'a takeover by the mob'. *La Nation* even speculated that, if the Noes were triumphant, M. Poher might not have time to reach the Elysée to take up the interim presidency. Whether he would be met by Leftist or Gaullist occupiers was not wholly clear. But although some desperadoes may have dreamed of a takeover, they were firmly discouraged by a declaration from the Paris police union that the police, the armed forces and the administration would obey the legitimate government or the interim president. Gaullist diehards were also restrained by their leaders' realisation that the only hope of survival lay in being seen as the party of stability.

In the highest referendum turnout since 1958 53 per cent of the voters replied No. The proposals were rejected in seventy-two of the ninety-five metropolitan departments. Only in parts of the Centre and the traditional bastions of Brittany and Alsace did the General still win a majority. There was no evidence that the electorate actually wanted de Gaulle to go, but with the threat of a new May receding and with Pompidou in the wings, the threat of his departure had clearly not weighed as heavily as in the past. While the bulk

---

[1] Forty-eight hours before the polls opened some senior Socialists were still refusing to believe that de Gaulle might lose.

[2] *Le Monde*, 28–29 April 1969.

Table VI   Five Referendums, 1958–1969

	1958 '000s	1961 '000s	1962(1) '000s	1962(2) '000s	1969 '000s
Electors*	26,603	27,184	26,992	27,582	28,656
Voting	22,597	20,791	20,402	21,302	23,091
Spoiled	304	595	1,098	560	632
YES	17,669	15,200	15,509	12,809	10,516
NO	4,625	4,996	1,795	7,933	11,943
Percentage of electorate					
Voting	84·9	76·5	75·6	77·2	80·6
Spoiled	1·1	2·2	4·1	2·0	2·2
YES	66·4	55·9	64·9	46·4	36·7
NO	17·4	18·4	6·6	28·8	41·7

*Usually at least one million people of voting age failed to register. All figures relate to metropolitan France only.

of the Noes came as usual from the Left, the balance was tilted by the defection of a large fraction of the Centre and moderate Right—the PDM and RI voters,[1] the middle class and residents of the smaller towns and the countryside rather than workers and city dwellers. Despite important regional and social nuances, the outcome also marked a further notable step towards the nationalization of French politics. Even before the full results were known, at 12.11 a.m. on 28 April came the terse communique from Colombey: 'I am ceasing to

---

[1] At parliamentary level both PDM and RI were divided and made no clear voting recommendation. Most of the Centrists campaigned for No, but many Giscardians supported the government — Giscard himself being sharply critical without actually advocating a No. The final SOFRES poll in April showed the proportions of Yes voters according to party identification: PCF 1 per cent; Federation 4 per cent; Centre 18 per cent; RI 48 per cent; UDR 87 per cent (Burnier, *op. cit.,* p. 19).

exercise my functions as President of the Republic. This decision takes effect at noon today'. Apart from an equally terse congratulatory message to his successor in June this was his last public pronouncement. Overnight, after a reign of ten years and 332 days, he returned to the shadows.

The country took de Gaulle's departure in total calm. With a minimum of sentimentalizing, attention turned to the 'war of succession'. Yet, quite apart from being the occasion of the General's withdrawal, the referendum marked a significant milestone in the development of the Fifth Republic. His resignation firmly established that, whatever the constitution might say, a President has a personal political responsibility. Again, this probably marked the end of the attempt to 'naturalize' the referendum—ironically enough at the very moment when de Gaulle's departure had diminished its anti-democratic reputation. It was equally clear that all prospect of Senate reform had now vanished. As the results came in all the proposals the senators had been canvassing so loudly disappeared into their pigeonholes, and the General's successors were careful not to raise the ghost. Despite its popularity, regional reform too was to be severely delayed. The prospects for political modernization had dimmed considerably.

The constitutional arrangements for a presidential transition now operated for the first time. Under article 7 the President of the Senate exercises presidential powers (except those relating to the dissolution and referendum) until a new president can be elected within fifty days. Poher's entourage were to express some rather disingenuous surprise that de Gaulle's staff had made off with all the Elysée's files and, more seriously, there was a delay in briefing the new Commander-in-Chief on his responsibility for the nuclear strike force. Otherwise the procedures worked as well as could be hoped with a potential Centre candidate for the Elysée presiding over a bereaved Gaullist cabinet. (Occasions for embarrassment were reduced by conducting much of the government's business in *conseil de cabinet* without the President.) The Couve de Murville government remained on a caretaker basis, excepting Capitant who refused to serve under one of de Gaulle's political assassins, and who felt no stake in providing the continuity which might elect Pompidou as successor. During the difficult transition Couve emerged as a more relaxed and effective Prime Minister than he had ever been under the General. His relations with Poher were courteous and correct throughout, while Debré launched into a long diatribe at the first cabinet on the theme that 'France has suffered a defeat in the eyes of the whole world', and leaked it fully to the press—having only recently stigmatized cabinet leaks as 'a sign of decadence in the *mores* of the Republic'. It was left to Poher to remind Debré sharply of the constitutional proprieties. He also intervened firmly to recall to the heads of ORTF their obligation to be fair, and to dismiss Jacques Foccart from his shadowy but disquieting duties as secretary for African and Malagasy Affairs.[1] Otherwise Poher confined himself to a quiet caretaker role, carefully avoiding even occupying the President's office.

With this careful blend of dignified inactivity and well publicized insistence on Republican virtue, Poher could play a waiting game. Other contenders for the presidency were launched into intense activity. Pompidou announced his candidacy within forty-eight hours, without reference to the Gaullist hierarchy. Some of the elders wanted to run a 'Gaullist of the first hour'; Pompidou successfully forced their hand. Giscard made an attempt to balk Pompidou, but then hastily made a pact with him. The Left were caught completely unprepared. The Federation had collapsed; the new Socialist Party was as yet officially unborn. Its founding conference on 4 May became a nominating convention in which the presidential election, the reform of the Left, and the battle for power between SFIO apparatchiks and the new men from the clubs were inextricably intertwined. Mollet refused to negotiate with the Communists and bent all his efforts to nominating a man of straw, paving the way for the election of Poher on the second ballot. Significantly, the new

---

[1] It has been said of Foccart that of the loyal Gaullists he had 'done the most to bestow upon the fraternity this secret-society atmosphere, to give it the appearance of a police regime, the flavour of clandestinity and false beards, . . . the tendency to think that secret funds, card-indexes, moral pressures and material interests are the best weapons of government. . . . It is the worst of the deviations of Gaullism, the most open to criticism and condemnation. Unhappily, it forms inseparably an integral part of the inheritance' (P. Viansson-Ponté, *Les Gaullistes*, p. 118).

Despite his dismissal Foccart continued operations from the embassy of the Ivory Coast until his reinstatement by Pompidou.

party refused to follow his preference for a mere 'arbiter President'. As Savary said: 'If the President of the Republic was to be nothing but an arbiter, the victory of a man of the Left would have no political or practical meaning.' From the bitter and confused wrangling which augured dismally for the expected 'renewal', the Socialists nominated Gaston Defferre, with his preference for Left-Centre alliances and his hopes of negotiating with the Communists from strength. That choice crystallized the Communist Party's resolve to run its own candidate, Jacques Duclos. Angry at the failure of a united Left candidacy, the PSU nominated its general secretary, Michel Rocard, to 'rally the forces of May', while Alain Krivine emerged on leave from his Verdun barracks as the standard-bearer of the trotskyist Ligue Communiste, a conscript private 2nd class contending for the post of Commander-in-Chief: both he and Rocard had their eyes less on the Elysée than on the free television time all candidates received. The united Left of 1965 had fragmented into four contending factions—and the Radicals had opted for Poher without even waiting for him to declare himself. Thus even before the campaign opened, Defferre's potential electorate had shrunk to roughly that of the SFIO, and his ambition to pushing the Communist into fourth place. To bolster his chances he took Pierre Mendès-France as running mate and prospective premier, but it was too late; he began and stayed a weak fourth in the polls.

Poher delayed the formal announcement of his candidacy until it was quite clear that he would have no competition from the Centre or Right, and that it was too late for the Left to unify. Almost unknown to the general public before 27 April he had won widespread praise for his behaviour since. Yet his principal asset was nothing he did or said; it was that he was not a de Gaulle, but a reassuring figure apparently embodying a certain tradition of worthy provincial respectability. His standing at the polls rapidly climbed to vie with Pompidou's, and the anxious Gaullists began to wonder whether he had robbed them of their asset of symbolizing stability. But Poher was an utterly unimpressive campaigner, tempted by his need to rally every possible non-Gaullist vote into increasingly hollow platitudes and flowery generalizations. Even his commitment to Europe became so imprecise and qualified as to be scarcely distinguishable from Pompidou's. With every speech he looked more like a weary survival of the Fourth Republic. His support gradually wilted, both from his ever more obvious personal inadequacies and because the Centre had collapsed both as a distinct political force and as the traditional pivot in the system.

As Poher flagged, Pompidou's underlying strength was steadily confirmed as he campaigned energetically on the theme of 'continuity and an open door'. Presenting himself as the bulwark of stability against the Red peril and a return to the Fourth Republic, he scattered shrewdly timed promises to disgruntled groups like the self-employed and the North African refugees, and courted the liberals with a pledge to establish political fair play at ORTF, eluding full exposition of his views with the grandly dismissive 'programme is not a Gaullist word'. In contrast, Defferre and Mendès-France (like Rocard) addressed themselves seriously to the issues facing the country; but with negligible support from the old SFIO national machine and many local federations working openly for Poher even before the first ballot, their campaign limped dismally. On 1 June Pompidou emerged in the first ballot with a commanding 43·9 per cent followed at a considerable distance by Poher, and Duclos—an unexpectedly strenuous and jovial campaigner who was alleged to have avoided ever using the word 'Communism'—a close third; between them they exceeded Pompidou's total. Though the minor parties fared as badly as expected, the outcome was a disaster for Defferre—who had once said that the Communists would not dare run against him for fear of making themselves look ridiculous. Without waiting for the second ballot the old Federation voters had deserted in droves, most to Poher, but many to Duclos as the only credible candidate of the Left. Failing to carry a single department, Defferre received only 5 per cent of the national vote, and even in his home fief of Marseilles he was a poor fourth with 12 per cent of the poll.

Although challenged to withdraw and let Pompidou fight it out with Duclos on the second ballot, Poher maintained his candidacy, and emerged as a more energetic and resolute campaigner. But although there seemed little doctrinally between Pompidou and Poher, as both pitched their appeal for liberal and left-wing votes, the outcome was never in doubt. Although Poher improved his share of a turnout depressed (from 78 per cent to 69 per cent) by calls for abstention from

Table VII 1965 and 1969 Presidential elections

	Gaullist	Centre and Right*	Non-Communist Left†	Communist
Votes (1st ballot) '000s				
1965	10,387	5,434	7,937	—
1969	9,761	5,486	2,178	4,780
Votes (2nd ballot) '000s				
1965	12,645	—	10,557	—
1969	10,686	7,871	—	—
Share of vote (1st ballot) %				
1965	43·7	22·8	33·4	—
1969	44·0	24·7	9·8	21·5
Share of vote (2nd ballot) %				
1965	54·5	—	45·5	—
1969	57·6	42·4	—	—

*Lecanuet, Tixier-Vignancour, Marcilhacy (1965); Poher and Ducatel (1969).

†Mitterrand, Barbu (1965); Defferre, Rocard, Krivine (1969).

the PCF, the PSU and the Ligue Communiste, Pompidou emerged the winner with 57·58 per cent of the vote, winning all but eight departments (seventeen more than the General in 1965).[1] Although the most striking aspect of his support was its breadth, he clearly drew stronger backing than the General from the middle class and the rural south, and less from the industrial north and the workers. In surviving, Gaullism had acquired a more conservative and rural basis, yet had also

[1] He received the support of 37·17 per cent of the electorate. 'Victory' and 'defeat' depend heavily on context. The Gaullist victories of 1968 and 1969 were won with 10,200,000 and 10,686,000 votes; but Mitterrand lost in 1965 with 10,557,000 votes and de Gaulle lost in 1969 with 10,516,000 votes.

strengthened its national hold. It was just five months since Malraux's assertion that after-Gaullism would never be based on the defeat of the founder, and seven weeks since the General himself had forecast disruption in the wake of his defeat. Pompidou succeeded remarkably in snatching victory from defeat—even if some of the faithful doubted whether what survived really merited the name of Gaullism. The new system of electing the President both confirmed its popularity with the voters and proved a valuable aid to legitimizing a crucial succession. Far from being the *mal-élu* opponents predicted, Pompidou took office on 20 June with his position unchallenged, and the prophets of doom confounded.

Gaullism without de Gaulle

'Continuity and an open door' remained the predictable watchword of the administration in its early days. This policy was most evident in the new government. Banishing Couve de Murville, Pompidou took as Premier Jacques Chaban-Delmas, President of the Assembly since 1959—and one of nine ministers who had held office under the old System.[1] The President took an active part in selecting the new cabinet which, with thirty-nine members, was the largest since 1958—one of the clearest indications of the need to consolidate political support. Twenty fresh ministers came in, and only four of Couve's government retained their previous posts. Edgar Faure was sacrificed to the Gaullist Right, and though Michel Debré stayed on as the seal of authentic Gaullism he was shunted to Defence, leaving foreign affairs to the more flexible Maurice Schumann. The lion's share of posts went to Gaullists of almost every hue and vintage, but as recompense for rallying to Pompidou, Giscard returned to Finance and four Centrists were given office, including Pleven and Duhamel who had campaigned for No in April. The balance of the new government was pro-Pompidou, neo-liberal, and more 'European' and 'political' than its predecessors. (All its members were deputies or senators, and only four had essentially technocratic backgrounds—none of them in a leading post.)

Pompidou was seeking to consolidate a personal electoral

---

[1] Chaban-Delmas, a wartime Gaullist, entered politics as a Radical. Ironically, during the campaign Poher had also let it be known that if elected he would take Chaban as Premier.

base which extended well beyond the UDR. In doing so he further disrupted the Centre. Duhamel and Pleven created a new Centre for Progress and Democracy as the 'progressive and European wing of the majority' and attracted a steady stream of recruits, including Pflimlin, the ex-president of MRP who had left the government in 1962 in protest at the General's European policy. PDM declared itself 'associated' with the majority, but since neither supporters nor opponents of the government were numerous enough to form an independent parliamentary group, it became more than ever an ambiguous syndicate of contradictory tendencies. But outside the Assembly its constituent elements, like Democratic Centre, still played a significant role in local politics and its ambitious politicians could still dream of piecing together the fragments of the Centre and Centre-Left. One who did was Jean-Jacques Servan-Schreiber. In 1969 he took over as general secretary of the moribund Radical party, with the encouragement of its president, Maurice Faure, and attempted to revive it in 1970 on the basis of a highly publicized manifesto embracing a neo-capitalism in which managerial efficiency was to be reconciled with social justice. His successful exploitation of local discontent to capture a safe Gaullist seat at Nancy in June 1970 showed that the anti-Communist opposition could also win by-election victories.

As Servan-Schreiber embarked on his uphill attempt to rescue one venerable party from extinction, Alain Savary was struggling to revitalize another. But although the new Socialist Party attracted some new blood, it was still dominated by the stultifying hand of the old SFIO. The new Socialist group in the Assembly counted among its forty-three members neither Mitterrand nor Rocard, who had just beaten the luckless Couve at a by-election. But if Rocard's success showed that a unified Left could still win unexpected victories, the departmental council elections in March 1970 confirmed the stagnation in the Socialists' popular support. As the age-old wrangling over alliances continued, devitalizing the party and creating fresh defections, French social democracy lay in pieces. Of the parties of the Left only the Communists could look forward confidently to survival as a significant political force. But with the choice of Georges Marchais to succeed Waldeck Rochet, the most limited and inward-looking apparatchiks seemed to have firmly regained control.

Meanwhile, the bereaved Gaullists were struggling to adjust to their changed situation. Heterogeneous, traditionally wearing their doctrines lightly, and held together for so long by a unique historical figure, they now had to search painfully for a fresh basis for their unity. Their leaders set about restoring the party's shaken confidence and preparing the ground for its survival. The evolutionary view of the party's development was put by Chaban: 'The problem is whether our future is to be limited to our past or whether, as in the past, we are to prepare for the future.'[1] But for some of the older loyalists such thoughts were treachery. The bitterest attacks came from Pompidou's old Left Gaullist enemies, Capitant and Vallon, who resurrected the old UDT (merged in the UNR in 1962), which proclaimed in its journal that as in 1940 the watchword of all true Gaullists was 'resist'. Vallon declared that the government contained only two genuine Gaullists, accused Pompidou of plotting the General's downfall with the Centrists, and even likened him to Pétain. Eventually he was expelled after publishing a tract about Pompidou entitled *L'Anti-de Gaulle*. But the true faith had more circumspect guardians like Couve de Murville and Messmer. The latter emerged as a highly partisan politician after years of docility to lead Presence and Action of Gaullism, which rallied some forty deputies under the slogan 'continuity and vigilance'. *La Nation* tartly reminded the ultras that 'fidelity to the principles of Gaullism does not consist in asking oneself each morning what General de Gaulle would have done had he remained in office'[2]. Despite severe pressure from both UDR headquarters and the Elysée, Messmer persisted with his movement, though agreeing to keep within the UDR and not to run candidates against the party's own nominees. Thus, from personal rancour, sentiment and ideological conviction a section of the UDR had yet to reconcile itself to the succession and was determined to keep Pompidou on a short lead.

The diehards received no encouragement from the General. Some of them continued for months hoping against hope for

---

[1] *Le Monde*, 2 Dec. 1969.

[2] *Le Monde*, 16 Sept. 1969. Outside parliament, however, Messmer's movement was simply Presence of Gaullism.

the return of the Guide.[1] But the word came down from Colombey that he would not break his silence; his departure was irreversible. Even so, it would be a long while before the party would cease to sense his silent presence. Although the ultras seemed more noisy than dangerous, and the virulence of a Vallon simply strengthened the President's hand, disquiet over the 'open door' to new political allies was widespread. Some simply disliked the more definite commitment to the Right and Centre; they had not come into the party to rub shoulders with Tixier-Vignancour (who had rallied to Pompidou in June). Others resented Pompidou's consolidating his personal electoral majority in a way which implied the abandoning of the strategy which had proved so profitable to the Gaullists in parliamentary elections up to 1968.[2] And others feared that the party was being edged out of its rightful role and heritage—and its share of the jobs. The UDR's chilly reception was indicated by Robert Poujade. Insisting that the UDR would fight to retain its primacy, he made it clear that 'our neighbours, allies and friends are nothing more than neighbours, allies and friends'—and thus not members of the Gaullist family. Although Chaban argued that the General himself had 'welcomed everyone who wanted to act, whether they were liberals, Christian Democrats or socialists', the party made clear its hostility to the open door being pushed any wider.[3] The greatest resentment was directed not at the Centrists but at Giscard, always an uncertain ally, and now decreeing unpalatable policies—still unforgiven for his sniping at the General and his defection at the referendum. The skirmishing even broke out into public polemics between the RI general secretary and UDR ministers, and an attack

---

[1] But public opinion was not with them: though 51 per cent regretted the General's departure, 62 per cent did not want him back (*Le Monde*, 7 Nov. 1969).

De Gaulle was back in Colombey writing his memoirs, having departed to Ireland for the duration of the presidential campaign. This was the occasion of Edgar Faure's comment on Chaban's cabinet: 'The Left has quit the government and emigrated to Ireland.'

[2] Cf. above, pp. 95–6.

[3] *Le Monde*, 16 Dec. 1969. Later, when Frey envisaged alliances with 'all who are not communists' in the 1971 municipal elections, Poujade vigorously retorted, 'There is no question of our creating a new RPF or opening the party to any Tom, Dick or Harry' (*ibid.*, 7 April 1970).

on Giscard by his ministerial colleague Chalandon. But such outbursts were important mainly as signs of the continuing uncertainty about the party's future. Chaban insisted that it must not become merely a 'vast conglomerate whose ambition would be to maintain itself in power'. Gradually, however, the UDR seemed to be seeing itself as the dominant partner in a dominant coalition—a neo-Conservative party with supporting parties to its Left and Right. Seeing themselves as both a party of government and the guardians of the General's heritage, the Gaullists now more than ever identified their own health and survival with that of the State itself.

Both continuity and the 'open door' were evident in policy matters. Continuity was essential if Pompidou was to confirm himself as the authentic successor in the eyes of the faithful, yet change was also needed if he was to consolidate his personal electoral majority and steer the country out of some of the impasses into which de Gaulle had led it. Continuity was most evident in foreign affairs, where the preservation of the General's policies was the touchstone of Pompidou's sincerity for the loyalists. Since these had also been generally popular (notwithstanding Israel and Quebec), and change was more pressing in domestic matters, Pompidou's early speeches were filled with reassertions of national independence and hostility to supranationalism and blocs. But although the old themes persisted, Maurice Schumann (now foreign minister) admitted that the 'accent could no longer be the same' as under de Gaulle. The old wounding arrogance with its gratuitous baiting of adversaries disappeared almost overnight—though a more courteous manner did not necessarily imply greater flexibility in content. While substance was slower to alter than style, the ostensibly global foreign involvement and the 'all horizons' defence policy appeared to be giving way to more limited ambitions—a more traditional defence orientation and a concentration on France's role in Europe and the Mediterranean.[1] And it soon became clear that with the passing of de Gaulle domestic policy was no longer merely the handmaid of external policy. At home, Pompidou inherited an economy which a mixture of political anaemia and electoral expediency had allowed to run out of control. In the short

---

[1] In fact all these trends were discernible in the closing months of de Gaulle's reign.

term there was nothing for it but devaluation, austerity, and an end to the long feud with the international monetary system. In the longer run there was the problem of restoring competitiveness and carrying through the transformation of France into a modern industrial power. Yet the continuing unrest in the universities, the militancy of such groups as the shopkeepers and small businessmen, and the hostility of the farmers to any acceleration of change all rapidly underlined to the new rulers the difficulty of modernizing a country in which, as one commentator put it, *contestation* had become institutionalized as one of the parameters of decision-making.

Nowhere was the concern for continuity greater than in institutional matters. One or two Gaullists pressed for a constitutional amendment to enact full presidentialism and to remove the irksome incompatibility between ministerial office and membership of parliament. The constitution, they argued, should not be treated 'as if it had been handed down by God the Father'. But the bulk of the party felt a reluctance to tinker with the constitution on the morrow of de Gaulle's departure and an instinctive hostility to a purely parliamentary revision procedure which once started, might prove difficult to contain. Thus formally the constitution remained unchanged, but informally the institutional balance naturally reflected the transition. Taking the lesson of the referendum the new leaders were loud in their promises of a closer relationship with parliament and a strengthening of the role of both houses and the Economic and Social Council.[1] Pompidou

---

[1] Public attitudes, as reported in a SOFRES poll in *Le Figaro*, 10 Nov. 1969 were as follows:

At present who mainly decides major policy issues, and who should decide them?

	Does(%)	Should(%)
Government	40	36
President	38	24
Parliament	13	33
No reply	9	7

Who should take decisions in the following fields?

	Economic Policy %	Justice %	Foreign Policy %	Social Problems %
Government	49	35	51	43
President	15	23	25	9
Parliament	30	33	17	43
No reply	6	9	7	5

sent a cordial message to parliament and there was an apparently full reconciliation with the Senate. Politically expedient though this was it left unresolved the problem of a largely rural and traditional second chamber in a period when governments are concerned predominantly with the problems of a modern urban society. Bolstered by the Assembly's vote of 369 to 85 for its declaration of policy, the government tried to avoid resort to some of the more resented procedural weapons like the package vote, and allowed a timid reform of standing orders. A new system of more rapid-fire and topical questions was introduced in a modest attempt to revitalize question time. Chaban sought to foster closer relations with the government's supporters through regular meetings and a series of letters explaining official policies to them. But if this assiduous cultivation of the majority brought some political dividends, it did not add up to any effective change in the power of parliament.

While the new President repeated tirelessly that he was 'not General de Gaulle', he seemed set on maintaining the ascendancy of his office:

I believe that the choice the French people have made shows their endorsement of General de Gaulle's conception of the role of the President of the Republic. At the same time head of the executive, guardian and guarantor of the constitution, he is doubly responsible for giving the lead on fundamentals, laying down the key guidelines, ensuring and watching over the proper functioning of the organs of government. He is both an arbiter and the holder of the highest responsibility in the nation. Such a conception does not, of course, encroach on the rights of parliament, either in respect of its legislative function or in its scrutiny of the work of the government. It leaves to the Prime Minister an extremely important and very heavy role (of which I myself have long experience) in the conduct of business, the running of ministries and relations with parliament. But such a conception bears with it the primacy of the Chief of State which springs from his national mandate and which he has a duty to maintain.[1]

---

[1] Press conference (*Le Monde*, 12 July 1969).

Thus, although Pompidou did not endorse de Gaulle's more extreme assertions of presidentialism, he appeared to accept the General's view that the President should settle matters of high policy, leaving the secondary and managerial functions to his Prime Minister. He also endorsed unequivocally the view that the President now has direct political responsibility to the people. Yet the new leaders were aware that the inherent difficulties of the Fifth Republic's double-headed executive structure had not been conjured away. Chaban himself recognized that

> our constitution has an Achilles heel . . .: the need for close, almost intimate relations between the President of the Republic and the Prime Minister, between whom there must be complete confidence. There must not be the slightest trace of envy or rivalry in the mind of the Prime Minister. Conversely there must be no rigorous or rigid subordination. The Prime Minister must state his feelings fully even if on occasion they are not those of the Chief of State. In the last analysis they must work together, it being understood that the decision must in the end lie with the Chief of State, and that once he has taken it, then it is the Prime Minister's responsibility to put it straight into force.

During the early months there were signs of difficulty in striking the delicate balance, but publicly Chaban accepted the President's lead, agreeing that it was for Pompidou to determine both the composition and the policy of the government. He never forgot, he said, that 'the pre-eminent man is at the Elysée'.

While retaining the principal role Pompidou imposed a different division of labour from the General. Although, like any modern chief executive, he was closely involved with foreign affairs, defence—that other pillar of the old reserved sector—reverted to normal ministerial control under Debré. Where de Gaulle monopolized one or two areas of policy and intervened intermittently elsewhere, Pompidou took a considerably wider brief. Increasingly, major decisions were made in *conseil restreint* or *tête-à-tête* at the Elysée. Though left with a significant role in social and economic affairs the Prime Minister appeared more frequently as spokesman, intermediary and negotiator than as a final arbiter.[1] Pompidou was personally decisive not only in major matters like devaluation, but also in imposing his own policies in the legislation extending white collar conditions of employment to manual workers, and the distribution of shares in the nationalized Renault company to its employees despite the manifest reticence of the ministers concerned. He even intervened in the debate about the secondary school curriculum over the head of the Minister of Education. For the UDR, Robert Poujade promised that Pompidou would be treated in the same way as de Gaulle (though it was not clear how far he spoke for the general public). He added diplomatically that 'the President of the Republic is our guide both institutionally and morally. He also inspires us, his inspiration adding to that of General de Gaulle', and for the moment at UDR meetings giant representations of the Founder still dominated those of his successor. But Pompidou seemed to be establishing himself both with the party and within the governmental system. Where the General had often been content to reign, Pompidou seemed intent on governing. His style was both inevitably and deliberately different from his predecessor's. The vocabulary of 'authority', 'prestige' and 'grandeur' gave way to the language of 'progress', 'realism' and 'happiness'. 'Today I am a Frenchman among Frenchmen,' remarked Pompidou in opening his first press conference—a comment as unthinkable under de Gaulle as the pictures of the President disporting himself in bathing trunks which filled the papers during his vacation. Under her new President France seemed to be moving from republican monarchy to an original form of presidentialism. But the underlying realities of government and administration had changed much less than the external trappings. It remained to be seen whether this new regime could succeed, where de Gaulle's had failed, in tackling the

---

[1] But it was Chaban who outlined the 'philosophy' of the new administration in his proposals for a 'new society' (see below, p. 382).
    Initially at least the blurring of the demarcation of responsibilities between the President and the Premier caused some hesitation and faulty coordination in the higher administration, and also confused the general public. Pompidou now seemed to be viewed widely as the 'head of the government', while one poll actually sought views on the 'Pompidou government'. The popularity curves of President and Prime Minister, once clearly demarcated, now tended to merge.

problems its Prime Minister outlined: a 'country of castes', a fragile economy, a 'tentacular and inefficient state', an 'archaic and conservative' social structure, which all went to make up the 'seized-up society'.[1] As Robert Poujade said, 'there is no longer an opposition in parliament, but in the country it is quite a different matter'. Each social group resorted to direct action to press its own claims, yet resented similar methods when used by others—and criticised the government both for brutal repression of its own justified protests and for weakness in face of the intolerable disorders provoked by everyone else. Despite the massive parliamentary majority, the main complaint against the new regime was its lack of effective authority; in theory it was better adapted for reform than its predecessors, but it seemed premature as yet for Chaban-Delmas to cry triumphantly: 'the war of the Republics is over at last!'

---

[1] *Le Monde,* 18 Sept. 1969. 'Seized-up society' translates very imperfectly Chaban's *société bloquée,* itself a highly approximate rendering of Stanley Hoffman's 'stalemate society'. The French phrase evokes machinery turning endlessly yet making no progress.

16

VISION AND REALITY

Quoi, tu veux qu'on t'épargne et n'as rien épargné!

CORNEILLE

A Balance Sheet

With Pompidou securely established in the Elysée, and de Gaulle rapidly receding into history, an illustrious shadow brooding over his memoirs at Colombey, the Fifth Republic has shown a greater capacity for survival than many critics forecast. This owed much to de Gaulle's own unflagging efforts to restore the authority of the State. But also the regime itself had gradually attracted an impressively broad spectrum of support from people whose loyalties were not purely personal, and who were prepared, at least provisionally, to back the new order after the passing of its founder. Many of them came from the groups which had done well from the economic and social changes of the Fourth and Fifth Republics—the managers, executives and technicians. Others belonged to the groups most threatened by these same changes —peasants, shopkeepers and independent craftsmen who looked to the State to halt or temper the onward sweep of economic modernization. The socio-political bases of Gaullism were heterogeneous and potentially precarious, both during and after the General's reign.[1] Yet it was a major achievement to have attracted and held for so long such a substantial

---

[1] The composition of the Gaullist coalition of course changed frequently, both while the General was there and after his departure. While to the end he personally won substantial support among the workers (and a poll in the summer of 1969 showed that his going was most regretted by the workers and the retired), it was largely the defection of both the upper bourgeoisie and the 'small men' of agriculture, industry and distribution which sealed his fate in April 1969. Pompidou held few of the workers but gained ground with the other groups which had deserted the General.

following. For throughout modern French history successive political systems have had great difficulty in retaining the social supports they needed to work effectively.

This long-standing imbalance between society's demands on the State, and the supports it was capable of generating took a particularly serious form after World War II. Gripped by both specific crises such as decolonization, and the more generalized stresses arising from her belated surge forward towards a modern economy, France could no longer—as under the Third Republic—seek a comfortable refuge in a form of government which simply divided Frenchmen least. Robbed of its last resort in immobilism, the Fourth Republic collapsed from the inability of its atomized and resistive society to mobilize the political forces the system required. While many welcomed de Gaulle in 1958 simply as a lesser evil than the Algiers fascists, much of his initial backing came from those (both voters and politicians) who had been most frustrated by the failure of the old System, and who eagerly grasped at the opportunities offered by a new political order. Even among de Gaulle's Mendèsist and PSU opponents many were covertly hoping that he would succeed in breaking down the elements in the social and political systems which had doomed democratic regimes to ineffectiveness. Thus, if the conservative forces were strong, in 1958 there were also significant elements in French society looking to de Gaulle to base his new system on the forces of change, and recognizing that the traditional Republican State was no longer adequate to the tasks expected of it by the groups most attuned to modern society. Financial crisis, foreign failure, imperial defeat and the knowledge that their political system was an international laughing stock brought home to ordinary Frenchmen the drawbacks of weak government in a dangerous world; and when the army and Algerian settlers vetoed any further retreat, the Fourth Republic (like the Third) found itself without defenders. De Gaulle therefore inherited two interlinked problems: to break the specific policy deadlocks he inherited from the Fourth Republic, and to promote the development of a modern political system in a country whose social structure and political attitudes were still rooted in the nineteenth century.

In addressing the French people for the first time after his return in 1958, de Gaulle himself set out his agenda in these terms: Algeria, Black Africa, financial and economic equilibrium, the assertion of French independence, and the construction of a strong, stable political order. His regime may fairly be assessed against the challenge he outlined then. The clearest success has been the smooth and speedy liquidation of colonial rule in Black Africa, including the skilful correction of the 'false start' with the Community. Helped by a relatively generous aid programme, relations between France and her former African possessions have—with the unforgiven exception of Guinea—remained markedly more cordial than Britain's. Today all that survives of the French colonial empire is a scattering of overseas departments and territories from the South Seas to the Gulf of St Lawrence, most seeking wider autonomy, but as yet finding a less sympathetic reception than the Africans did.

While de Gaulle carried through the liberal evolution in Black Africa begun by Gaston Defferre, in Algeria he had a far less enviable legacy—partly due to his own past policies. Historically this settlement is probably his greatest achievement, even though so pitifully little was salvaged from the wreck of *Algérie française*. Not because he willed an outcome which was in any case 'in the nature of things', but because he prevented the affair from inflicting a lasting scar on France which could have hindered progress towards greater political community for decades. However, despite de Gaulle's determination to show the world a model relationship between ex-colonizer and ex-colonized, and consequent readiness to tolerate the liberties taken by self-consciously 'revolutionary' Algerian governments with the Evian agreements, relations between the two countries have become steadily less cordial since 1965.

In foreign affairs, the belief that 'France cannot be France without grandeur' led to the development of a nuclear strike force whose rationale was more diplomatic than military, and to the tireless proclamation of a distinctively French position on every world problem. To many this abrasively assertive foreign policy was ultimately to prove a futile failure: futile because national independence is an anachronistic chimera, a failure because while de Gaulle was adept at thwarting his adversaries over European integration, nuclear testing, the United Nations and the Atlantic Alliance, he was unable to muster sufficient international support for his own policies or leadership to prevail. His characteristic combination of hypersensitivity to French interests with a ruthless disregard of the feelings of others built up such irritation and distrust that minds were closed to any merits his views had. However, his intentions should not be misread. At times a provocative gesture seemed to be intended less for immediate success than as a catalyst; he calculated that after the first outraged reactions had faded his ideas would make headway. This approach was most effective in such areas as EEC and NATO where he had some chance of making his prophecies self-fulfilling; its limitations elsewhere were cruelly exposed when the invasion of Czechoslovakia laid in ruins his hopes of disintegrating the eastern bloc. Again, his pronouncements on such matters as Santo Domingo, Vietnam, Cyprus, Biafra and Quebec were self-justifying in his terms by the controversy and attention they aroused—they demonstrated that France was playing a world role; any practical outcome was simply a bonus. De Gaulle in fact exploited systematically France's relative weakness and her limited responsibilities to play the classic card of the second-rank power: 'moral leadership'. It says much for his political skill that he contrived with some success to present himself as the champion of self-determination for the oppressed while running a profitable arms trade with South Africa. In the end he embittered relations with practically all of western Europe, North America and Israel (unsentimentally brushed aside in the pursuit of a rapprochement with the Arabs), but won widespread popularity in much of the Third World and eastern Europe. Cynical and unscrupulous, de Gaulle's policy brought little progress towards his positive objectives, but as long as he was there France appeared larger than life on the world stage. In spite of his bomb, his paratroops in his African satrapies, his support of Portugal and Katanga at the UN, and his sales of arms to South Africa, his hostility to the United States earned him the enthusiastic admiration of left-wingers everywhere, and above all in France. Even after the outcry over such issues as Quebec and the Israel arms embargo, his assertive policies remained to the end a source of domestic satisfaction and political strength.[1]

---

[1] In February 1965 and March 1968 national samples were asked: 'Are you satisfied or dissatisfied with the role France is currently

On the other hand, the Fifth Republic has often received rather more than its due for economic achievement. The crucial changes in attitudes to growth were, after all, under way well before its birth, while the Fourth Republic bequeathed to its successor a basically strong economy and a long-term investment programme which bore fruit in the sixties.[1] It also made the courageous decision, over fierce Gaullist protests, to join EEC—which has been a spur to modernization ever since. But de Gaulle can take credit for driving home and popularizing the need for change, which he depicted as 'the mainspring of modern civilization, the wish of the entire people, and the condition of French independence, power and influence'. Economic development became part of the call to greatness: 'This gigantic renewal must be the chief concern and capital ambition of France.' Throughout his years in office, no themes recurred more frequently in his public utterances (apart from the unvarying denunciations of the parties), than the challenge and promise of 'renovation', 'change' and 'transformation'. The new readiness of the French to look to the future must surely owe something to his insistent, confident vision.

Economic modernization has been carried forward. While it is still far from complete, there is now a sounder balance between industry and agriculture. But although France has consistently expanded her economy faster than a flagging Britain, in neither growth nor price stability has she outstripped her EEC partners.[2] The capital market remains

---

playing on the international level?'. In 1965 44 per cent were satisfied, 16 per cent dissatisfied and 40 per cent made no reply. In 1968 the figures were, respectively, 56 per cent, 25 per cent and 19 per cent. However, when asked whether France could really be independent militarily, economically and politically, in 1968 only 28 per cent thought this possible militarily, 26 per cent economically and 34 per cent politically. Cf. *Sondages*, 1968 (2), p. 42.

[1] Though rarely acknowledging that anything of value was achieved during his years in the wilderness, de Gaulle agreed (13 June 1958) that he inherited 'an economy which has broken free of routine once and for all, and is advancing technically'.

[2] Taking 1958 = 100, in April 1968 the French retail price index was 144, compared with West Germany 125, Italy 139, Holland 141, Belgium 126, UK 134, USA 119. Over 1958–66 French GNP per head at constant prices rose 49 per cent, West Germany 53 per cent, Italy 55 per cent and Holland 55 per cent.

VISION AND REALITY

grossly underdeveloped; the legal structure still reflects at many points the old restrictionist philosophy; and only limited headway has been made against the jungle of obstacles to expansion (by groups as varied as meat wholesalers, chemists and taxi-drivers) which were stigmatized in the Rueff-Armand report of 1960. Preoccupied with grandeur abroad, and as susceptible as the demagogues of the old System to prestige projects like Concorde and the Mont-Blanc tunnel, the Fifth Republic has often shirked the basic reforms which are needed to carry modernization through. Wavering erratically between neoliberal economic policies and greater *dirigisme*, unsuccessfully seeking to stem the American challenge through economic nationalism,[1] the regime has too often taken stability as a virtue in itself rather than as a basis for further progress.

Financially, the outstanding achievement was the successful devaluation and austerity programme of December 1958, which enabled France to honour engagements to EEC on which the committed 'Europeans' of the Fourth Republic would surely have had to renege. By preventing devaluation being squandered through rapid inflation, Pinay and Debré helped to hold a competitive edge for exports, and so build up the record exchange reserves which backed de Gaulle's foreign policy. For a decade the Fifth Republic brought greater financial coherence and stability than at any time within living memory—though Giscard's attempt to return to classically balanced budgets proved short-lived. It was no small feat to make the despised franc so strong that de Gaulle could challenge the international monetary system and threaten the dollar. But then came May 1968. After paying so high a price for stability it seemed the regime had simply concentrated all discontents into one huge and immensely costly explosion. Attitudes engrained by decades of inflation and unstable currency, which had been lying latent for several years, now brusquely revived. One inevitable result flowed from the slow deterioration in the competitiveness of French products (which had developed long before May) and the sudden disappearance of confidence. Though de Gaulle himself defiantly

[1] Even under de Gaulle France failed in her bid to persuade Europe to adopt the French colour TV system, and in her attempt to preserve a wholly French computer industry; the even more costly attempt to develop French-designed nuclear power stations was abandoned within months of de Gaulle's departure.

resisted the inevitable, like the Fourth Republic he left to his successor a strong economy, but an inescapable devaluation and a convalescent currency.

To de Gaulle, however, there could ultimately be no successful financial economic or external policy without a solution to the political problem, which was capital. 'The French nation', he declared, 'will bloom again or perish depending on whether or not the State has the strength, steadfastness and authority to lead it along the path it must follow.' Oversimplified though this diagnosis was, it touched a responsive chord in a people with such unfortunate political memories. Early in 1958 a poll enquired whether Frenchmen considered certain countries to be governed better or worse than their own. The proportions judging the foreign systems superior were: Britain 39 per cent, Italy 10 per cent, USA 58 per cent, West Germany 52 per cent and USSR 31 per cent. After seven years of the Fifth Republic the response to an identical question was eloquently different: Britain 14 per cent, Italy 3 per cent, USA 30 per cent, West Germany 21 per cent and USSR 15 per cent. When asked what was the best thing de Gaulle had done during his first presidential term, 27 per cent mentioned stable government and only 14 per cent Algeria.[1] Even among the opposition there was widespread satisfaction that France's political troubles were no longer the subject of world-wide derision. The General was well aware that this satisfaction was a major source of political strength. He sought tirelessly to identify his opponents with the instability of the past (habitually referred to in flesh-creeping flashbacks); and although, like any 'bad old days' argument, this was a wasting asset, to the end it remained one of his most potent campaigning ploys.[2]

De Gaulle's achievement in restoring to the French their political self-respect and giving his country the longest period

---

[1] Cf. *Sondages*, 1966(1), pp. 22–5.

[2] A characteristic passage from his closing speech in the 1965 presidential election: 'There is . . . the regime of the past, in which the State, the nation, destiny were at the discretion of the parties; the regime of politicians' little games, of fraudulent coalitions, of house-of-cards cabinets; the regime of impotence, abasement and failure. If it reappeared nobody can doubt it would bring with it the frightful confusion of the past.'

of calm she had known for decades is not to be underestimated, particularly against the confusion, incoherence and impotence of the Fourth Republic's dying months, and the indifference amid which it expired. But if the Fifth Republic is to be more than a mere historical parenthesis, it must also promote some solution to the underlying problem of political community, without which there is little hope of breaking permanently free from the cycle of weak representative governments leading to the personal rule of a 'great man', followed by a reaction to a fresh representative regime. This was what Debré set out to do in 1958 with a constitution which he hoped would provide France at last with a true parliamentary system. But the ink was scarcely dry on the constitution before there was talk of amending it to allow direct election of the President. The controversial revision procedure employed in 1962 led to differences between the Gaullists and the Senate hardening into a feud which left the fate of the upper house (and thus of both the legislative process and the interim presidential succession) in doubt for over six years. The future of the Economic and Social Council was never really clear throughout the General's reign. Finally the 1969 referendum proposals would have repealed or modified no fewer than 21 of the constitution's 92 articles. Below the constitutional level were the creation and suppression of special courts at the President's pleasure, the succession of changes and proposals for regional institutions and the government of Paris, and the tinkering with the system of city elections for partisan ends.

The regime has repeatedly stretched, evaded or violated its own system. Debré's arbiter-President became a monarchical ruler who, long after the Algerian crisis, continued to consolidate himself as the hub of the political universe. De Gaulle was clearly not the man to content himself with simply 'the power to solicit other powers', but few imagined that article 20 would count for quite so little, that the initiative for referendums would pass completely to the President despite articles 11 and 89, or that de Gaulle would dismiss a Prime Minister with only the barest genuflection to article 8. Apart from this overall tilting of the constitutional balance there were episodes like the constitutional short-cut used in giving independence to the Community states to avoid having the parliamentarians meet in Congress under the orthodox procedure of article 89; the refusal to call a special session of parliament requested by a majority of deputies; the improper (if excusable) exclusion of Algeria from the April 1962 referendum, and the improper (and inexcusable) resort to the referendum for constitutional revision in 1962 and 1969; the President's unethical intervention on the eve of poll in both the 1967 and 1968 elections, and the refusal of the Pompidou government to test its parliamentary standing in a confidence vote after the 1967 elections.[1]

Similar psychological traits appeared in the predilection for exceptional grants of authority: special powers for Algeria, transitional powers in 1958–59, delegations of the right to legislate by ordinance from parliament or through referendum, together with permanent standby powers to handle emergencies and, most apocalyptic of all, article 16. For about half de Gaulle's reign some form of exceptional powers operated to cut through normal legislative, administrative or (more rarely) judicial procedures. While these were mainly invoked to cope with the Algerian war and its aftermath (when they were often put to curiously trivial use),[2] the Pompidou government's immediate reaction to almost losing its parliamentary majority in 1967 was to call for powers to legislate by ordinance. Even within the executive the superimposition of republican monarchy on the structure of cabinet government meant that the chain of decision-making was often uncertain. It was often hard for the minister or civil servant operating outside the 'reserved sector' to know when normal procedures might be disrupted by a sudden intervention from the Elysée. The consequences were apparent in the collapse of authority in May 1968.

However unexceptionable some of the ends may have been, cumulatively these methods showed the regime's proclivity for riding roughshod over its own constitution (while applying it with the strictest legalism to opponents), and shortcircuiting normal procedures to impose its will or simply suit its convenience. Reproached for violating the constitution de Gaulle is said to have retorted, 'You cannot rape your own wife'.[3]

---

[1] This list is not exhaustive. For further examples relating to parliament, see above, pp. 221–2.

[2] Cf. above, p. 190.

[3] Pursuing the analogy, however, there is an instructive French jurisprudence on *excès, sévices et injures* — as grounds for divorce.

This pungent revelation of his brutally proprietary attitude towards 'his' system exposes the major source of the uncertainty about institutional relationships which persisted throughout his reign.

Leadership, style and consensus

De Gaulle's perception of the problem of the succession seemed torn by the inner uncertainties characteristic of that complicated man. At times he seemed to contemplate the question with a fatalistic recognition that once a heroic leader leaves the stage France tends to slide thankfully back into a less demanding routine. This could lead to a period of weak government and a gradual descent into decadence until eventually a new *homme providentiel* emerged to save her from mediocrity or catastrophe. Fanciful though the scenario sounds, it is fully in keeping with the fairytale vision with which the General opens his memoirs. Yet at other times he seemed determined to break out of the historic cycle once and for all. Early in the Fifth Republic the emphasis was on new institutions and new men, almost as if they were an answer in themselves, though it was the technocratic Jacobin Debré who placed the highest hopes in purely mechanical change, rather than de Gaulle, whose historian's eye had scanned the wreckage of so many earlier attempts. Over the years an even greater awareness of the limitations of constitutional remedies crept into his utterances.

A constitution is simply an envelope [he said in 1965]. The question is, what is inside . . .? If, despite the envelope and despite the terms and the spirit of what was adopted in 1958, the parties again take over the institutions, then the Republic and the State are reduced to nothing. The purpose of the confessional is to try to repel the devil. But if the devil gets inside the confessional itself, then that's quite a different matter![1]

Nevertheless, with the 1962 constitutional reform he attempted to build a bridge between the traditions of personal rule and of representative government, between his own historic legitimacy and a new institutional one. While, as he

---

[1] TV interview, 15 Dec. 1955.

put it, the form of presidential election system could neither 'determine my own responsibilities towards France nor, by itself alone, express the confidence the French people have in me, it will be a very different question for those who, not necessarily having received the same national mark from events, will come after me to occupy my present post in turn'.[1] He constantly tried to shift expectations and traditions in the direction of the stronger leadership which republican monarchy requires. Not without success. All the main challengers in the 1965 and 1969 campaigns adopted personal and assertive styles far removed from the customary practice of the Fourth Republic; all campaigned on programmes which they would have felt obliged to fight for if successful. De Gaulle clearly hoped that, even allowing for any post-Gaullist reaction against strong Presidents, he would mark his office so indelibly that successors would draw authority from his example (though MacMahon is a reminder that over-assertive Presidents may also weaken their office).

Yet the hybrid structure of presidential-cum-cabinet government which has evolved since 1958 is peculiarly difficult to operate. The system of double responsibility can work only if the cabinet retains the confidence of both the President and a parliamentary majority. Even de Gaulle found this difficult to achieve at times. In the event Pompidou, inheriting a massive majority, was able to bridge the immediate transition successfully, but it will not be easy to maintain this in a system with so limited a tradition of political cooperation. Differences between the President and parliament will tend inevitably to produce a struggle for ascendancy over the cabinet, with each having considerable scope for obstruction (refusal to legislate on the one hand, and to sign decrees on the other). The President can seek an issue by dissolving the Assembly (unless he has already dissolved it prematurely during the previous year), and then he will either be vindicated by the electorate or be obliged to give in or go—failing some patched-up compromise. The original 1958 President, elected by 80,000 elderly provincial bigwigs, was singularly ill-equipped for any such confrontation. The 1962 revision left the potential contenders more evenly matched. Future Presidents will be men with a personal policy to defend, and

---

[1] TV address, 20 Sept. 1962.

they will be armed with both the moral backing of popular election and the precedents created for them by de Gaulle. Even so, the President's success in such situations is far from sure. Ultimately, a procedure as risky as dissolution is not a satisfactory regulator for an entire system. Dual responsibility —or stable government in any form—can rest only on a party machine coherent enough to sustain strong leadership.

In his way, de Gaulle recognized the problem while rejecting the solution, with his assertion that 'no constitutional texts, even if interpreted to match the circumstances; no declarations, however skilfully balanced; no promises, however freely distributed, can ensure that a Chief of State in France really is a Chief of State, if he issues not from the profound confidence of the nation but from a momentary bargain between professional tricksters'. While recognizing the personal qualities of politicians as diverse as Maurice Thorez, Pierre Mendès-France and Edgar Faure, he never showed the least acknowledgement of the value of political parties. Over the years a gradual grudging acceptance of the services of the UNR crept into his speeches, but no occasion was missed for a ritual vituperation of the *régime des partis*. Except for moments when he needed them he treated the parties as irredeemable moral delinquents—and admittedly their behaviour not infrequently matched his expectations. His supporters systematically thwarted or ridiculed the few faltering attempts of the opposition towards modernizing itself. The Gaullist jubiliation at the collapse of the Defferre candidature and the failure of the Federation revealed that the attitudes of the old System had not all died with it.[1] Reacting with a partisan determination to cling to power and privilege, they showed the Fifth Republic as far from developing a concept of loyal opposition as the Fourth had been from accepting the need for democratic leadership.

To the extent that a solution to France's political ills can be had on a political level, it lies neither in new men nor in fresh institutions (though these may have their place), but in the development of a party system capable of sustaining firm representative government. But the very characteristics of Gaullist rule which led to the sweeping away or humbling of

---

[1] This jubilation was not shared by Left Gaullists like Capitant, who wanted to see a genuine democratic left-wing opposition.

so many traditional parties have tended to militate against the modernization which should follow. De Gaulle neither employed his great didactic talents to educate the parties to an acceptance of fresh attitudes towards leadership and responsibility, nor offered an alternative vision of how to operate an effective modern democracy without healthy parties.

Towards the end of the General's reign the fashionable solution to this dilemma became 'participation'—the watchword of the reforming Left in the early sixties before becoming the Gaullist panacea in the wake of May. In a country with so strong a tradition of the 'absent people' (and under de Gaulle even ministers learned of the Israeli arms embargo in the newspapers), the superficial attractions of such a nostrum are strong. But genuine participation is difficult enough in any complex advanced society; in France the dangers of degeneration into corporatism or technocracy are obvious and already present. Moreover, many of the more recent protagonists have seen participation more as a substitute for politics than as a means of deepening or democratizing them—reflecting a lingering belief that some fundamental unity will be found beyond the partisan cries of professional politicians. This is especially wishful thinking in France, where the problem is precisely an absence of fundamental unity, which makes strong government and extensive participation particularly hard to reconcile.

For participation to knit Frenchmen together rather than merely mirror their divisions there would have to be a determined onslaught on traditional, centralized hierarchical authority and the attitudes arising from it, to ensure a greater voluntarism in social action and a wider area of open debate. The Plan, the educational system, the factories and broadcasting would be good places to begin. But so far the experience of the CODER, and the Economic and Social Council, has been that the ruling style of the Fifth Republic inhibits the emergence of more positive attitudes. Scornful of elites and intermediaries, de Gaulle composed with them when need be, overruled and neglected them whenever he could. He was never able to integrate them fruitfully into his system. Yet in large measure meaningful popular participation must lie through just such bodies.

Under de Gaulle the system was in fact less participatory even than Debré had conceived it in 1958. From the beginning it functioned as a republican monarchy dominated by a man who pre-eminently belonged to the French tradition of *hommes providentiels*. 'Heroic leadership', as Stanley Hoffmann has described it, is less a change of system than a switch in procedures within an essentially unchanging tradition of authority. It tends accordingly to exist in an oddly symbiotic relationship with its avowedly mortal enemy—the routine leadership characteristic of representative government.[1] In either case the existing hierarchy of ranks and statuses is basically unchanged, and authority remains equally remote and centralized. One system puts power in the hands of a relatively small 'political class', and the other personalizes it in the hero —but neither provides genuine popular participation. Crisis leadership in fact serves to preserve the continuing long-term system from the consequences of the representative regime's chronic tendency towards immobilism, and to prevent a major change to either despotism or participant democracy. This function of crisis leadership was tacitly recognized by the traditional politicians when they turned to de Gaulle in 1958, considering him as *un mauvais moment à passer* until they could reclaim their lost prerogatives.

Thus, although the distinctive flavour of the Fifth Republic was inseparable from the personality and career of the man who dominated it for more than a decade, his style touched many historical chords in a nation with a greater awareness than most of its past. The 1958 constitution, as moulded by de Gaulle to his own wishes, proved an exceptionally convenient framework for a style of leadership which drew constantly on the example of earlier heroic figures. Having ministers who were prepared to be his faithful executants, de Gaulle, unlike American presidents or British premiers, was able to rid himself of anything he deemed trivial, while retaining the right to intervene anywhere at any time; to use his ministers as buffers between himself and the outside world and to

---

[1] Cf. S. Hoffmann, 'Heroic Leadership: the Case of Modern France', in L. J. Edinger, ed., *Political Leadership in Industrialized Societies* (New York, 1967), pp. 108 ff. In this highly perceptive if slightly oversystematized analysis Hoffmann makes it clear that the 'heroic leadership' style can appear in representative regimes (Clemenceau and Mendès-France); Second Empire and Vichy experience suggests that 'routine leadership' can also be found in personal regimes.

associate himself with success while avoiding contamination by failure. Screened by his ministers in all but the gravest crises, freed from the need to answer either in parliament or in unfettered press conference, subject to election only after seven years, he could reveal as little or as much of himself as he chose, when he chose, in minutely prepared addresses to the nation or press levées. This ability to avoid the constant public explanations and comments required of other democratic political leaders was indispensable to preserving that reserve, mystery and surprise he considered essential to effective leadership.[1]

Thus aided by the institutional structure, de Gaulle adopted the heroic, monarchical stance of presenting his actions as working above and beyond the mundane trivialities of factional politics towards a great enterprise: national ambition and greatness. Although the exegetist can detect the way de Gaulle steadily edged towards acknowledgement that he led a distinctive political force, even his most direct endorsement of his supporters was formally noncommittal. He was the man above the battle, judiciously weighing the contending interests, discerning where the national interest lay and ordaining accordingly, then maintaining his decision *envers et contre tout*. While this is a game that countless conventional politicians try to play, such was de Gaulle's skill that, although devoid of political scruples, to the end he remained a figure above politics to a high proportion of his countrymen.

This lofty form of consensus politics was also characterized by a concern for national unity and reconciliation. Occasional exceptions like the 1968 election apart, de Gaulle set a deliberate contrast with the strident divisions of partisan politics, wooing Communists, Vichyites, OAS and even individual politicians of the Fourth Republic back to the fold. Only the 'parties of the past' remained firmly unredeemed in a vengeful purgatory. There was more to this than a sentimental quest for unanimity. A leader who, like de Gaulle, looks for support directly to the people rather than to organized political forces, must ceaselessly be preoccupied with consensus. This same end was served by most familiar external features of Gaullist leadership: the triumphal progressions through the provinces, the protocol of State occasions calculated minutely

---

[1] *Le Fil de l'épée*, pp. 77–89.

for historical resonance and political effect, the magnificent sense of timing, the sheer performance element in the memorized press conferences with their supremely ambiguous phrases, the mildly anachronistic language of his speeches with their careful blending of the ritual with the unexpected. The dramatic spectacle offered by this superb political actor compelled the admiration of the most hostile critic. This was more than mere outward trapping: the inimitable style was one of the most carefully thought through aspects of his statecraft.[1]

Yet, apart from occasional moments of crisis like the Generals' revolt, France is even today notoriously lacking in underlying consensus. Fragmented, resistant to change, hostile to political command, it is exceptionally difficult to govern. The heroic style impressed with its colourful rituals, its Olympian fiats, its repeatedly proclaimed rejection of petty haggling and compromise, and its boast that where the national interest was involved *le pouvoir ne recule pas*. The reality behind this spectacular façade was inevitably less magnificent. De Gaulle was obliged to proceed by equivocation, prevarication and the slow elimination of every alternative if the heroic image was not to be shattered. His handling of the Algerian war was a classic example of the technique. Mystery, concealment and cunning were constantly needed to camouflage the inevitable indecision, the deals and the failures which contrasted tellingly with the proud mythology of a monarch determined to set himself apart from the shabbiness of routine leadership. Aided somewhat by his ministerial buffer, even more by his talent for concealing his objectives until victory was within his grasp, de Gaulle showed exceptional skill in concealing his own defeats or deflecting them on to others. Exceptions like his miscalculated committal of his prestige in the 1963 miners' strike were remarkably rare, until May 1968 brought its cruel revelation of the querulous indecision of the ageing monarch.

---

[1] 'Lesser men are concerned simply to behave correctly before their men; the greatest arrange their interventions carefully. They make an art of this, as Flaubert realized very well; in *Salammbô* he depicted for us the effect produced on flagging troops by Hamilcar's carefully calculated arrival on the scene. Every page of the *Commentaries* shows us how Caesar weighed his every movement in public. We know what thought Napoleon always took to show himself in such a way as to impress those who saw him.' *Le Fil de l'épée*, pp. 79–80.

379

The weakest feature of his statecraft was his personal medio-crity as a negotiator. The recognition of equality and the element of personal revelation involved in face-to-face bargaining are at bottom incompatible with heroic leadership. De Gaulle preferred to proceed by unilateral commands or concessions rather than true negotiation—a failing which served both him and France badly during the search for an Algerian settlement.

De Gaulle's approach to the problem of consensus was always complex. He worked constantly to maintain a rather vague and generalized assent at the popular level, but he seemed less comfortable with sustained backing from among the organized participants in the political system. While he preferred to hold his followers by deploying all his con-siderable capacity for ambiguity, few politicians have been as skilful, unsentimental or systematic about shifting the basis of their support. This was demonstrated early in his reign over Algeria, and at the end, in 1968, by his characteristic attempt to shift within days from appealing electorally to the most conservative elements in society to seeking an opening towards the Left. He saw every ally as a potential adversary, and every adversary as a potential ally—as he tacitly recognized in claiming that every Frenchman had been, was or would be a Gaullist. Consequently he was always concerned to maintain a diversity of forces, hoping to escape being the prisoner of his friends. Thus in 1958 he was concerned that the electoral system should not be gerrymandered to produce a UNR landslide; he opposed proposals to create a vice-presidency, and he always encouraged a number of factions within Gaullism. While his identification with the Gaullist party increased as the years went by, to the end he avoided unequi-vocal acceptance of it as 'his' party. Such an attitude led naturally to the emergence of court politics, with ruler and courtiers ceaselessly, watchfully jockeying for position.

This concern of the republican monarch to be as many things to as many men as possible goes far to explaining the character of Gaullist rule, and the surprisingly timid and unimaginative record of reform. For de Gaulle personally was no rock-ribbed conservative. While inescapably a man of his time, in many areas he grasped the need for change and fresh ideas to a degree remarkable in someone of his years. Committed to a vision of France in history, he was totally pragmatic and quite unhampered by attachment to existing institutions or social groups. Far from being the man of any particular caste or interest, de Gaulle always had uneasy relations with politicians, industrialists, soldiers, prelates and intellectuals (and none whatever with workers). His isolation from the nation's elites was sometimes an advantage to him as a reformer, though elsewhere it was a political weakness. In some matters, such as agricultural and university reform, he was willing to go further than his supporters.

Unlike the General, the Gaullist elite were mostly bound by their origins, education or occupation to the attitudes of the industrial, commercial or administrative elites—a comfortable milieu where proletarian or reforming voices are few. Typically, when Pompidou was confronted by proposals to reform the *grandes écoles*, as a former *normalien* he ruthlessly emasculated them—and equally typically de Gaulle did not intervene. Time and again change was stifled or watered down by the timidity or heterogeneity of administrators and politicians (itself the outcome of the ambiguous breadth of Gaullism's appeal).[1] Yet although the Gaullist electorate spanned the political spectrum, its centre of gravity was always the solid, the cautious and the satisfied, who wanted a quiet life without surprises.

De Gaulle himself, preoccupied with international grandeur, and treating society and the economy as mere handmaids of foreign policy, was often ready enough to accept change, but rarely to initiate it. He would provoke and weather the fiercest storms over Israel or Quebec, but he would not risk the unpopularity of fundamental domestic reforms jeopardizing his relationship with the people—and thus the free hand on foreign issues which really mattered. A man so preoccupied with ambiguity and blurring issues (yet with such a capacity, when it suited his purpose, for brutal clarification of matters which others wanted blurred), was constantly tempted to evade awkward domestic choices and water down reforms. He was keenly aware of the need for extensive social, legal and economic change, and he had exceptional opportunities to promote it. But to those who pressed him to speed this transformation early in 1968 he made the defeatist

[1] One notable instance was the continuing division in the UNR and the government between the economic liberals like Pompidou and the interventionists like Debré.

reply, 'My means are limited'.[1] 'France', he once said, 'only reforms in the wake of revolution'—a tacit recognition that even nominally strong government may sink into the quicksands of inertia. But even after the near-revolution of 1968, the long overdue reform of the universities was considerably diluted before de Gaulle intervened, while another chance (his last) was missed to implement his views on relations between labour and capital. The appeal, the style, the priorities, and the urge to maintain consensus with which he ruled meant that ultimately, under the General, Gaullism and thoroughgoing reform could not go hand in hand.

Scarcely had de Gaulle left the stage when Chaban-Delmas was attributing the malaise from which France was suffering to a 'seized-up society'. The economy was fragile, with an over-narrow industrial base, and a permanent tendency to inflation. The State was 'tentacular and inefficient', its appetite for new responsibilities constantly outrunning its capacity to deal with them effectively. It had 'little by little put the whole of French society into tutelage', and its actions were often unintelligible, incoherent or unjust. The social structure was so 'archaic and conservative' that it nurtured extremism. France was a 'country of castes', with 'excessive inequalities of income, and inadequate social mobility' which sustained the separation of social groups. Though the General's name was never uttered during this sombre catalogue of failings, the call to begin the creation of a 'new society' was by inescapable implication the cruellest epitaph on his decade of power. But the General's successors would in turn be unable to escape the fact that their electoral support, like his, came disproportionately from groups like peasants, small shopkeepers and independent craftsmen, who were the most threatened by social and economic change. It remained to be seen whether they could succeed in overcoming this contradiction between the attack on the 'seized-up society', and the conservative nature of Gaullism's electoral (and parliamentary) base.[2]

---

[1] Reported by J.-M. Domenach, *Le Monde*, 11 Nov. 1969.

[2] *Le Monde*, 18 Sept. 1969. Some critics suggested that Chaban launched into his vision of a distant 'new society' because he had nothing more concrete to offer. Mitterrand's comment, though, was: 'When I look at you I do not doubt your sincerity, but when I look at your majority, I doubt your success.'

Legitimacy and the succession

In keeping with the tradition of crisis leadership, de Gaulle's rule was neither despotic nor truly democratic. He admitted having considered dictatorship when he departed for the wilderness in 1946, but claimed to have set his face against this both because it was essentially vulgar and because 'no man can be a substitute for a people'—even a people he privately dismissed as 'soft' or 'sheep'.[1] There were illiberal blemishes on his rule, such as the internments and press seizures of the Algerian war, and the continuing unchecked excesses of the police. Yet these were mostly characteristic of French regimes generally rather than of his in particular—although sometimes, as with the subjugation of broadcasting, they took an accentuated form.[2] One characteristic, though again not unprecedented, failing of the Fifth Republic has been its readiness to lapse into arbitrary behaviour, whether in constitutional or administrative matters or in affairs like the trying of OAS criminals. Although the opposition has only been restricted at the extremes, an ugly illiberal streak has always lurked in the spirit of the Fifth Republic. One of its

---

[1] Cf. his classic denunciation from his Bayeux speech of 1946. 'What is dictatorship but a gamble? No doubt it seems to offer advantages at first. Amidst the enthusiasm of some and the resignation of others, with the strict order it imposes, and with the aid of a glittering decor and one-sided propaganda, it at first takes on a dynamic air which contrasts sharply with the preceding anarchy. But dictatorship is destined inevitably to overreach itself in what it undertakes. As impatience with compulsion and regret for the freedom they have lost spread among its citizens it must at all costs offer them vaster and vaster successes in compensation. The nation becomes a machine which its master accelerates with ever-increasing frenzy. Whether in foreign or domestic matters its aims, risks and efforts gradually exceed all measure. At every step a host of obstacles rise in its path at home and abroad. At last the mainspring breaks. The grandiose structure collapses in blood and tribulation. The nation is shattered more gravely than before the adventure began.'

[2] One illiberal trait peculiar to the Fifth Republic has been the spate of prosecutions for insulting the President of the Republic, under a law enacted when Presidents were mere figureheads. By 1965 there had been over 300 prosecutions compared with only six in the Third and Fourth Republics combined. Convictions were secured for booing the President in the Champs-Elysées, shouting 'Retire!' at him, and caricaturing him on a restaurant tablecloth.

least attractive forms has been the unsavoury demi-monde of 'parallel police' and semi-secret networks which have from time to time been so useful to the authorities. They have ranged from the counter-terrorist bands which fought the OAS (and kidnapped one of its leaders from Germany after the struggle was over), to the Civic Action Committees — gangs of hard-core Gaullists and strong-arm men which sprang up in response to the General's call for 'civic action' to meet the challenge of May 1968, under the inspiration of one of his closest advisers in the Elysée — Jacques Foccart.[1] Yet, despite this tendency to disregard proprieties or legality, de Gaulle substantially preserved traditional liberties even under the exceptional pressures of the Algerian war. France under his rule was no dictatorship, but a basically free political system — subject to backsliding.

Gaullists have claimed that the regime has actually extended democracy through the referendum, presidential elections, and de Gaulle's 'direct' relationship with the people. But while the new presidential electoral system lends this boast some substance, against it lie the repeated concealment of policy changes until a week or so after polling day, and the attempt to keep details of the 1969 referendum from the public as long as possible. Television communication was almost wholly unilateral. Though under de Gaulle France was said to be governed by the word, it was always a monologue, never a dialogue. Not once in his eleven years of power did the General expose himself publicly to free discussion or questioning. The referendum, mingling related but distinct issues in a single question, was a weapon for confounding the President's foes rather than a way of extending the people's choice. Their role was to accept and support rather than to participate. The most typical expression of Gaullist 'direct democracy' was the 'crowd bath', when the General dived into a forest of murmuring and deferentially enthusiastic bystanders, communicating in snatches and slogans, to emerge revivified with his legitimacy ratified anew.

For legitimacy was one of de Gaulle's recurring preoccupations. By seeking the Assembly's investiture in 1958 he marked his determination to preserve the thread of legality. But neither the overwhelming ratification of the constitution

---

[1] On Foccart, see above, p. 350n.

by referendum nor his eventual stigmatizing of the 'military subversion' preceding his return quite removed the stigma of the original sin. In 1940 too de Gaulle had played an irregular if heroic role, and his authority was challenged even by France's allies until the very eve of the Liberation. Thus 1958 reopened wounds which had never really healed. Such was his unremitting bitterness towards the Fourth Republic that in 1960 he repudiated its authority (and thereby his own legacy from it), invoking 'the national legitimacy which I have embodied for twenty years' (i.e. since his appeal of 18 June 1940). His claim was personal rather than legal and institutional, resting on his unique historic actions—renewed and confirmed by election and the informal plebiscites of the 'crowd bath'. It was only a short step to identifying the Fifth Republic with himself; he did this in 1968 with his contention that his opponents had raised 'the issue of the regime—in other words of the Chief of State'. It may well have been the need to demonstrate his own continuing legitimacy after the May 1968 humiliation—which no mere parliamentary triumph could assuage—that led him to his final and politically fatal referendum.

By its nature Gaullist leadership, with its compelling overshadowing virtuoso performances, was unrepeatable. The evident impossibility of transmitting so personal a heritage was a major reason for the persistently provisional air which hung over the Fifth Republic as long as the General was there. Ultimately this uncertainty was dispelled by his own immediate acceptance of defeat and the uninterrupted normality of the succession. The installation of M. Pompidou at the Elysée, the propriety of which was challenged by no significant political force, showed that the Fifth Republic had at last acquired its own legitimacy, independent of its founder.

Yet although the initial transfer went smoothly, the problem of promoting stable and effective democracy remained one of the least enviable elements in Pompidou's heritage. For, as always, the problem was not simply one of political personnel, but of the nature of wider political attitudes, and of society itself. France today is less stratified and fragmented, her people are less socially and psychologically isolated than in the past, and social cooperation is greater than it was a generation ago. Yet none of these changes has produced the conditions required for long-term political stability. The prospect of a modernized party system seems as distant as ever. The gap between the 'real' and 'legal' country is still unbridged. The State towers above its subjects as it always has. Though now more personalized, it remains impersonal, suspect and remote. The upheavals of 1968 emphasized the persistence of the old traditions of *incivisme* and the all-or-nothing approach to social relationships, with its endemic tendency to direct action or even violence. Even now the social modernization which is a precondition of political modernization is very far from complete. Indeed, the tensions inherent in bringing the 'seized-up society' through the urban-industrial revolution to which France is committed for at least another generation seem liable to nurture and exacerbate just those weaknesses of social fragmentation and resistive political culture which have so long prevented the emergence of an effective democratic political community. During the Gaullist years France has moved forward both economically and socially towards the General's vision of her 'marrying her century'. But despite the encouraging normality of the first succession, the long overdue task of political modernization is incomplete, and in some respects it has scarcely begun. Without this France will still not be a wholly modern nation, and without it, too, politically France could easily relapse once more into being one of the sick men of Europe.

INDEX

Important references are set in bold type

Chaban-Delmas, Jacques
as Gaullist, 89, 95, 177, 193
as Pres. Assembly, 54, 89, 192, 354
as PM, 207, 342n, 354, 356–7,
361, 362n, 363, 382
Chalandon, Albin, 89–90, 92, 305,
315, 358
Challe, Gen. Maurice, 34–35, 265,
267
Chambres d'agriculture, 148–9,
292, 298
Chambres de Commerce, 298
Chambres de Métiers, 298
Champs-Elysées, 25, 27, 58, 383n
Chaplin, Charles, 322
Charonne, 36
China, 44, 47, 133, 138
Christian Democrats — see MRP
Church — see Catholicism
Church schools, 20, 30, 144, 153–4,
159, 164, 202, 216, 324
Cinema, 166, 321–3
Cinémathèque Française, 321–3,
331
Civic Action Committee, 384
Civil liberties, 190, 261, 384
Civil service, 29, 122, 144, 146, 195–
197, 213n, 232, 236–48, 250, 291,
321, 336, 372, 383–4; and see
administration
Clair, René, 322
Class, 18, 22, 63, 112, 114, 141,
212, 308; and see bourgeoisie,
workers
Clemenceau, Georges, 262, 377n
Clericalism, 63, 110; and see anti-
clericalism
Club Jean Moulin, 244–5, 342n
Clubs, political, 121–2, 157, 244–
251, 252, 342n, 380
Cold War, 7, 64
Colombey (-les-deux-Eglises), 24,
57, 348, 357, 364
Colonial policy, 26, 31, 52n, 88, 97,
104, 208
Comités interministériels, 202n
Comité Maurice Audin, 156, 262n

Comité National de Conciliation,
163
Commission (European), 48, 244,
297
Commission on the Reform of
Higher Education, 324
Committees for the Defence of the
Republic, 100
Commission de l'Intéressement, 303
Committee of Public Safety, 24
Committees, parliamentary
in IV Rep., 144, 161
in V Rep., 92, 201
ad hoc, 161, 225, 303
conference, 210, 227–8
permanent, 161, 210, 218–19, 225,
233
Communautés Urbaines, 258
Common Market — see European
Economic Community
Communes, 204–9, 238, 249
Communist Party, French (PCF)
character, 20, 131, 141–3, 338
support, 28–9, 40–1, 64, 66, 68–9,
77–83, 94, 104, 120, 131–43,
257, 338, 353
organization, 131, 133, 143, 338
policies, 43, 46, 55, 57, 69, 103,
129, 131–43, 289, 304, 309, 330,
338
and Algeria, 34, 36n, 90, 132, 134,
137–8
and de Gaulle, 25, 40, 52, 57–8,
66, 94, 113, 132, 136–9, 141,
199, 378
and elections, 26, 45–6, 53, 58,
63–85, 131–2, 135–6, 140, 143,
300–2
and other parties, 46, 50–2, 54,
65, 70, 74, 76, 79, 94, 104, 111,
119, 121, 123, 126–30, 135–6,
138–40, 144, 335
in May 1958, 25, 136
in May 1968, 142–3
Community, 26, 31n, 177, 181, 187,
194, 272, 366, 371
Compagnies Republicaines de

Plan, Planning—*cont.*
  3rd Plan, 247
  4th Plan, 164, 245–7
  5th Plan, 47, 165, 205, 218, 245–8, 252, 300
  6th Plan, 165n
Plan, Commissioner-General of, 9, 244–5, 298
Pleven, René, 102n, 252, 271, 284, 285, 286, 319, 337, 354
Pnom-Penh, 52
Poher, Alain, 233, 344, 347, 349–53, 354n
Poirier, J.-M., 218
Poland, 133
Police, 33, 36, 56, 156, 190, 221, 262–3, 266, 267n, 268–9, 313, 318, 322, 324, 336, 347, 350n, 383–4
Policy, statements of, 53, 182–3, 209, 221, 231, 360
Polls, opinion, 19n, 21n, 22, 22n, 43n, 44, 49–50, 55, 74, 75n, 93, 95n, 129, 168, 180n, 206, 234, 335n, 336n, 345n, 346n, 348n, 351, 357n, 359n, 362n, 364n, 367n, 370
Polynesia, 26n
Pompidou, Georges
  directeur de cabinet, 275
  member Const. Council, 275
  P.M.
    and de Gaulle, 37, 56–7, 92, 99, 183, 195, 198, 201–6, 217, 305–7
    and Gaullists, 75, 78, 98–9, 102, 205, 234, 319, 340n
    and ministers, 106, 109, 197–200, 218, 246, 309, 315–16
    and office, 46, 53–4, 56–9, 182, 184, 186, 195, 202–5, 226, 231–3, 340n
    views, 99, 165, 247–8, 257, 303, 305, 372, 381
  deputy, 328, 345, 347
  Pres. aspirant, 46, 56, 58, 82–3, 99, 205, 345, 439–54

Pres. of Rep., 17, 196n, 206, 234, 254, 270, 354, 356, 358, 360–3, 374, 385
Popular Front, 138
Population, 8–9, 15–16, 64
Portugal, 367
Poujade, Pierre; Poujadism, 12, 66, 99, 103, 106n, 107, 116, 147, 162, 303, 313
Poujade, Robert, 99, 328, 347, 362, 363
Prague, 114, 337, 338
Prefects, 167, 202, 238, 242, 249–254, 312
Premier, *see* Prime Minister
Presence and Action of Gaullism, 356
President of the Community, 177, 181
President of the National Assembly, 35, 54, 89, 158, 189, 193, 234, 274, 354
President of the Senate, 111, 187n, 189, 217, 274, 345, 349. *See also* Monnerville, Poher
President of the Republic
  in III Rep., 188n
  in IV Rep., 183
  in V Rep.
    election, 29, **39–40**, 46–51, 66, 68, 74, 99, 109, 121–4, 177–8, 180, 185, 208, 213, 217
    insults to, 215, 383n
    powers, 35, 46, **173–207**, 208–209, 260–1, 274–5
    staff, 195–7, 201
    vacancy, 187, 345n
    and ministers, 175, 177–8, 181–4, 193–207, 208–9, 354, 360
    and parl., 177–8, 185–7, 191–2, 374
  And see de Gaulle, Pompidou; Elections, Presidential
Presidents' Conference, 222, 283
Press, 63, 88, 133, 134, 162, 190, 213, 268, 273, 350, 378